POSER® 7 REVEALED:
THE E FRONTIER
OFFICIAL GUIDE

Kelly L. Murdock

THOMSON

™

COURSE TECHNOLOGY

Professional ■ Technical ■ Reference

**Publisher and General Manager,
Thomson Course Technology PTR:**
Stacy L. Hiquet

Associate Director of Marketing:
Sarah O'Donnell

Manager of Editorial Services:
Heather Talbot

Marketing Manager:
Heather Hurley

Acquisitions Editor:
Megan Belanger

Marketing Assistant:
Adena Flitt

Project Editor:
Kezia Endsley

Technical Reviewer:
Chris Murdock

PTR Editorial Services Coordinator:
Erin Johnson

Copy Editor:
Kezia Endsley

Interior Layout Techs:
Jill Flores, Susan Honeywell,
& Robin Roberts

Cover Designer:
Mike Tanamachi

Indexer:
Larry Sweazy

Proofreader:
Kim Benbow

THOMSON

COURSE TECHNOLOGY

Professional ■ Technical ■ Reference

25 Thomson Place
Boston, MA 02210
http://www.courseptr.com

ISBN-10: 1-59863-296-5

ISBN-13: 978-1-59863-296-5

Library of Congress Catalog Card Number: 2006927151

Printed in the United States of America

07 08 09 10 11 PH 10 9 8 7 6 5 4 3 2 1

I've always loved the beauty of the rose,
Their delicate simplicity is like love that grows.
But roses haven't always graced my life,
And I've relied on other flowers to quell my strife.

My father gave me a daisy when I was just young,
to comfort me after a bee left me stung.
I remember being crushed when it wilted days later.
And losing the flower was a pain much greater.

The night I remember when I stole my first kiss,
I was wearing a carnation and feeling great bliss.
I offered my thanks with a squeak in my voice,
But neither the boy nor his flower were my first choice.

Everything was perfect on my wedding day,
Except for the lilies that graced my bouquet,
After the ceremony where we exchange love and our rings,
I realized I should get hung up on such things.

As our young children played together outside,
I planted rows of tulips that spread far and wide,
Roses weren't practical with young ones around,
With no thorns, the gardens were safe and sound.

Years later my youngest daughter was married,
In her hands an arrangement of irises she carried.
I was so happy for her on her special day.
And I cried because I knew she would soon go away.

I now have time to spend with my beloved roses.
I don't regret time spent with other flower poses.
Because of my sacrifice, this thing I have learned
That time spent with flowers is not taken, it's earned.

To my dear mother for wisdom, sacrifice and love, 2006

Acknowledgments

When you write the first edition of a book, you don't think about the possibility that there someday may be a second edition, but when it happens, the feeling is like visiting an old friend that was once very close to you. It also represents a second chance where you can clean up all the mistakes that appeared in the first edition while simultaneously creating a whole new set of mistakes.

Second editions are also a great chance to share all the experience that you've gained since the first edition. This experience comes through working with the product, but also from all the new friends in the Poser community that I've made since the first book appeared.

First on the list of friends is the wonderful people at Thomson who remain my friends through thick and thin. Leading the pack is Megan who is always so quick to follow up with an encouraging word when it is sorely needed. Thanks also to Kezia who handled the editing tasks and caught many of the glaring errors that I missed. Thanks also to my brother, Chris, who took over the technical editing and for providing all the valuable insights and the polite criticisms.

I've also really enjoyed working closely with the team at e frontier. I got a chance to spend some time with them at Siggraph and was impressed with their dedication to the product and their willingness to address any issues or questions I had. Huge kudos to Daryl Wise, Tori Porter (the race car queen), Uli Klumpp, Steve Rathmann, Steve Yatson, and Vespiri. I even had the honor to meet with Takihiro, the head of e frontier.

As always, I'd like to thank my family, without whose support I'd never get to the end of a book. To Angela, for her patience, maybe we should work on finishing the basement now, eh; to Eric, who will spend the next six months playing the Wii system, and to Thomas, for all his help in doing work around the house. Okay, guys. This book's done and before Christmas even. Now how about watching some of the summer blockbusters.

A big thanks out to Addy Norton, who created that image used on the cover and chapter openers. I contacted Addy many months ago to get an image for an early marketing version of the book cover and was so impressed with her amazing Poser images that it ended up being on the final cover. She is truly an inspiration to all of us.

About the Author

Kelly L. Murdock has a background in engineering, specializing in computer graphics. This experience has led him to many interesting experiences, including using high-end CAD workstations for product design and analysis, working on several large-scale visualization projects, creating 3D models for several blockbuster movies, working as a freelance 3D artist and designer, 3D programming, and a chance to write several high-profile computer graphics books.

Kelly's book credits include seven editions of the *3ds max Bible, Edgeloop Character Modeling for 3D Professionals Only, LightWave 3D 8 Revealed, Maya 6 Revealed,* two editions of both the *Illustrator Bible,* and the *Adobe Creative Suite Bible, Adobe Atmosphere Bible, gmax Bible, 3d Graphics and VRML 2.0, Master Visually HTML and XHTML,* and *JavaScript Visual Blueprints.*

In his spare time, Kelly enjoys rock climbing, mountain biking, skiing, and running. He works with his brother at his co-founded design company, Logical Paradox Design.

ABOUT THE AUTHOR

CONTENTS

Chapter 4
Working with Files and
Accessing Content Paradise   124

CONTENTS

C O N T E N T S

**Chapter 8
Creating and Applying Materials 248**

Chapter 9
Creating a Face and
Facial Expressions   **288**

CONTENTS

Chapter 12
Rigging a Figure with Bones   368

C O N T E N T S

**Chapter 16
Rendering Scenes**   **464**

Chapter 17
Using Poser with Other Software   500

Chapter 18
Writing Python Scripts   520

Revealed Series Vision

A book with the word *Revealed* in the title suggests that the topic that is being covered contains many hidden secrets that need to be brought to light. For Poser, this suggestion makes sense. Poser is a powerful piece of software, and finding out exactly how to accomplish some task can be time-consuming without some help. Well, you're in luck, because the help you need is in your hands.

As you dive into the *Revealed* series, you'll find a book with a split personality. The main text of each lesson includes a detailed discussion of a specific topic, but alongside the topic discussions are step-by-step objectives that help you master the same topic that is being discussed. This unique "read it and do it" approach leads directly to "understand it and master it."

—The *Revealed* Series

Author Vision

When I was approached to write a book on Poser, I thought, "Okay, I'm a Poser user." It's a great program to use to enhance my other 3D projects if I ever need a figure in some unique pose. But, after having spent most of my waking hours looking at every control and fiddling with every option over the past several months, I've happily discovered that there is a whole lotta Poser that I never even knew existed. Cloth simulation, dynamic hair styles, ethnic faces, morphed expressions, a bones system that's easy to use, and a elegantly simple set of animation tools. Wow! This stuff is great.

The more I researched and discovered, the more amazed I became. I can see now why this unique piece of software has been so popular for so long. It does one incredibly hard task, that of posing characters, very well, but it has so much more to offer than just positioning figures.

The Poser interface is one of the "love 'em" or "hate 'em" designs with no middle ground. By dividing the entire interface into separate rooms, you can quickly focus your efforts on the task at hand without having to wade through all the tools that you don't need. The ability to rearrange entire sets of controls on-the-fly is also very handy when you need just a little more room to see the right side of the rendered image.

If you're new to Poser, don't be put off by the simplicity of the program. Beneath the slick uncluttered interface is a powerful piece of software that can be used to create, render, and animate entire scenes and projects. A good example of this power can be found with Poser's animation tools. Basic animation tasks are handled using the Animation Controls, a side bar shelf of controls that rise the bottom of the interface to take up only a narrow band of desktop space, yet from this basic set of graphical icons, you can create keyframe animations. For more functionality, one click opens a grid of cells known as the Animation Palette that lets you manipulate keyframes for all scene items. One more click opens editable animation graphs for the selected key. And that's it. No hidden panels with endless knobs and switches or command written in code. Just the features you need when you need them.

Now that I've gushed over the software in a way that would make any Marketing Director proud, let me explain the most logical approach to learning Poser. I've organized each chapter to cover a logical set of features, starting with an overview of the Poser interface found in Chapter 1.

From this interface tour, I jump right into a couple of chapters on posing and working with figures. This is the main purpose of Poser and represents some of the most important chapters in the book.

The next several chapters march through the available rooms of features including coverage of the features for working with materials, props, lights, cameras, face, hair, cloth, and bones.

The book concludes with chapters covering animation, rendering, and using Python scripts.

Throughout the book, several special graphical elements are used to highlight special comments including Notes, Cautions, and Tips. These comments provide a way to present special information to you the reader. Be sure to watch for them.

Along with every discussed task are several step-by-step objectives that show you a simplified example of the discussed topic. Each of these examples was created to be extremely simple to keep the number of steps to a minimum. I've tried to add some variety here and there, but none of these examples should be overwhelming (or will win a prize at the county fair). The real creative work is up to you, but these simplified examples will be enough to show you how to use a feature and give you some practice.

Each objective example begins from the default setting that appears when the program is first loaded, but you don't need to close and reopen the software to begin each example; just select the File, New menu command, and you'll be ready to go. For some of the more complex examples, the steps instruct you to open an example file. You can download these files from the Course Technology Web site, or you can use your own files as a beginning point. Included with the downloadable files at the Course Technology Web site are the final saved files from each example. These are available for you to compare with your own work to learn where you might have made a mistake (check out http://www.courseptr.com).

Poser is an amazing piece of software, but it isn't overwhelming. And in this book, most every feature is covered, providing you with a reference that you can use whenever you get stuck or to give you some creative inspiration.

—Kelly L. Murdock

chapter

1

LEARNING THE
POSER INTERFACE

1. Learn the interface controls.

2. Explore the Pose Room.

3. Use the Document Window.

4. Discover the other rooms.

5. Configure the interface and set preferences.

6. Get Help.

LEARNING THE
POSER INTERFACE

The Poser interface is one of the most unique and interesting interfaces found in any software. Yes, it has the traditional menus and windows, but the entire interface is fluid, allowing you to move and place each set of controls precisely where you want it. Even the main view window, called the Document Window, is portable. So if you want to place the Editing Tools right under the menus or in the lower corner of the interface, you simply need to grab the Editing Tools' title bar and drag it where you want it.

Each set of specific features is divided into what Poser calls rooms, with each room accessed using tabs that run along the top of the interface. The available Poser rooms include Pose, Material, Face, Hair, Cloth, Setup, and Content. The room tabs are one aspect of the interface that cannot be changed. You also cannot delete or add rooms, but I'd like to be able to add a Wash room to clean my figures.

The interface also has hidden palettes that slide in from the right and bottom side of the interface. These side controls let you access a library of content and animation controls, but because these controls aren't needed all the time, they can be cleverly tucked away until they are needed.

The main default room is the Pose Room. In this room, you can work with the Document Window and several other control sets to view the exact part of the figure you want to see. The Light Controls let you set how light strikes the figure, the Camera Controls lets you focus the view on specific body parts, and the Display Style controls let you change how the preview figure is rendered. The Document Window is divided into two panels used to display a preview of the scene and to render the current scene. It also includes controls that you can use to change the number of views, and several other display options such as shadows and background colors.

All interface controls and additional interface dialog boxes can be hidden or made active using the Window menu. The menus also include commands for accessing the various features and for setting preferences that you can use to configure the interface. Finally, the menus include a Help option for accessing the PDF-based documentation. This chapter is meant as an introduction to the software and its interface. Once you become familiar with the various interface elements, you can look to the later chapters for more specifics on how these features are used (and maybe even discover the means for cleaning up figures since the Wash room can't be found).

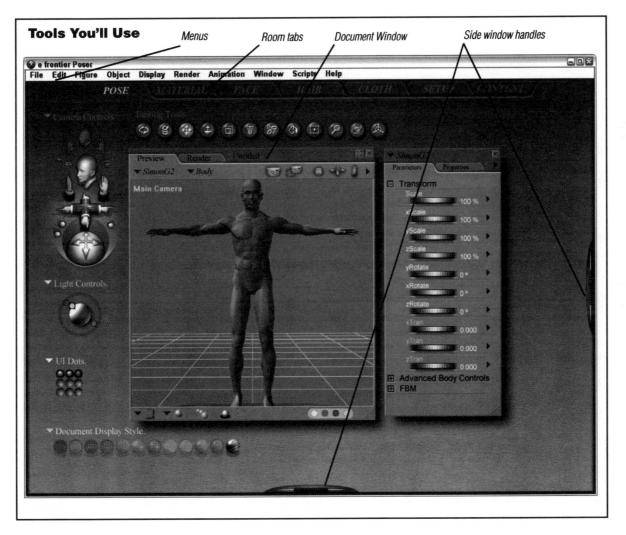

Tools You'll Use — Menus — Room tabs — Document Window — Side window handles

LEARN THE
INTERFACE CONTROLS

What You'll Do

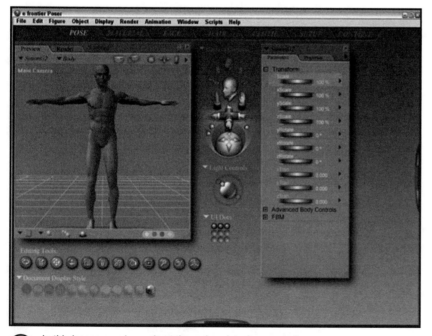

In this lesson, you learn about the various interface controls.

You start Poser by clicking its icon or selecting it from a menu of applications just like other software. When Poser first opens, a default figure is displayed, letting you get right to work.

NOTE The default figure in Poser 7 is named SimonG2. The G2 stands for Generation 2, and you can find expressions, hairstyles, and clothes that fit him in the Library.

When Poser first launches, you'll see several sets of controls sprinkled about the center view window. Although each set of controls has a position, you can place the control exactly where you want it. To reposition an item, simply click on its title and drag it where you want it. However, the room tabs cannot be moved.

QUICKTIP You can even move the background graphic if you want to. Just Alt-click the faint interface background image to cycle through the available background images.

Using Menus

The one interface element that Poser has in common with other software is its menus, shown in Figure 1-1, located at the top of the interface.

These menus work by clicking and dragging to select the specific menu command that you want to execute. You also can access menu commands by using keyboard shortcuts, which are listed to right of the menu command. Arrow icons to the right of a menu command indicate that a submenu of additional options is available, and menu commands that are followed by an ellipsis (three small dots) open a dialog box. If a menu command is unavailable, the menu is light gray and cannot be selected.

Using the Room Tabs

Directly below the menus are seven room tabs with the current room highlighted. The room tabs include Pose, Material, Face, Hair, Cloth, Setup, and Content, as shown in Figure 1-2. Clicking these tabs opens a separate interface with specialized features. For example, the Material Room includes all the controls for creating materials that you can apply to the figure, and the Hair Room includes controls for creating and editing hairstyles. The Pose Room opens by default when Poser first starts.

> **NOTE** Not all menu commands are available for every room. For example, most of the options in the Window menu are disabled when the Face and Content Rooms are open.

FIGURE 1-1
Sample menu

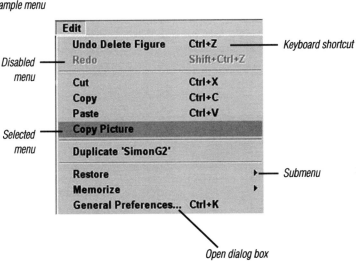

FIGURE 1-2
Room tabs

Using Floating Controls

Located about the interface are several floating sets of controls. These controls have a transparent background, and you can move them around the interface by clicking and dragging their titles. For the Pose Room, the floating controls include the Light Controls, Camera Controls, Display Style, Memory Dots, and the Editing Tools. Other sets of floating controls are available in the other rooms.

The floating control's title changes as you move the mouse over the various buttons and icons in the set, revealing the name of the icon that the cursor is over. All of the floating controls, except for the Editing Tools, include a small down arrow icon, which opens a pop-up menu of options.

> **QUICKTIP**   Double-clicking a floating control's title bar will roll up the controls so that only the title is visible. This is a great way to hide a set of controls until you need them.

Disabling Tool Titles

If you want to hide the title text for each of the floating control sets, you can use the Window, Tool Titles toggle command to turn off the control text. By disabling the text, the interface looks even cleaner than before (see Figure 1-3). Even though the tool titles are disabled, if you move the mouse over the top of each control set, its title will appear briefly and then slowly fade out.

FIGURE 1-3
Disabled tool titles

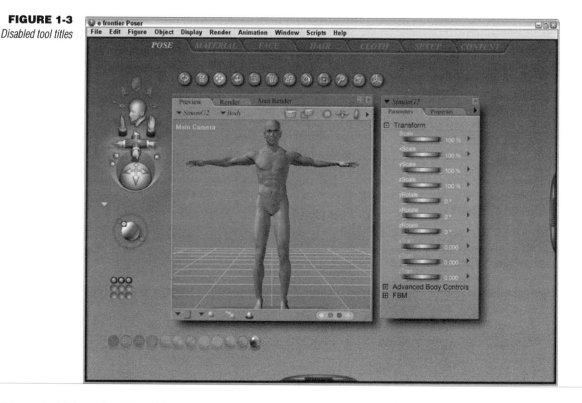

Moving the Document Window

The figure you are working on is displayed in the Document Window. You can reposition this window by dragging its title bar and resize it by dragging on its lower-right corner. The Document Window is divided into two panels—Preview and Render.

The Preview panel displays the figure using the selected display style, and the Render panel displays the final scene with all lights, shadows, and textures computed into the final image. The process of rendering the scene can take a few seconds to several minutes, depending on the specified rendering options. The Preview panel is covered in more detail later in this chapter and the Render panel is covered in Chapter 16, "Rendering Scenes."

Click the tabs at the top of the Document Window to access each of these panels. In the upper-right corner are two icons. The left one is the Maximize toggle button and the right one is used to close the Document Window. Figure 1-4 shows the Document Window maximized.

> **NOTE** Closing the Document Window closes the current file. You will be prompted to save the file if you have made any changes to it.

FIGURE 1-4
Maximized Document Window

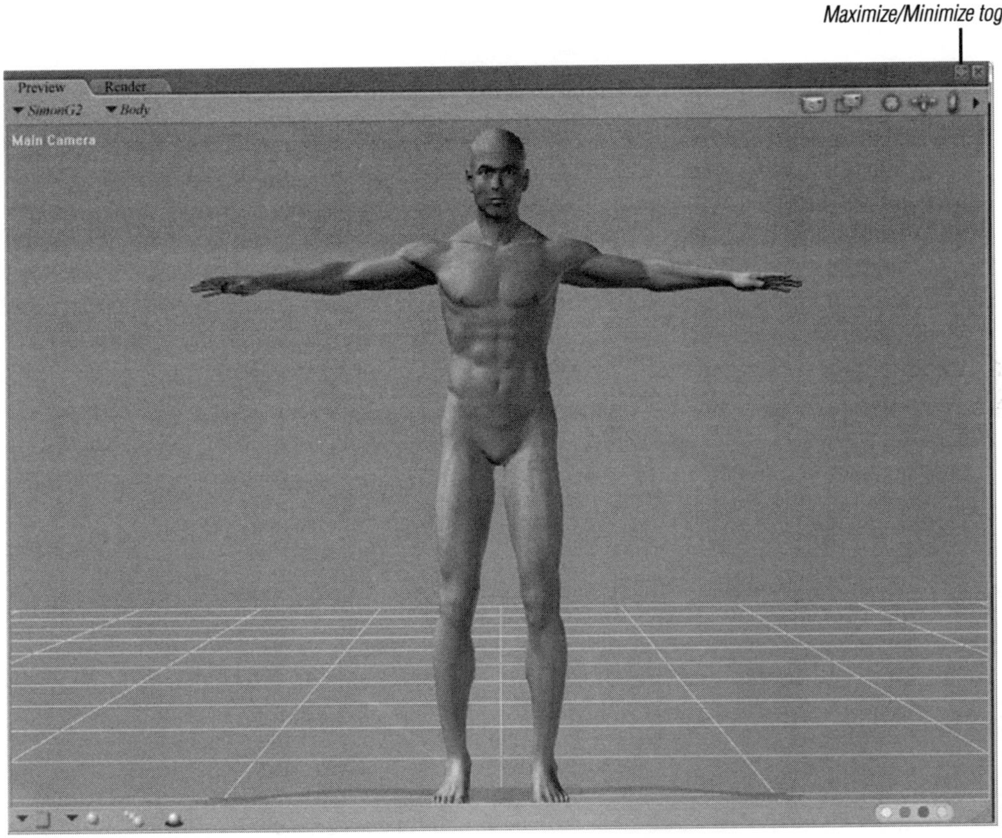

Maximize/Minimize toggle button

Using the Parameters/Properties Palette

Another useful floating control is the Parameters/Properties palette. You can open this palette, shown in Figure 1-5, using the Window, Parameter Dials menu command. It includes tabs for accessing the parameters and properties for the current selection. Within the palette are parameter dials that you can drag to the right or left to change a parameter's value. The parameters define the selected element such as its position and orientation. You can also click each numeric value on the right side of the palette and change its value by entering numbers on the keyboard. To the right of the numeric value is an arrow icon that opens a pop-up menu of options. These options are covered in Chapter 3, "Editing and Posing Figures."

FIGURE 1-5
Parameters/Properties palette

Parameter dial

Pop-up menu

Numeric value

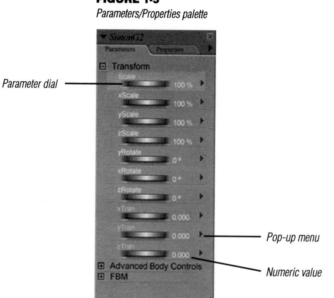

Introducing the Side Window Palettes

If you look closely along the right and bottom edges of the interface, you'll notice two side window handles. If you click these controls, an interface panel slides in from the edge.

The side window control to the right opens the Library palette and the side window control to the bottom opens the Animation Controls, as shown in Figure 1-6. You close the side window control panels by clicking again on the side window handle, or for the Library palette, you can also close it by clicking the Close button in the upper-right corner of the panel. The Library palette is covered in more detail in Chapter 2, "Using the Poser Library," and the Animation Controls are covered in Chapter 13, "Animating Figures and Scenes."

Showing and Hiding Interface Elements

The Window menu includes commands for displaying and hiding all the various interface elements. When a listed interface element is visible, a checkmark appears to the left of its menu command. Each interface element also has a keyboard shortcut to quickly hide it. You can also use the Window, Show All Tools (Ctrl+\) and the Window, Hide All Tools (Ctrl+0) commands to show or hide all interface elements except for the Document Window. When tools are hidden, only their title is visible if the Window, Tool Titles menu is enabled.

FIGURE 1-6

Side Window palettes

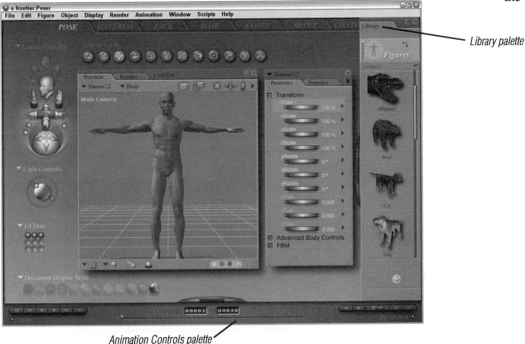

Library palette

Animation Controls palette

1. Click the Start button on the Taskbar, point to All Programs, click eFrontier, click Poser 7, and then click Poser (Win) or double-click the hard drive icon, navigate to and double-click the Poser folder, then double-click the Poser icon  (Mac).

   The Poser interface loads using the default settings. The Pose Room displays the default SimonG2 figure.

2. Click Window on the menu bar, and then click Show All Tools. All of the tools are visible in the interface.

3. Click and drag the Document Window to the upper-left corner of the interface. Then drag the Light and Camera Controls and the Memory Dots to the right of the Document Window. Position the Parameters/Properties palette to the right of the Light and Camera Controls.

4. Drag the Editing Tools under the Document Window and drag the Document Display Style controls underneath the Editing Tools. As you position the interface elements, leave enough room at the bottom and right of the interface for the Library and Animation Controls to appear without overlapping the other controls, as shown in Figure 1-7.

5. Click File on the menu bar, click Save As, type **Custom interface layout.pz3** in the File name text box, and then click Save.

FIGURE 1-7

Interface elements in custom positions

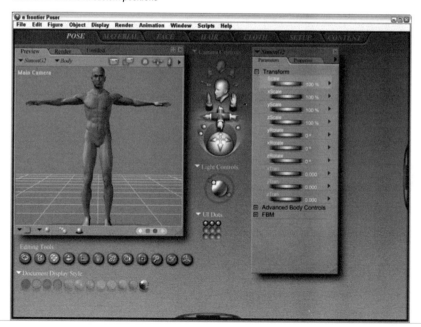

EXPLORE THE
POSE ROOM

What You'll Do

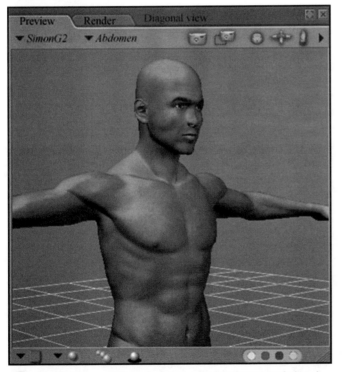

In this lesson, you learn how to use the interface controls found in the Pose Room.

The Pose Room is the default room that opens when Poser is first started. It is the main interface for posing figures and will be the room where you'll probably spend the most time. Posing and editing figures is covered in Chapter 3, "Editing and Posing Figures," but this lesson covers the various controls that change how the figure is displayed in the Document Window. The controls covered in this lesson include the Camera, Light, and Display Style controls, so if you're a director, by the end of this chapter, you'll have the lights and camera, and will only need the action.

QUICKTIP This lesson covers only the basics of using the Light and Camera Controls. Cameras are covered in detail in Chapter 6, "Establishing a Scene—Cameras and Backgrounds," and lights are covered in depth in Chapter 7, "Adding Scene Lighting."

Using the Camera Controls

The Camera Controls are also a critical set of controls that you can use to zoom in and rotate around a specific body part for a close-up view. These controls, shown in Figure 1-8, have a direct and immediate impact on the figure displayed in the Document Window. By using these controls, you can control precisely which part of the figure is displayed.

The top three icons in the Camera Controls are used to change the camera's view to focus on the right hand, the left hand, and the face. The key icon toggles animating the camera on and off. The key icon is colored red when animating is enabled. Animating is covered in Chapter 13, "Animating Figures and Scenes." The Flyaround button spins the camera about the figure's center, and you can use it to get a quick look at all sides of your character.

QUICKTIP You can change the view that's stored in one of the top three icons to the selection in the larger camera preset icon by holding down the Alt key and clicking on one of the top three icons.

FIGURE 1-8
Camera Controls

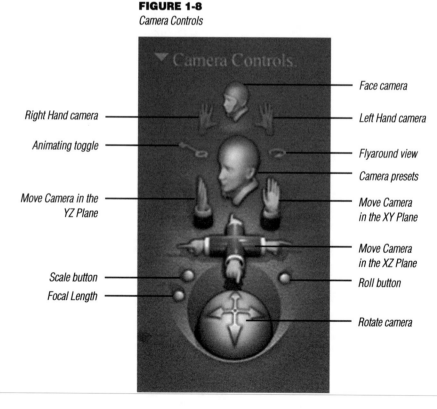

Face camera

Right Hand camera

Left Hand camera

Animating toggle

Flyaround view

Camera presets

Move Camera in the YZ Plane

Move Camera in the XY Plane

Move Camera in the XZ Plane

Scale button

Roll button

Focal Length

Rotate camera

Using Camera Presets

The centered head icon lets you switch between preset camera views including the Main, Auxiliary, Left, Right, Front, Back, Top, Bottom, Face, Posing, Right Hand, Left Hand, and Dolly cameras. To display the camera name in the upper-left corner of the viewpane, enable the Display, Show Camera Names option. Each of these cameras has its own icon, which you can access by clicking repeatedly on the icon to cycle through the available cameras or by clicking and dragging to the left or right. You can also select each of the preset cameras from the Camera Control pop-up menu and from the Display, Camera View menu.

Moving a Camera

The hand icons are used to move the camera view within the YZ plane, the XY plane, or XZ plane. To use these icons, just click them and drag in the direction that you want to move the camera. The figure in the Document Window is updated as you drag. For example, dragging down on the XY plane pans the camera in the Document Window upward, causing the figure's view to sink downward.

Rotating a Camera

The sphere with arrows on it at the bottom of the Camera Controls is called the trackball. It is used to rotate the camera. It is used like the move icons, by clicking and dragging in the direction you want to rotate the camera. The Roll button spins the figure within the Document Window about its center.

> **QUICKTIP** Small move and rotate camera icons also exist in the top-right corner of the Document Window. These small controls work just like their large counterparts in the Camera Controls.

Changing a Camera's Scale and Focal Length

The final two buttons to the left of the Rotate Camera control are for adjusting the camera's scale and focal length. Dragging on the Scale button changes the size of the figure within the viewpane and dragging with the Focal Length button changes the center focus point for the camera, which affects how close or far the figure appears from the camera.

> **NOTE** The Camera Scale button doesn't work when one of the face or hand cameras is selected.

Using the Light Controls

The Light Controls directly affect the figure in the Document Window. By surrounding a figure with lights, you'll be better able to see its details. Enabling shadows can give you a sense of depth, but too many bright lights can wash out the figure.

The Light Controls, shown in Figure 1-9, are used to set the lighting effects for the figure in the Document Window. The large sphere in the center of the Light Controls is a sample that shows the current lighting settings. Surrounding this large sphere are three smaller circles connected to the larger one. These smaller circles are the individual lights. You can change their location relative to the figure's center by dragging them about the larger sphere.

When you select a circle representing a light, controls for changing its intensity, color, and properties appear about the larger sphere. There are also buttons for removing the selected light and creating new lights.

> **QUICKTIP** When a light icon is behind the large center sphere in the Lighting Controls, it appears dimmed.

FIGURE 1-9
Light Controls

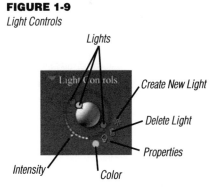

Changing Display Styles

The more details that are displayed with a figure, the longer it takes to be updated when a change is made. For example, a figure with lots of details and textures could take quite a while to be redrawn in the Document Window every time a change is made. By changing between the various styles in the Display Style controls, shown in Figure 1-10, you can control how much detail and what kind of detail is displayed in the Document Window. For example, complex scenes might work best when a simple Wireframe style is used, but for looking at a close-up of the face, you might want to switch to the Texture Shaded style.

You can apply display styles to the entire scene, to a single figure, or to a single element or body part. You select the application level from the pop-up menu at the top of the Document Display Style toolbar or from the Display menu.

QUICKTIP You can make the Display Style controls (along with the Editing Tool) vertical by holding down the Alt key while clicking one of its buttons.

The styles available in the Display Style controls include the following. Some of these styles have shortcut keys, indicated in parentheses:

- **Silhouette (Ctrl+1):** Displays the entire figure as if cut out and displayed against the gray background. This style is good for isolating edges.

- **Outline (Ctrl+2):** Displays just the figure lines that outline the various body parts.

- **Wireframe (Ctrl+3):** Displays all the mesh lines that make up the entire figure.

- **Hidden Line (Ctrl+4):** Displays only those lines that are facing the camera. Lines on the backside of the figure aren't shown.

- **Lit Wireframe (Ctrl+5):** A wireframe view that is colored based on the scene lights.

- **Flat Shaded (Ctrl+6):** Displays the figure using the correct material colors for each mesh face without any smoothing.

- **Flat Lined:** Displays flat shading with lines.

- **Cartoon:** Displays the figure as a hand-drawn cartoon rendering style.

- **Cartoon with Line (Ctrl+7):** Same as the Cartoon style, but with distinct black outlines.

- **Smooth Shaded (Ctrl+8):** Displays the figure using the correct material colors.

- **Smooth Lined:** Same as Smooth Shaded style, but with visible lines.

- **Texture Shaded (Ctrl+9):** Displays the figure using full textures as if it were rendered.

NOTE If you select one of the Cartoon styles, you can set the number of tones used for the style by right-clicking the Document Window and selecting the Toon Tones menu. The options include One Tone, Two Tones, Three Tones, Three Tones + Hilite, and Smooth Toned.

FIGURE 1-10

Display Style controls

FIGURE 1-11

Display styles

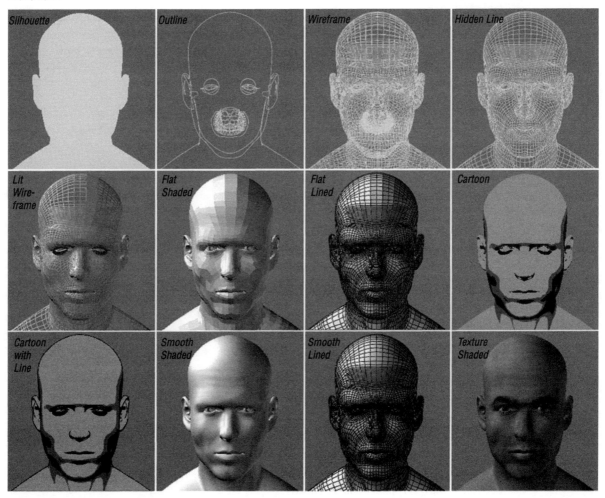

How each of these styles looks up close on a face.

Control Cameras

1. Click the Camera Presets icon 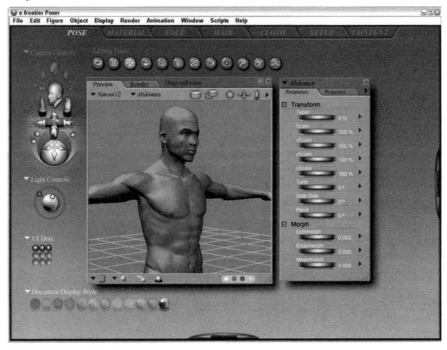 in the Camera Controls until the Main Camera view is displayed in the Document Window.

2. Click the Move Camera in XZ Plane icon and drag down until the center of the figure is visible around the hips.

3. Click the Move Camera in YZ Plane icon and drag down until the figure is visible from the chest up.

4. Drag the Rotate Sphere control to the right to rotate the figure about its center.

   After you rotate the camera, the view in the Document Window is updated to show a diagonal view of the figure, as shown in Figure 1-12.

5. Select File, Save As and save the file as **Diagonal view.pz3**.

FIGURE 1-12
Diagonal view

FIGURE 1-13

Modified lights

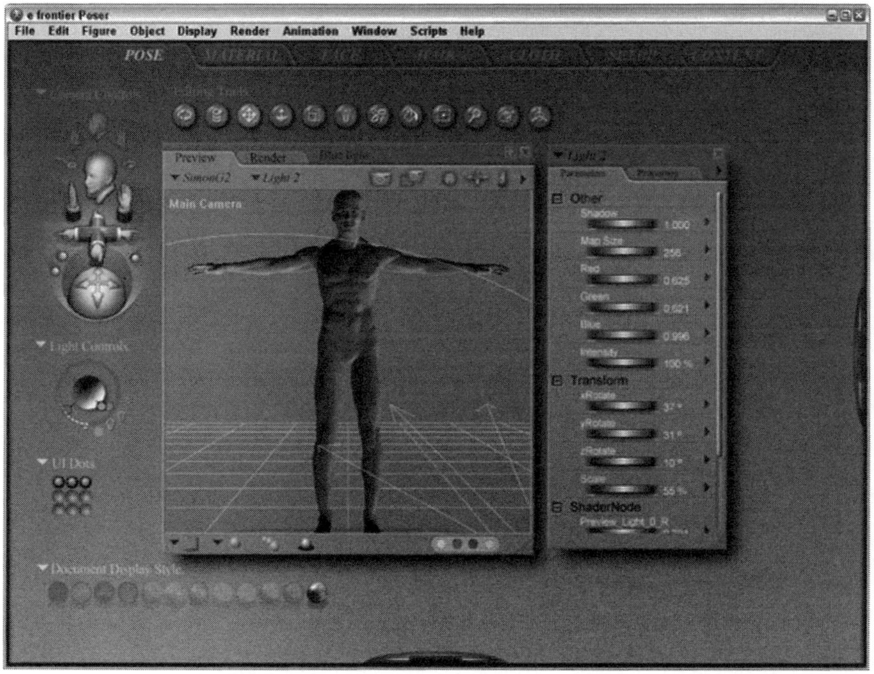

Control Lights

1. With the default figure loaded, click and drag the light circle icon in the upper-left of the Light Controls to the lower-left.

   The light's position changes, and the updated light is displayed in the Document Window.

2. Click and drag the center light circle in the Light Controls to the lower-right side of the centered larger sphere.

3. With the center light selected, click the Light Color icon and select a blue color. The center light changes position and color, as shown in Figure 1-13.

4. Select File, Save As and save the file as **Blue light.pz3**.

Change the Display Style

1. Open Poser with the default figure visible.

2. Click Window on the menu bar, and then click Preview Styles to make the Display Style options visible if they aren't already.

3. Drag the mouse over the various styles. Each style icon sphere is highlighted as the mouse is rolled over it.

4. Click the Cartoon with Lines style icon sphere.

   The view of the figure is updated with the Cartoon with Lines style, as shown in Figure 1-14.

5. Choose File, Save As and save the file as Cartoon figure.pz3.

FIGURE 1-14
Cartoon style

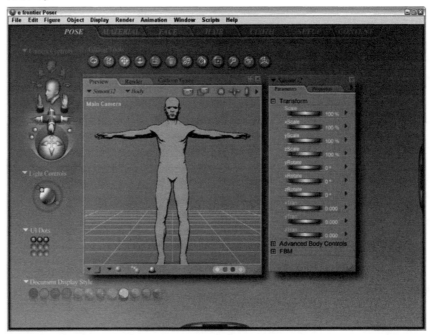

USE THE
DOCUMENT WINDOW

What You'll Do

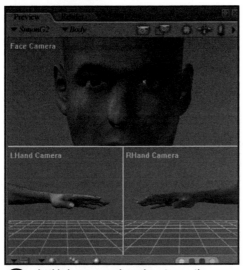

▶ In this lesson, you learn how to use the interface controls found within the Document Window.

The Document Window, shown in Figure 1-15, displays the current figure using the light and camera settings in the selected display style. The title bar displays the name of the saved file along with buttons to maximize and close the window. Directly below the title bar are two tabs that let you switch between the Preview and Render panels. The Preview panel displays a figure as a rough approximation that can be easily manipulated and posed. The Render view lets you render the figure using textures, materials, and effects, but this process can take some time depending on the complexity of the figure and the render settings. The rendering process and all of the available render settings are covered in Chapter 16, "Rendering Scenes."

NOTE The title of the Document Window displays the saved file name. If the file hasn't yet been saved, the title bar displays "Untitled."

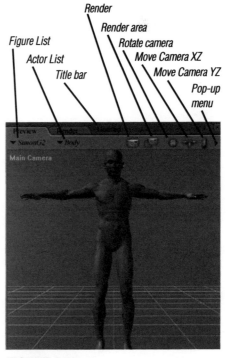

FIGURE 1-15
Document Window Controls

Beneath the panel tabs are two drop-down lists called the Figure List and the Actor List, where you can select the figure to work on and the specific body part or actor you want to work on. To the right of these lists are the icon buttons Render and Render an Area, which renders the entire scene or just a selected area, respectively. There are also buttons to Rotate and move the camera view. The Rotate and Move Camera icons work just like the controls found in the Camera Controls.

Displaying Additional Ports

At the bottom of the Document Window are several controls for changing the display settings for the Document Window. The Viewpane Layout list in the lower-left corner includes several options for configuring the ports that fill the Document Window. The options include Full Port, Four Ports, Three Ports—Big Top, Three Ports—Big Bottom, Three Ports—Big Right, Three Ports—Big Left, Two Ports—Left/Right, and Two Ports—Top/Bottom. Each separate port can have its own selected camera, but only one port can be active at a time. A red border identifies the active port. The Camera Controls affect the camera view in the active viewpane only. You can quickly change the camera view for any port by right-clicking within the port and selecting a view from the Camera View menu. You can manually resize each port by dragging its interior border. Figure 1-16 shows the Four Ports layout.

QUICKTIP Pressing the F key cycles through the available viewpane layout options and pressing the D key switches between a single port and the last selected multiple port layout.

FIGURE 1-16
Four Ports viewpane option

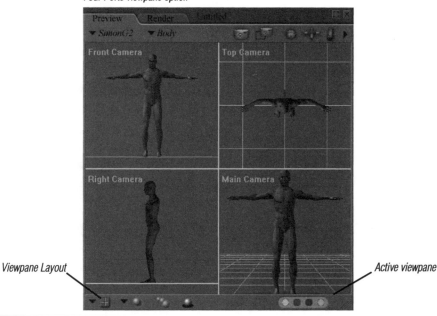

Viewpane Layout

Active viewpane

Setting Tracking Modes

To the right of the Viewpane Layout options is a drop-down list of three tracking modes. These modes are Box, Fast, and Full. By changing these modes, you can affect how quickly the figure in the Document Window is updated as changes are made. The Box tracking mode displays all body parts as simple rectangular boxes, as shown in Figure 1-17. It is the quickest update mode. The Fast tracking mode displays the figure in its high-resolution form when the figure is static and displays the figure as boxes when the figure or its camera is moving. The Full tracking mode displays the high-resolution figure at all times.

Enabling Depth Cueing and Shadows

The Depth Cue toggle, to the right of the tracking modes, turns depth cueing on and off in the Document Window. When on, objects get fainter the farther back in the scene they are located, and objects closer to the camera are shown in greater detail, as shown in Figure 1-18. Note how the hand farthest from the camera isn't as clear as the hand closest to the camera. Depth cueing has no effect when the scene is rendered.

FIGURE 1-17
Box tracking mode

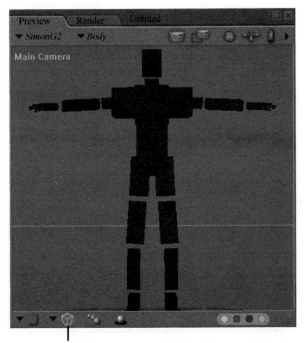

Tracking modes

FIGURE 1-18
Depth Cueing enabled

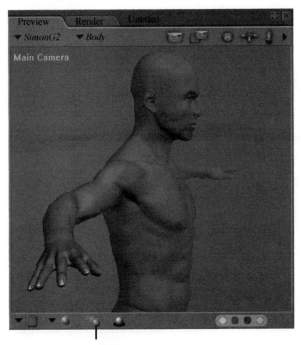

Depth Cue toggle

When the Shadows toggle is enabled, a simple shadow for the figure and any scene props is shown on the ground plane in the Document Window. Document Window shadows, like depth cueing, are also not rendered. Re-positioning the lights in the Light Controls also has no effect on these shadows. Rendered shadows can be enabled for scene lights. Figure 1-19 shows the figure with Document Window shadows enabled.

Changing the Document Window Colors

In the lower-right corner of the Document Window are four radio buttons. Moving the mouse over these buttons changes the cursor to a small eyedropper. If you click any of these buttons, a pop-up color selector palette appears, as shown in Figure 1-20.

> **QUICKTIP** If you drag the eyedropper cursor away from the Color Selector dialog box, you can select any color visible on the computer screen.

FIGURE 1-19
Shadows enabled

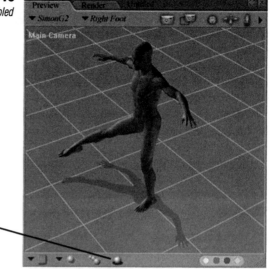

Shadows toggle

FIGURE 1-20
Pop-up color palette

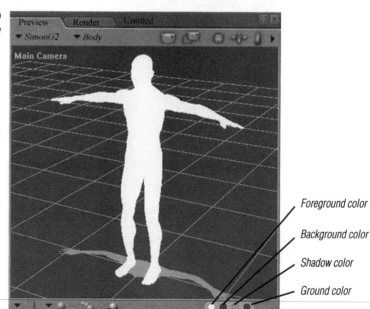

Foreground color

Background color

Shadow color

Ground color

The four radio buttons correspond to the following scene elements:

- Foreground: Changes the color of the grid lines for the ground plane and the figure's line color in Silhouette, Outline, Wireframe, and Lit Wireframe display styles.

- Background: Changes the color of the background.

- Shadow: Changes the shadow color if the shadow is enabled.

- Ground: Changes the ground color.

Figure 1-21 shows the Document Window with several custom colors.

FIGURE 1-21
Document Window with custom colors

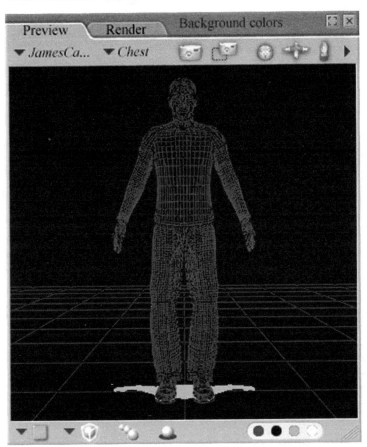

Changing the Document Window Size

You can change the size of the Document Window by dragging on the lower-right corner of the window, but you can also size the Document Window to precise dimensions using the Window, Document Window Size menu command. This command opens the Preview Dimensions dialog box, shown in Figure 1-22, where you can enter the desired size of the Document Window. The size of the Document Window is the default size used for rendered images and animations unless the dimensions are changed. If a background is loaded, you can automatically have the Document Window match the size of the background image, or you can have the Document Window match the specified Production Aspect, as defined in the Render Dimensions dialog box.

FIGURE 1-22
Preview Dimensions dialog box

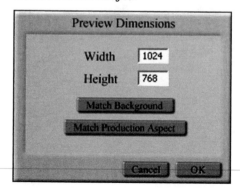

QUICKTIP Double-clicking the lower-right corner of the Document Window opens the Preview Dimensions dialog box.

Enabling Hardware Acceleration

Another way to speed up the update rate of the Document Window is to enable hardware acceleration using **OpenGL**. Many modern video cards include capabilities that let them compute redrawing the Document Window using the video card hardware instead of the computer's central processing unit (CPU). This leaves the CPU, which is the main brain of the computer, free to handle other tasks such as dealing with the interface. The language that makes this hardware acceleration possible is OpenGL, and it is automatically detected and enabled if your system includes the capabilities to use it. You can also manually select it by right-clicking the Document Window and selecting the OpenGL option. The SreeD option is a software option.

NOTE Using hardware acceleration can cause display problems under certain circumstances. If you notice any trouble with your display, switch the display to the SreeD option.

Change Viewpoint Layout and Tracking Mode

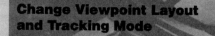

1. Click the lower-left corner icon [ ] in the Document Window and select the Three Ports – Big Top option.

   The Document Window is split into three panes with the largest pane on top.

2. Click the icon next to the viewpane layout [ ] and select the Full option as the tracking mode.

   The figures in the viewpanes are displayed in high resolution, as shown in Figure 1-23.

3. Select File, Save As and save the file as Three ports.pz3.

FIGURE 1-23
Three ports

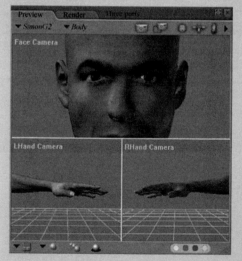

FIGURE 1-24

Modified Document Window

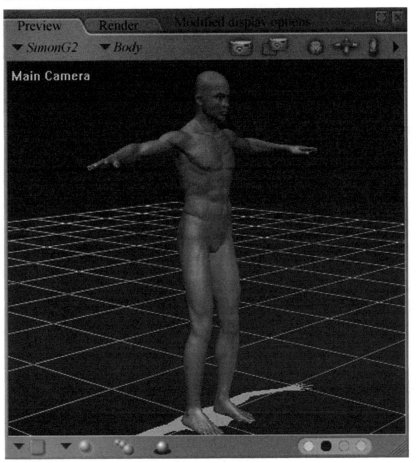

1. Click the Depth Cue icon button ![icon] at the bottom of the Document Window, and then drag the Rotation control in the Camera Controls to turn the figure sideways.

   The arm that is farther from the camera starts to fade with the Depth Cue option enabled.

2. Click the Shadow toggle icon ![icon] to enable a shadow in the Document Window (if necessary).

3. Click the Background color button ![icon] , select a black background color, click the Shadow color, and then change it to light gray.

   The display of the Document Window changes, as shown in Figure 1-24.

4. Select File, Save As and save the file as **Modified display options.pz3**.

1. Choose Window, Document Window Size.

2. In the Preview Window dialog box, enter 640 as the Width and 480 as the Height values, and then click OK.

   The size of the Document Window changes, as shown in Figure 1-25.

3. Select File, Save As and save the file as **Resized window.pz3**.

FIGURE 1-25

Resized Document Window

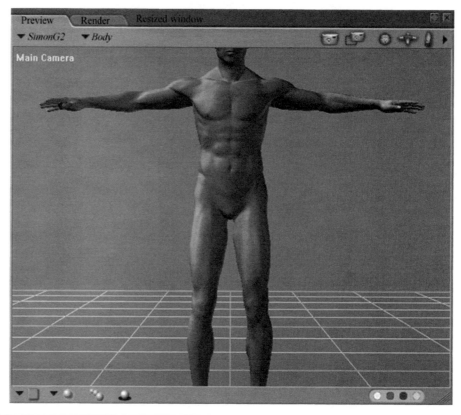

LESSON 4

DISCOVER THE
OTHER ROOMS

What You'll Do

In this lesson, you learn how to access the other Poser rooms using the room tabs.

Although the Pose Room is the default room, Poser includes several other rooms, each with its own set of features. Each of these rooms is covered in a separate chapter, but this lesson introduces each room and shows some features that are common among them all. To switch between the various rooms, you simply need to click the room tabs located at the top of the interface.

Using the Material Room

The Material Room, shown in Figure 1-26, includes an interface used to apply materials to the various body parts. You apply these materials using an interface dialog box for Diffuse Color, Highlight, Ambient, Reflection, Bump, and Transparency. The resulting material is shown in the Material Preview panel. In addition to these simple material properties, the Advanced panel includes many additional material properties. The Material Room also includes all the interface controls found in the Pose Room including the Document Window. The Material Room is covered in more detail in Chapter 8, "Creating and Applying Materials."

Using the Face Room

The Face Room interface, shown in Figure 1-27, includes controls for specifying the details included in the figure's face. It includes support for loading front and side view photos of the face you want to use along with tools to map the images onto the figure's face. The Face Room interface also includes the Face Shaping Tool dialog box, which lets you change the various attributes of the current face including the position of the various facial features, its gender, age and ethnicity. The Face Sculpting pane lets you see a preview of the current face settings. The Face Room is covered in Chapter 9, "Creating a Face and Facial Expressions."

FIGURE 1-26
Material Room interface

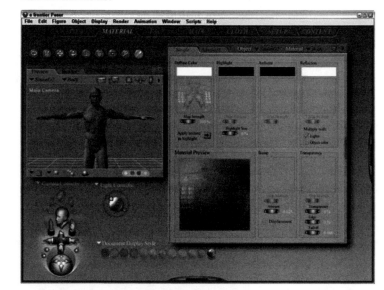

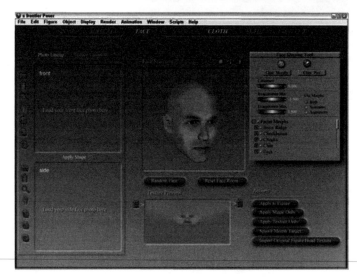

FIGURE 1-27
Face Room interface

Using the Hair Room

The Hair Room, shown in Figure 1-28, includes all the controls needed to grow and style hair for the figure. You can grow hair for any body part and view the hair using the Texture Shaded style in the Document Window. The Hair Room also includes the standard Pose Room interface controls. The Hair Room is covered in detail in Chapter 10, "Adding Hair."

Using the Cloth Room

You use the Cloth Room, shown in Figure 1-29, to clothe the current figure and to define the dynamics of those clothes. These controls can make clothes that are smooth and flowing or clothes that fit tightly. You can use dynamic objects to add forces such as wind and gravity for animation sequences. The resulting clothes are viewed in the Document Window. Creating cloth and using clothes are presented in Chapter 11, "Working with Dynamic Cloth."

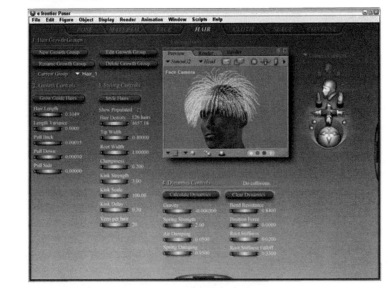

Using the Setup Room

The Setup Room, shown in Figure 1-30, overlays the figure in the Document Window with a set of bones that are positioned about the figure's joints. Using this room, you can add new custom bones to the figure as needed. These new bones are used to animate custom imported objects. The Setup Room and using bones are covered in Chapter 12, "Rigging a Figure with Bones."

Using the Content Room

The Content Room, shown in Figure 1-31, provides a convenient way to add new figures, materials, and props to the Library. It also provides access to Content Paradise, an online repository of available content. The Content Room and using Content Paradise are covered in Chapter 4, "Working with Files and Accessing Content Paradise."

FIGURE 1-30
Setup Room interface

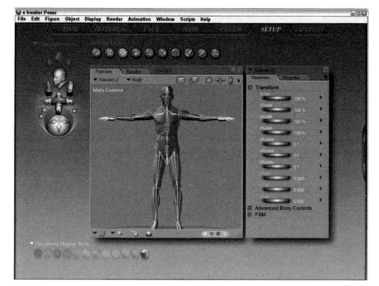

FIGURE 1-31
Content Room interface

1. Click the Content tab at the top of the interface.

   The Content Room interface, shown in Figure 1-32, is displayed.

2. Browse to the content category that you want to download.

3. Follow the online instructions for completing the download.

FIGURE 1-32

The Content Room and Content Paradise

CONFIGURE THE INTERFACE
AND SET PREFERENCES

What You'll Do

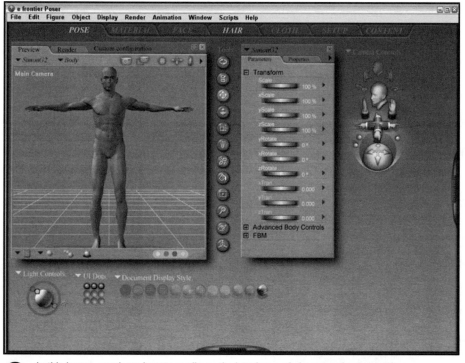

Once you are happy with the layout of the interface controls, you can use the UI Dots, shown in Figure 1-33, to save the configuration. For the Document Window, you can use the General Preference dialog box to set its preferred state. There are several other preferences that impact the interface you can set as well.

NOTE The preference settings are stored separately from where Poser is installed. On Windows computers, the preferences are saved in the Documents and Settings\Username\Application Data\Poser 7 directory, and on Macintosh systems, they are saved in theUsers\ username\Library\Preferences\Poser 7 folder. If you reinstall Poser, it's likely the preferences will remain.

FIGURE 1-33
The UI Dots

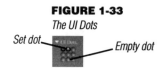

Set dot — — Empty dot

In this lesson, you learn how to configure the interface and change preference settings.

Using the UI Dots

If you like to use several different interface configurations, you can save each interface configuration using the UI Dots options in the Memory Dots control. To use a Memory Dot, simply click a dot to save the current UI layout. Clicking again on the dot recalls the saved layout. Holding down the Alt key while clicking a dot clears it.

QUICKTIP You can use Memory Dots also to save poses and camera settings.

Using Preferences

Poser lets you access the General Preferences dialog box with the Edit, General Preferences (Ctrl+K) command. This General Preferences dialog box includes five separate panels—Document, Interface, Library, Render, and Misc. The Library panel options are covered in Chapter 2, "Using the Poser Library," and the Render panel options are covered in Chapter 16, "Rendering Scenes."

The Document panel of the General Preferences dialog box, shown in Figure 1-34, includes a button to Set Preferred State. You can use this button to have Poser remember the current Document Window's state and figure. So, if you load a custom dragon model and you want this figure to appear as the default figure from then on, you can click the Set Preferred State button, and the dragon will become the default figure as long as the Launch to Preferred State option is selected. If you grow tired of the default dragon, enable the Launch to Factory State option to return to the original default figure.

NEW POSER 7 FEATURE

The Render panel in the General Preferences dialog box is new to Poser 7.

FIGURE 1-34
Document panel of the General Preferences dialog box

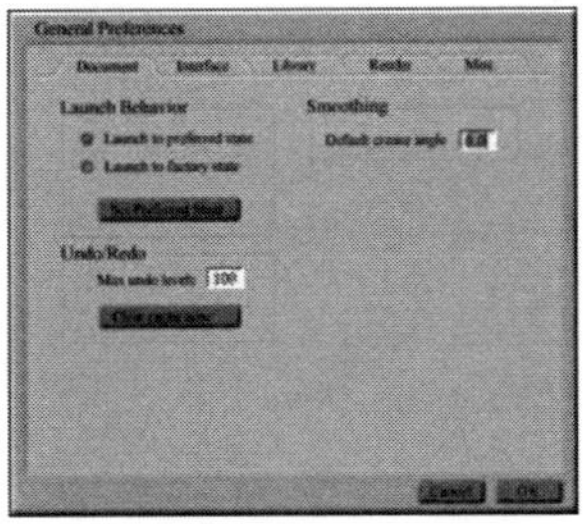

Using Undo/Redo

The Document panel also includes an option to set the maximum number of undo levels that Poser remembers. Poser will remember and let you undo all the previous commands up to this value. To move back and forward through the stored commands, use the Edit, Undo (Ctrl+Z) and Edit, Redo (Shift+Ctrl+Z) commands. There is also a button to Clear Cache Now, which eliminates any stored commands and frees up memory.

NEW POSER 7 FEATURE

The ability to undo multiple commands is new to Poser 7.

Setting the Global Smoothing Angle

The default crease angle sets the angle for all adjacent polygon faces required to smooth between them. If the angle between two adjacent polygon faces exceeds this value, the shared edges are not smoothed, but remain a hard edge. You can learn more about smoothing options in Chapter 8, "Creating and Applying Materials."

Restoring the Interface's Factory State

If you make changes to the interface, including the position and size of the Document Window and the location of the various controls, you can set these changes to be remembered next time you restart Poser using the Launch to Previous State option in the Interface panel, shown in Figure 1-35. If you enable Launch to Factory State, the default factory settings are used for the size and position of the Document Window and the interface window.

FIGURE 1-35
Interface panel of the General Preferences dialog box

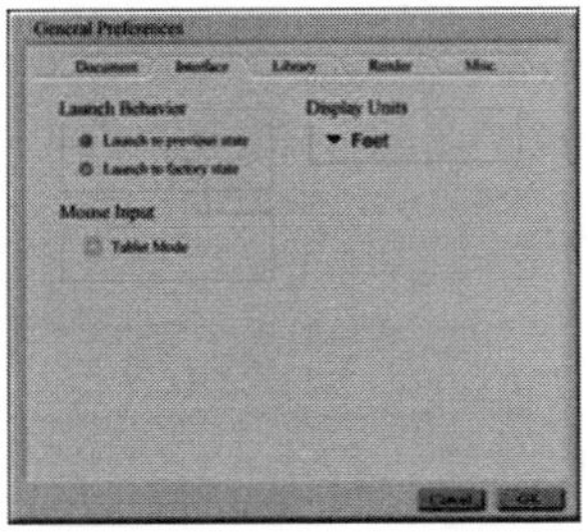

Enabling Tablet Mode

In the Interface panel of the General Preferences dialog box, you can enable the Tablet Mode option, which gives you support for a graphics tablet.

Changing Display Units

This Interface panel also includes a setting for the Display Units. The available options include Poser native units, Inches, Feet, Millimeters, Centimeters, and Meters. One native Poser unit is equal to roughly 8.6 feet or 2.6 meters.

Checking for Updates

The Misc panel of the General Preferences dialog box, shown in Figure 1-36, includes an option to Check for Updates on Launch. If this option is enabled, Poser will automatically check for updates every third time Poser launches using the Internet. You can also manually check for updates at any time via the Poser Web site using the Check Now button. If an update is found, a dialog box presents a link where you can download the update.

FIGURE 1-36
Misc panel of the General Preferences dialog box

Configure and Save the Interface

1. Drag the titles of the various interface elements, including the Document Window, to your liking.

2. Click on one of the empty dots in the UI Dots control to store the interface configuration.

3. Select and move each of the interface controls to a new location. Then click on the stored UI Dot selected earlier.

   The interface reverts to the saved configuration, as shown in Figure 1-37.

4. Choose File, Save As and save the file as **Custom configuration.pz3**.

FIGURE 1-37
You can recall saved interface configurations

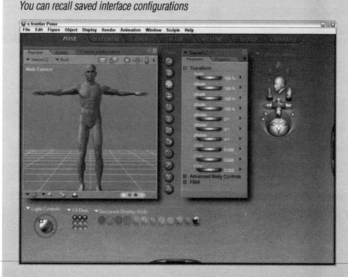

Save Interface Layouts

1. Pose the default figure and add some clothes to the scene.

2. Choose Edit, General Preferences (or press Ctrl+K).

   The General Preferences dialog box opens with the Document panel selected.

3. In the Document panel, enable the Launch to Preferred State option and click the Set Preferred State button.

4. Select the Interface panel, enable the Launch to Previous State option, and click OK.

5. Close and relaunch Poser.

   The layout configuration is retained from the previous session.

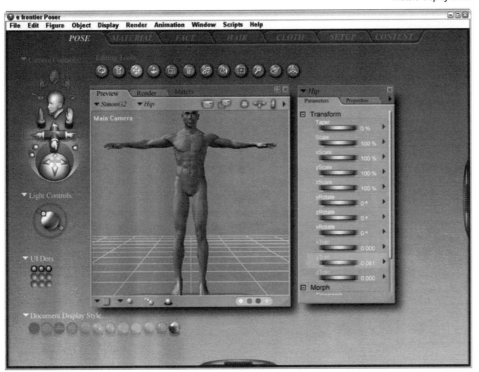

FIGURE 1-38

Meters display units

Change Display Units

1. Choose Edit, General Preferences (Ctrl+K) and click the Interface panel tab.

   The Interface panel of the General Preferences dialog box opens.

2. Select Meters as the Display Units option and click OK.

3. Select the hip object and open the Parameters/Properties panel.

   The translation values are listed in meter values, as shown in Figure 1-38.

4. Choose File, Save As and save the file as **Meters.pz3**.

GET
HELP

What You'll Do

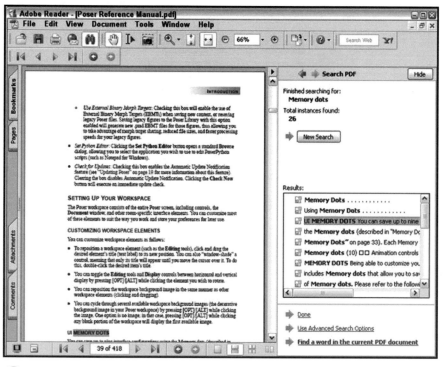

If you're looking for more help, Poser includes a detailed PDF-based set of help files that have all the answers. Poser also includes help for each room that you can access and an overall Quick Start dialog box with several project guides.

In this lesson, you learn how to access the Poser Help documentation.

Using Poser Documentation

To access the Poser documentation, select the Help, Poser Reference Manual menu command. This command opens the PDF Help files in Acrobat Reader, as shown in Figure 1-39. The Acrobat Reader interface lets you open specific topics using the pane on the left or search for specific words with its search feature.

Accessing Poser Tutorials

Many people learn better by seeing how a certain task is accomplished. You can learn from the Poser tutorials using the Help, Poser Tutorial Manual menu command. These tutorials are also PDF-based and open in Acrobat Reader.

Enabling Room Help

If you need help with a particular room, you can enable Room Help with the Window, Room Help menu command. When enabled, a pop-up Help window appears, as shown in Figure 1-40, with help specific to the current room.

FIGURE 1-39

Poser Reference Manual

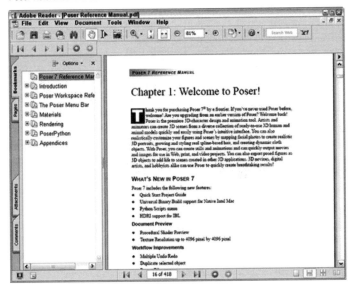

FIGURE 1-40

Room Help window

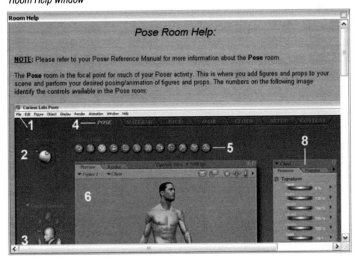

Using Quick Start

The Quick Start window, shown in
Figure 1-41, includes several project guides,
which are a set of steps for accomplishing
specific tasks. It appears when Poser is first
started, but can be accessed at any time using
the Window, Quick Start menu command.
The available project guides include Getting
Started, Rendering Styles, Pose Figure,
Add Props, and Lighting.

NEW POSER 7 FEATURE

The Quick Start feature with its various Project Guides
is new to Poser 7.

Accessing Online Help

At the bottom of the Help menu are several
commands for accessing helpful Web pages at
Content Paradise, e frontier, and the general
Poser community. Selecting any of these menu
commands opens a Web browser with the
selected Web page. In particular, the e frontier
pages include pages for registering Poser, getting support, and additional Poser tutorials.

Getting Help on the Web

The Help, Other Web Links include links to
several community pages that aren't
sponsored by e frontier. These sites provide
additional resources for locating Poser content
and tools.

FIGURE 1-41
Quick Start project guides window

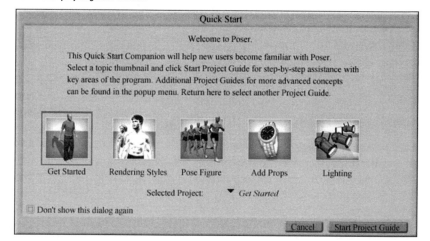

FIGURE 1-42

Searching Poser Help

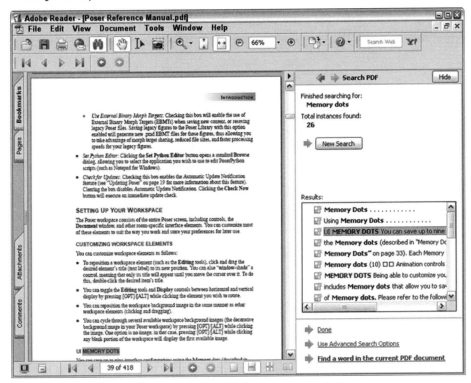

Access Poser Help

1. Choose Help, Poser Reference Manual.

   The Poser 7 Reference Manual PDF file is opened within Acrobat Reader.

2. Click the Search button in the Acrobat Reader toolbar and type Memory Dots in the Search field.

   After Poser searches the PDF file, it displays the available links, as shown in Figure 1-42.

3. Click a link to see the information on a topic.

CHAPTER REVIEW

Chapter Summary

This chapter introduced the Poser interface, including the various floating controls and the Document Window. It also introduced the different rooms that are available. You read about methods for configuring the interface, along with the General Preferences. The final lesson explained how to get help.

What You Have Learned

In this chapter, you

- Learned to work with the various interface controls, including menus, floating controls, and the Document Window.

- Accessed the Library and Animation Control palettes.

- Used the Camera and Light Controls and changed the display styles.

- Changed the number of views displayed in the Document Window.

- Altered the Document Window display options, including the tracking method, depth cueing, shadows, and colors.

- Explored the remaining rooms using the interface tabs.

- Configured the interface using the UI Dots and preference settings.

- Accessed the Poser Help files as a way to get additional help.

Key Terms from This Chapter

- **Display ports.** Additional sections of the Document Window that can display a different view of the scene.

- **Display styles.** Render options for the Document Window.

- **Document Window.** The main window interface where the posed figure is displayed.

- **Floating control.** An interface object that isn't attached to the interface window and can be placed anywhere within the interface window.

- **Interface.** A set of controls used to interact with the software features.

- **Keyboard shortcut.** A key or set of keys that can be used to execute a command.

- **OpenGL.** An option used to enable hardware acceleration for fast Document Window updates.

- **PDF file.** (Portable Document File) A document format created by Adobe used in Poser to view the Poser Refer-

ence Manual. PDF files require a Web browser or the Adobe Reader to read the files.

- **Preferences.** An interface for setting defaults and for configuring the interface.

- **Quick Start.** An interface with step-by-step project guides for accomplishing specific tasks.

- **Room tabs.** A set a tabs located at the top of the Poser interface that allow access to various feature interfaces.

- **Side window handle.** A simple control positioned on the side of the interface used to open another set of controls.

- **SreeD.** An option used to enable software rendering to be used if the OpenGL option causes display problems.

- **Tool titles.** The text that appears above each control set to help identify it.

- **Tracking mode.** Modes that define the detail of the objects displayed in the Document Window.

- **UI.** User interface.

- **UI Dots.** Interface controls used to remember and recall a specific interface configuration.

chapter 2
USING THE
POSER LIBRARY

1. Work with the Library.

2. Load Library figures.

3. Discover the Library categories.

4. Save content to the Library.

5. Remove content from the Library.

6. Use Content Collections.

chapter 2 USING THE POSER LIBRARY

When you first launch Poser, it loads the default SimonG2 Casual figure. This figure is a nice piece of work, but if you want to add your own clothes, you can find several versions of Simon in the Library, including figures with and without clothes. Luckily, the Library palette includes an assortment of clothes that you can put on Simon along with several additional figures that you can load if you think that Simon is too shifty eyed. There is even a folder full of animal figures if you're more interested in a furry figure.

You can access the Library by clicking on the interface handle located on the right side of the interface. This slides the Library palette out into the main interface, or you can also undock the Library palette from the interface and expand it to make it larger and easier to work with.

The Poser Library comes pre-populated with an ample selection of content—

including figures, poses, expressions, hair, props, and more—spread across several different categories. Each item within the Library displays a thumbnail of the selected object along with buttons to add the selected item to the current scene. There are also buttons to add and remove content from the Library.

The Library is also extensible, allowing you to save your own content to the Library in each of the various categories. You can even create your own content folders and library sets. The Library also features Content Collections that let you organize specific sets of content into an easy-to-access collection.

All content displayed within the Library palette is mirrored on the local hard drive, where it can manually be manipulated to move large numbers of content objects at once including copies of other shifty eyed figures that you come across.

Tools You'll Use

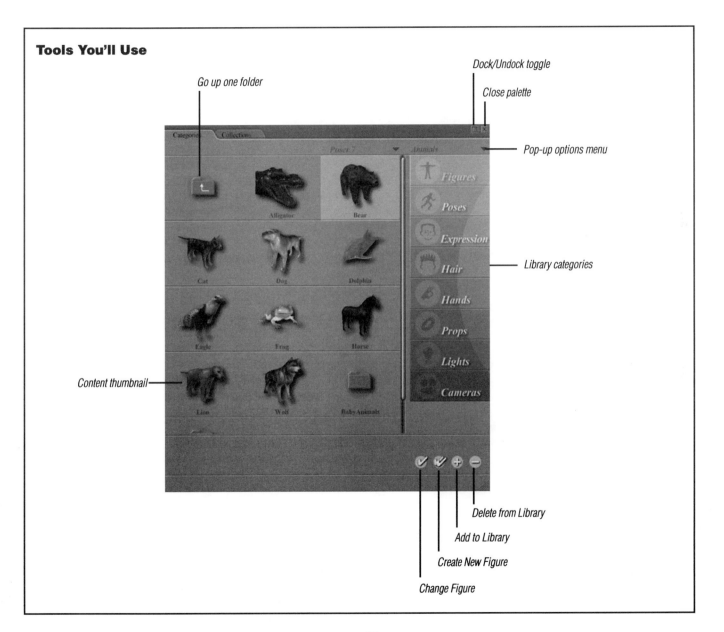

Go up one folder

Dock/Undock toggle

Close palette

Pop-up options menu

Library categories

Content thumbnail

Figures

Poses

Expression

Hair

Hands

Props

Lights

Cameras

Delete from Library

Add to Library

Create New Figure

Change Figure

WORK WITH THE
LIBRARY

What You'll Do

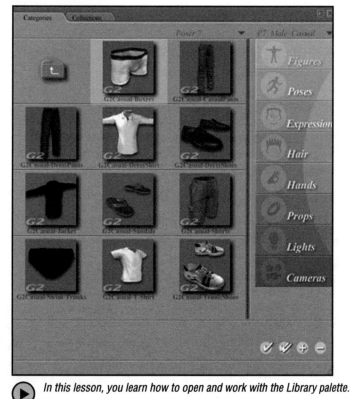

The Poser Library is a hidden palette located along the right side of the interface, but you can change it to a floating palette that can be positioned anywhere and resized as needed.

▶ In this lesson, you learn how to open and work with the Library palette.

Opening the Library Palette

To open the Library palette, simply click on the handle located to the right of the interface. This causes the Library palette to slide out towards the middle of the interface, as shown in Figure 2-1. The palette can be returned to its hiding spot by clicking again on the palette handle or by clicking the Close palette button in the upper-right corner. You can also open the Library palette with the Window, Libraries menu command.

Undocking the Library Palette

If you click the Dock/Undock button in the upper-right corner of the Library palette, the palette becomes a floating window, shown in Figure 2-2, that you can move by dragging its title bar and resize by dragging its lower-right corner. The undocked palette also shows both thumbnails and the categories at the same time.

Expanding the Library Palette's Width

While the Library palette is undocked, you can increase its width by dragging on the lower-right corner of the palette. This allows more content to be viewed within the palette, as shown in Figure 2-3.

Close button
Dock/Undock button

FIGURE 2-1
Library palette

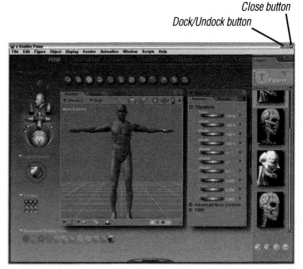

FIGURE 2-2
Unlocked Library palette

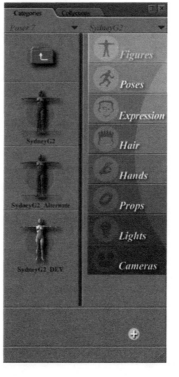

FIGURE 2-3
Unlocked Library palette with increased width

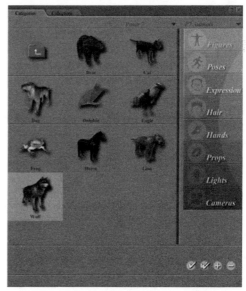

Navigating the Library Palette

All of the content in the Library is hierarchically organized into folders. To open a folder, simply double-click on the folder icon. To go up a level, double-click on the folder at the top of the palette with an up arrow on it. If you keep clicking up the hierarchy of folders, you'll eventually reach two folders labeled Poser 7 (with a red dot by it) and Downloads, as shown in Figure 2-4. The Poser 7 folder is the default folder that includes all the content that ships with Poser 7, and the Downloads folder includes all the content that is downloaded and installed using the Content Room.

You can also jump to a specific Library folder using the Root folder drop-down list or to a specific Content folder using the pop-up menu, which lists all the available folders as menus and submenus. The drop-down lists are updated to include any new folders as they are added.

NEW POSER 7 FEATURE
The ability to select specific Library and Content folders from the drop-down lists is new to Poser 7.

FIGURE 2-4
Root folders in the Library palette

Root folder drop-down list

Content folders drop-down list

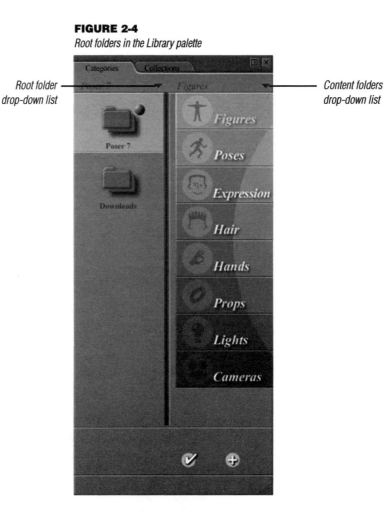

Switching Between Libraries

The red dot next to the Poser 7 folder marks the active library. Only the active library can be navigated. You can make a library the current folder by selecting it and clicking on the Make Current button at the bottom of the palette, or you can just double-click on the Library folder to open the folder and make it active.

Over time, you'll add new content folders to the Library and you can use the Root folder drop-down list to jump straight to a root folder instead of having to navigate all the way up the existing folders and then back down again.

> **NOTE** Several categories include a folder named Poser 7, but the root folder is all the way at the top of the available folders and is marked with a red dot.

Setting Library Preferences

The Library panel of the General Preferences dialog box, shown in Figure 2-5, includes options for defining the action of double-clicking on the thumbnails found in the Library palette. The options include Add to Scene (which adds another figure to the scene) or Replace Existing (which replaces the current figure with the one from the Library).

> **NOTE** Only the Figures and Lights categories include an option to replace the current object; all other categories will only let you add the content to the scene.

FIGURE 2-5
Library panel of the General Preferences dialog box

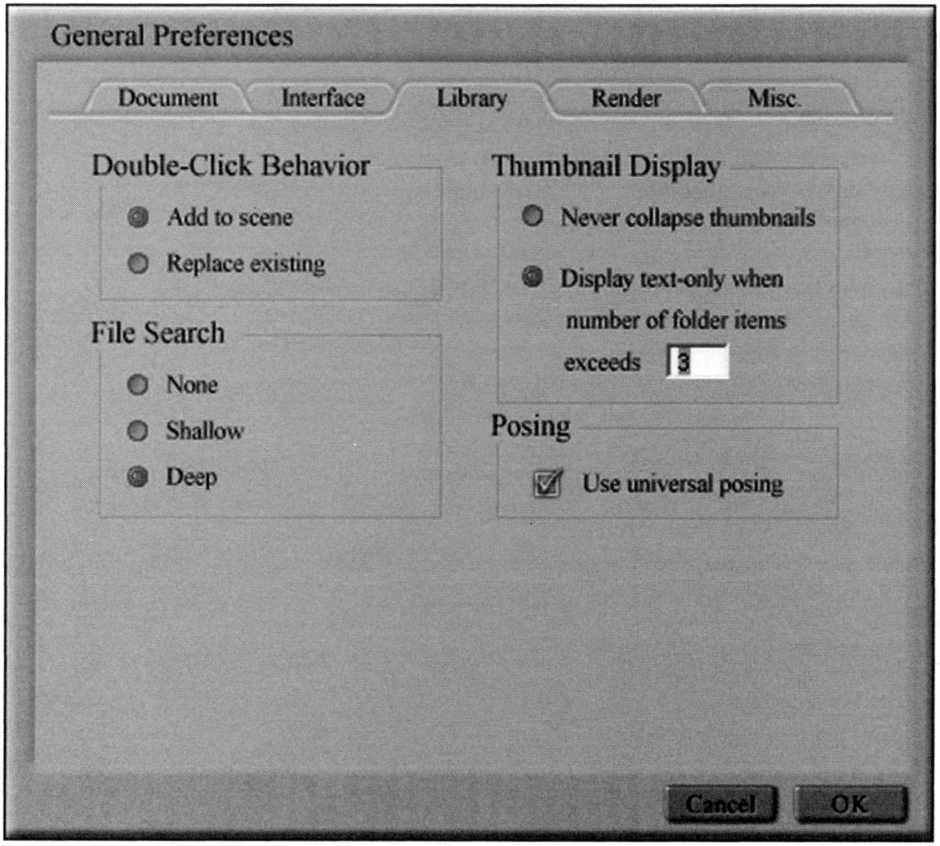

When a complex piece of content (such as a figure) is loaded, it often includes multiple files for textures. The File Search setting determines how aggressively to search for referenced files. The None option doesn't search at all and simply presents a warning dialog box with a message that some content files couldn't be found. It also includes a Browse button for locating the missing file. The Shallow option searches the surrounding folders, and the Deep option searches extensively through all the content folders, which could take some time.

You can also select to never collapse thumbnails (which requires more memory) or to display text-only when the number of items in the folder exceeds a designated value. The value of thumbnails is that they show what the item looks like, but with many items in a Library folder, showing all thumbnails can slow down the system.

NOTE If you select the Display Text-Only option, the items in the Library aren't really collapsed. The spacing stays the same; only the thumbnail images are replaced with a question mark.

The Use Universal Posing option enables Poser 7 to use a new format for saving poses. This new format allows older Poser models to assume any saved Library pose even if its skeleton doesn't exactly match the current structure. For example, some older Poser skeletons didn't have defined finger joints, so applying a pose that involved posed fingers was problematic. With the Universal Posing format, these poses will work just fine. If the Use Universal Posing option is selected, all poses saved to the Library are converted to this new format.

NEW POSER 7 FEATURE
The Use Universal Posing format is new to Poser 7.

Open and Unlock the Library Palette

1. Open Poser with the default man visible.
2. Click on the side handle at the right of the interface.

   The Library palette extends from the side of the interface.

3. Click the Dock/Undock button to the upper right of the palette.

   The Library palette becomes a floating palette.

4. Drag the lower-right corner of the palette to increase its width.

5. With the Figures category selected, double-click on the G2/G2 Male Clothes/P7 Male Casual folder.

   The thumbnails for the set of male casual clothes are displayed within the Library palette, as shown in Figure 2-6.

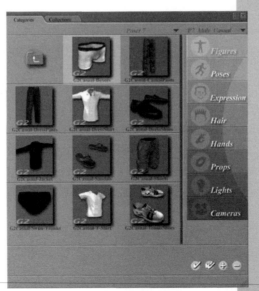

FIGURE 2-6
The male casual clothes thumbnails are shown in the Library palette

LOAD LIBRARY FIGURES

What You'll Do

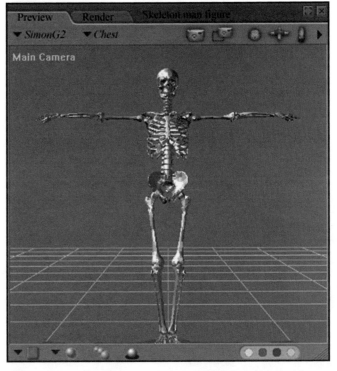

In this lesson, you learn how to load new figures from the Library.

The first place to look if you want to work with a new **figure** is the **Library palette.** In addition to Library figures, you can use models created in other 3D packages by importing them using the File, Import command. Keep in mind that a bone structure needs to be attached to imported models before you can pose them. All default Library figures already have bones attached. Importing files is covered in Chapter 4, "Working with Files and Accessing Content Paradise," and building a bone structure is covered in Chapter 12, "Rigging a Figure with Bones."

Viewing the Library Figures

To select and load new figures from the Library palette, click the Figures category. Several folder images of the available Library figures are displayed. Double-clicking a folder will open it to reveal its contents. Within the folders are thumbnails of the various available figures, as shown for the Jessi figure in Figure 2-7. When a figure thumbnail is selected, four buttons appear at the bottom of the palette. These buttons are Change Figure, Create New Figure, Add to Library, and Remove from Library.

> **NOTE** If the number of thumbnails exceeds the palette space, dragging the scroll bar to the right of the figure thumbnails shows additional figure thumbnails.

Replacing the Current Figure

Selecting a figure thumbnail and clicking the Change Figure button replaces the current Poser figure with the selected thumbnail figure. When you click the Change Figure button, the Keep Customized Geometry dialog box, shown in Figure 2-8, appears. Using the options in this dialog box, you can maintain any modified geometries and keep any props or deformers attached to the figure. There is also a button to cancel the figure change.

> **NOTE** Some clothing items are added to the scene as figures and not as props.

FIGURE 2-7
Figure thumbnails

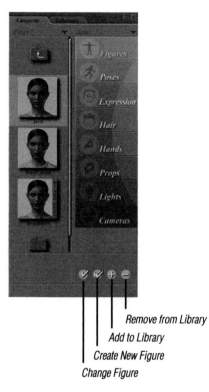

Remove from Library
Add to Library
Create New Figure
Change Figure

FIGURE 2-8
Keep Customized Geometry dialog box

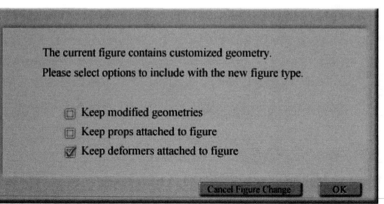

The current figure contains customized geometry.
Please select options to include with the new figure type.

☐ Keep modified geometries
☐ Keep props attached to figure
☑ Keep deformers attached to figure

Cancel Figure Change   OK

Following the Keep Customized Geometry dialog box, the Keep Scales dialog box, shown in Figure 2-9 appears where you can select to maintain the current figure proportions. Figure 2-10 shows the mannequin figure that has replaced the default figure.

> **QUICKTIP** If you spent some time posing and moving a figure, you can keep the work even though you're loading a new figure by selecting the options in the Keep Customized Geometry and Keep Scales dialog boxes.

Adding a Figure to the Current Scene

Clicking the Add New Item button in the Library palette adds the selected figure to the scene without removing the existing figure. Using this button, you can add multiple figures to a single scene. Figure 2-11 shows the default man sharing the scene with mannequin figure loaded from the Library.

> **QUICKTIP** When new figures are added to the scene, they are placed in the center of the scene right on top of the existing figure. To see both figures side by side, you'll need to move one or the another.

FIGURE 2-9
Keep Scales dialog box

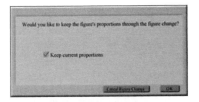

FIGURE 2-10
Replaced figure

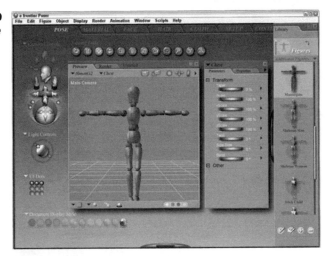

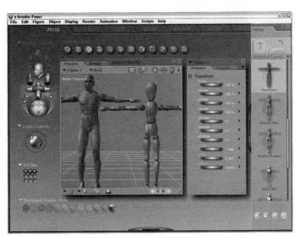

FIGURE 2-11
Multiple figures

1. Open the Poser interface.

2. Click the side interface control to open the Library palette.

   The Library palette is displayed.

3. Select the Figures category icon. Several figure thumbnails are displayed within the Library palette.

4. Double click on the Additional Figures folder and scroll downward in the Library palette and select the Skeleton Man thumbnail.

5. Click the Change Figure button ✔ at the bottom of the Library palette.

6. Click OK in the Keep Customized Geometry and the Keep Scale dialog boxes that appear.

   The new figure replaces the default figure in the Document Window, as shown in Figure 2-12.

7. Select File, Save As and save the file as **Skeleton man figure.pz3**.

FIGURE 2-12

Skeleton Man figure

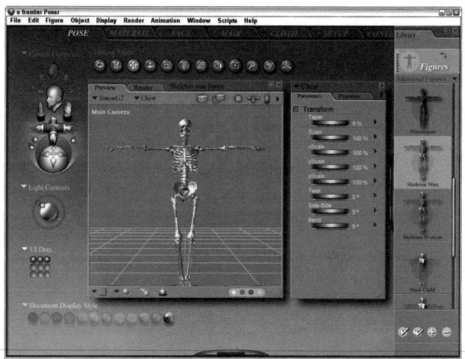

DISCOVER THE
LIBRARY CATEGORIES

What You'll Do

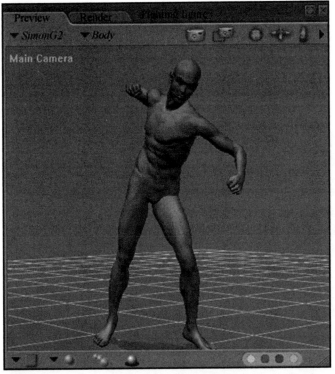

The Library palette includes much more content than just figures. It has a repository of content organized by category, including figures, poses, expressions, hair, hands, props, lights, and cameras.

▶ *In this lesson, you learn about the other categories in the Library.*

Accessing Other Library Categories

From the figure thumbnails, you can access the Library categories again by clicking the Category button located at the top of the Library palette, as shown in Figure 2-13. You can also access the various categories directly using the small circle category buttons to the left of the current category title or from a list using the pop-up menu.

> **NOTE** There is actually another Library category. The Materials category is only accessible from the Material Room.

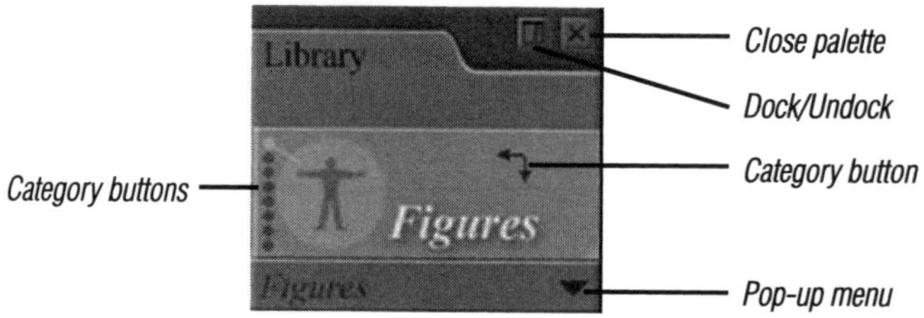

Loading Library Poses and Motions

The second category in the Library holds figure poses. To access the available poses from the Library, click the Poses category and navigate to the folder containing the types of poses you want to apply to the current figure. Within each folder are thumbnails of the various poses. With a pose thumbnail selected, click the Change Pose button at the bottom of the Library palette. The selected pose is then applied to the current figure. Figure 2-14 shows several pose thumbnails contained in the Action folder with one applied to the default figure.

FIGURE 2-13
Library palette navigation controls

Close palette
Dock/Undock
Category buttons
Category button
Pop-up menu

FIGURE 2-14
Library palette navigation controls

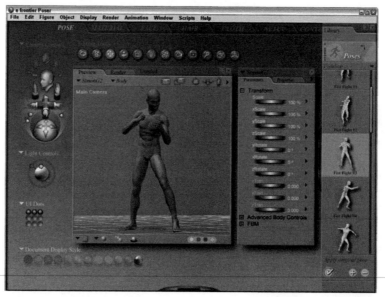

In addition to poses, the Poses category also holds some animated motions. Motion thumbnails are identified by the number of frames listed in the upper-right corner of the thumbnail, as shown in Figure 2-15.

Loading Facial Expressions

The Expressions category in the Library holds various expressions to show emotion, as shown in Figure 2-16. These expressions can be edited using the settings found in the Face Room. The Face Room is covered in more detail in Chapter 9, "Creating a Face and Facial Expressions." To load an expression from the Library, simply select it and click the Apply Library Preset button. The selected expression will replace the current face setting on the current figure.

QUICK TIP If you're unsure about which expression to load, you can select to load the Random Face option located at the bottom of most of the default Expression folders. This option randomly changes the face to different and unique expressions every time it's applied.

FIGURE 2-15
Motion files in the Library

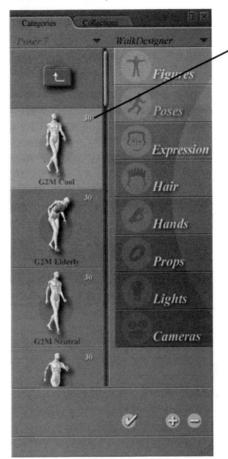

Number of frames

FIGURE 2-16
Expressions in the Library

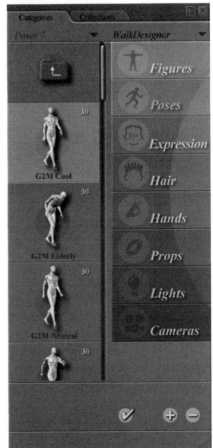

Loading Hair

The next three categories let you load hair, hands, and props. The Hair category includes both the older prop-based hair and the newer dynamic strand-based hair. Strand-based hair is identified by a label to the right of the thumbnail that says, "Strand," as shown in Figure 2-17. Strand-based hair can be edited using the controls in the Hair Room. You can learn more about using prop-based hair in Chapter 5, "Dealing with Props," and more about using strand-based hair in Chapter 10, "Adding Hair."

NOTE The Hair category in the Library also includes some thumbnails that are denoted as "Trans Map." This label indicates that the hair includes a transparent texture map for greater realism.

Loading Hand Poses

Posing hands can be time-consuming, so you might want to load a default hand pose from the Library to save you the work. When applying a hand pose, a simple dialog box, shown in Figure 2-18, appears asking if you want to apply the pose to the Left Hand or the Right Hand. To apply the pose to both hands, you'll need to apply it twice.

FIGURE 2-17
Strand-based hair thumbnail

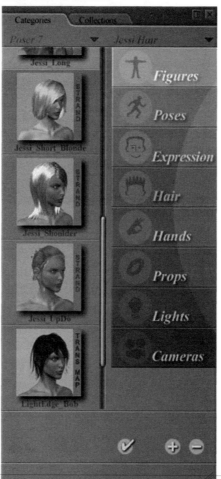

FIGURE 2-18
Hand poses can be applied to either hand

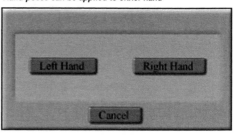

Loading Props

The Props category can include a variety of objects from scene objects such as furniture, as shown in Figure 2-19, to figure-specific objects like clothing. Some clothing thumbnails within the Props category are identified with a "Conforming" label. These items can be made to conform to a figure for proper fit using the Figure, Conform To menu command. You can learn more about using conforming clothes in Chapter 5, "Dealing with Props."

FIGURE 2-19
Prop Library folder

Loading Library Light and Camera Settings

To access the available lights and cameras from the Library, click either category and navigate the folders until you find just the light or camera you want to apply to the current scene. Each light and camera thumbnail shows the default figure using the lighting or camera setup.

For the Lights category, both the Apply Library Preset and the Create New Light buttons are enabled, thus allowing you to replace the existing set of lights or add to the existing set.

NEW POSER 7 FEATURE
The ability to add a new light set to the current light set is new to Poser 7.

With the desired thumbnail selected, click the Change Item button at the bottom of the Library palette, and the selected light or camera set is loaded into the Document Window. Figure 2-20 shows several light and camera thumbnails found in the Library.

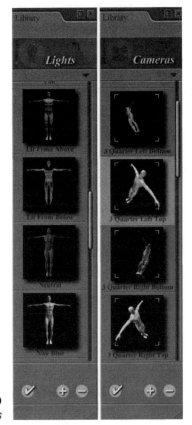

FIGURE 2-20
Some available Library lights and cameras

Loading Materials from the Library

To access the available materials from the Library, you need to have the Material Room open, and then click the Materials category and navigate to the folder containing the types of materials you want to apply. Several unique sets of material folders are available in the default installation. Within each folder are thumbnails of the various materials. With a material thumbnail selected, click the Apply Library Preset button at the bottom of the Library palette, and the selected material is loaded into the Shader Window and applied to the selected material group. Figure 2-21 shows several material thumbnails contained in the Basic Materials folder with the Fireball material loaded.

> **NOTE** For some loaded materials viewed in the Simple panel, a small exclamation point icon is visible in the upper-right corner of the various properties, as shown in Figure 2-21. This icon indicates that some additional parameter values are available for this property that can only be accessed from within the Advanced panel.

FIGURE 2-21
Loaded Library material

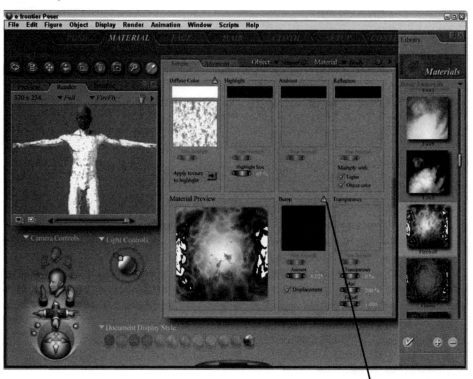

Additional parameters exist

Load Content from the Library

1. Open Poser with the default man visible.

2. lick the side control to the right of the interface to open the Library palette or select Window, Libraries.

3. Click the Poses category at the top of the Library palette and locate and open the G2/G2 Male/Action/Fighting folder. Then select the Fist Fight 05 thumbnail. Click the Change Item button 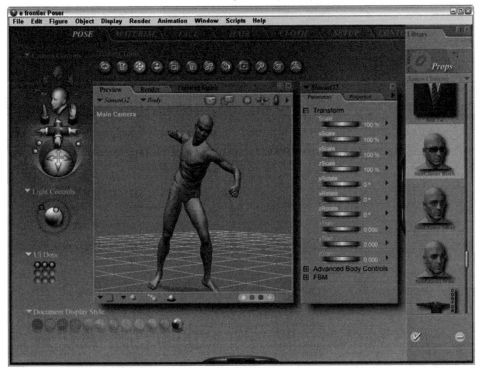 at the bottom of the Library palette.

   The figure assumes the selected pose.

4. Select the Expression category and open the Poser 7/SimonG2 folder. Then select the Simon Disgust thumbnail and click the Apply Library Preset button.

   The figure assumes an angry expression to accompany his fighting stance.

5. Select the Props category and open the Poser 6/James Clothing folder. Select the SunGlasses Black thumbnail and click the Apply Library Preset button.

   The figure now is wearing glasses, as shown in Figure 2-22.

6. Select File, Save As and save the file as **Fighting figure.pz3**.

NOTE You didn't add clothes to this figure yet because they require an additional step to conform the clothes to the body, which is covered in Chapter 5, "Dealing with Props."

Load Light and Camera Settings from the Library

1. Open Poser with the default man visible.

2. Click the side control to the right of the interface to open the Library palette or select Window, Libraries.

3. Click the Lights category at the top of the Library palette and open the Light Sets folder. Locate the Lit from Below light setting. Then click the Change Item button 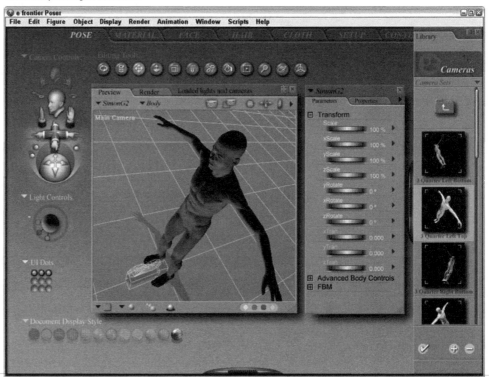 at the bottom of the Library palette.

   The scene is updated with the new light settings.

4. Click the Cameras category at the top of the Library palette and open the Camera Sets folder. Locate the 3 Quarter Left Top camera setting. Then click the Change Item button at the bottom of the Library palette.
   The scene is updated with the new camera settings, as shown in Figure 2-23.

5. Select File, Save As and save the file as **Loaded lights and camera.pz3**.

FIGURE 2-23

Scene with preset lights and camera

SAVE CONTENT TO THE LIBRARY

What You'll Do

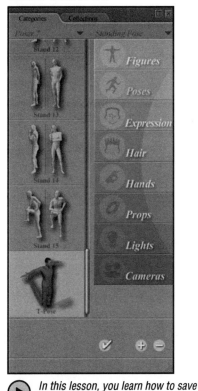

In this lesson, you learn how to save content and settings to the Library.

Although Poser ships with a fairly extensive library of content, it won't be long before you'll want to add your own figures and content to the Library. Poser allows you to intermingle your saved content with the default library, or you can create your own library folder to hold all your creations. When content is saved to the Library, data files are saved to the hard drive using the following file types:

• Figures are saved as .CR2 files.

• Poses are saved as .PZ2 files.

• Expressions are saved as .FC2 files.

• Hair is saved as .HR2 files.

• Hands are saved as .HD2 files.

• Props are saved as .PP2 files.

• Lights are saved as .LT2 files.

• Cameras are saved as .CM2 files.

• Materials are saved as .MT5 files.

Creating New Content Folders

When a typical content folder is opened, the bottom of the Library palette's pop-up menu has an option to Add New Category. If you select this option, a dialog box appears asking you to type a name for the new content folder. The new folder is added to the current open Library folder, thus providing you a place where you can save new content.

Creating a New Runtime Folder

By default, Poser 7 includes two libraries, the Poser 7 library and the Download library. You can see both of these library folders by navigating to the top of the folder hierarchy. When these two default library folders are visible, you can select the Add New Runtime menu from the pop-up menu or click on the Add Runtime button at the bottom of the palette to create a new library folder. Using either of these commands opens a file dialog box, shown in Figure 2-24, where you can browse to an existing folder and name the folder. There is also a button to Make New Folder.

When a new runtime library folder is created, it automatically creates subfolders for each of the default categories at the same time. All of the new subfolder names match the library categories except that figures are placed in the Character folder and expressions are saved in the Face folder.

Adding Content to the Library

With the Library palette open, you can add the current selection of content to the Library using the Add to Library button located at the bottom of the Library palette (it looks like a plus sign). The type of content that is saved depends on the Library category that is currently opened. For example, if you have the Figures category in the Library open, selecting the Add to Library button will save the current figure in the library, but if you have the Props category in the Library open, the Add to Library button is only active if you have a prop selected in the Actor List.

FIGURE 2-24
The Browse for Folder dialog box lets you create a new library

When the Add to Library button is clicked, a simple dialog box, shown in Figure 2-25, appears where you can name the new content.

FIGURE 2-25
The New Set dialog box lets you name the thumbnail

Setting the Library Thumbnail

The thumbnail that appears in the Library palette when content is added to the Library is taken from the current view in the Document Window. To create a better thumbnail, position the camera and change the display style before adding the content to the Library.

Creating a Custom Library Thumbnail

When content is added to a library, several files are saved to the hard drive, and one of these files is a .PNG file that is named the same as the content's name located where the content was saved. The thumbnail images are 91 by 91 pixels. If you locate this .PNG file, you can edit it in a program like Photoshop. If you don't change the file's name, the edited image will appear in the Library palette when the palette is refreshed.

Saving Poses and Subsets

When the Poses category is selected in the Library palette, the Add to Library button offers the option to save just a subset of the entire figure hierarchy. The New Set dialog box for poses, shown in Figure 2-26, includes a button called Select Subset, which opens the Select Objects hierarchical list of body parts. Using this dialog box, you can select just the specific body parts to include with the pose.

FIGURE 2-26
You can choose to save only a subset of the pose

After the New Set dialog box closes, an extra dialog box, shown in Figure 2-27, appears that gives you the option to save morph channels and body transformations with the pose. Morph channels are intermediate positions of the body that you can animate between. More on creating morph channels is covered in Chapter 14, "Morphing Figures."

> **CAUTION** If a scene includes multiple objects with morph targets or a prop with morph targets that is parented to a figure, only the morph targets for the selected item will be saved to the Library if the Use External Binary Morph Targets option is enabled in the General panel of the Preferences dialog box. To save all morph targets, disable this option before saving to the Library.

The Body Transformation option saves any movements to the body object such as repositioning the figure in the scene.

> **NEW POSER 7 FEATURE**
> The ability to save body transformations with a figure's pose is new to Poser 7.

FIGURE 2-27
Additional Information can be saved with a pose

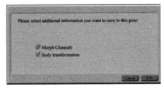

Saving Motions

Following the dialog box to save morph channels and body transformations, a Save Frames dialog box, shown in Figure 2-28, appears when saving a pose. Using this dialog box, you can save the current motion keyframes to the Library along with the pose. When a motion is saved with the pose, the number of frames included in the pose is listed in the upper-right corner of the pose thumbnail automatically. This helps remind you that this saved file includes motion and not just a pose.

> **NOTE** If the motion you are saving is divided into animation layers, a Select Layers button appears in the Save Frames dialog box. Clicking this button opens a dialog box where you can select the specific layers to save.

FIGURE 2-28
Poses can also hold motion

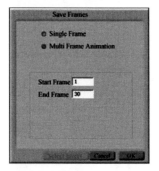

Saving Props

When parented props are saved to the Library, a dialog box opens asking if you want to save the prop as a smart object. If you click Yes, the parent relationships between the prop and its parent are preserved, but clicking No causes the parent-child link to be broken.

> **QUICKTIP** When you save a prop to the Library, the current figure is included with the prop thumbnail. To capture a thumbnail without a figure, simply hide the figure with the Figure, Hide Figure menu command before clicking the Add to Library button.

Saving Hair and Cloth

Strand-based hair can be saved to the Library in the Props category, but you'll need to save the prop object that it is grown from or you'll lose the positional information for the hair. The easiest way to do this is to create a prop based on the selected polygons where the hair is set to grow. If you click on the Edit Growth Group in the Hair Room and click on the Create Prop button in the Group Editor, a prop will be created that is identical to the hair growth group. You can learn more about this procedure in Chapter 5, "Dealing with Props." Once a new prop is made, you can grow hair on it, and the hair and prop can be saved to the Library. Be sure to use the Select Subset button to select both the prop and hair objects. When a prop with hair is saved to the Library, all the hair settings specified in the Hair Room are also saved.

> **CAUTION** Hair that has been applied directly to a body part cannot be saved in the Library.

If you've specified some dynamic cloth objects within your scene, the best way to save your settings is to save the cloth as part of the scene file using the File, Save As menu command. If you save the cloth object to the Props library, all of the custom dynamic cloth settings and simulation keys will be lost.

Saving Materials

The current material selected in the Material Room can also be saved to the Library using the Add to Library button located at the bottom of the Library palette. This button opens the New Material Set dialog box, shown in Figure 2-29, where you can name the current material set and the thumbnail for the current material is added to the open Library folder. The dialog box also includes options to save a Single Material or a Material Collection. If the Material Collection option is selected, you can click the Select Materials button to open a separate dialog box, shown in Figure 2-30, where you can select which materials to include in the collection. The thumbnail for the material collection shows the current scene.

FIGURE 2-29
You can choose to save materials as collections

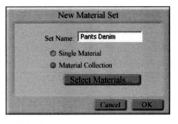

FIGURE 2-30
Select Materials dialog box

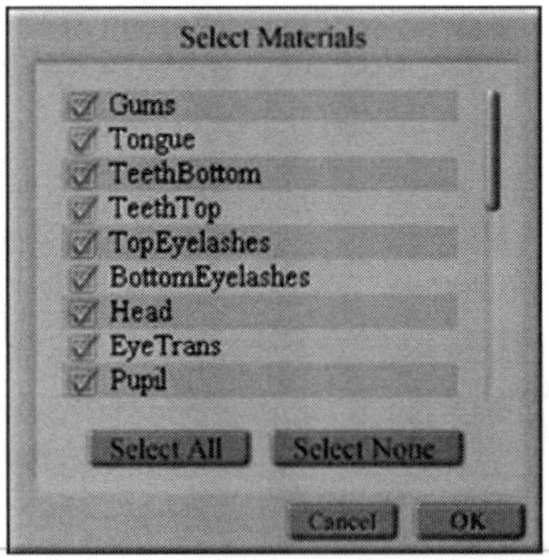

Create a New Library

1. Click the side interface control to open the Library palette or select the Window, Libraries menu command (if necessary).

2. Double-click on the folder with an up arrow displayed on it until you see the Poser 7 folder.

3. Select the Add New Category option from the pop-up options menu.

   The Browse for Folder dialog box appears.

4. Browse to the location on the hard drive where the new library will be saved and select or create a new folder. Click the OK button.

   A new folder appears below the Poser 7 folder, as shown in Figure 2-31.

5. Double-click the new folder to select and open it.

6. Select the Add New Category option from the pop-up options menu to add a new folder for the selected category.

FIGURE 2-31
A new library folder

Add a Figure Pose to the Library

1. Click the side interface control to open the Library palette or select the Window, Libraries menu command (if necessary).

2. Select the Poses category and double-click to open the James Pose, Standing, Standing Pose folder where the pose will be saved.

3. Click on the Texture Shaded option in the Display Style toolbar.

4. Click the Add to Library button ⊕ at the bottom of the Library palette. The New Set dialog box appears.

5. Type the name, T-Pose, in the Set Name dialog box and click OK.

   The Morph Channels/Body Transformation dialog box appears.

6. Keep both options disabled and click the OK button.

   The Save Frames dialog box appears.

7. Select the Single Frame option and click the OK button.

   The default figure is added to the Library with its thumbnail listed in alphabetical order, as shown in Figure 2-32.

FIGURE 2-32
New pose added to the Library

Create a Custom Library Thumbnail

1. Load the T-Pose pose from the Library and rotate the camera around to show an angled view of the figure.

2. Open the Render, Render Dimensions dialog box and set the Width and Height values both to 91. You'll need to select the Render to Exact Resolution option and disable the Constrain Aspect Ratio option. Then, click on the Render button at the top of the Document Window to render the current figure.

3. Click on the Document Window pop-up menu and choose the Export Image option. Name the file the same as the loaded pose, T-Pose, and save it as a PNG file in the same directory as the existing thumbnail. A warning dialog box appears asking if you want to replace the existing file.

4. Click the Yes button to replace the existing file. Then open the Library palette again and notice how the thumbnail has changed, as shown in Figure 2-33.

FIGURE 2-33
The library shows an updated thumbnail

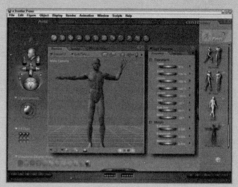

Save Motions to the Library

1. Choose File, Open and select and open the Waving figure.pz3 file.

2. Click the side control to the right of the interface to open the Library palette or select Window, Libraries.

3. Click the Poses category at the top of the Library palette and open the Walk Designer folder.

4. Drag the Timeline ▼━━━━━ in the Animation Controls to the final frame.

5. Click the Add to Library button ⊕ at the bottom of the Library palette and name the motion **Waving Figure** in the Set Name dialog box that appears. Then, click OK. A simple dialog box will then ask if you want to include morph channels. Click Yes.

6. In the Save Frames dialog box that appears, select the Multi Frame Animation option and click OK.

   The new motion thumbnail appears in the open folder, as shown in Figure 2-34.

FIGURE 2-34
New motion added to the Library

FIGURE 2-35

New prop added to the Library

1. Select File, Open and open the Imported
   table prop.pz3 file.

2. Select SimonG2 from the Figure List at the
   top of the Document Window.

3. Select the Figure, Figure Hide menu.

   *The scene figure is hidden, leaving only the
   table prop object.*

4. Drag on the Camera Controls until the table
   is centered within the Document Window.

5. Select the table prop from the Actor List at
   the top of the Document Window.

6. Click the side interface tab to open the
   Library palette and select a folder where you
   want to save the prop thumbnail.

7. Click the Add to Library button ⊕ at the
   bottom of the Library palette.

   The Set Name dialog box appears.

8. Enter Table as the name of this prop and
   click OK.

   *The new prop appears in the folder
   thumbnails, as shown in Figure 2-35.*

REMOVE CONTENT
FROM THE LIBRARY

What You'll Do

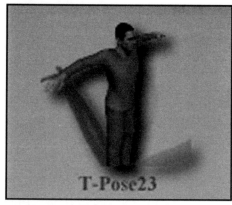

In this lesson, you learn how to create and work with Content Collections.

You use the right-most button at the bottom of the Library palette (the one with a minus sign on it) to remove the selected thumbnail from the Library. This can help to keep your Library content organized.

> **CAUTION** Removing items from the Library removes them from your computer's hard drive also.

Removing Library Content

The Remove from Library button is only enabled when a thumbnail is selected. When the Remove from Library button is clicked, a warning dialog box, shown in Figure 2-36, appears. Clicking the Yes button permanently deletes the content from the Library and from your hard drive, and clicking the No button cancels the action.

FIGURE 2-36
Remove content warning

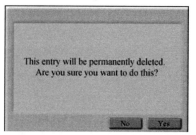

This entry will be permanently deleted.
Are you sure you want to do this?

No   Yes

Removing a Runtime Library

When a root library folder is selected, clicking on the Remove Runtime option removes the library folder without any

warning. This action doesn't remove the content from the hard drive, it only severs the link to the content. To reestablish the connection, simply use the Create a New Library command from the pop-up menu again.

To permanently remove an entire library of content, locate the library's name on the local hard drive and delete its folder along with all its subfolders.

Renaming Library Content

There isn't a command to rename any of the content thumbnails, but if you rename all the files (there are typically three files with each content object) associated with a piece of content on the hard drive, the new name will appear within the Library palette. This works for category folders also, but to rename the library folder, you need to create a new link to the renamed folder using the Add New Runtime pop-up menu command.

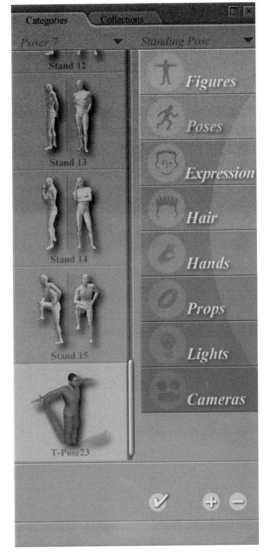

1. Open the Library palette and locate a thumbnail that you want to rename.

2. Search the local hard drive for the thumbnail's name.

3. Locate and rename all three files that have the same name as the selected thumbnail.

4. Navigate up a folder and back down to the folder with the renamed content.

   The thumbnail now has a new name, as shown in Figure 2-37.

FIGURE 2-37

Renamed library content

USE CONTENT
COLLECTIONS

What You'll Do

The Library is great for gathering together content into the various categories, but if you want to gather several different types of content into a single group, you can use the Collections panel to create a unique group of content from all the different categories.

NEW POSER 7 FEATURE
Content Collections are new to Poser 7.

Creating a Collection

If you right-click on any thumbnail in the Library, an Add to Collection menu option appears. If you select the Add to Collection, Add New Category menu option, the New Library Name dialog box, shown in Figure 2-38, lets you name the new collection.

Adding Items to a Collection

Once you've created a new collection, its name appears in the right-click pop-up menu under the Add to Collection menu. If you right-click on a thumbnail, you can add the selected piece of content to any of the collections.

FIGURE 2-38
New Library Name dialog box

 In this lesson, you learn how to create and work with Content Collections.

Viewing a Content Collection

To view a collection of content, you'll need to undock the Library. When undocked, a Collections tab appears at the top of the Library palette. If you select this tab, the available collections are displayed as folders, as shown in Figure 2-39, and the various content added to each collection is contained within each folder.

Using a Content Collection

All the content contained within a Content Collection can be used in the same manner as using the content from the Library. Selecting a thumbnail and clicking the Add New Item button adds the content to the scene.

Managing a Content Collection

You can remove thumbnails within collections by using the Delete from Library button. However, when content is deleted from a collection, it is removed from the collection, but not from the original Library category.

FIGURE 2-39
Collections panel

1. Open and undock the Library palette.

2. Right-click on a content thumbnail and select the Add to Collection, Add New Category menu. In the Library Name dialog box, type the name, **My Collection**.

3. Navigate the Library and locate a figure thumbnail that you want to add to a collection. Right-click on the thumbnail and select Add to Collection, My Collection menu.

4. Select a different category and add another thumbnail to the My Collection folder.

   The selected thumbnails are placed in the new collection, as shown in Figure 2-40.

FIGURE 2-40
Collection thumbnail

CHAPTER REVIEW

Chapter Summary

This chapter showed how the Library palette is used to access new content from several different categories, including figures, poses, expressions, hands, hair, props, lights, and cameras. The Library can also be used to save existing content that you might use later. Content from several different categories can be gathered together into a collection.

What You Have Learned

In this chapter, you

- Opened and undocked the Library palette.

- Discovered how to navigate the Library palette to locate content.

- Explored the various categories of content available in the Library.

- Changed the Library preferences.

- Loaded new figures from the Library and saved the altered figures back to the Library.

- Learned to edit the content's thumbnail image.

- Loaded new content, including poses, motions, expressions, hair, hands, props, lights, cameras, and materials.

- Created new library and category folders.

- Saved existing content to the Library for each of the different categories.

- Removed existing content from the Library.

- Learned to use Content Collections to gather content from several different categories.

Key Terms from This Chapter

- Content Collection. A group of content gathered together that can include content from several different categories.

- Figure. A character loaded into Poser that can be posed using the various interface controls.

- Library. A collection of data that can be loaded into the scene.

- Prop. An object that exists in the scene independent of the figure and that can be saved as a separate object.

- Smart object. A piece of content that is parented to another object in the scene.

- Thumbnail. A small image that displays the selected content.

- Undocked palette. A palette that is no longer constrained to the interface and can float freely as a separate window.

chapter

3 EDITING AND
POSING FIGURES

1. Position figures within the scene.

2. Set figure properties and style.

3. Select figure elements.

4. Use the basic editing tools.

5. Use the parameter dials.

6. Use symmetry, limits, balance, and inverse kinematics.

7. Work with hierarchies.

chapter 3 EDITING AND
POSING FIGURES

Posing figures is surprisingly easy; you just grab a body part and move it into position. All attached body parts will move along with the selected part in the same way they move in real life, unlike when you're on the dance floor. In other words, if you raise the upper arm of a model, the lower arm, wrist, and hand will move with it.

Once you have loaded a figure in the Document Window, you can select and move it into position within the scene before starting to pose the figure. Moving a figure moves the entire figure as one unit and lets you separate multiple figures within a single scene.

Several commands are available for working with figures, including changing its height, locking a figure in place, and hiding a figure to speed the update within the Document Window. Most of these commands are located within the Figure menu, but you can also change a figure's parameters and properties using the Parameters/Properties palette.

The first step in posing a character is being able to select the individual figure elements such as the upper arm or the lower leg. You can select figure elements directly in the Document Window using the mouse or by using the Actor List at the top of the Document Window.

To help with the task of positioning figure body parts, you can use the **Editing Tools**. Within the Editing Tools are tools to **translate**, rotate, twist, **scale, taper,** and even color the various elements. Understanding how to effectively use the edit tools will enable you to create good poses. Another way to position elements is to alter their parameter values using the parameter dials that appear in the Parameters/Properties palette.

Poser includes several menu options that you can use to help you as you pose figures in the scene. The Figure, **Symmetry** menu includes options for copying the element poses on the left side of the object to the right side and vice versa. You can also copy arm and leg poses between opposite sides, swap poses on either side, and straighten the torso. The Figure, Use Limits option restricts the movement of elements to be within designated values, and the Figure, Auto Balance option automatically moves figure elements to maintain the figure's center of gravity.

The Figure, Use **Inverse Kinematics** options enable you to move all the elements in a pre-set chain by positioning the last (or goal) element in the chain. This is particularly convenient for positioning hands and feet and having the arms and legs follow naturally. This chapter concludes by looking at the

Hierarchy Editor, which is an interface listing all the elements in the entire scene. It provides an interface for parenting elements.

Tools You'll Use

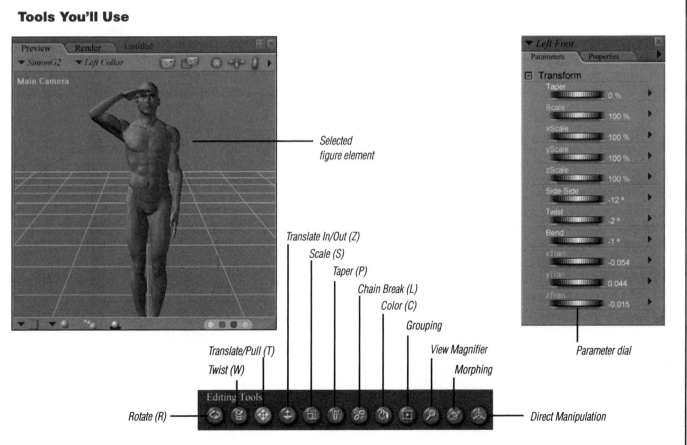

Selected figure element

Translate In/Out (Z)
Scale (S)
Taper (P)
Chain Break (L)
Color (C)
Grouping
View Magnifier
Morphing
Translate/Pull (T)
Twist (W)
Rotate (R)
Editing Tools
Direct Manipulation
Parameter dial

POSITION FIGURES
WITHIN THE SCENE

What You'll Do

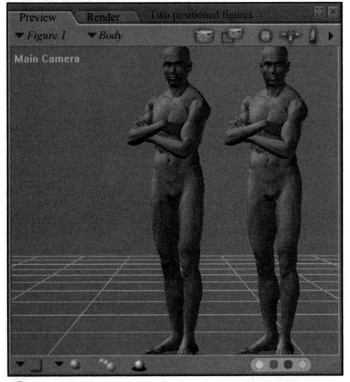

Loaded figures appear in the center of the Document Window at a point known as the *origin*. The origin is the point in 3D space where the X, Y, and Z coordinate values are all 0. But you can move the scene figures as needed using the Document Window controls.

Selecting Figures

If the scene includes multiple figures, you can select an individual figure using the Figure Selection list located in the upper-left corner of the Document Window. Each figure is given a name when first loaded from the Library. The default names are "Figure" and a number such as Figure 1, Figure 2, and so on, but you can change a figure's name using the Properties palette.

Using the Figure Circle Control

Dragging over a figure in the Document Window highlights the various body parts, but if you move the mouse cursor towards the edges of the figure, a large circle appears that surrounds the figure, as shown in Figure 3-1. This circle is the Figure Circle control and it enables the entire figure to be translated. Clicking and dragging on this control lets you edit the entire figure using the various Editing Tools, including translating, rotating, and scaling the entire figure. A complete description of the various Editing Tools appears later in this chapter.

> **NOTE** You can also make the Figure Circle control appear by selecting the Body option in the Actor List.

Changing Figure Parameters

In addition to the Figure Circle control and the Editing Tools, you can also change a figure's position and orientation using the parameter values found in the Parameters palette. You change these parameter values by dragging on the dial controls or by entering a new value. Doing so updates the figure in the Document Window.

Dropping a Figure to the Floor

As figures are moved, you can position them above or below the ground plane, which can make it look like they are walking on air or in the ground. The figure shadow is a good indication if the figure is above the ground plane, but there is a feature that can return the figure to the ground plane. The Figure, Drop to Floor (Ctrl/Command+D) menu command moves the selected figure downward or upward until it contacts the ground plane. The Drop to Floor command also works if part of the figure is positioned below the ground plane.

Figure Circle control

Figure Selection list

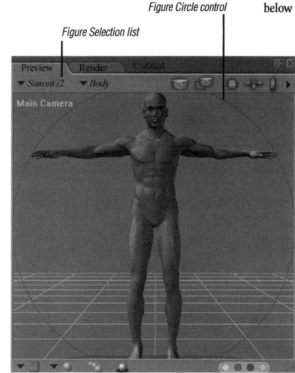

FIGURE 3-1
Figure Circle control

NOTE The Drop to Floor command simply moves the figure until the lowest body part is touching the floor. This could be a finger or a toe; the command doesn't compensate for body weight.

Locking Figures

Once you have a figure positioned exactly where you want it, you can lock it so it won't be moved by accident. To lock the selected figure, select Figure, Lock Figure. Body parts of a locked figure also cannot be moved. A check mark appears in the Figure menu next to the Lock Figure menu when it is enabled. To unlock a figure, simply select Figure, Lock Figure again.

NOTE The Figure menu also includes a command to Lock Hands Parts. Locking the hands is helpful. Because the hands include so many different parts, it is easy to select the wrong part accidentally.

Memorizing and Restoring a Figure

If you make a mistake while positioning a figure, you can use Edit, Undo to undo the previous edits, or you can restore the figure to its last saved, loaded, or memorized position using the Edit, Restore, Figure (Ctrl+Shift+F) (or Command+Shift+F on the Mac) menu command. To memorize a figure's current position so you can restore it, use Edit, Memorize, Figure (Alt+Ctrl+F) (Mac: Option+Command+F)

QUICKTIP In addition to figures, you can also use the Memorize and Restore commands on Elements, Lights, Cameras, and All items.

Using the Pose Dots

Another useful way to save a current pose without using the menus is to use the Pose Dots. The Pose Dots, shown in Figure 3-2, can be selected from the Memory Dots by selecting them from the options under the title. To remember the current pose for the selected figure, simply click on one of the empty Pose Dots. You can recall set poses at any time by clicking on the appropriate Pose Dot. Clicking on a Pose Dot with the Alt key held down (the Option key on the Mac) causes the dot to be reset.

FIGURE 3-2
Pose Dots

Set dot —

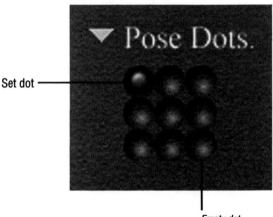

Empty dot

Duplicating a Figure

To duplicate an entire figure, including its expression, hair, pose and animation keys, use the Edit, Duplicate menu command. This command always lists the figure name that you will be duplicating to help ensure that you are duplicating the correct figure. The duplicated figure appears directly on top of the original figure and one will need to be moved to reveal the other.

NEW POSER 7 FEATURE
The Edit, Duplicate menu command is new to Poser 7.

FIGURE 3-3
Two positioned figures

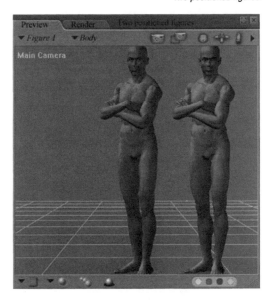

Lesson 1   Position Figures Within the Scene

1. Open Poser with the default figure visible.

2. Open the Library palette and select the Poses category. Then open the G2, G2 Male, Business, Standing folder and locate and the apply the Bsns Stand 06 pose.

3. Select the Edit, Duplicate SimonG2 menu to create a clone of the current figure.

   The duplicate figure is positioned in the same location as its original.

4. Choose the Figure 1 figure from the Figure Selection List at the top of the Document Window. Then drag the circle surrounding the figure to the right, away from its original.

5. Select the Figure, Drop to Floor menu to align the figure with the floor.

   The figures are now positioned apart from one another and aligned with the ground plane, as shown in Figure 3-3.

6. Select File, Save As and save the file as **Two positioned figures.pz3**.

1. Select File, Open and open the Two positioned figures.pz3 file.

   This file includes two separate figures positioned side by side.

2. From the Figure Selection drop-down list at the upper-left of the Document Window, select the Figure 1 option.

3. Select Edit, Memorize, Figure.

4. In the Document Window, click and drag on the circle surrounding the figure and move the figure to the right. Then select and drag one of the figure's arms.

5. Select Edit, Restore, Figure.

   The default figure is returned to its memorized position.

SET FIGURE
PROPERTIES AND STYLE

What You'll Do

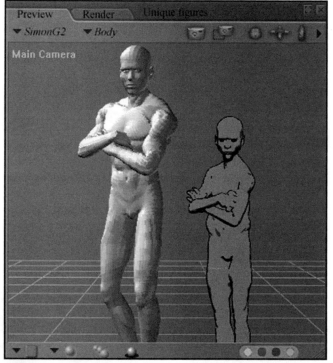

 In this lesson, you learn how to set figure properties, height, and style.

When a figure is selected, you can use the Properties panel of the Parameters/Properties palette, shown in Figure 3-4, to change several properties that are unique to the selected figure, such as its name and whether it is visible

> **NOTE** The properties that are displayed in the Properties palette depend on the element that is selected. The figure properties will only be visible when the figure is selected.

Naming Figures

The default names of Figure 1 and Figure 2 can get confusing if you have several figures in the scene, so you should try to name your figures something descriptive like "Scary dude with a bad attitude who likes to kick dogs that cross his path." Accessing the Properties palette lets you type a new name for the selected figure. Once a figure has a new name, this name will appear in the Figure Selection list.

Hiding Figures

With several figures in a scene, the redraw time can slow down, but you can speed up the redraw time by hiding the figures that you aren't working with. To hide the selected figure, simply disable the Visible option in the Properties palette. This won't delete the figure, but only hides it from view. Enabling the Visible option will make the figure visible in the Document Window again. You can also hide the current figure using Figure, Hide Figure (Ctrl/Command+H). The Figure, Show All Figures menu command makes all hidden figures visible.

NOTE If you're worried about the redraw time in the Document Window, you can also look into using the Tracking option at the bottom of the Document Window.

FIGURE 3-4
Figure Properties palette

Setting Other Properties

The Visible in Ray Tracing option causes the figure's reflection to be cast to other objects in the scene when ray tracing is enabled during the rendering phase. Raytracing is covered in Chapter 16, "Rendering Scenes."

The Displacement Bounds value is used to set the maximum depth that a displacement map can indent an object. Displacement maps are discussed in more detail in Chapter 8, "Creating and Applying Materials."

Setting a Figure's Height

The default figure appears using a standard adult height, but you can change the selected figure's height using the Figure, Figure Height menu command. The height of each option is measured relative to the size of the head. The height options include Baby, Toddler, Child, Juvenile, Adolescent, Ideal Adult, Fashion Model, and Heroic Model.

Figure 3-5 shows each of the various figure heights for the James figure. Notice how the body's proportion is changed along with its height.

> **CAUTION** Some of the default figures don't change height very well. For example, the default SimonG2 cannot change into most of the smaller heights.

Adding Genitalia

Most of the older Poser models without clothes are anatomically correct, but you can enable and disable whether the genitalia is visible using the Figure, Genitalia menu. Enabling this option enables it for all models in the scene, as shown for the James and Jessi figures in Figure 3-6. Many of the newer models, including SimonG2, include genitalia as a separate figure that can be conformed to the figure just like clothing.

Not all figures include genitalia. Enabling this option for figures that don't have modeled genitalia will have no effect. It also has no effect for figures that are covered with clothes.

> **NOTE** During installation there is a Custom install option labeled General Audience. If this installation option is selected, no nude figures are installed.

FIGURE 3-5
Various figure heights

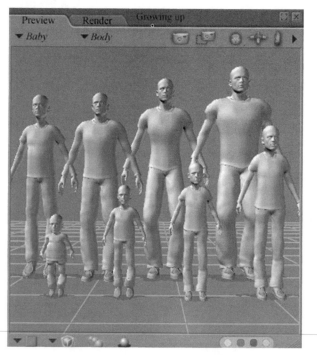

FIGURE 3-6
Anatomically correct figures

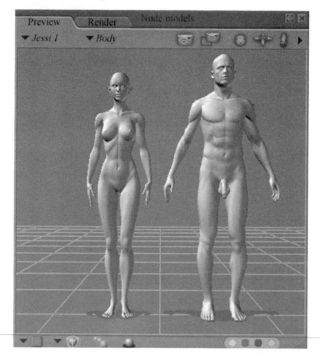

Setting Figure Style

The Display Style control sets the display style for all items in the scene, but you can also set the display style for just the selected figure using Display, Figure Style, or by clicking the Display Style pop-up menu. The default option is Use Document Style, or you can select one of the 12 display styles. Figure 3-7 shows three figure display styles applied to the same figure.

Using Display Guides

The Display, Guides menu command includes several useful display guides that can help to keep the relative size of the different figures consistent. The Display, Guides, Head Lengths guide divides the figure into seven evenly sized head lengths shown as simple rectangular boxes, as shown in Figure 3-8. Because all adult humans are about seven head lengths in size, you can use these guides to determine if the figure's size has the correct proportions.

Another useful display guide is the Hip-Shoulder Relationship guide. This guide shows the width of the hip and the shoulders as two boxes. You can access it from the Display, Guides menu command.

FIGURE 3-7

Figure display styles

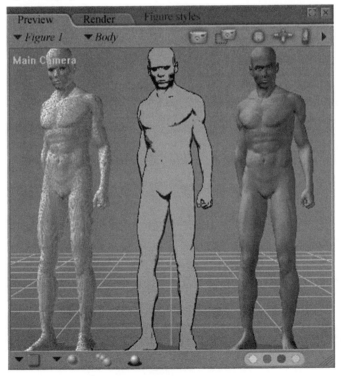

FIGURE 3-8

Head lengths guide

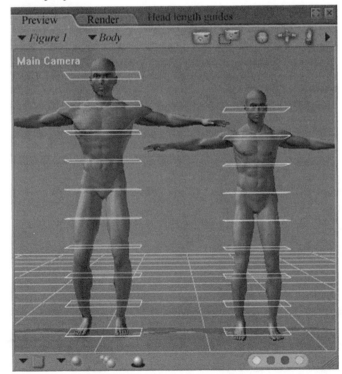

1. Select File, Open and open the Two positioned figures.pz3 file.

2. From the Figure Selection drop-down list at the upper-left of the Document Window, select the Figure 3 option.

3. Select Window, Parameter Dials to open the Parameters/Properties palette if it isn't already open.

4. Click the Properties tab in the Parameters/ Properties palette.

5. In Name field, type the name, **SimonG2 Clone**.

   Each of the figures now has a unique name.

6. From the Figure Selection drop-down list at the upper-left of the Document Window, select the SimonG2 option.

7. Select Figure, Figure Height, Heroic Model.

8. Select Display, Figure Style, Flat Shaded.

9. From the Figure Selection drop-down list at the upper-left of the Document Window, select the SimonG2 Clone option.

10. Select Figure, Figure Height, Adolescent.

11. Select Display, Figure Style, Cartoon with Lines.

    *Each of the figures is displayed using a differ-
    ent height and style, as shown in Figure 3-9.*

12. Select File, Save As and save the file as **Unique figures.pz3**.

Deleting Figures

You can delete selected figures from the scene using Figure, Delete Figure or by pressing the Delete key. When you select this command, a warning dialog box appears asking if you want to delete the figure. Clicking Yes permanently deletes the figure from the scene.

CAUTION The Delete key will only delete figures and not elements. If an element is selected and you press the Delete key, Poser will attempt to delete the entire figure.

FIGURE 3-9

Cartoon style figures of different heights

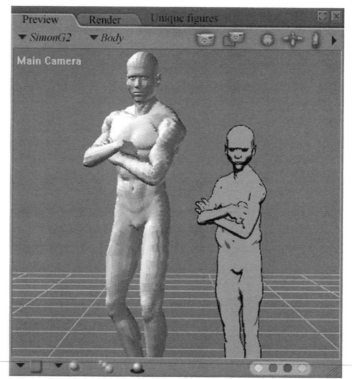

SELECT
FIGURE ELEMENTS

What You'll Do

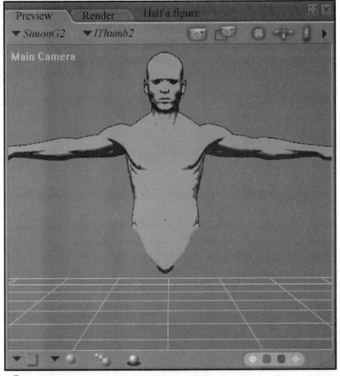

In this lesson, you learn various methods for selecting figure elements.

Each figure is made up of several distinct body parts that you can select independently. Any object that can be selected from the Actor List is an element consisting of body parts, props, lights, and cameras. Selecting specificelements is the key to being able to pose a figure.

Selecting from the Document Window

When you drag over an element in the Document Window, it becomes highlighted. If you click the element when it is highlighted, the element is selected and its name appears in the Actor List at the top of the Document Window and in the title bar of the Parameters/Properties palette.

Many times, multiple elements can be positioned in the same place, making it difficult to highlight the exact element you want to select. If you right-click in the Document Window, all elements that are currently under the mouse cursor are listed in the Select menu. They are listed in order from the elements closest to the camera to the ones farther back. The element's distance from the camera view is stored in memory in an array called the Z-Buffer. This feature is very helpful when selecting individual parts of the fingers.

NEW POSER 7 FEATURE

The Z-Buffer Actor Selection option in the right-click menu is new to Poser 7.

Selecting from a List

Another way to select figure body parts is by selecting them from the Actor List at the top of the Document Window and in the title bar of the Parameters/Properties palette, as shown for the Chest element in Figure 3-10. Both of these lists are identical and include menu options for selecting Body Parts, Body, Props, Cameras, and Lights. Selecting the Body Parts menu presents a long list of body parts. Only one figure element can be selected at a time.

NOTE Selecting the Body option from the Actor List selects the entire figure.

FIGURE 3-10

Selected element

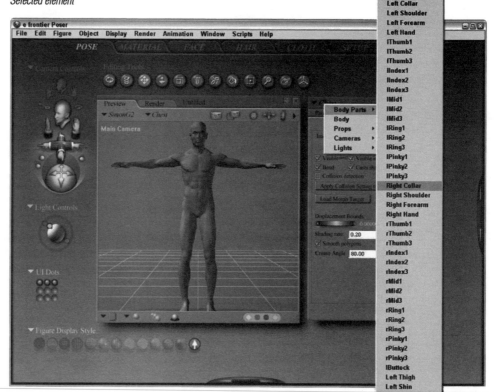

Naming Elements

The default names in the Actor List match the various body parts such as Chest, Right Hand, and Left Forearm, but you can use the Name field in the Properties palette, shown in Figure 3-11, to change the name of any selected element. Once an element has a new name, this name will appear in the Actor List, but Poser also maintains an internal name that it uses to coordinate the body part with its adjacent body parts.

FIGURE 3-11

Element properties

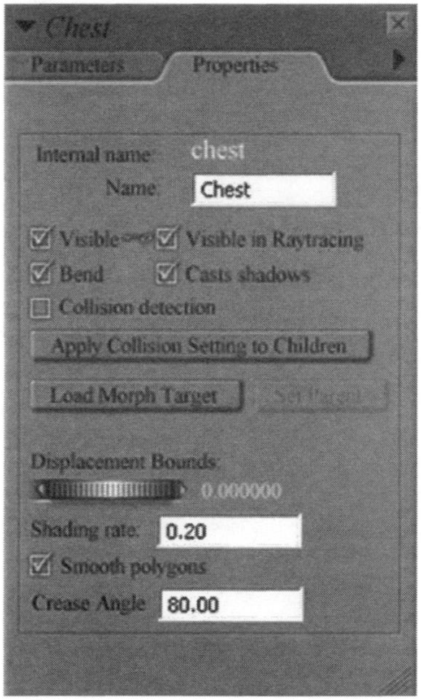

Hiding and Locking Elements (Actors)

You can hide elements by disabling the Visible option in the Properties palette. This won't delete the element, but only hide it from view. Figure 3-12 shows a figure with its chest element hidden. To make a hidden element visible again, you'll need to select the element from the Actor List and enable the Visible option again.

FIGURE 3-12

Hidden elements

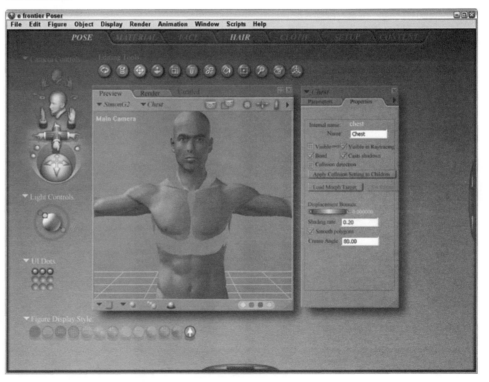

Setting Other Element Properties

The Visible in Ray Tracing option causes the element's reflection to be cast to objects in the scene when ray tracing is enabled during the rendering phase. Raytracing is covered in Chapter 16, "Rendering Scenes."

The Bend option lets you specify whether the selected element bends to stay connected to its adjacent parts when moved. Disabling this option can cause gaps to appear in the figure. The Casts Shadows option causes the element to display a shadow in the Document Window when the Shadow toggle is enabled. The other properties are covered in subsequent chapters.

Setting Element Styles

Just as setting a specific figure style is possible, you can also set the display style for a specific element using the Display, Element Style menu command. The default option is Use Figure Style, or you can select one of the 12 display styles. Figure 3-13 shows a figure that uses several element display styles.

FIGURE 3-13
Different element styles

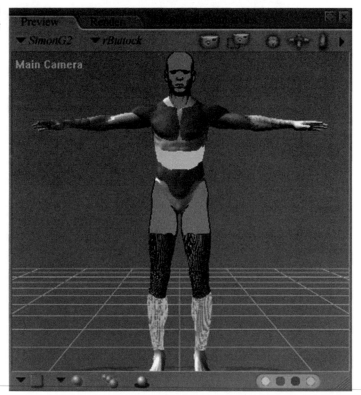

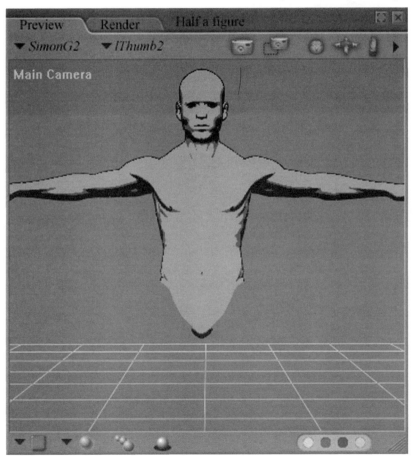

FIGURE 3-14

Half a figure shaded using Cartoon style

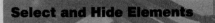
1. Open Poser with the default man figure visible.

2. Click the Left Thigh element in the Document Window to select it.

   The element is highlighted, and its name appears in the Actor List at the top of the Document Window.

3. Select Window, Parameter Dials to open the Parameters/Properties palette, if it isn't already open, and click the Properties tab.

4. Disable the Visible option.

5. Repeat Steps 2 and 4 for the Right Thigh, Left Shin, and Right Shin elements.

6. Click the Head element in the Document Window to select it.

7. Select Display, Element Style, Cartoon with Lines.

8. Repeat Steps 6 and 7 for the other visible body parts.

   The visible elements are displayed using the Cartoon with Lines style to look like a Genie, as shown in Figure 3-14.

9. Select File, Save As and save the file as **Half a figure.pz3**.

LESSON 4

USE THE
BASIC EDITING TOOLS

What You'll Do

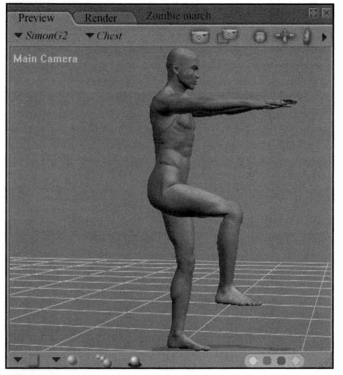

 In this lesson, you learn how to pose figure elements using
the basic editing tools.

In order to pose figures, you need to learn
how to move, rotate, twist, and scale the
different figure elements. The Editing Tools
in Figure 3-15 can help you accomplish
these tasks. You can open this set of tools
using Window, Editing Tools. You can select
only one editing tool at a time, with the
current tool being highlighted in yellow.

QUICKTIP You can use all the Editing Tools also
on figures and props in addition to body parts.

Moving Figure Elements

One of the first places to start when posing a figure is to move the various elements. A good example of this is dragging the upper arm to raise or lower the entire arm. There are a couple of Editing Tools you can use to move figure elements, including the Translate/Pull tool and the Translate In/Out tool.

QUICKTIP When translating body parts, the body part highlighted in white moves when you drag in the Document Window. The red highlighted object is the current selection.

The Translate/Pull tool (T) is the one tool that is selected when Poser is first started. It allows you to move figure elements within the XY plane.

The Translate In/Out tool (Z) moves the selected element in and out of the Z plane, which is towards or away from the current camera view. Figure 3-16 shows a simple pose accomplished by translating the upper arms using these two tools.

FIGURE 3-15

Editing tools

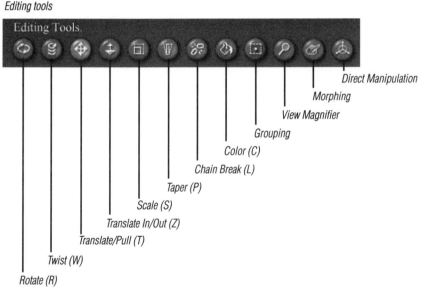

Direct Manipulation

Morphing

View Magnifier

Grouping

Color (C)

Chain Break (L)

Taper (P)

Scale (S)

Translate In/Out (Z)

Translate/Pull (T)

Twist (W)

Rotate (R)

FIGURE 3-16

Translated arms

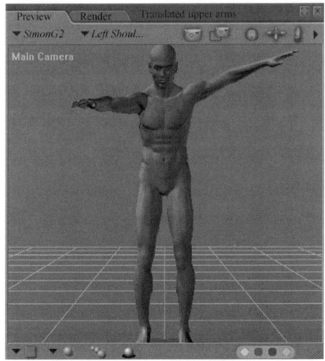

Rotating and Twisting Elements

You use the Rotate tool (R) to rotate elements about their joints. For example, if you drag on the selected forearm object with the Rotate tool, it will rotate about the elbow joint. Dragging an element with the Twist tool (W) causes it to rotate about its joint axis. For example, dragging the abdomen element with the Twist tool makes a figure twist about its waist. Figure 3-17 shows a figure whose forearms have been rotated with the Rotate tool and whose waist has been twisted with the Twist tool.

Scaling and Tapering Elements

The Scale tool (S) changes the size of the element along a single axis, but you can cause the element to be uniformly scaled along all axes at the same time by holding down the Shift key while dragging.

The Taper tool (P) is similar to the Scale tool, except it scales only one end of an element, leaving the other unchanged. The result of a tapered element is to make the object long and thin or short and fat. Figure 3-18 shows a figure whose chest and collarbones have been scaled.

FIGURE 3-17
Rotated forearms and twisted waist

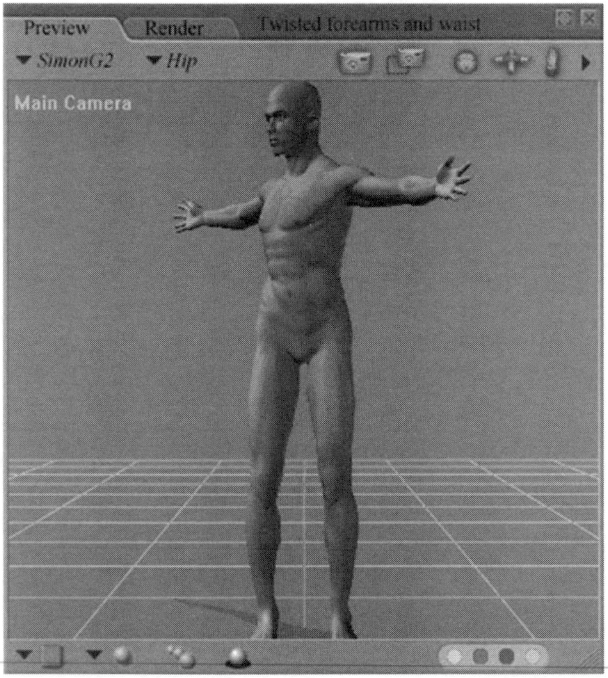

FIGURE 3-18
Scaled chest

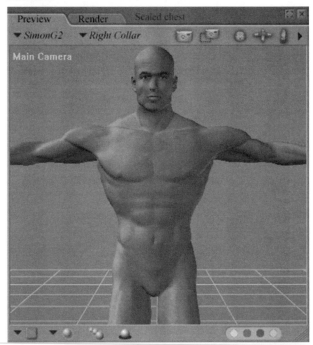

Coloring Elements

Although the real place to apply colors and textures to a figure element is in the Material Room, which is covered in Chapter 8, "Creating and Applying Materials," you can place basic flat colors to elements using the Color tool (C). Clicking with this tool on an element causes a pop-up color palette, shown in Figure 3-19, to appear. You can select a color from this pop-up color palette by dragging over the color that you want to select. Clicking a color in the palette closes the pop-up color palette. Figure 3-20 shows a figure with several colors applied.

NOTE The Color tool adds colors to material groups such as Shirt, Pants, Skin Color, and so on, instead of to elements. More on material groups is covered in Chapter 8, "Creating and Applying Materials."

FIGURE 3-19
Pop-up color palette

Open Color selector

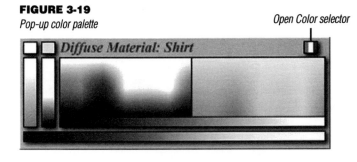

FIGURE 3-20
Figure with colors

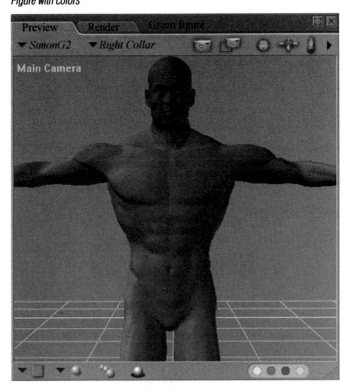

Using the View Magnifier Tool

The View Magnifier tool allows you to zoom in on an area without changing the parameters of the current camera. To use it, simply click the area that you want to zoom in on. Each successive click zooms further in on an area. Clicking with the **Ctrl** key (or **Command** key on the Mac) held down zooms out. You can also zoom in on a region by dragging over the zoom area with the View Magnifier tool. Figure 3-21 shows a zoomed figure that used the View Magnifier tool.

Using the Direct Manipulation Tool

The Direct Manipulation tool surrounds the selected element with icons that can be used to move, rotate, and scale the selected element, as shown in Figure 3-22.

By dragging these controls, you can change the element's position, rotation, and scale in the X, Y, and Z axes. These controls have the same effect as dragging the corresponding parameter dial.

NOTE The mouse cursor changes to match the corresponding action when moving it over the top of the various controls.

FIGURE 3-21
Zoomed figure

FIGURE 3-22
Direct Manipulation Tool controls

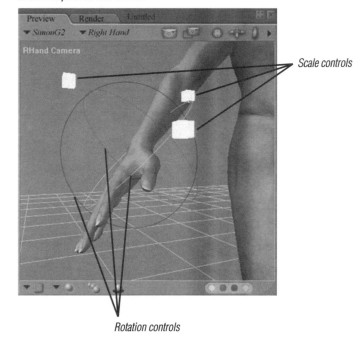

Scale controls

Rotation controls

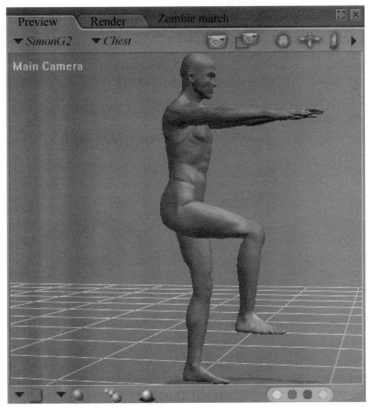

FIGURE 3-23

Zombie march pose

1. Open Poser with the default man visible.

2. Select Window, Editing Tools to make the Editing Tools buttons visible if they aren't already visible.

3. Click the Translate/Pull tool (or press the T key) ⊕ and drag on the left shoulder to raise it to be horizontal with the ground. Repeat for the right shoulder so both arms are outstretched.

4. Click the Translate In/Out tool (or press the Z key) ⊕ and drag the left shoulder until it is stretched in front of the figure. Repeat for the right shoulder so both arms are stretched out in front of the figure.

   The chest of the figure will lean forward as you pull the arms forward.

5. Select From Left from the Camera Controls pop-up menu.

6. Click the Rotate tool (or press the R key) ◎ and drag the abdomen until the figure's torso is vertical again.

7. Click the Translate/Pull tool (or press the T key), select and drag the left foot and pull it out and up from the figure as if the figure were taking a step.

   The side view of the figure shows the figure with both arms outstretched taking a step forward, as shown in Figure 3-23.

8. Select File, Save As and save the file as **Zombie march.pz3**.

Color Elements

1. Open Poser with the default man visible.

2. Open the Library palette and select the Props category. Then open the Poser 7/P7 Male Clothes/Poser 7 Casual folder and apply the G2 Casual Dress Shirt using the Create New Figure button. Then add the G2 Casual Swim Trunks using the same method.

3. Select Window, Editing Tools to make the Editing Tools buttons visible, if necessary.

4. Click the Color tool (or press the C key) and click the figure's shirt.
   A pop-up color palette appears with the title Diffuse Material: Shirt.

5. Select a green color.

   The shirt area of the figure is colored green and the pop-up color palette is closed, as shown in Figure 3-24.

6. Select File, Save As and save the file as **Green shirt.pz3**.

> **CAUTION** The G2 Casual Swim Trunks were removed from the Poser 7 Library at the last second, but will be included using the content updater at a future time.

FIGURE 3-24
Figure with green shirt and black pants

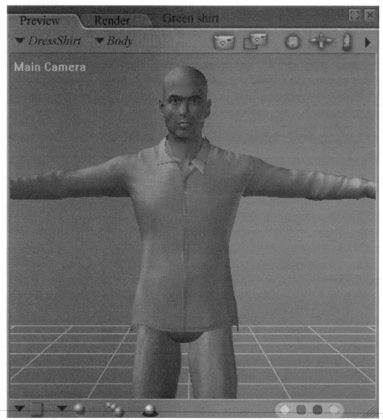

FIGURE 3-25

Scaled and rotated element

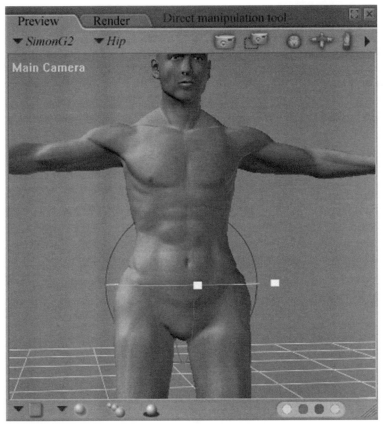

Use the Direct Manipulation Tool

1. Open Poser with the default figure visible.

2. Select Window, Editing Tools to make the Editing Tools buttons visible (if necessary).

3. Select the hip object in the Document Window and drag the Move Camera in XZ Plane control in the Camera Controls to zoom in on the hip region.

4. Select the Direct Manipulation tool from the Editing tools.

   Manipulation controls surround the hip element.

5. Drag the right Scale control icon to the right in the Document Window.

6. Drag the red Rotation control to rotate the figure slightly forward.

   The figure now has a larger belly section, as shown in Figure 3-25.

7. Select File, Save As and save the file as **Direct manipulation tool.pz3**.

USE THE
PARAMETER DIALS

What You'll Do

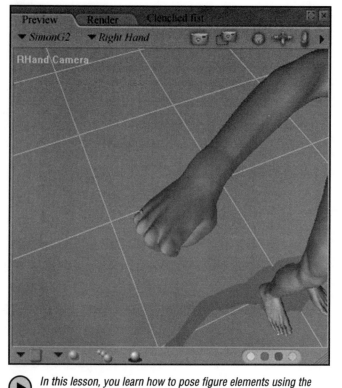

In this lesson, you learn how to pose figure elements using the parameter dials.

For more precise changes to a pose, you can use the parameter dials found in the Parameters/Properties palette, shown in Figure 3-26. You can open this palette by selecting Window, Parameter Dials. The parameter dials affect the selected element that is listed at the top of the palette.

| NOTE The available dials are different depending on the item and figure that is selected.

FIGURE 3-26
Parameters/Properties palette

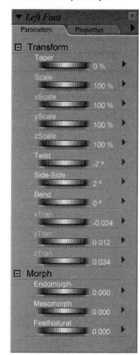

Changing Dial Values

To the right of each parameter dial is its value. To change this value, click and drag the dial to the right to increase its value or to the left to decrease its value. If you click the value itself, the value is selected within a text field where you can type a new value using the keyboard.

Resetting Dial Values

To the right of each parameter dial is a black arrow icon that opens a pop-up menu of options. If you select the Reset option, the value changes to its last memorized value. You can set the memorized value for a figure, element, light, or camera using the Edit, Memorize menu command.

> **QUICKTIP** You can also reset a parameter value by clicking the parameter dial with the Alt/Option key held down.

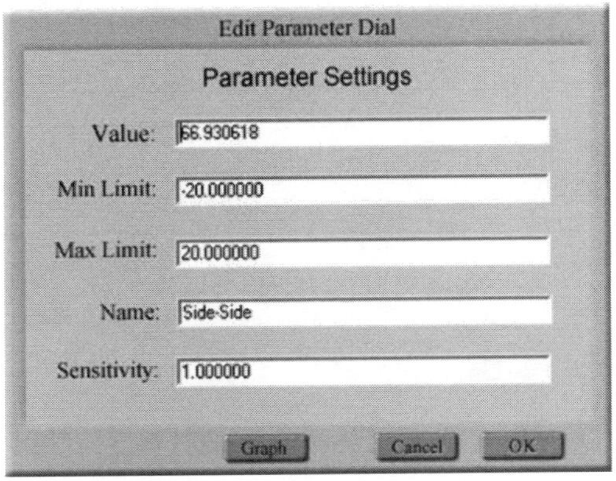

Changing Parameter Settings

Double-clicking the parameter dial or selecting the Settings option from the pop-up menu opens the Edit Parameter Dial dialog box, shown in Figure 3-27. Using this dialog box, you can change the current value, Minimum and Maximum Limit values, the Parameter Name, and its Sensitivity. Lower sensitivity values require a larger mouse drag to change the parameter value.

FIGURE 3-27
Edit Parameter Dial dialog box

Understanding Unique Morph Parameters

Most of the parameter dials relate directly to the Editing Tools such as Taper, Scale, Twist, and Translate, but several of the dials found in the Parameters palette are unique. These unique parameters are actually morph targets and you can alter them by changing the parameters' values. Some example morph targets include the following:

- Side-Side, Bend, Up-Down, Front-Back: Causes elements to be rotated in a specific direction based on the element. For example, the Side-Side parameter rotates the torso and feet to the side, the Bend parameter rotates the torso forwards and backwards and the feet up and down, and the Front-Back parameter moves the arms forwards and backwards.

- Eye Dilate: When an eye element is selected, a unique parameter called Dilate is available for changing the size of the pupil and iris.

- Face Morphs: If the head element is selected, a number of face morph parameters are available for changing the brows, eyes, nose, and so on. These parameters can be used to create unique expressions and are covered in Chapter 9, "Creating a Face and Facial Expressions."

- Hand Controls: When hand objects are selected, the palette includes parameters for clenching all fingers together and the thumb together and spreading the figures apart.

- Body Controls: When a figure is selected, the Parameters palette includes a set of Advanced Body Controls parameters. These parameters let you work with the upper body, arms, and legs.

- Ectomorph, Endomorph, Mesomorph: These morph parameters define the body shape. An Ectomorph body shape is thin, an Endomorph body shape is heavy set, and the Meshmorph body type is muscular, as shown in Figure 3-28.

QUICKTIP Chapter 14, "Morphing Figures and Using Deformers," shows how you can create your own morph targets.

FIGURE 3-28

Ecto-, Endo-, and Mesomorph body shapes

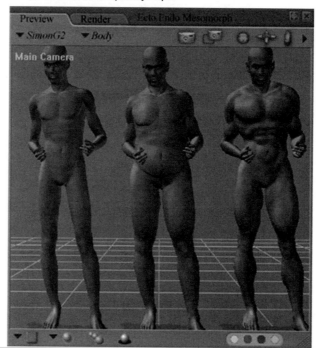

Creating Parameter Groups

Custom figures can have many parameters. For example, many animal figures include custom parameters for controlling the curve of their tails. To handle figures with a large number of parameters, you can create a parameter group using the pop-up menu located at the top of the Parameters/Properties palette. Selecting the Create New Group option from the pop-up menu opens a simple dialog box where you can name the new parameter group. This group name then appears in the Parameters palette.

To add parameters to the group, simply drag the parameter title and drop it on the new group name. Clicking the plus or minus icon to the left of the group name lets you expand and contract the parameter group. Figure 3-29 shows a new group named New-Group added to the Parameters/Properties palette. You can delete selected groups by selecting the Delete Selected Group option in the pop-up menu.

QUICKTIP The order of the parameters in the new group follows the order that they were dropped into the group, but parameters can be rearranged by dragging and dropping parameters above or below other parameters.

FIGURE 3-29

Custom parameter group

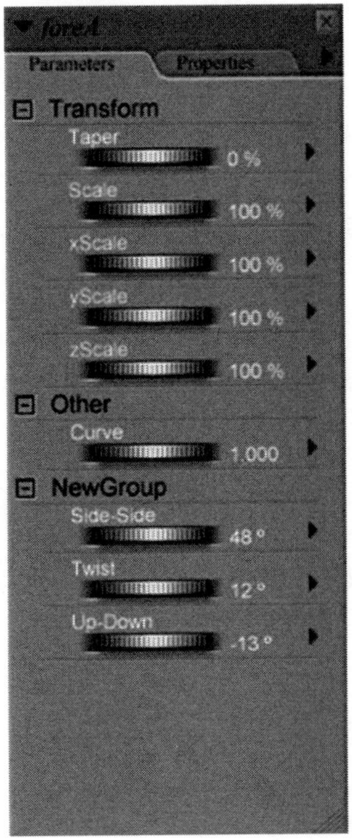

Use the Parameter Dials

1. Open Poser with the default man visible.

2. Select Window, Parameter Dials to make the Parameters/Properties palette visible, if necessary.

3. Select the abdomen element in the Document Window and drag the Side-Side parameter dial ▬▬▬ to the right to 45 degrees.

4. Select the left foot element and click the xTran parameter, and then type the value 0.531.

   The figure's torso bends to the right, and its left foot is pointed away from the body, as shown in Figure 3-30.

5. Select File, Save As and save the file as Pointed toe.pz3.

FIGURE 3-30
Pointed toe pose

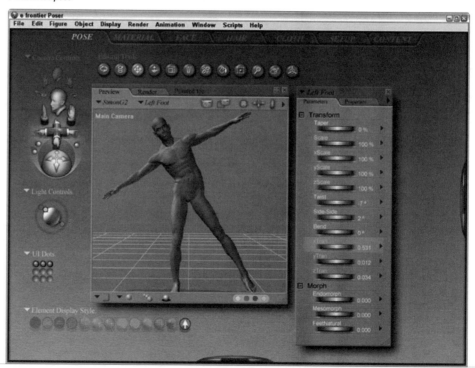

1. Open Poser with the default man visible.

2. Select Window, Parameter Dials to make the Parameters/Properties palette visible, if necessary.

3. Click the right hand camera 🖐 in the Camera Controls.

4. Select the right hand element in the Document Window and drag the Grasp parameter dial to the right and the Thumb Bend parameter dial to the left.

   Changing the custom Grasp and Thumb Bend parameters results in a clenched fist, as shown in Figure 3-31.

5. Select File, Save As and save the file as **Clenched fist.pz3**.

FIGURE 3-31

Clenched fist

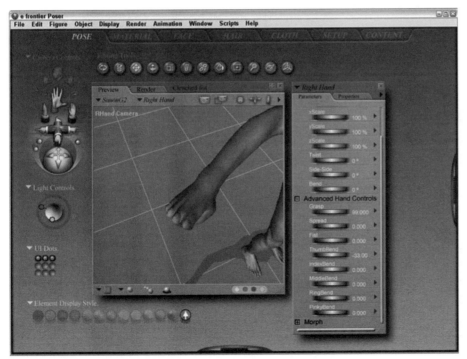

Create a Parameter Group

1. Open Poser with the default man visible.

2. Select Window, Parameter Dials to make the Parameters/Properties palette visible, if necessary.

3. Select the hip element in the Document Window.

4. Select the Create New Group option from the pop-up menu at the top of the Parameters/Properties palette.

5. In the New Group Name dialog box that opens, name the group X-axis parameters.

6. Select and drag the xScale, xRotate, and xTran parameters and drop them on the new group name.

7. Repeat Steps 4-6 to create groups for the Y-axis and Z-axis parameters.

   After expanding each of the new groups, the Parameters palette looks like the one shown in Figure 3-32.

8. Select File, Save As and save the file as **Custom parameter groups.pz3**.

FIGURE 3-32

Custom parameter groups

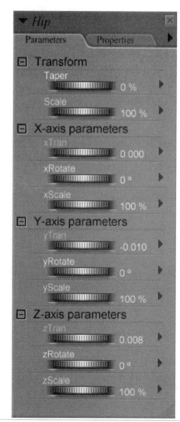

LESSON 6

USE SYMMETRY, LIMITS,
BALANCE, AND INVERSE KINEMATICS

What You'll Do

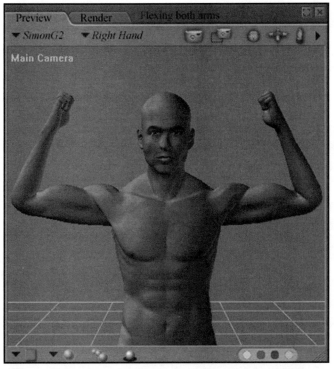

In this lesson, you learn how to control figure poses using the Symmetry, Limits, Auto Balance, and Inverse Kinematics options.

Human figures have a wonderful symmetry that you can use to your advantage. If you work to get the right arm in a perfect position, you can use the Figure, Symmetry menu command to copy this pose to the left arm. Two other common properties that you can mimic using commands found in the Figure menu are limiting the movement of the various body parts to be realistic and having Poser compute the center of mass to have the figure maintain its balance.

Using Symmetry to Copy Settings Between Sides

If the pose you are trying to realize is symmetrical, you can make it perfectly symmetrical by copying all parameter values applied to the left side of the figure to the right side and vice versa. Simply select the Figure, Symmetry, Left to Right or Right to Left menu commands. This causes a dialog box to appear asking if you want to copy the joint zone's setup also. Figure 3-33 shows a simple figure whose left arm and foot were moved and its poses copied to the opposite side.

Copying and Pasting Arm and Leg Poses

To copy the assumed pose of just an arm or a leg to the opposite arm or leg, select Figure, Symmetry. The options include Left Arm to Right Arm, Right Arm to Left Arm, Left Leg to Right Leg, and Right Leg to Left Leg.

Swapping Sides

If you've spent some time posing a figure only to realize that you've got the right side confused with the left side, you can use Figure, Symmetry, Swap Right and Left to fix the problem. This command symmetrically swaps all poses on either side of the figure's midline. There are also options to swap right and left arms and legs.

Straightening the Torso

As you pull on a hand or an arm to position the arm, you'll often find that the torso will follow. To straighten the torso, select Figure, Symmetry, Straighten Torso. This option leaves the arm and leg poses in place, but straightens the torso.

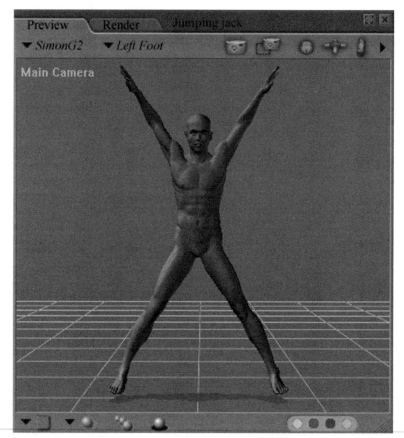

FIGURE 3-33
Left and right side symmetry

Using Limits

Poser is aware of exactly how far each body part can actually bend in order to maintain a realistic pose, but you can also disable this option to allow body parts to move through one another. The Figure, Use Limits option is a toggle that you can enable or disable. When enabled, Poser restricts the movement of the body parts to realistic positions. For example, when dragging a figure's arm straight up with the Use Limits option enabled, Poser prevents the arm from moving farther than the head, as shown in Figure 3-34. Limits also prevent the head from rotating all the way around.

NOTE You can set and edit limits by using the Parameter Settings dialog box. You can access this dialog box by clicking on the pop-up menu to the right of any parameter dial.

FIGURE 3-34
Using limits prevents unnatural poses

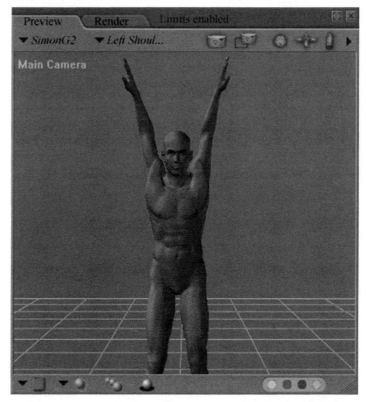

Using Auto Balance

Another helpful setting that can aid you in creating realistic poses is the Figure, Auto Balance option. This option, like Use Limits, is also a toggle button. When enabled, counter body parts are moved in order to maintain the centered weight of the figure. The pose, shown in Figure 3-35, was created by moving the right foot with the Auto Balance option enabled. Poser moved the top half of the figure to the right to counter the foot's position.

Enabling Inverse Kinematics

Normally when you pose body parts, you position the objects by moving the parent object and having all its **children** follow. The children can then be moved independently. This method of positioning objects is called *Forward Kinematics* because it follows the hierarchy structure, but another method exists called **Inverse Kinematics (IK)**. IK works by allowing the child object to control the position of the parent object.

You can enable or disable IK for each arm and leg using the Figure, Use Inverse Kinematics menu command. When enabled, IK lets you position a figure's hand or foot, and the rest of the body parts move to accommodate the motion.

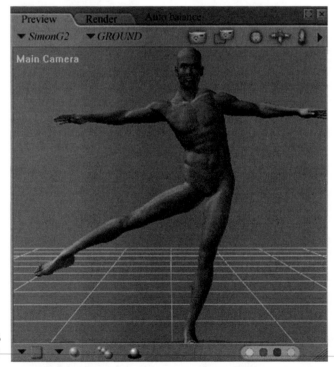

FIGURE 3-35
Auto Balance center-balances figures

FIGURE 3-36
Symmetrical flexing arms

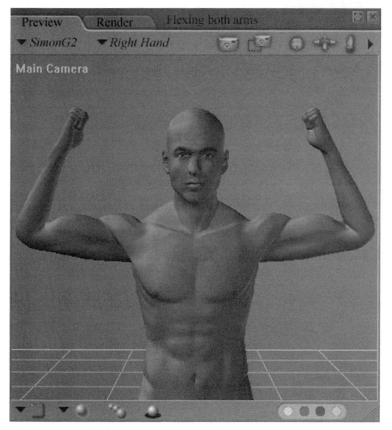

1. Open Poser with the default man visible.

2. Enable the Figure, Use Limits option.

3. Select the Twist tool and twist the left forearm and upper arm. Then use the Rotate tool to rotate the forearm towards the head.

4. Select the left hand element and use the Grasp and Thumb Bend parameters to make a fist.

5. Select Figure, Symmetry, Left to Right. A dialog box appears asking if you want to copy the joint zone's setup. Click Yes to accept this option.
   The pose for the left arm is then copied to the right arm, as shown in Figure 3-36.

6. Select File, Save As and save the file as **Flexing both arms.pz3**.

Use Inverse Kinematics

1. Select File, Open and open the Two positioned figures.pz3 file.

2. Select the figure on the right and drag the left foot away from the body.

   Since this figure has Inverse Kinematics enabled for the left leg, the rest of the leg follows the foot as the foot is moved.

3. Select the figure on the left and disable the Figure, Use Inverse Kinematics, Left Leg option. Then drag the left foot element away from the figure's body.

   The figure with IK disabled moves the foot independent of the rest of the leg before finally pulling the leg with it. Figure 3-37 shows the differences between these two moves.

4. Select File, Save As and save the file as **Using Inverse Kinematics.pz3**.

FIGURE 3-37
Inverse Kinematics poses

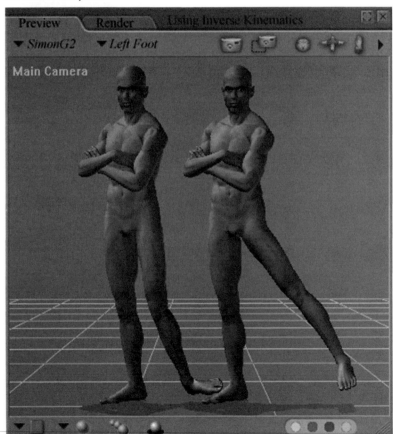

WORK WITH
HIERARCHIES

What You'll Do

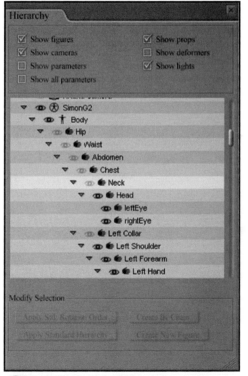

In this lesson, you learn how to use the Hierarchy Editor.

A **hierarchy** is a list of elements ordered in such a way that the **parent-child relationships** between the elements are evident. These relationships are established by linking (or parenting) child objects to parent objects. When the parent object is moved, the child object follows along, thus helping to maintain the hierarchy. To see a complete hierarchy of the selected figure, you can open the Hierarchy Editor.

Using the Grouping Tool

When the Grouping tool is selected, the Group Editor opens. This editor is used in many different ways to collect objects together. It is used to create material groups, hair and cloth groups, and custom polygon groups for defining how body parts move in relation to one another. Details on using the Group Editor are presented in the subsequent chapters.

Opening the Hierarchy Editor

You can open the Hierarchy Editor, shown in Figure 3-38, using the Window, Hierarchy Editor menu command. It includes a list of all the items that are included in the current scene indented to show the parent-child relationships of the scene items. The default figure and the Library figures all have a pre-defined hierarchy.

Selecting View Options

The options at the top of the editor window let you select which types of items to make visible, including Figures, Cameras, Parameters, All Parameters, Props, Deformers, and Lights.

To the left of each item name are three icons. The first icon is a plus or minus sign.

By clicking this icon, you can expand or collapse the children listed underneath the current item. For example, the Forearm is a child of the Shoulder element. Clicking the collapse icon hides the Forearm element and all its children and changes the icon to a plus sign.

FIGURE 3-38
Hierarchy Editor

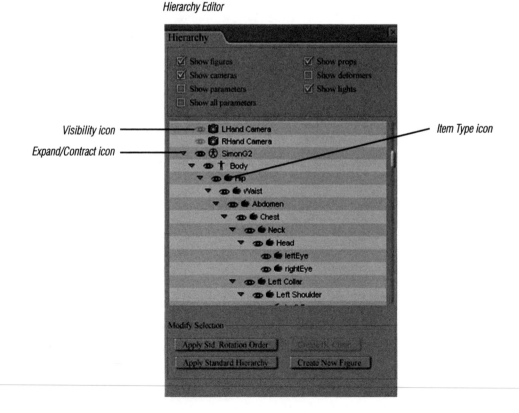

Hiding Items

The second icon is the Visibility icon. Clicking this icon hides the selected item in the Document Window, but not any of its children. The third icon identifies the item. For example, all body parts are identified with a hand icon, all props have a ball icon, the entire scene (called the Universe) has a world icon, the Body object has a stick figure, lights have a light bulb icon, cameras have a camera icon, deformers have a small magnet, IK chains has a chain link icon, and parameters have a wheel icon.

Selecting and Renaming Items

Selecting an item in the Hierarchy Editor automatically highlights the item and selects the same item in the Document Window. Double-clicking an item title in the Hierarchy Editor selects the item's name in a text field where you can type a new name for the selected item. You can also delete certain items, including props and figures.

> **QUICKTIP** The Hierarchy Editor is also a convenient place to delete objects. Individual body parts, cameras, and the ground plane cannot be deleted.

Setting a Figure's Parent

By default all figures in the scene are children to the Universe item, which is the top (or root) item in the scene, but you can change the figure's parent using the Figure, Set Figure Parent menu command. This command causes the Object Parent dialog box, shown in Figure 3-39, to open. From within this dialog box, you can select a new parent for the figure. For example, you might want to parent a figure to a bicycle or an elevator prop.

> **NOTE** You can parent figures only to the items listed in the Object Parent dialog box, including lights, cameras, and props.

A new figure parent can also be assigned using the Hierarchy Editor. To do this, simply select and drag the figure title to the item that you want to be its parent, and the hierarchy will be reordered to show the change.

FIGURE 3-39

Object Parent dialog box

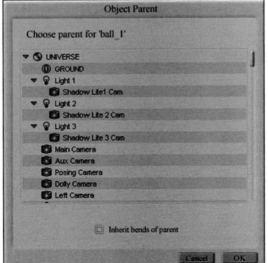

Setting an Item's Parent

Figures aren't the only items that can be assigned a new parent. Most items, including elements, cameras, and props, can be made children objects. To assign a new item to be the selected item's parent, select the Object, Change Parent menu command. This causes the Choose Parent dialog box to appear, which is similar to the Object Parent dialog box shown previously, where you can choose the item to be the parent.

You can also drag the item's title in the Hierarchy Editor and drop it on the item that you want to be its parent. A third way to choose an item's parent is to click the Set Parent button in the Properties palette for the selected item. This opens the Change Parent dialog box.

QUICKTIP The Hierarchy palette is also very helpful in creating Inverse Kinematics chains, and is covered in Chapter 12, "Rigging a Figure with Bones."

Use the Hierarchy Editor to Hide Elements

1. Open Poser with the default man figure visible.
2. Select Window, Hierarchy Editor.
   The Hierarchy Editor opens.
3. Click the Visibility icon to the left of the Hip, Abdomen, Chest, and Neck items.
   The selected elements are hidden, as shown in Figure 3-40.
4. Select File, Save As and save the file as **Quickly hidden elements.pz3**.

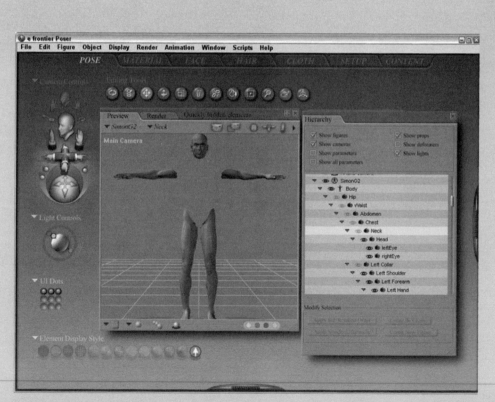

FIGURE 3-40
Elements hidden using the Hierarchy Editor

FIGURE 3-41

The Hierarchy Editor shows the relationships

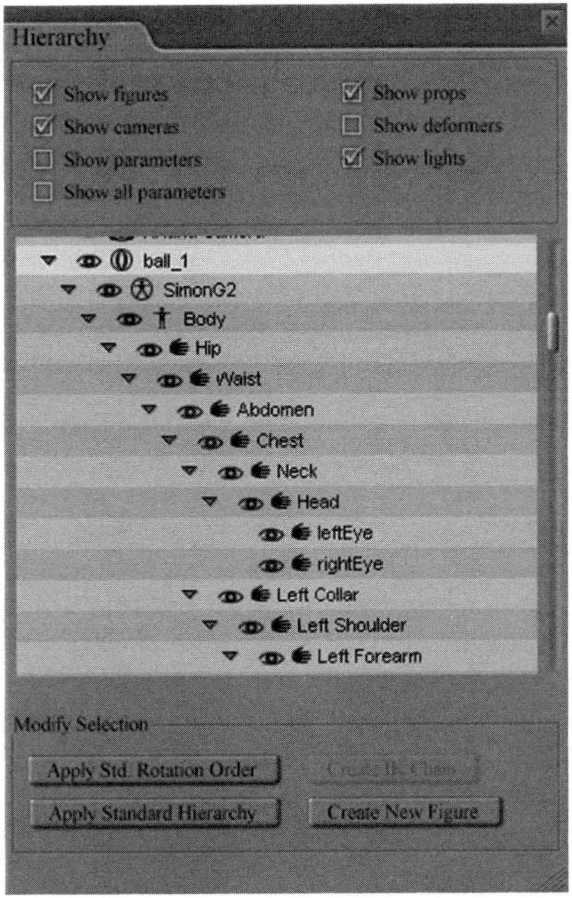

Hierarchy

- ☑ Show figures
- ☑ Show cameras
- ☐ Show parameters
- ☐ Show all parameters

- ☑ Show props
- ☐ Show deformers
- ☑ Show lights

▼ ⊙ ◯ ball_1
  ▼ ⊙ ⊗ SimonG2
    ▼ ⊙ ♀ Body
      ▼ ⊙ ⋐ Hip
        ▼ ⊙ ⋐ Waist
          ▼ ⊙ ⋐ Abdomen
            ▼ ⊙ ⋐ Chest
              ▼ ⊙ ⋐ Neck
                ▼ ⊙ ⋐ Head
                  ⊙ ⋐ leftEye
                  ⊙ ⋐ rightEye
                ▼ ⊙ ⋐ Left Collar
                  ▼ ⊙ ⋐ Left Shoulder
                    ▼ ⊙ ⋐ Left Forearm

Modify Selection

[Apply Std. Rotation Order]   [Create IK Chain]

[Apply Standard Hierarchy]   [Create New Figure]

Set a Figure's Parent

1. Open Poser with the default man figure visible.

2. Open the Library palette and select the Props category. In the Primitives folder, select and add the Ball object to the scene.

3. From the Figure Selection drop-down list at the upper-left of the Document Window, select the SimonG2 option.

4. Select Figure, Set Figure Parent.

5. In the Figure Parent dialog box, select the Ball1 object and click OK.

   The default figure becomes a child of the ball item. Now if you select and move the ball object, the figure follows. You can also see in the Hierarchy Editor, that the SimonG2 figure is located under the Ball 1 object, as shown in Figure 3-41.

6. Select File, Save As and save the file as **New figure parent.pz3**.

CHAPTER REVIEW

Chapter Summary

This chapter explained how to work with figures in the Pose Room, including moving figures within the scene and changing figure parameters and properties. You can use several menu commands in the Figure menu to alter a figure's height and style. You also learned how to select body parts in the Document Window and in the Hierarchy Editor. This chapter also showed you how figures can be edited and posed within the Pose Room using the Editing Tools, the parameter dials, and several menu commands in the Figure menu, including Symmetry, Set Limits, and Auto Balance. Inverse Kinematics was also explained briefly and demonstrated.

What You Have Learned

In this chapter, you

- Selected and moved figures about the scene and aligned the current figure to the floor.
- Saved a specific pose using the Pose Dots.
- Changed a figure's properties, including its name and visibility.
- Altered the figure's height and style using menu commands.
- Selected various body parts using the Actor List in the Document Window.
- Moved, rotated, twisted, scaled, and tapered figure body parts using the Editing Tools.
- Changed body parts colors using the Color tool.
- Used the View Magnifier tool to zoom in on an area in the Document Window.
- Changed a figure's body part using the parameter dials.
- Used the Symmetry, Use Limits, and Auto Balance Figure menu commands to control a figure while being posed.
- Learned how Inverse Kinematics can be used to position parent objects by moving their children.
- Used the Hierarchy Editor to select, hide, rename, and re-parent scene elements.

Key Terms from This Chapter

- **Body part.** The defined pieces that make up a figure.
- **Child.** The following object in a hierarchy chain. Child objects can move independently of the parent object.
- **Editing Tools.** A selection of tools used to manipulate and transform scene elements.
- **Element.** Any scene object that can be selected, including body parts, props, cameras, and lights.
- **Figure.** A character loaded into Poser that can be posed using the various interface controls.
- **Figure Circle control.** A circle that surrounds the figure and enables the entire figure to be moved as one unit.
- **Genitalia.** Male and female sex organs that can be visible or hidden.
- **Hierarchy.** A linked chain of objects connected from parent to child.
- **Inverse kinematics.** A unique method of calculating the motion of linked objects that enables child objects to control the position and orientation of their parent object.
- **Library.** A collection of data that can be loaded into the scene.
- **Origin.** A point in the scene where the X, Y and Z coordinate values are all 0.
- **Parent.** The controlling object in a hierarchy chain. Child objects also move along with the parent object.
- **Pose Dots.** An interface control used to remember and recall a specific figure pose.
- **Rotation.** The process of spinning and reorienting an object within the scene.
- **Scaling.** The process of changing the size of an object within the scene.
- **Symmetry.** A property that occurs when one half of an object is identical to the opposite side.
- **Tapering.** A scaling operation that changes the size of only one end of an object.
- **Translation.** The process of moving an object within the scene.
- **Z-Buffer.** A portion of memory whereby each of the element's distance from the camera view is stored.

4 WORKING WITH FILES AND
ACCESSING CONTENT PARADISE

1. Work with Poser files.

2. Import 3D objects into Poser.

3. Import other content.

4. Export from Poser.

5. Access Content Paradise.

6. Load custom content.

chapter 4 WORKING WITH FILES AND
ACCESSING CONTENT PARADISE

Although the Poser Library can be used to save and restore content in different categories, the Library is really intended to just hold certain content like expressions and poses for quick recall. The permanent method for saving all the content of a scene file is to use the File menu to save and open files.

All Poser files are saved using the .PZ3 file format, although you can also save them using a compressed format, which has a .PZZ extension. Morph files can also be saved as a separate file with the .PMD extension. A saved Poser file contains all the content associated with a scene, including the default figure, its pose, materials and expression, and all the settings for the saved scene.

When working with other 3D packages, the Import and Export features allow objects to be transported back and forth between these external packages. Poser includes several options for importing externally created 3D objects. Poser can

also import background images, sound files, and **motion capture** data. Scene files can also be exported to formats that can be opened within other software packages.

Another way to access content is to load content from an online repository. The Poser interface is linked to a Web site called **Content Paradise** that you can access using the Content Room. Content Paradise lets you browse through custom content created by e frontier and multiple other third-party vendors.

Still another way to access custom content is to load it from an external file shipped via CD-ROM or downloaded from a Web site. Installing custom content is a simple process, and the Content Room includes buttons to automate this process.

Tools You'll Use

WORK WITH
POSER FILES

What You'll Do

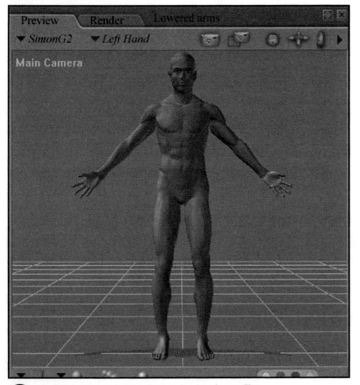

In this lesson, you learn how to load and save files.

The File menu on the menu bar includes several commands for working with the various Poser file formats. In addition to loading and saving files, the File menu includes commands that let you start a new file or revert to the original file after changes have been made.

Creating a New File

The File, New menu command creates a new scene with the default figure. If the current scene includes any changes, a confirmation dialog box appears asking you if you want to save the current changes.

Loading Saved Files

You load saved files into Poser using the File, Open command. This command opens the Open Poser Scene dialog box, as shown in Figure 4-1. This dialog box can load several different file types, including:

- **All Poser Scene Files:** All Poser file types.

- **Poser Scene Files:** Saved with the .PZ3 file extension.

- **Compressed Poser Scene Files:** Saved with the .PZZ file extension. Compressed files are smaller than regular files, but take an extra step to decompress them when opening.

- **Poser 1 Scene Files:** Saved with the .POZ file extension used for the first edition of Poser.

- **Poser 2 Scene Files:** Saved with the .PZR file extension used for the second edition of Poser.

The Open as Read-Only option opens a file for viewing, but does not allow changes. The File, Revert menu command throws away any current changes and reverts to the last saved state of the file.

QUICKTIP The File, Close button closes all interface elements and presents an empty interface with only the menus visible.

FIGURE 4-1

Open Poser Scene dialog box

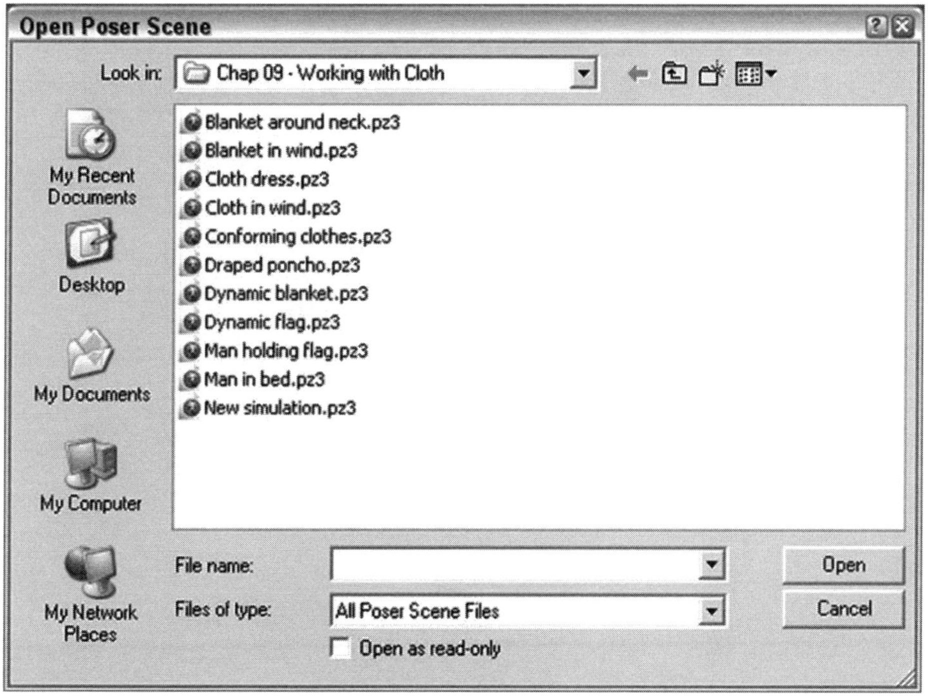

Saving Files

The File, Save menu command saves the current scene file using the same file name. The File, Save As command lets you rename the current scene file. Files saved in Poser 7 are saved by default using the Poser 3 file format with the .PZ3 extension. You can also save them as compressed scene files with the .PZZ file extension if the Use File Compression option is enabled in the Misc panel of the General Preferences dialog box.

> **QUICKTIP** You can select to compress all saved files using the General Preferences dialog box.

Accessing Recent Files

The File, Recent Files menu lets you access the most recently opened files. The running list keeps track of the 10 most recently opened files with the newest files at the top of the list. This list only includes files with the .PZ3 and .PZZ extension and doesn't remember any imported files.

> **NEW POSER 7 FEATURE** The ability to open recent files is new to Poser 7.

Using File Preferences

The Misc panel of the General Preferences dialog box, shown in Figure 4-2, includes an option saving files in a compressed format. When this option is enabled, all scene files and runtime library files are saved using a compressed file format. Compressed files save disk space, but require time for the file to be uncompressed before it can be opened. All default Poser 7 content is compressed.

FIGURE 4-2
The Misc panel in the General Preferences dialog box

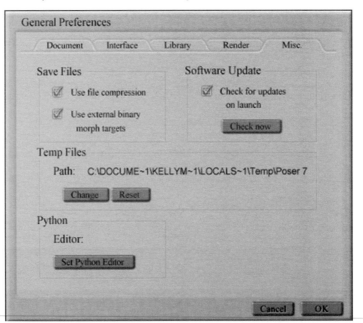

You can also enable the Use External Binary Morph Targets option, which saves morph targets as a separate file with the .PMD extension. This results in smaller scene files that load quicker. Several scene files with the same figure can access the same .PMD file if the morph targets haven't been changed.

Finally, you can select the editor to use to edit Python scripts and check the Curious Labs Web site for Poser updates.

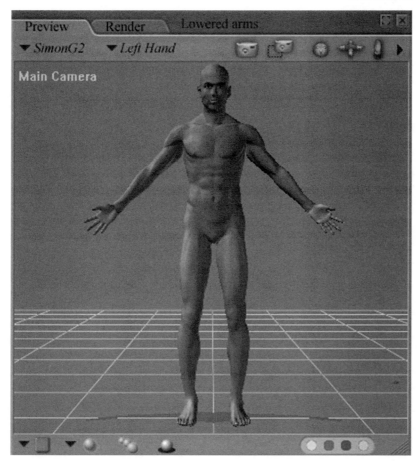

FIGURE 4-3

Saved scene file

1. Click File on the menu bar, click Open, navigate to the drive and folder where your data files are stored, click Raised arms.pz3, and then click Open.

   A scene file containing the default figure with raised arms is loaded.

2. Select and lower the figure's arms.

3. Save the file as **Lowered arms.pz3**.

   The modified scene file is saved using the new name, as shown in Figure 4-3.

IMPORT
3D OBJECTS INTO POSER

What You'll Do

In this lesson, you learn the options for importing 3D models into Poser.

The File, Import menu includes multiple different options for importing different types of content, including 3D models, backgrounds, sounds, and even motion capture data. This provides the means for bringing in external files to the current scene.

Importing 3D Models

Several formats are available for importing 3D objects. All imported models appear as props. The available 3D formats include the following:

- **QuickDraw 3DMF:** Imports geometry objects using the QuickDraw 3DMF file format (available for Macintosh systems only).

- **3D Studio:** Imports geometry objects using the .3DS file format from 3D Studio Max.

- **DXF:** Imports geometry objects using the .DXF file format.

- **Lightwave:** Imports geometry objects using the .LWO file format from Lightwave.

- **Wavefront OBJ:** Imports geometry objects using the .OBJ file format.

You can learn more about these various import options for the various 3D packages in Chapter 17, "Using Poser with Other Software."

QUICKTIP If you have a choice of which 3D format to use, stick with the Wavefront .OBJ format for objects without materials. It tends to provide the cleanest import models. If the model includes materials, use the 3D Studio or Lightwave options.

Setting Object Position

The Import Options dialog box, shown in Figure 4-4, appears when any of the previously mentioned formats are selected from the File, Import menu. It is used to set the initial position and scaling of the imported prop object and includes options for fixing certain problems. The Centered option causes the imported prop to appear centered about the grid origin within the Document Window. The Place on Floor option causes the lowest portion of the imported prop to be aligned on the grid floor.

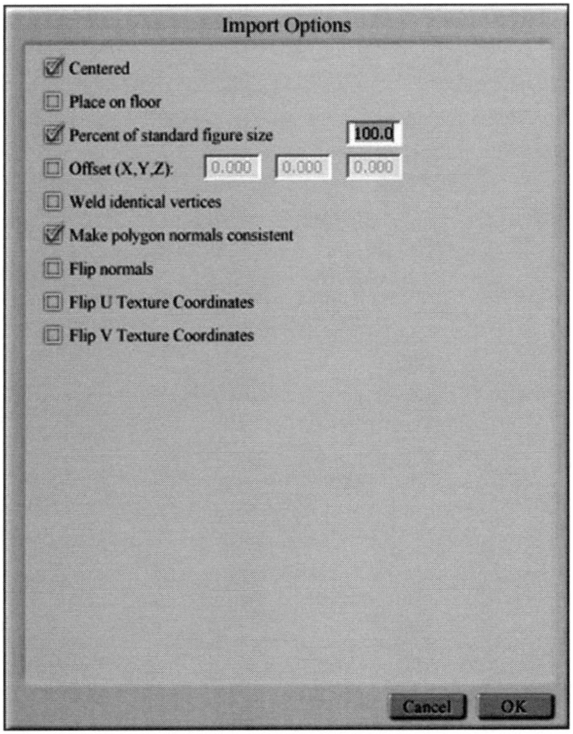

Scaling Imported Objects

The Percent of Standard Figure Size option lets you scale the imported prop based on the size of the current figure. Setting this value to 100 will import the prop using a scale that is equal to the default figure, but a setting of 50 would scale the object to be half the size of the default figure. You can use the **Offset** value to move the prop's initial position from the grid center.

QUICKTIP Don't be too concerned if the imported prop isn't in the exact position or scaled to the right size because you can use the Editing Tools to change its position and scale.

FIGURE 4-4
Import Options dialog box

Import Options

- ☑ Centered
- ☐ Place on floor
- ☑ Percent of standard figure size   100.0
- ☐ Offset (X,Y,Z):   0.000   0.000   0.000
- ☐ Weld identical vertices
- ☑ Make polygon normals consistent
- ☐ Flip normals
- ☐ Flip U Texture Coordinates
- ☐ Flip V Texture Coordinates

Cancel   OK

Reducing Duplicate Vertices

The Weld Identical Vertices option reduces the total number of vertices by combining any vertices that have the same coordinates. This is especially common for mirrored objects along the center mirroring axis. Duplicate vertices can cause trouble for some game and rendering engines. They also can increase the file size of the model.

> **CAUTION** If the imported model has a lot of details represented by vertices that are close together, enabling this option might cause the tight vertices to be combined. You would then lose any details in the model.

Controlling Normals

If the model being imported appears inside out, or if some of its normals appear to be colored dark, it could be that the polygon's normals are pointing inward, as shown for the bookcase on the right in Figure 4-5. A **normal** is an invisible vector that points outward from the center of the surface polygon and is used to tell the rendering engine which way a polygon is pointing.

If the normal is flipped (which can happen occasionally when exporting and importing models), the back side of a polygon becomes visible and its front side becomes invisible, thus making the object appear inside out. Using Polygon Normals

Consistent causes all normals to point inward or outward based on the direction of the majority of the normals. If the majority of the normals are pointing incorrectly inward, you can use the Flip Normals option to change their direction.

FIGURE 4-5
The left bookcase has correct outward pointing normals, but the bookcase on the right has inward pointing normals.

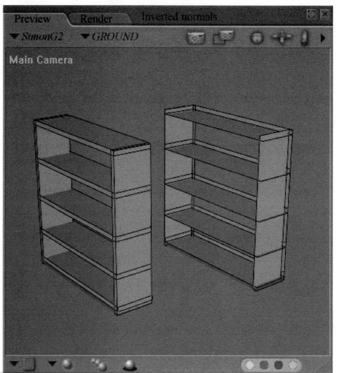

Flipping UV Textures

When a texture is mapped onto the surface of an object, its position on the surface is defined by a coordinate system with U for the horizontal position of the upper-left corner and V as the vertical position of the upper-left corner. If the imported bitmaps on an object come in upside down or flipped left to right, you can use the Flip U and V Texture Coordinates to correct the problem. Figure 4-6 shows an image with a mapped image that is imported with the texture upside down.

FIGURE 4-6
The bitmap on this object is mapped upside down

Import a 3D Object

1. Open Poser with the default man visible. Select the Figure, Hide Figure menu to hide the current figure.

2. Click File, Import, Wavefront OBJ menu.

   The Import Options dialog box appears where you can specify the import settings.

3. In the Import Options dialog box, select the Centered, Place on Floor, and Scale options and then click the OK button.

   A file dialog box appears.

4. Select the Super Fizzy Pop.obj file from the Chap 04 folder and click the Open button. Then select the Super_fizzy_pop_label.tif file from the same folder and click the Open button again.

   The object with its mapped image is imported as shown in Figure 4-7, but the label is upside down.

5. Press the Delete key to delete the current object. Then choose the File, Import, Wavefront OBJ menu again.

6. This time, enable the Flip U Texture Coordinates and Flip V Texture Coordinates options and load the same model again.

   This time the object and its label are imported correctly, as shown in Figure 4-8.

FIGURE 4-7
The 3D model is imported, but has problems

FIGURE 4-8
The 3D object is imported correctly this time

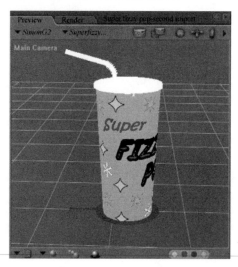

IMPORT
OTHER CONTENT

What You'll Do

In this lesson, you learn how to import additional content into Poser, including images, movies, sound, and motion capture data.

Within the File, Import menu are several additional options for importing other types of content. Some of this content can be older Poser files, but other content types include images and movies to be used as backgrounds, sound files, and motion capture data. The remaining options in the File, Import menu include

- **Background Picture:** Imports image files. Formats that you can import include .SGI, .BMP, .DDS, .EXR, .GIF, .HDR, .JPEG, .MAC, .PCD, .PNG, .PSD, .TGA, and .WBMP files. These images also appear in the background behind the figures.

- **Poser Document/Prop:** Imports the selected scene or prop file into the current scene file. This command is useful for combining figures and props into a single scene file.

- **Poser 1.0 Library:** Imports a Poser 1.0 Library that has a unique format.

- **LipSync Audio:** Loads .WAV sound files for use by the Talk Designer.

- **Sound:** Loads .WAV sound files for use in an animation sequence.

- **BVH Motion:** Loads a Biovision motion capture file, which is a format that describes how the figure should move between poses.

- **AVI Footage/QuickTime:** Imports movies, including the .AVI file format for Windows and QuickTime (.MOV) files for Macintosh systems. The imported movie appears in the background of the Poser figures.

NEW POSER 7 FEATURE
Support for the .EXR and .HDR image formats is new to Poser 7.

Importing Backgrounds

Backgrounds can add a lot to a scene, but they can also be used to work with the current scene. A background image can be rendered as part of the scene to add some variety. Background images can also be used as a template to match the position of a character's body parts.

When a background image is imported, a dialog box appears stating that the width/height ratio of the background is different than the Document Window and offers to change the Document Window's size to match the background. If you select Yes, the window is resized, as shown in Figure 4-9. If you choose No, the background image is resized to match the current window.

Merging Existing Poser Content

The File, Import, Poser Document/Prop menu command lets you select any existing Poser file, and the contents of the selected file are loaded into the current scene. This is an excellent way to reuse content from other scenes in the current scene.

CAUTION Be aware that when a Poser file is loaded, all the current objects, figure, and scene elements are loaded, which might result in duplicate figures.

FIGURE 4-9
Document Window is resized to match the background image

Importing Sound Files

Sound files can be imported and used within an animation sequence or with the Talk Designer to lip synch a character's talking motions. Both the Sound and LipSync Audio options look for .WAV files. The difference between the two import options is where the sound file shows up. LipSync audio files are routed directly to the Talk Designer interface, and sound files are loaded into the Animation palette where it can be viewed. You can learn about Talk Designer and using LipSync audio files in Chapter 15, "Lip Synching with Talk Designer," and how audio files are used with animation in Chapter 13, "Animating Figures and Scenes."

Loading External Motion Capture Data

You can import motion files from an external source using the File, Import, BVH Motion menu command. Biovision files are typically created using **motion capture**, a system that enables computers to record actual motions into an importable file format. The imported file replaces any existing keyframes. After selecting a file to load, a dialog box, shown in Figure 4-10, asks you to specify whether the arms are aligned along the X-axis or along the Z-axis. Then another dialog box gives you the option to scale the data point automatically or to not scale them at all. Following this, warning dialog boxes appear for all the figure elements that aren't included in the imported motion set.

> **NOTE** It is normal for motion sets to not include motion data for all the figure elements, such as the figure's toes.

FIGURE 4-10

BVH Export/Import Options dialog box

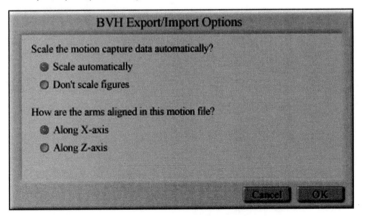

1. Open Poser with the default man visible.

2. Choose the File, Import, Background Picture menu command. Locate and open the Man balancing.tif file. In the Change Window to Match Background dialog box, choose the Yes option.

   The background image is loaded, and the Document Window is resized to match.

3. Rotate and move the camera to match the figure's position and scale to the background image.

4. Rotate and move the feet with the Rotate tool to align with the background image. Next, rotate the neck and the arms into place, and then adjust the hands to match.

5. Finally, choose an expression from the Library to match the background picture's expression.

   After adjusting the pose, the figure roughly matches the background image, as shown in Figure 4-11.

6. Select File, Save As and save the file as **Background match.pz3**.

Importing Video

Video sequences can be loaded into the Poser interface as backgrounds using the .AVI format for Windows machines and using the QuickTime (.MOV) format for Macintosh machines. When loaded, a dialog box appears asking if you want to change the Document Window's size to match the background video, the same as for background images. You can scrub through the frames of the video using the Animation Controls located at the bottom of the interface. More on using images and videos for background is covered in Chapter 6, "Establishing a Scene—Cameras and Backgrounds."

FIGURE 4-11
Figure matched to background image

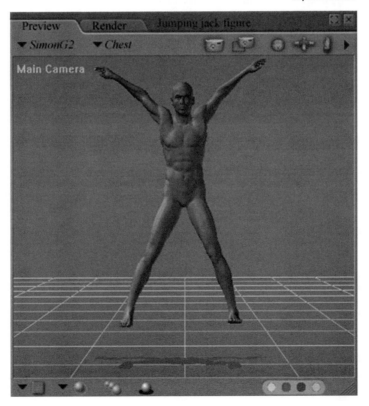

FIGURE 4-12
Imported motion

1. Open Poser with the default man visible.

2. Choose the File, Import, BVH Motion menu command. Locate and open the Jumping jack.bvh file. In the BVH Export/Import Options dialog box, choose the Don't Scale Figures option and the Along X-Axis option, and then click the OK button.

   Several warning dialog boxes appear; simply click OK to clear each of them.

3. Click the sidebar control at the bottom of the interface or select Window, Animation Controls and click Play.

   The figure is animated, as shown in Figure 4-12.

4. Select File, Save As and save the file as **Jumping jack figure.pz3**.

EXPORT
FROM POSER

What You'll Do

In this lesson, you learn how to export objects from Poser for use in other 3D packages.

The File, Export menu includes several options for exporting the current Poser scene so it can be used in other 3D packages. This is a huge benefit when you're using other packages that don't work so well with figures. Posed figures can be exported from Poser and reused in other packages.

Exporting 3D Objects

There are several formats for exporting the current Poser scene. Each of these options can be found in the File, Export menu, including the following:

- **RIB:** Exports to the Renderman .RIB file format.

- **3D Studio:** Exports geometry objects to 3D studio max using the .3DS file format.

- **QuickDraw 3DMF:** Exports to the QuickDraw .3DMF file format. This format is available for Macintosh only.

- **DXF:** Exports geometry objects using the .DXF file format.

- **HAnim:** Exports geometry objects using the .HANIM file format.

- **Lightwave:** Exports geometry objects to Lightwave using the .LWO file format.

- **Wavefront OBJ:** Exports geometry objects using the .OBJ file format.

- **VRML:** Exports geometry objects using the .WRL file format.

CAUTION The 3D Studio export option can only output scene files that are fewer than 65,000 polygons. You can check the number of polygons in the current scene using the Scripts, PrintInfo, PrintFigandActorInfo menu.

When one of these options is selected, the first dialog box to appear is the Export Range dialog box, shown in Figure 4-13. This dialog box lets you choose to export only the current frame or multiple frames, and you can choose the frame range.

FIGURE 4-13
Export Range dialog box

FIGURE 4-14
Select Objects dialog box

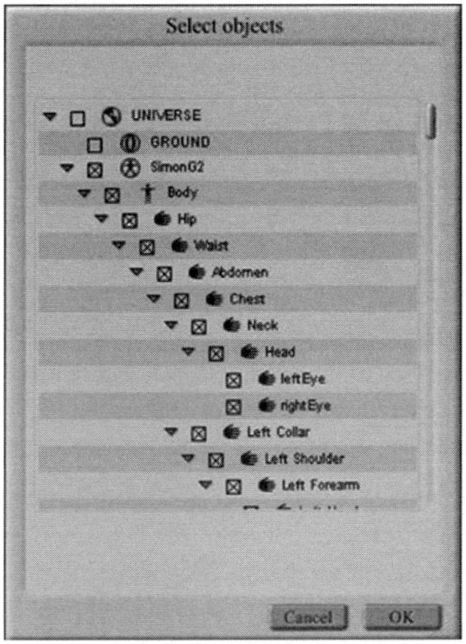

The next dialog box to appear is the Export Options dialog box, shown in Figure 4-15. The options available in the Export Options are the same for all the various formats, and they include

- **Export Object Groups for Each Body Part:** Causes each designated Poser body part to be exported as a separate group that is recognized in the external 3D application.

- **Weld Body Part Seams:** Causes the vertices along the seam between body parts to be welded together so the individual body parts can't be moved independently.

- **As a Morph Target:** Exports the figure pose as a morph target, allowing several targets to be morphed in between.

- **Include Body Part Names in Polygon Groups:** Names each group according to the Poser body part name that it represents.

- **Use Exact Internal Names Except Spaces:** Causes the internal name minus any spaces to be used as the polygon group name.

- **Include Figure Names in Polygon Groups:** Adds the figure name to the polygon group name, such as Figure1LeftHand.

- **Include Existing Groups in Polygon Groups:** Adds the existing group name to the polygon group name.

FIGURE 4-15
Export Options dialog box

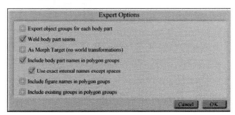

Finally, a file dialog box appears so you can locate a folder where the exported file can be saved and give it a name.

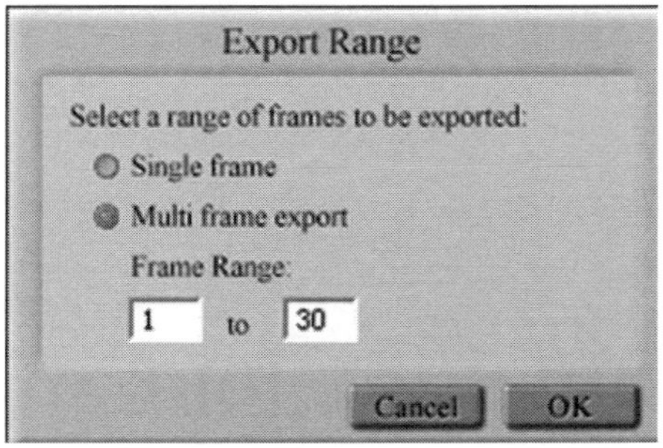

Following the Export Range dialog box, the Select Objects dialog box, shown in Figure 4-14, appears. This dialog box lets you select which objects get exported. For example, if you don't want the Ground plane exported, you can just deselect the check box to the left of the Ground object.

Exporting Images

Rendered images can be saved using the pop-up menu found in the Document Windows, but the current Document Window can be exported using the File, Export, Image menu. The file dialog box includes options to save the exported image using one of the following formats: .BMP, Flash Pix, .JPEG, .PICT, .PNG, .PSD, .TGA, and .TIF. Some image formats have a separate dialog box of save options that you can access. For example, the .JPEG format includes a dialog box where you can set the compression ratio.

| **CAUTION** The File, Export, Image menu will only export the active view in the Document Window. If multiple ports are displayed, only the active view is exported and the size of the view is used.

Exporting Motions

You can export motions from Poser to the .BVH file format using the File, Export, BVH Motion menu command. This causes the same BVH Export/Import Options dialog box to open where you can specify whether the motion capture data is scaled and how the arms are aligned.

Additional Exporting Options

In addition to the options found in the File, Export menu, Poser has several other places where content can be exported.

Within the Sketch Designer is a button that lets you export the Sketch Designer settings to a script that can be read by Painter. These exported files are simple text files that Painter can read to recreate a sketch effect. Rendered images can be exported as images or as movies using the Render Settings dialog box. You can learn about these export options in Chapter 16, "Rendering Scenes."

You can save rendered images also by using the Export Image option in the Document Window's pop-up menu. The formats that you can export include many of the same formats available in the File, Export, Image menu. You can export rendered animations to the numbered image files or to the .AVI, QuickTime (.MOV) or Flash (.SWF) formats by using the settings found in the Movie Settings panel of the Render Settings dialog box. You can learn more about saving rendered images and animations in Chapter 16, "Rendering Scenes."

Converting Hier Files

Poser 3 enabled figures to be created using text-based hierarchy files (**hier files**). The File, Convert Hier File menu command opens a file dialog box where you can select and covert these hierarchy files to a figure. In Poser 7, new figures can be defined using the Setup Room instead of hierarchy files, but this comman d is included for backwards compatibility.

1. Open Poser with the default man visible.

2. Open the Library and choose the Poses category. Then navigate to the Walk Designer folder and apply the G2M Cool motion to the figure.

3. Select the File, Export, Wavefront OBJ menu.

   The Export Range dialog box appears.

4. Select the Multi Frame Export option from frame 1 to 30 and click the OK button.

5. In the Select Objects dialog box, deselect the Ground object and click the OK button.

6. In the Export Options dialog box, enable the Weld Body Part Seams and the Include Body Part Names in Polygon Groups options and click the OK button.

   A progress dialog box appears showing the progress of the exporting process, as shown in Figure 4-16.

NOTE The export process may take some time, depending on the complexity of the scene.

FIGURE 4-16

Exporting progress dialog box

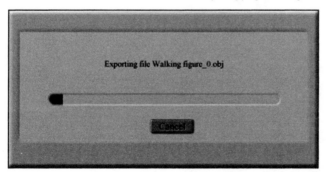

Exporting file Walking figure_0.obj

Cancel

ACCESS
CONTENT PARADISE

What You'll Do

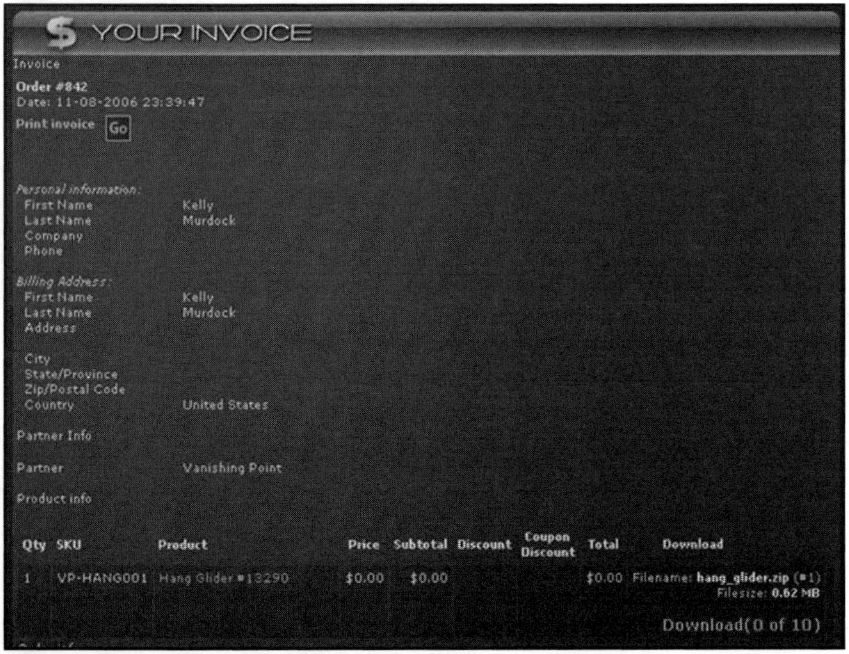

YOUR INVOICE

Invoice
Order #842
Date: 11-08-2006 23:39:47

Print invoice [Go]

Personal information:
First Name   Kelly
Last Name   Murdock
Company
Phone

Billing Address:
First Name   Kelly
Last Name   Murdock
Address

City
State/Province
Zip/Postal Code
Country   United States

Partner Info

Partner   Vanishing Point

Product info

Qty	SKU	Product	Price	Subtotal	Discount	Coupon Discount	Total	Download
1	VP-HANG001	Hang Glider #13290	$0.00	$0.00			$0.00	Filename: **hang_glider.zip** (#1) Filesize: **0.62 MB**

Download(0 of 10)

▶ *In this lesson, you learn how to access and use Content Paradise.*

If you've used all the presets in the Library and you're ready for some new content, you can open the Content Room, which gives you access to a ton of new content via an online connection and the Content Paradise Web site, as shown in Figure 4-17. Old figures can be revitalized with a new hairstyle or a new set of clothes.

NOTE You can also access the Content Paradise Web site using a normal Web browser by entering www.contentparadise.com.

Setting Up an Account

Although you don't need to be a member to browse the site, it is helpful, and you can receive promotional information via e-mail if you choose. If you're a member of Content Paradise, you can take advantage of the site's weekly freebies and special offers. To set up an account on the Content Paradise Web site, click on the Sign Up link above the Featured Image on the left.

Then fill out the information presented on the site and click on the Submit button. As part of the sign up options, you can choose to disable the display of nudity on the site.

CAUTION When you're browsing the Content Paradise site in the Content Room, the Tab button doesn't work, which makes it tough to fill out forms.

After you've signed up to be a member, a confirmation e-mail will be sent you. You'll need to click on a link in this e-mail before you can log into the site.

CAUTION On Macintosh systems, Content Paradise opens within a separate window, and the Auto Install feature is not available.

Logging in to Content Paradise

After your account has been verified, you can log in to the site using the username and password that you entered as part of your setup. After logging in, your username appears at the top of the site along with a new link in the QuickLinks section to View My Stuff. The My Stuff page lets you see a synopsis of the support tickets you've created, your recent purchases, a wishlist, a list of your favorite vendors, your active subscriptions, and any membership rewards you've earned. You can log out of the site by clicking on the Exit door icon to the right of your name.

FIGURE 4-17
The Content Room

Browsing the Site

Along the top edge of Content Paradise are tabs that you can use to access different parts of the site. The tabs include the following:

- **Members:** Includes the Sign Up pages, links to the Forums, Passport (which is a discount program for purchasing Poser content), and Gift Certificates.

- **Software:** A shopping site for purchasing e frontier products including Poser, Shade, Anime Studio, Manga Studio, Amapi, Vue, MotionArtist, and Utilities.

- **3D Content:** Includes a broad range of 3D models and props for several different e frontier products, including Poser, Shade, Amapi, Vue and Others. Figure 4-18 shows the 3D Content tab for Poser.

- **2D Content:** Includes 2D assets for MotionArtist, Manga Studio, and Anime Studio.

- **Audio:** Several categories of sound files, including Ambient, Loops, Collections and Podcasts.

- **Resources:** Includes sections covering various Poser-related resources, including Tutorials, Books, Characters, Featured Partner, Gift Certificates, and Press Info.

FIGURE 4-18

The 3D Content tab for Poser in Content Paradise

Searching Content Paradise

To give you an idea of the amount of content available in this paradise, my browser is set to display 25 items in one page, and the 3D Content tab for Poser shows over 480 different pages or close to 12,000 items.

With this many items, it can be difficult to find exactly what you're looking for. Luckily, the site's search engine is pretty powerful. If you click the Advanced Search button in the QuickLinks section, a search page appears where you can filter the search by keyword, category, software package, and partner, as shown in Figure 4-19.

FIGURE 4-19
The Advanced Search in Content Paradise

Selecting and Purchasing Content

Below each object is the object's cost. Clicking the thumbnail displays a page with more detailed information on the selected object, such as the one in Figure 4-20. To purchase the item, click the shopping cart icon to add it to your cart. Clicking the Cart tab in the top-right corner lets you check out and pay for your selected objects. You need an account in order to purchase content online.

> **QUICKTIP** Within the Hot Searches section below the Login section is a link to free stuff.

After you've made your purchase, you'll receive an online invoice that includes a Download button. Clicking on this button begins the download and installation.

FIGURE 4-20
Detailed item information

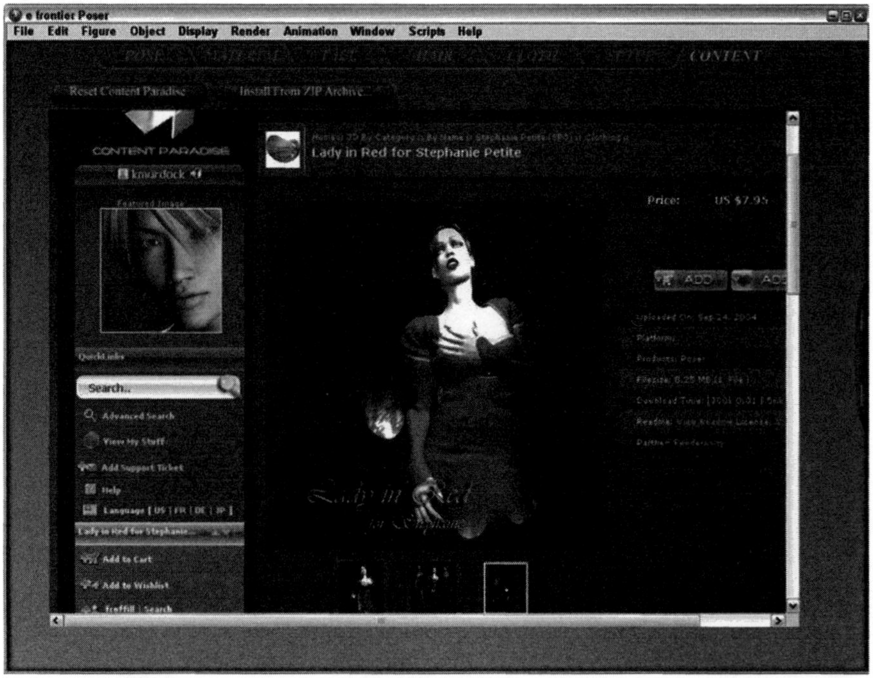

FIGURE 4-21
The invoice includes the Download link

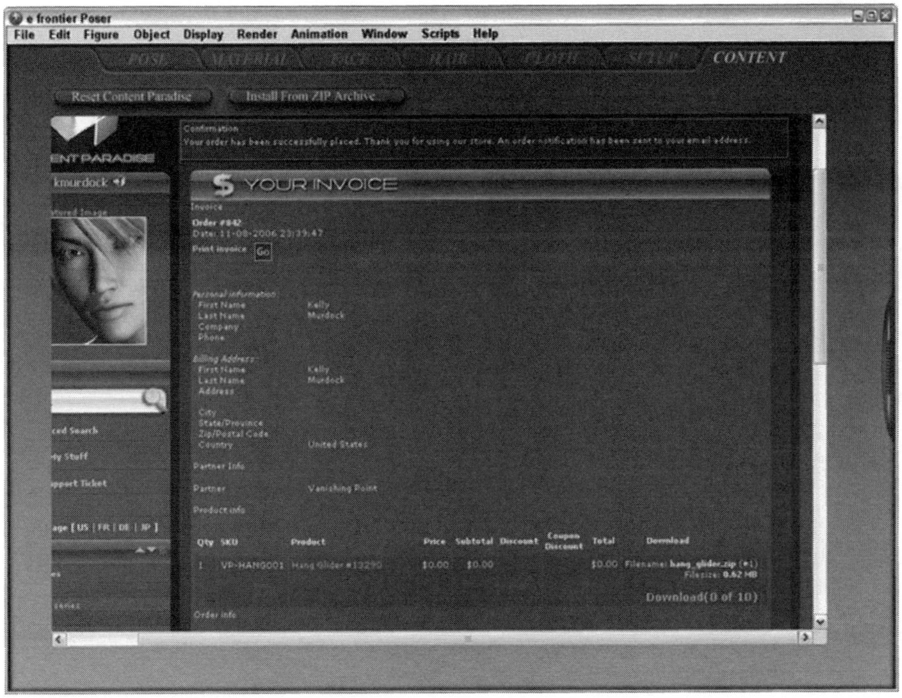

Search Content Paradise

1. Open Poser with the default man visible.

2. Click on the Content tab to open the Content Room where Content Paradise is visible.

3. Click on the Sign Up link to create an account. A confirmation e-mail is sent to you. Click on the e-mail link to verify and activate your account.

NOTE Signing up for an account doesn't require any credit card information, only an e-mail address. You need to enter a credit card only when you purchase items.

4. Log in to the site using the username and password that you've been set up with.

5. Click on the Advanced Search link. Enter the keyword for the type of content you want to find and click the Search button.

6. To purchase any of the searched items, click on the Add to Shopping Cart button. Then proceed to checkout, where you can enter your payment method.

   After you complete your purchase, an invoice for the purchase is displayed that includes a download option, as shown in Figure 4-21.

Lesson 5   Access Content Paradise

LOAD
CUSTOM CONTENT

What You'll Do

In this lesson, you learn how to install and access content downloaded from Content Paradise and other Web sites.

There are several ways to install custom content, whether downloaded from the Content Paradise site or obtained online from a different site.

Downloading and Installing Content

Once you have purchased the selected content, a download progress box appears for each selected object. Once all items are downloaded, the Install Options dialog box, shown in Figure 4-22, appears. Clicking the Install button automatically installs the content into the selected directory. Clicking the Copy button opens a file dialog box where you can select to save the content to the hard drive. If the Web page fails to load for some reason, you can click the Reset Content Paradise button at the top of the Content Room, and the first page will be reloaded.

QUICKTIP It is always a good idea to save a Copy of the downloaded file as a backup in case your system crashes.

Installing from a Zip Archive

Files that are downloaded are contained within a compressed archive with a .ZIP file extension. If a friend sends you a figure via an e-mail, you can save the Zip file to your hard drive and auto install it using the Install from Zip Archive button at the top of the Content Room. This button opens a file dialog box where you can select a Zip file to auto install using the same Install Options dialog box.

FIGURE 4-22
Install Options dialog box

Install Options

Click the Install Button to auto-install content.
Click the Copy Button to copy the downloaded file to a specific directory

Install path:

C:\Program Files\e frontier\Poser 7\Downloads

Note: If you choose 'copy', you will need to manually install this content later

Cancel   Install   Copy

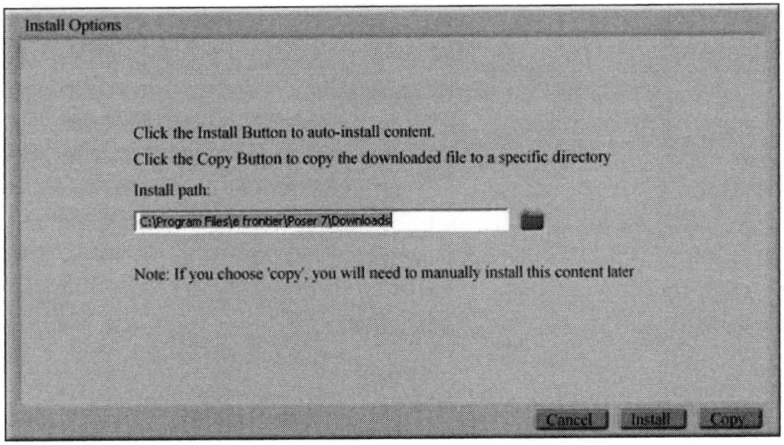

Installing from an Executable File

Some content is bundled as part of an executable file with its own installation routine. By running the executable, you can begin the installation process, as shown for a Daz Production model in Figure 4-23. These installation routines walk you through the installation process and let you choose the folder where the content is installed. Often, these installation routines scan your system looking for a Poser installation. The downloaded content is then typically uncompressed within a Runtime folder.

If you create a new runtime folder and point it to the folder where the uncompressed content is located, the downloaded assets will appear and can be accessed from the Library palette, as shown in Figure 4-24.

FIGURE 4-23

The DAZ Production installation wizard guides you through installing new content

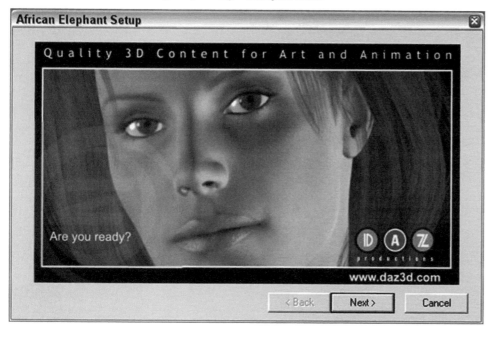

FIGURE 4-24

Installed content can be accessed from the Library palette

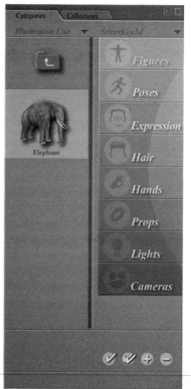

Accessing Downloaded Content

Files that are auto installed are placed by default in the Downloads folder where Poser is installed. You can access the down-loaded content by double-clicking the up arrow at the top of the Library palette. At the top of each category are several folders, including a folder labeled *Poser 7* and another labeled *Downloads,* as shown in Figure 4-25. The red circle marks the active folder. All downloaded content by default is in the Downloads folder.

FIGURE 4-25
Top Library folders

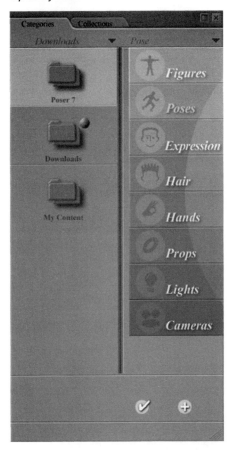

Add New Content

1. Proceed through the process of selecting and purchasing an object from Content Paradise.

   Content Paradise responds by showing you an invoice that includes a download link.

2. Click the Download link on the Invoice page.

   The Install Options dialog box appears.

3. Select a folder where the new content should be downloaded and click the Install button to proceed.

   The file is downloaded and saved to the local hard drive.

4. Open the Library palette and click on the up arrow icon until you reach the top folder. Then double-click on the Downloads folder to see the newly installed item, as shown in Figure 4-26.

FIGURE 4-26
Downloaded item

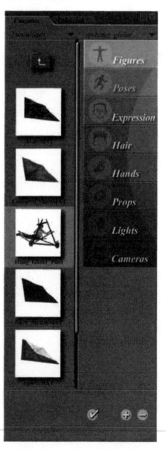

Install New Content from an Executable File

1. Purchase and download new content from the vendor's Web site, such as the Lemur model created by DAZ Productions.

   The file is delivered as an executable file (.EXE for Windows or .SIT for Macintosh).

2. Locate and double-click on the executable file to begin its installation.

   The Setup wizard runs and begins by searching for an installation of Poser.

3. The setup process then asks if you want to install an Uninstall routine. Click the No button to continue.

   The Setup wizard then presents an License Agreement and has you accept the license terms.

4. The next step of the wizard asks you specify the target application, which could be one of the many different versions of Poser or DazStudio.

5. You can then specify which folder to save the content into, as shown in Figure 4-27. This folder can be the Runtime folder located where Poser is installed, but it is often easy to locate the new content if you install it into a separate folder.

6. Start Poser and open the Library palette. Then navigate to the top of the folders and select the Add New Runtime pop-up menu option. Locate the folder that contains the new Runtime folder where the new content is saved and click the OK button.

7. The new content can then be accessed from within the Library palette and loaded into the Document Window, as shown in Figure 4-28.

FIGURE 4-27
Installed content lets you choose the folder

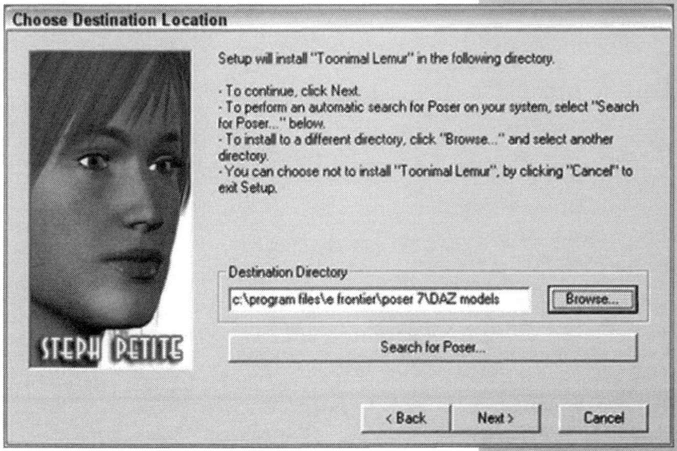

FIGURE 4-28
Installed content can be loaded into the scene

CHAPTER REVIEW

Chapter Summary

This chapter introduced the commands for working with files, including opening, saving, and reverting files. It also covered the various import formats for importing new 3D models. There are also options for importing background images, videos, sound files and motion capture data. Many of the exporting formats are similar to those for importing.

This chapter also covered the Content Room and showed how Content Paradise can be used to search for, purchase, and download new content. This new content can be installed directly into the Downloads folder of the Library.

What You Have Learned

In this chapter, you

- Learned how to work with files, including loading, saving, and reverting them.

- Accessed the File preferences to save compressed files.

- Imported 3D objects created externally into Poser using several different formats.

- Discovered how the import options can be used to change the imported object.

- Imported background pictures and videos.

- Merged content from other Poser files into the current scene.

- Imported sound files and LipSync audio files.

- Imported motion capture data to animate a figure.

- Exported content from Poser for use in other 3D software packages.

- Used the Content Room to access Content Paradise.

- Learned how to sign up with, log in to, search, and purchase objects from Content Paradise.

- Downloaded and installed content purchased from Content Paradise.

Key Terms from This Chapter

- **Compressed file.** The file that is reduced in size by compacting the data contained therein. Compressed files need to be uncompressed before they can be used. The decompression process happens automatically when Poser files are loaded.

- **Content Paradise.** A Web site connected to Poser that lets users purchase and download custom content that can be used within Poser and other e frontier products.

- **Exporting.** The process of saving Poser files to a format to be used by an external program.

- **File format.** The file type used to describe the contents of the file.

- **Hier file.** Short for *hierarchy file.* An older file format based on hierarchical data used in Poser 3 to create figures.

- **Importing.** The process of loading externally created files into Poser.

- **Motion capture.** A process of collecting motion data using a special sensor attached to real humans performing the action.

- **Normal.** A vector extending outward from the center of a polygon face used to determine which side of the polygon is visible.

- **Zip archive.** A compressed file format that reduces the size of files that need to be downloaded.

chapter 5
DEALING
WITH PROPS

1. Import external props.

2. Select, position, and edit props.

3. Attach props to elements.

4. Replace an element with a prop.

5. Create props from a selected group.

6. Use prop and conforming hair and cloth.

chapter 5 DEALING WITH PROPS

Although posing figures is the main purpose behind Poser, you aren't limited only to populating scenes with figures. Poser also supports objects known as **props** that can be placed anywhere within the scene. Props can be used to enhance the scene, such as the ground plane, a tree, or a light post; to interact with a figure, such as a chair, a weapon, or a basketball; or to enhance the figure directly, such as a hairdo, clothing, or jewelry.

Props can be loaded into a scene from the Library palette or created in another 3D package and imported into Poser. Once in Poser, props can be selected and edited using the same Editing Tools that are used to edit figures. You also can alter props by changing their parameters and properties. Props can also be grouped and given materials.

By parenting props to figure elements, you can make the prop move along with a figure element, such as a briefcase or a weapon. You can also replace figure body parts with props to create some interesting characters, such as a pirate by replacing a hand with a hook and the lower leg with a wooden leg.

New props can be created using the Group Editor dialog box. Any selection of polygons can be converted into a prop using the Create Prop button. This lets you quickly create props, such as breastplate armor or a facemask based on the existing figure.

Of all the available types of props, two specific types are unique—prop hair and prop clothes. These two categories are identified as prop objects to distinguish them from their dynamic versions. Dynamic hair and cloth can realistically react to forces in the scene, but there are times when the older prop-based versions of hair and cloth are sufficient.

Tools You'll Use

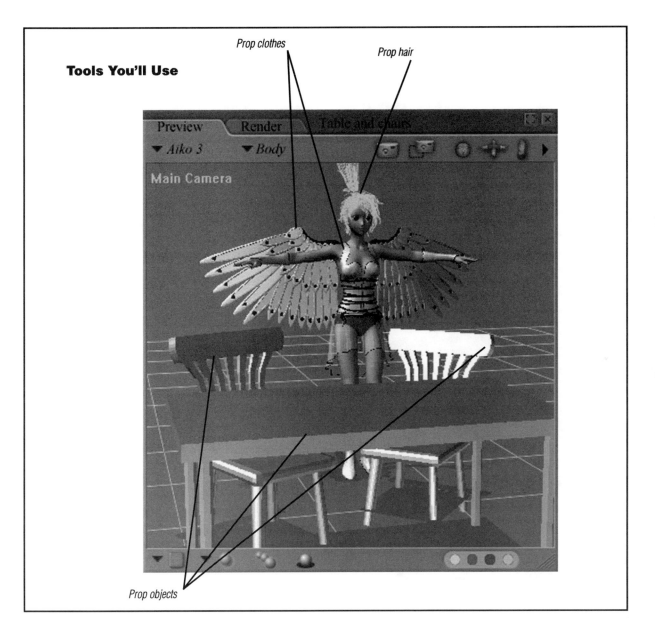

Prop clothes

Prop hair

Prop objects

IMPORT
EXTERNAL PROPS

What You'll Do

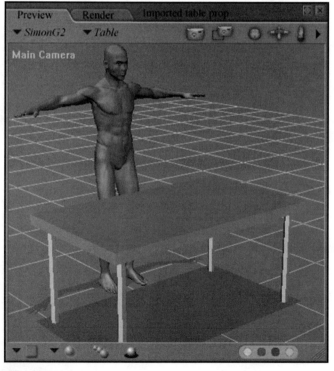

Although the Library palette contains some great props, it doesn't include all the props you may want to use. Any 3D object can be used as a prop, including objects created in external 3D packages. You simply import the object into Poser.

CAUTION The imported objects must be in one of the 3D formats that Poser supports in order to be imported. Also, Poser can only import polygon models.

 In this lesson, you learn how to import external props.

Preparing Prop Models for Importing into Poser

When building external models to be imported into Poser, keep the following in mind:

- The coordinate origin for the external 3D package corresponds the center of the floor in Poser. To have your props correctly positioned above the floor when imported, move them so they are above the origin along the Y-axis.

- Eliminate any duplicate polygons from the 3D model. Most external 3D packages include tools for automatically identifying and eliminating duplicate polygons.

- Avoid any internal polygons within the model. For example, creating a cylinder object that intersects with a sphere object leaves several polygons embedded within the sphere object. Using Boolean commands can eliminate these internal polygons. If left, the polygons will appear in their original place when bones are applied and the object is posed.

- Convert the model to polygons before saving. Poser's import features cannot handle NURBS, patches, or splines.

- Include enough resolution for the object if it needs to be posed. If an imported figure has an arm made from an extended cube, the object will not have enough polygons to bend.

- If you import a prop with groups, make sure each polygon is only included in a single group. If you're unsure whether polygons are in isolated groups, eliminate the groups and use Poser's grouping functions.

- Material definitions aren't imported along with the model, but material groups are recognized and imported.

- For optimal results, build objects to be imported into Poser using *quads* (polygons with four edges) whenever possible.

FIGURE 5-1
Import Options dialog box

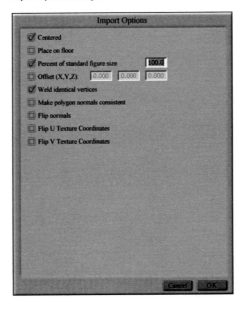

Loading External Props

To load an external 3D object as a prop, select File, Import and choose the 3D format that matches your 3D object. The available 3D formats that Poser can import include QuickDraw .3DMF, 3D Studio .3DS, .DXF, LightWave .LWO, and Wavefront .OBJ. After you select an import format, the Import Options dialog box, shown in Figure 5-1, is displayed. After setting the import options and clicking OK, a File dialog box appears where you can locate the specific file to open. Select the file and click the Open button. To learn more about these import options, see Chapter 4, "Working with Files and Accessing Content Paradise."

1. Open Poser with the default man visible.

2. Select File, Import, Wavefront OBJ.

   The Import Options dialog box appears.

3. In the Import Options dialog box, enable the Centered, Place on Floor, and Offset options. Set the Z-Axis Offset values to –0.5 and click OK.

   A file dialog box appears.

4. Locate and import the Table.obj file and click Open.

   The imported table object is displayed in front of the figure, as shown in Figure 5-2.

5. Select File, Save As and save the file as **Imported table prop.pz3**.

Deleting Props

Selected props can be deleted using the Object, Delete Object menu command. This command is different from the Delete Figure command found in the Figure menu.

FIGURE 5-2
Imported table prop

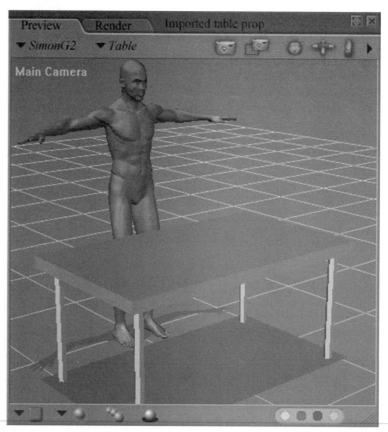

SELECT, POSITION,
AND EDIT PROPS

What You'll Do

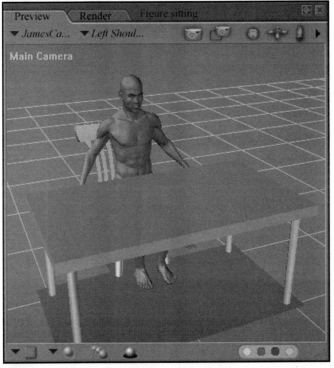

In this lesson, you learn how to select, position, and edit props.

You can select props by using the Props submenu of the Actor List located at the top of the Document Window and at the top of the Parameters/Properties palette. You can also select props from the Hierarchy Editor, which is opened using the Window, Hierarchy Editor menu command.

Using the Editing Tools

Once selected, props can be edited using all the standard buttons found in the Editing Tools. The Rotate (R) and Twist (W) tools are used to spin the prop about its view axis or about its center vertical axis. The Translate/Pull (T) and Translate In/Out (Z) tools can position the prop within the scene. The Scale (S) tool changes the size of the prop and the Taper (P) tool scales one end of the prop. Finally, the Color (C) tool can change the color of the prop. After selecting a tool, drag within the Document Window when the prop is highlighted in white. All of the Editing Tools are covered in more detail in Chapter 3, "Editing and Posing Figures."

Using the Parameter Dials

The position, orientation, and scale of the selected prop can also be controlled using the various parameter dials found in the Parameters palette, shown in Figure 5-3.

Dropping to the Floor

Selected props can also be moved vertically until their lowest point is in contact with the ground floor using the Figure, Drop to Floor (Ctrl/Command+D) menu command. This command can also be used to raise a prop that is positioned below the ground plane.

Locking Props

When the prop is positioned exactly where you want it to be, you can lock its position and orientation using the Object, Lock Actor menu command. This prevents the prop from being accidentally moved. To unlock a locked prop, just select Object, Lock Actor again to disable the toggle.

Naming Props

Imported props carry the name assigned to them in the external 3D program, but you can change this name in the Name field found in the Properties palette, shown in Figure 5-4. You can open the Properties palette by selecting the Object, Properties menu command. The other properties are the same as those for figures, which are covered in Chapter 3, "Editing and Posing Figures."

FIGURE 5-3
Prop parameters

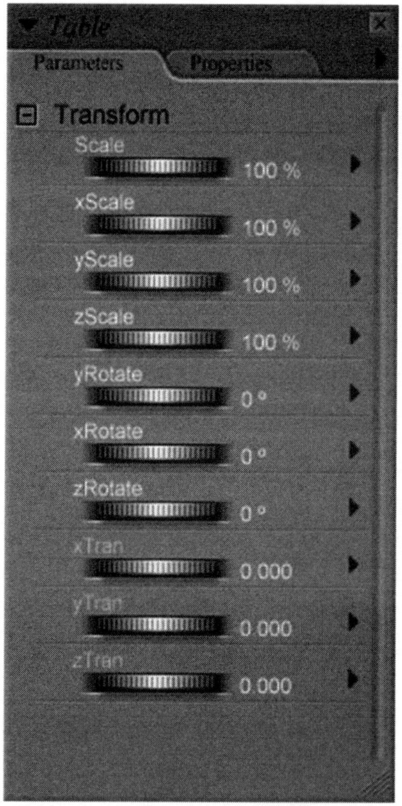

FIGURE 5-4
Prop properties

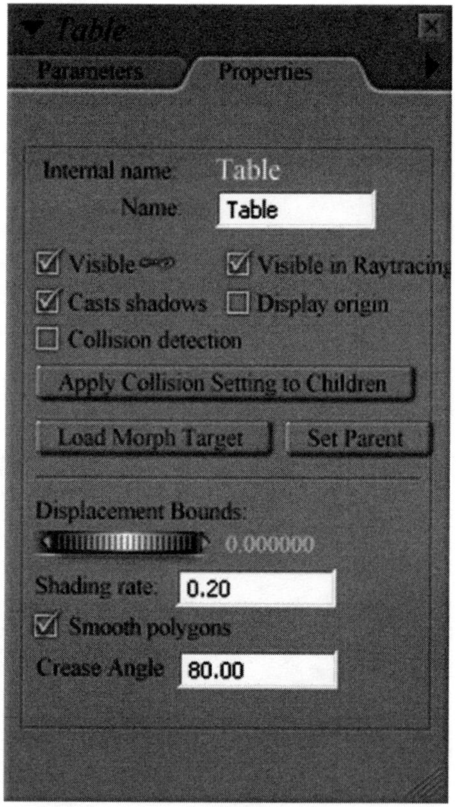

1. Select File, Open and open the Imported table prop.pz3 file.

2. Select File, Import, Wavefront OBJ and import the chair.obj file into the current scene.

3. With the chair prop selected, click the Scale tool 🔲 in the Editing Tools control. Hold down the Shift key and drag within the prop circle to uniformly reduce the size of the chair prop.

4. Select Figure, Drop to Floor (or press Ctrl/Command+D).

   The chair prop should now be aligned with the floor like the table.

5. Select the Translate In/Out tool 🟢 from the Editing Tools and drag the chair prop behind until it is positioned behind the table.

6. Select the From Left camera from the Camera Controls to see the scene from a side view.

7. Click the Translate/Pull tool 🟢 in the Editing Tools, select the figure's hip element, and drag backwards until the figure is in a sitting position. Then, drag on the figure circle to move the entire figure backward until it is sitting in the chair.

8. Select the Main Camera from the Camera Controls and rotate and move the camera until the view is zoomed in to the figure.

   The figure is positioned about the table and chair props, as shown in Figure 5-5.

9. Select File, Save As and save the file as **Figure sitting.pz3**.

FIGURE 5-5

Figure sitting at table and chair props

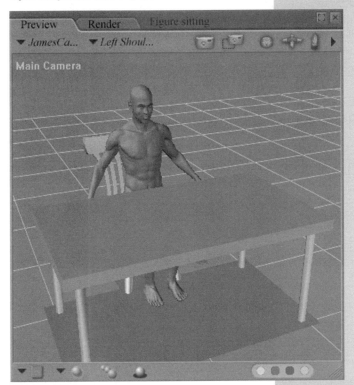

ATTACH PROPS
TO ELEMENTS

What You'll Do

In this lesson, you learn how to attach props to elements and point elements at a prop.

If you look through the types of props that are included in the Library, you'll find many figure accessories, such as clothing items, jewelry, watches, hats, and ties. These props won't help you much if you need to reposition them every time you change a figure's pose. Luckily, you can attach and conform these props to the figure so that when the figure is posed, the prop moves with it.

Attaching a Prop to a Figure Element

You attach a prop to a figure element by making the figure element the prop's parent with the Object, Change Parent menu command or by clicking the Set Parent button in the Properties panel. Both of these commands cause the Object Parent dialog box, shown in Figure 5-6, to appear.

Once parented to a figure element, the prop will move with the element as it is posed. Figure 5-7 shows a figure with a microphone prop attached to its left hand element. As the hand element is posed, the prop is moved with it.

QUICKTIP Be sure to position and orient the prop before selecting an element as its parent. It is more difficult to orient it once it is attached to an element.

Making an Attached Prop Bend with Its Parent

Enabling the Inherit Bends of Parent option in the Object Parent dialog box causes the attached prop to bend along with the parent. This is correct behavior for props that are attached to the body parts, like a shirt or a necklace, but can distort the prop incorrectly for objects that don't move with the body, like a hat or a sword.

FIGURE 5-6

The Object Parent dialog box

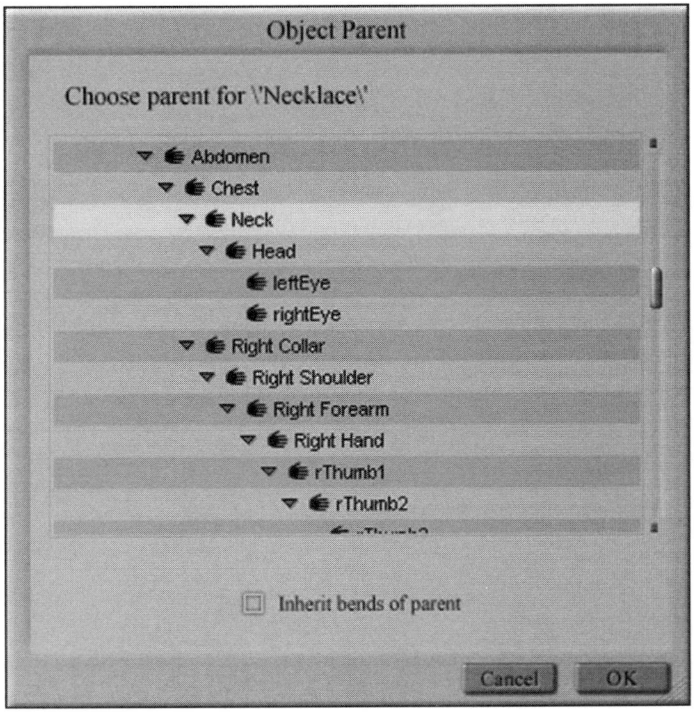

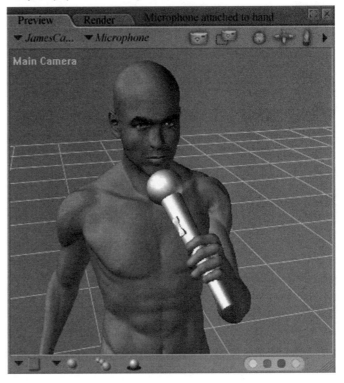

FIGURE 5-7

Microphone prop attached to the figure's hand

Changing the Prop's Parent

Once a prop is made a child object of another object, the assignment isn't permanent. You can change a prop's parent at any time using the Object, Change Parent menu command or the Set Parent button in the Properties palette. To remove a prop from its parent, simply make the root Universe object the new parent. Since objects can only have a single parent, the set parent is dropped and the root becomes the new parent.

Setting a Prop's Parent in the Hierarchy Editor

The Hierarchy Editor shows the parent-child relationships of all scene objects using an indented list. The Hierarchy Editor can also be used to reassign parents. To assign a new parent for a prop in the Hierarchy Editor, simply select the prop in the Hierarchy Editor and drag and drop it on the object that you want to be the new parent. Once dropped, the new child appears as a sub-object under its parent, as shown in Figure 5-8.

Pointing an Element at a Prop

Another way to link a prop to an element is with the Object, Point At menu command. This creates a link between the two objects that only affects the object's orientation. In some situations, this is very helpful. For example, you could use this command to

have a figure's eyes follow an object around the room, or you could cause a figure's head to tilt back and forth as if watching a tennis game. Figure 5-9 shows a figure's neck set to follow a ball about the scene, so the ball can be used to rock the figure's head back and forth.

The Point At command can be used between any two types of objects, so you could have figure elements follow a prop or you could have a prop rotate to follow a figure element. Props and figure elements can also be set to follow lights or camera

objects. Once you have identified the Point At object, a new parameter dial appears in the Parameters palette. Using this dial, you can set the amount of exaggeration the figure experiences in following the object.

Deleting a Point At Link

If you ever need to remove a Point At link between two objects, select the object that moves and choose the Object, Point At menu command again. In the Object Parent dialog box, choose the None button and the link is removed.

FIGURE 5-8
Parents can be set using the Hierarchy Editor

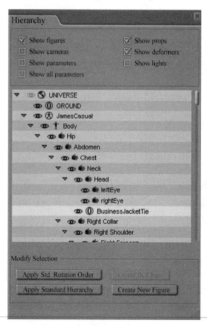

FIGURE 5-9
Figure elements can be set to point at a prop

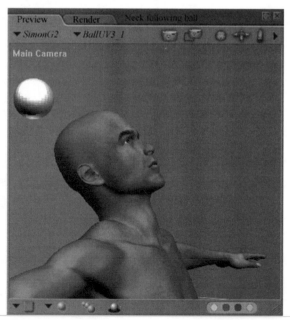

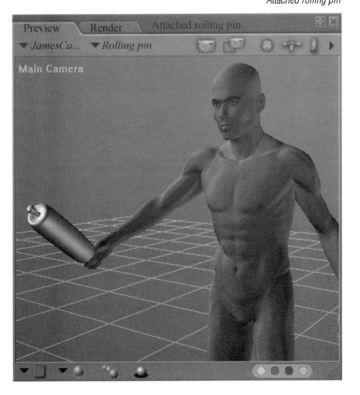

FIGURE 5-10
Attached rolling pin

Attach a Prop to a Figure Element

1. Open Poser with the default figure visible.

2. Select File, Import, Wavefront OBJ and import the Rolling pin.obj file into the current scene.

3. With the rolling pin item selected, click the Scale tool in the Editing Tools control. Hold down the Shift key and drag within the prop circle to uniformly reduce the size of the rolling pin prop.

4. Select the Rotate tool from the Editing Tools and rotate the rolling pin prop until it is parallel to the figure's right hand. Select the Translate/Pull tool to move the rolling pin prop close to the right hand.

5. Select the right hand element and drag the Grasp and Thumb Grasp dials in the Parameters palette to close the hand's fingers.

6. Position and orient the rolling pin prop within the right hand. Select the right hand camera from the Camera Controls to see it up close.

7. Select the rolling pin prop and select Object, Change Parent.

8. Select the Right Hand element in the Change Parent dialog box that appears and click OK.

   The prop will now move with the attached element, as shown in Figure 5-10.

9. Select File, Save As and save the file as **Attached rolling pin.pz3**.

Make a Figure Element Point at a Prop

1. Open Poser with the default figure visible.

2. Select File, Import, Wavefront OBJ and import the Striped ball.obj file into the current scene.

3. With the ball item selected, open the Parameters palette and change the Scale value to 12 to reduce the size of the ball. Then drag the xTran, yTran, and zTran dials until the ball object is in front and to the right, about eye level of the figure.

4. Select the left eyeball element and choose the Object, Point At menu command.

   The Object Parent dialog box opens.

5. In the Object Parent dialog box, scroll to the bottom of the dialog box and select the Striped ball object. Then click the OK button.

   The eyeball immediately rotates so the pupil faces the ball object.

6. Repeat Steps 4 and 5 for the right eyeball element.

7. Select and drag the ball object in front of the figure.

   The eyes both rotate towards the ball object as it moves, as shown in Figure 5-11.

8. Select File, Save As and save the file as **Eyes following ball.pz3**.

FIGURE 5-11

Eyes following ball

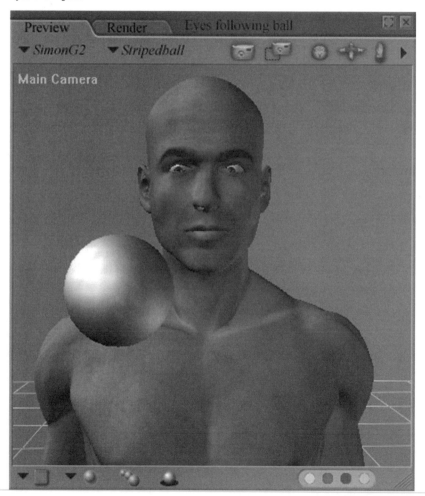

REPLACE AN
ELEMENT WITH A PROP

What You'll Do

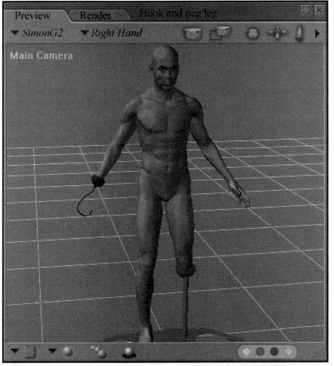

In this lesson, you learn how to replace a figure element with a prop.

If a figure has most of the elements that you want in a character, but it just needs a few little tweaks, there is no need to reinvent the wheel. For example, consider a cyborg character who has a laser cannon for his left forearm. To create this character, you can simply model the laser cannon weapon, position it where it should be, and replace the forearm with the new prop.

QUICKTIP Using the Replace Body Part with Prop command, you can quickly swap the default head with a customized one.

Replacing an Element with a Prop

Another way to attach a prop to an element is to actually replace an element with a prop. A good example of this is modeling a pirate who has a hook for a hand or a peg instead of a leg. To replace an element with a prop, load the prop into the scene, position the prop where it should be in place of the body part, select the body part that you want to replace, and choose the Object, Replace Body Part with Prop menu command. This opens a Replace Body Part dialog box where you can select the prop to replace the selected element. Figure 5-12 shows a silly figure where the head has been replaced by a hatchet prop.

> **CAUTION** The chain break icon for the hip cannot be removed. Replacing a body part with a prop is one of the few commands that cannot be undone using the Edit, Undo command.

Disabling the Bend Option

When you replace a body part with a prop, a warning dialog box appears stating that replaced parts usually work best when the Bend option in the Properties palette is disabled. To disable this option, open the Properties palette and click on the Bend option to disable it.

Deleting Figure Elements

Replacing a body part with a prop may require that you delete some figure elements. For example, if you replace the forearm with a hook, the hand and fingers are still there and need to be removed to complete the figure. There actually isn't any way to delete figure elements, but you can hide them. To hide figure elements, disable the Visible option in the Properties palette.

> **QUICKTIP** If several elements need to be hidden, use the Hierarchy Editor. It allows you to hide multiple body parts quickly.

FIGURE 5-12
Hatchet head

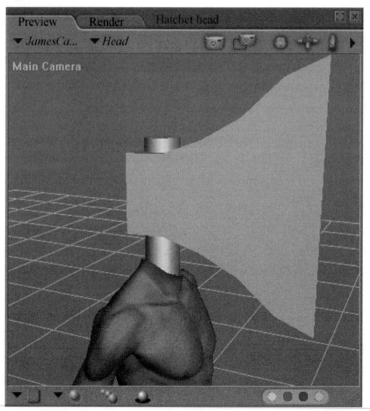

Replace a Figure Element with a Prop

1. Open Poser with the default figure visible.

2. Select File, Import, Wavefront OBJ and import the Arm hook.obj and the Peg leg.obj files into the current scene.

3. Select each imported object in turn and use the Editing Tools and the parameter dials to position them in place of the forearm and the lower leg.

4. Select the forearm object and choose the Object, Replace Body Part with Prop menu command.

   The Replace Body Part dialog box opens.

5. In the Replace Body Part dialog box, select the Arm hook object. Then click the OK button.

   The forearm element is replaced with the hook prop.

6. Repeat Steps 4 and 5 with the lower leg element and the peg leg prop.

7. For both replaced elements, open the Properties palette and disable the Bend option.

   The forearm and lower leg elements are replaced with the selected props, but the hand and foot objects are still visible.

8. Select the Window, Hierarchy Editor menu command to open the Hierarchy Editor. Then locate and disable the Visible option for the hand and foot elements that are still visible.

   Figure 5-13 shows the resulting character after the hand and foot become invisible.

9. Select File, Save As and save the file as **Hook and peg leg.pz3**.

FIGURE 5-13

Hook and peg leg

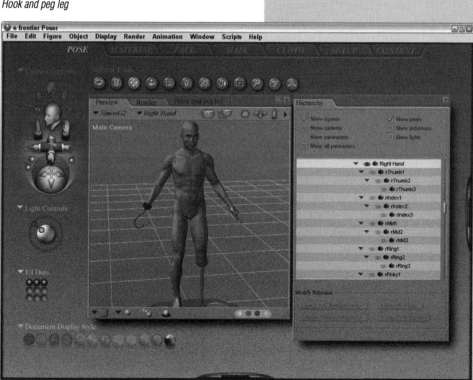

CREATE PROPS
FROM A SELECTED GROUP

What You'll Do

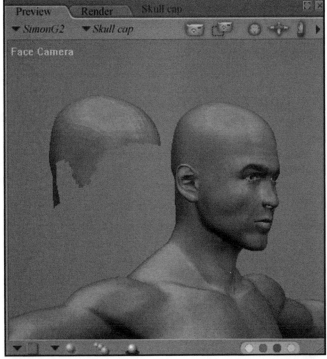

▶ *In this lesson, you learn how to create new props using the Group Editor.*

If you want to create a prop from part of a figure, you can use the Group Editor, shown in Figure 5-14, to select the exact polygons that make up the prop. You open the Group Editor by clicking the Grouping tool in the Editing Tools control. You can use the Group Editor to create material, hair, and cloth groups. Other Group Editor features are presented in other chapters.

FIGURE 5-14
Group Editor dialog box

Selecting Polygons

Within the Group Editor dialog box are two buttons for selecting polygons—one for selecting and one for removing selected polygons. By dragging over polygons in the Document Window with the Grouping tool, you can select polygons as part of the group. The selected polygons are highlighted in red in the Document Window. To remove polygons from the current selection, click the Deselect button at the top of the Group Editor and click the polygons to remove.

QUICKTIP You can also access the Deselect button by holding down the Ctrl/Command key.

Creating a Prop

Clicking the Create Prop button converts the selected polygon group into a prop. A dialog box opens where you can name the new prop. Figure 5-15 shows a new face mask prop that was created using the polygons in the front of the head element.

QUICKTIP An excellent use of the Create Prop feature is to create a separate surface prop that defines where body hair will grow. For the head, this prop is called a skullcap.

Spawning Multiple Props

Clicking the Spawn Prop button creates multiple props by converting all newly created groups into props.

FIGURE 5-15
New prop

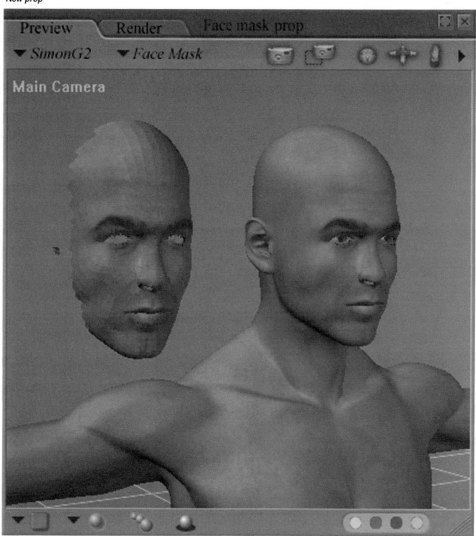

Create a Scullcap for Hair

1. Open Poser with the default figure visible.

2. Click the Hidden Line button in the Document Display Style controls.

3. Click the HeadCam icon in the Camera Controls.

4. Click the Grouping tool button [image] in the Editing Tools controls.

   The Group Editor panel appears, and the figure in the Document Window goes dark.

5. Click on the New Group button and name the new group **Skullcap**.

6. Drag over the top section of the head in the Document Window. Then rotate the camera around to the side and select the portions of the head where the hair grows above and behind the ear, as shown in Figure 5-16. Rotate the camera to the opposite side of the head and choose the remainder of the area where hair grows.

7. Click the Create Prop button in the Group Editor panel.

   The New Prop Name dialog box appears.

8. Type the name, **Skullcap**, in the New Prop Name dialog box and click OK.

9. Close the Group Editor and select the Skullcap prop from the Actor List at the top of the Document Window. Move it to the side of the original head object.

10. Click the Smooth Shaded button in the Document Display Style controls.

    The skullcap prop is positioned next to the figure's head, as shown in Figure 5-17.

11. Select File, Save As and save the file as **Skullcap.pz3**.

FIGURE 5-16
Group selection

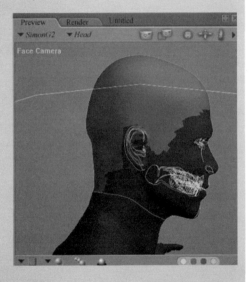

FIGURE 5-17
Skullcap prop

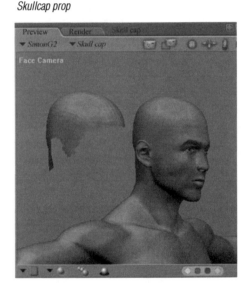

USE PROP AND
CONFORMING HAIR AND CLOTH

What You'll Do

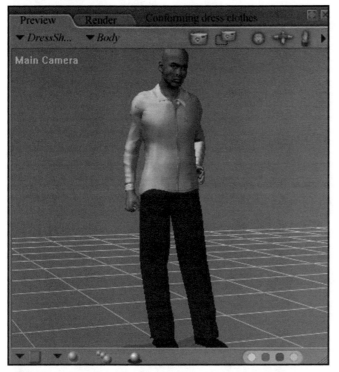

In this lesson, you learn how to use hair and cloth props.

Earlier versions of Poser used prop objects to create hair and clothes for figures. These prop objects are manually fitted on the figure and can be selected from the Props section of the Actor List. Although conforming and dynamic hair and cloth solutions are available in the current Poser version, you can still use the prop-based hair and cloth.

Another solution for hair and cloth is conforming hair and cloth objects. These objects are applied to the scene as figure items and can be made to conform to the current pose for the current figure. Once conformed, the hair and/or clothing items move along with the figure.

NOTE Conforming hair and clothes objects load from the Library as figure elements instead of as props, so don't look for them in the Actor List.

Loading Prop Hair

If you're not sure where to start, you can check the Library for several preset prop hairstyles that you can apply directly to the current figure. To access available hair from the Library, click the Hair category and navigate to the folder containing the prop hairstyles you want to apply. Within each folder are thumbnails of the various hairstyles. With a prop hairstyle thumbnail selected, click the Change Hair button at the bottom of the Library palette; the selected hairstyle is loaded into the Document Window.

NOTE You can actually load both prop and dynamic hair from within any room.

Loading Library Prop Clothes

Although almost any object, including body parts, can be treated as cloth, you'll typically want to look for cloth objects in the Props Library category. Within each folder are thumbnails of the various cloth objects. With a cloth object thumbnail selected, click the Change Prop button at the bottom of the Library palette, and the selected object is loaded into the Shader Window. Figure 5-18 shows the default SimonG2 figure with a set of prop hair and clothes added. I guess clothes do make the man.

QUICKTIP The Figures category also includes a Casual version of SimonG2 that includes clothes.

FIGURE 5-18
SimonG2 with prop clothes and hair

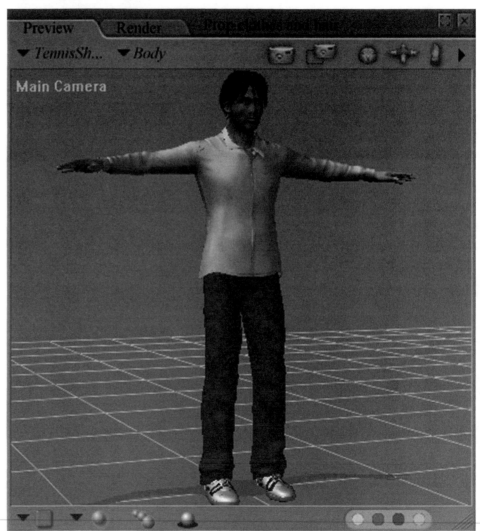

Loading Library Conforming Clothes

Many objects in the Props category of the Library are identified as **conforming objects**. These objects are created to fit exactly on the matching figure. To conform these clothing props to their matching figure, choose the Figure, Conform To menu command. This opens a dialog box where you can select the figure to conform the prop object to.

CAUTION Clothes that conform to a figure shouldn't be used in a dynamic simulation. For cloth to be simulated properly, it needs to be free of any intersections with the scene objects. Also, conforming clothes are set to move with the body, and including conforming clothes in a cloth simulation will make it so the clothes no longer move with the body.

Conforming Clothing Props to a Figure

Another way to attach props to an object is to make clothing props conform to a figure's shape using the Figure, Conform To menu command. Conforming clothes are best applied to naked figures. All conforming props in the Library are easily identified with the *Conforming* label. Most clothes are loaded as figures and can be selected from the Figure List at the top of the Document Window. Selecting the Figure, Conform To menu command opens the

Conform To dialog box, shown in Figure 5-19, where you can select the figure to which to conform the clothing. Figure 5-20 shows a shirt and pair of pants conforming to a figure.

QUICKTIP When loading a clothing item from the Library, use the Add New Item button instead of the Replace Figure button, or the current figure will be removed.

FIGURE 5-19
Conform To dialog box

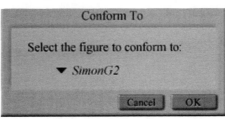

FIGURE 5-20
Conforming shirt and pants

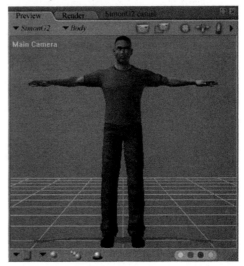

Handling Skin Poking Through Clothes

If the scale of the conforming clothes isn't exactly right, some skin may show through the clothes, as displayed in Figure 5-21. This happens frequently when clothes for different figures are interchanged, but you can fix this problem in several different ways. The easiest fix is to simply scale or rotate the clothing item until the skin is covered.

Another solution is to simply make the underlying body part that is showing through invisible. Because the clothing item holds the figure's shape, hiding the body part won't even be noticeable.

Clothing objects can also be morphed to cover the skin in a particular area. Be sure to save out the morph target before continuing.

FIGURE 5-21
Skin poking through clothes

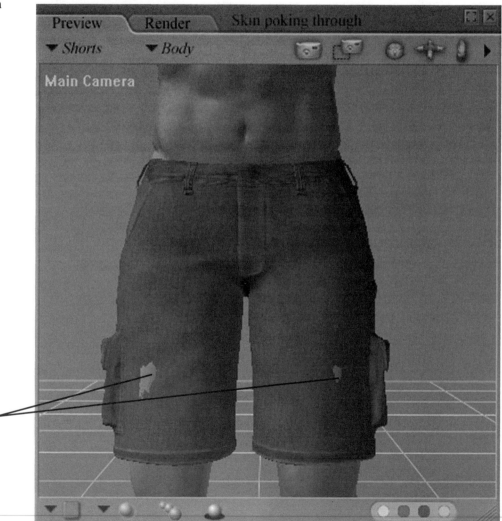

Note the skin poking through these shorts

FIGURE 5-22

Clothing mismatched with figure

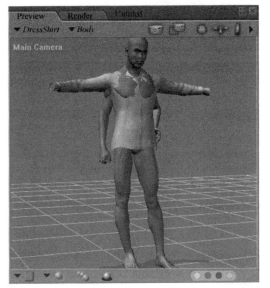

FIGURE 5-23

Conforming dress clothes

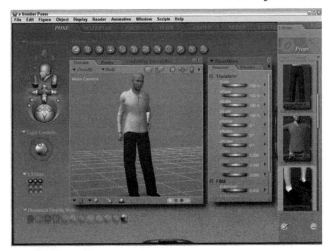

1. Open Poser with the default figure visible.

2. Click the side control to the right of the interface to open the Library palette or select Window, Libraries.

3. Select and apply a pose from the Poses category.

4. Click the Props category at the top of the Library palette and navigate to the Poser 7/P7 Male Clothes/Poser 7 Casual folder.

5. Select the G2 Casual Dress Shirt thumbnail and click the Apply Library Preset button at the bottom of the Library palette.

   The selected clothing item is loaded into the Document Window, but it doesn't quite match the figure, as shown in Figure 5-22.

6. With the Casual Dress Shirt item selected in the Figure List at the top of the Document Window, select Figure, Conform To.

7. In the Conform To dialog box that appears, select the SimonG2 object and click OK.

   The clothing item is conformed to fit the figure, as shown in Figure 5-23.

8. Repeat Steps 5, 6, and 7 for the dress pants and dress shoes.

   With all the various clothing conformed to the figure, he is ready for a night on the town, as shown in Figure 5-23.

9. Select File, Save As and save the file as **Conforming dress clothes.pz3**.

CHAPTER REVIEW

Chapter Summary

This chapter explained how prop objects can be used to enhance the scene. Props can be loaded from and saved to the Library and can include external objects, such as a mailbox or a motorcycle or figure accessories, such as watches, jewelry, hairstyles or clothes. Props can also be created in an external package and imported into Poser. Props are selected and positioned just like figure elements using the Editing Tools. Finally, props can be attached to existing figure elements, set to point at specific objects, replace figure elements, or created from existing body parts. This chapter concluded by showing you how to use conforming clothes and hair to dress a figure.

What You Have Learned

In this chapter, you

- Discovered how external props can be imported into Poser using a number of different formats and options.

- Selected, positioned, and edited props using the various Editing Tools.

- Attached props to figure elements using the Set Parent feature.

- Changed the orientation of props using the Point At feature.

- Replaced body parts with props.

- Created new props from a selected group of polygons.

- Made clothes conform to a figure.

Key Terms from This Chapter

- **Conforming prop.** An object that is deformed in order to fit the designated figure.

- **Locked prop.** A locked prop is one whose position and orientation is set and cannot be changed unless the object is unlocked.

- **Offset.** The location of an imported prop as measured from the scene's origin point.

- **Parent.** The controlling object that a child object is attached to. When the parent moves, the child object moves with it.

- **Prop.** Any external object added to the scene to enhance the final image. Props may include scenery, figure accessories, clothes, and hair.

chapter

6 ESTABLISHING A SCENE—
CAMERAS AND
BACKGROUNDS

1. Learn the available cameras.

2. Work with cameras.

3. Change camera parameters.

4. Aim and attach cameras.

5. Change the background.

chapter 6 ESTABLISHING A SCENE—
CAMERAS AND BACKGROUNDS

The real advantage of the 3D world is the ability to view the scene from any position—upside, downside, and even inside out. This is made possible using virtual cameras that are positioned within the scene. Poser includes several default camera types that you can choose. These camera types include a set of **orthographic cameras**, cameras that can be rotated and cameras that can be focused on specific body parts, like the face and hands.

Once a camera is selected, you can use the Camera Controls to change its position and orientation. The Camera Controls also let you change specific camera motions, such as rolling the camera and toggling Flyaround mode.

Cameras can also be selected from the Action List that makes the camera parameters and properties visible. Camera parameters offer a way to precisely move cameras to specific positions and orientations. You can also change camera properties, such as **focal length**, **F-stop**, and **clipping planes**.

Poser also includes some specialized features that let you point cameras at specific items in the scene. For example, you can quickly animate the rotations of a camera by pointing the camera towards the figure's head or torso, or you can have a specific body part set to point at a camera.

You can load a custom background of the Document Window to display a color, a picture, a movie, or particular texture. This background is displayed in the Document Window and can be included when the image is rendered.

Tools You'll Use

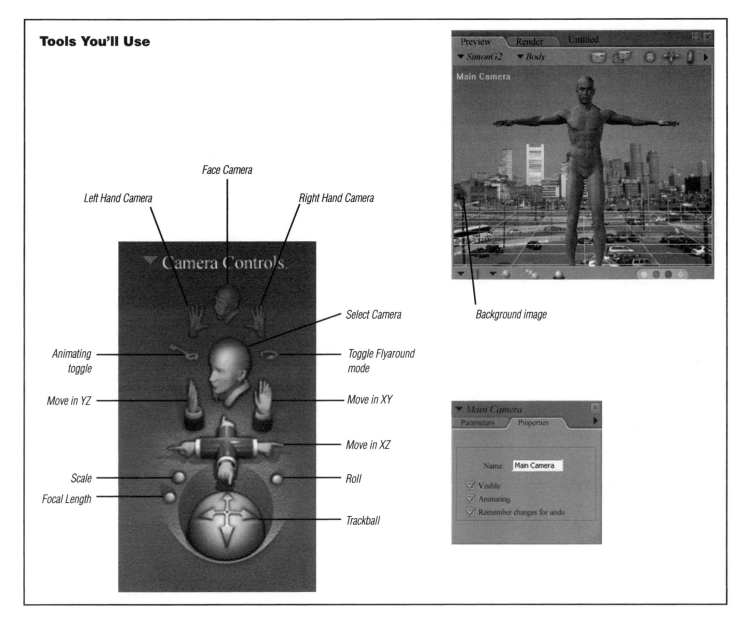

Left Hand Camera

Face Camera

Right Hand Camera

Camera Controls.

Select Camera

Animating toggle

Toggle Flyaround mode

Move in YZ

Move in XY

Move in XZ

Scale

Roll

Focal Length

Trackball

Main Camera

Background image

Preview   Render   Untitled

SimonG2   Body

Main Camera

▼ Main Camera

Parameters   Properties

Name: Main Camera

☑ Visible
☑ Animating
☑ Remember changes for undo

LEARN THE
AVAILABLE CAMERAS

What You'll Do

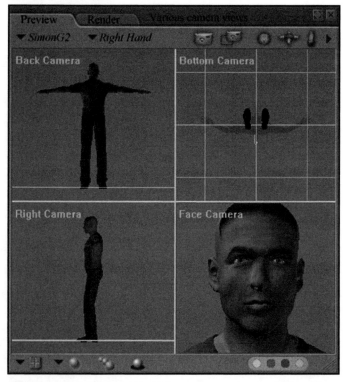

In this lesson, you learn which preset cameras are available and how to select them.

Cameras provide you a view of the scene and can be manipulated to show you the exact portion of the scene that you want to concentrate on. You can select preset cameras from the Display, Camera View menu, the Select Camera icon, and the pop-up menu in the Camera Controls. You can also select a camera for the current view by right-clicking on the Document Window and selecting Camera View from the pop-up menu.

NOTE You can also select from the various cameras using the Actor List at the top of the Document Window and the Parameters/Properties palette, but doing this only selects the camera icon and does not change the view.

Cameras within the current scene are represented by a camera icon, but most are set to be invisible by default. To see the camera icons, simply enable the Visible option in the Properties palette. Figure 6-1 shows a camera icon in front of the default figure.

Using Camera Presets

The available preset camera views include the Main, Auxiliary, Left, Right, Top, Bottom, Front, Back, Face, Posing, Right Hand, Left Hand, Dolly, and Shadow Light cameras. Each of these camera types has its own icon in the Camera Controls, as shown in Figure 6-2, which you can access by clicking the Select Camera icon or by clicking and dragging to the left or right. If the Display, Show Camera Names option is enabled, the camera name appears in the upper-left corner of the Document Window.

POSER 7 NEW FEATURE

Poser 7 allows you to create Dolly and Revolving cameras.

Using the Main and Auxiliary Cameras

The Main and Auxiliary cameras can be rotated about the center of the scene and are the main cameras that you'll probably want to use. These cameras are not affected by the movement of the figures in the scene. The Main and Auxiliary cameras work exactly the same, but the Auxiliary camera lets you maintain the Main camera's position while you investigate another view.

FIGURE 6-1
Cameras are displayed as icons in the scene

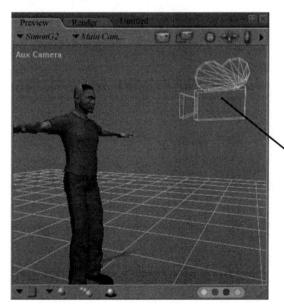

Visible camera icon

FIGURE 6-2
Select Camera icons in the Camera Controls

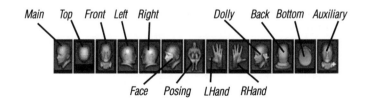

Main   Top   Front   Left   Right   Dolly   Back   Bottom   Auxiliary

Face   Posing   LHand   RHand

Using Orthographic Cameras

The Left, Right, Top, Bottom, Front, and Back cameras are all orthographic cameras that are located at the end of each axis. Orthographic cameras are special views that show the scene as a 2D image without any perspective and all dimension measurements are correct. Figure 6-3 shows the scene using the Four Ports layout, which includes three orthographic views. Orthographic cameras also cannot be rotated, and the Trackball in the Camera Controls is disabled when any of these cameras are selected.

NOTE If the Four Ports option is selected from the Layout List at the bottom of the Document Window or if the Display, Camera View, Four Cams menu command is selected, three of the views will be orthographic cameras.

Using the Posing Camera

The Posing camera can also be rotated about the scene, but it is focused on the selected figure. If the selected figure is moved, the Posing camera follows along with the figure. If a different figure is selected, the camera view changes to focus on the new figure.

Using the Face and Hand Camera

The Face and Hand cameras work like the Posing camera, except they are focused on the current figure's face or individual hands. These provide a quick close-up of the face and hands so you can check their details without having to maneuver the camera. The Face and Hand cameras also rotate about the face and hands of the selected figure. The Three Ports—Big Top layout displays views using the Face and both Hand cameras, as shown in Figure 6-4.

CAUTION The Face and Hand cameras look for objects named Face, Left Hand, and Right Hand. If you rename these elements, these cameras will not work.

FIGURE 6-3
Front, Top, and Right orthographic cameras

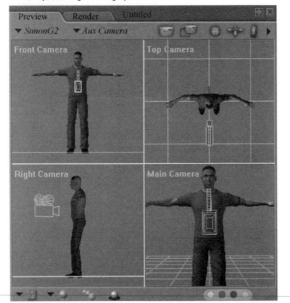

FIGURE 6-4
Face, Left Hand, and Right Hand cameras

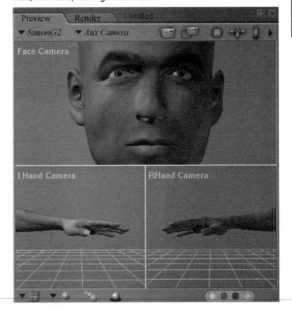

Using the Dolly Camera

The Main and Auxiliary cameras orbit around the center of the screen, but the Dolly camera pivots about its own axis, making it act just like a real camera. For animation sequences where the camera is moving, you'll want to use this specialized camera.

Using Shadow Light Cameras

The pop-up menu in the Camera Controls also includes a Shadow Light camera for each light in the scene. These cameras are positioned and oriented to point the same direction as its light and provide a look at how the shadows will be cast when rendered. Shadow cameras, like orthographic cameras, cannot be rotated. Figure 6-5 shows the Shadow camera for Light 2. Notice in the figure how the highlighted areas are facing the camera.

FIGURE 6-5
Shadow camera

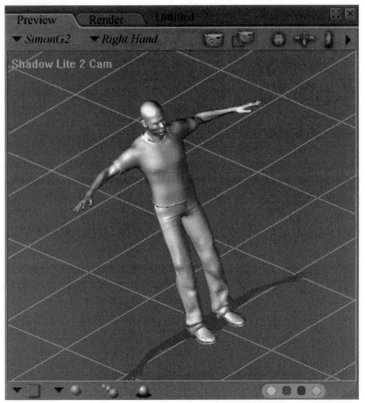

Change Cameras for Viewports

1. Open Poser with the default figure visible.

2. At the bottom of the Document Window, select the Four Ports option from the Layout List.

   The Document Window is divided into four different views.

3. Select the upper-left port.

   A red border that indicates the active port surrounds the port view.

4. Select the From Back option from the pop-up menu at the top of the Camera Controls.

5. Select the upper-right port, right-click on the Document Window, and select Camera View, Bottom Camera from the pop-up menu.

6. Select the lower-left port and change the camera to the left view using the Display, Camera View, From Right menu.

7. Select the lower-right port, click on the Select Camera icon in the Camera Controls, and drag to the right until the Face Camera is selected.

   All the cameras for the various ports have now been changed using various methods, as shown in Figure 6-6.

8. Select File, Save As and save the file as **Various camera views.pz3**.

FIGURE 6-6
Various camera views

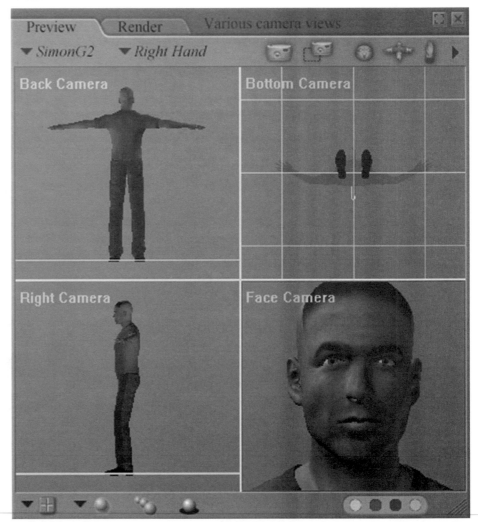

WORK WITH
CAMERAS

What You'll Do

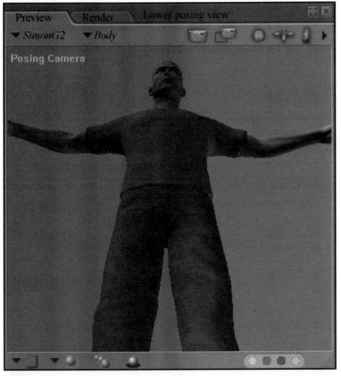

▶ *In this lesson, you learn how to work with cameras and the Camera Controls.*

Once a camera is selected, you can change its position and where it is pointing using the Camera Controls. The Parameters/Properties palette also includes several settings for controlling the cameras.

> **NOTE** You can manipulate the cameras also by selecting the camera icon or by selecting a camera from the Actor List and using the Editing Tools, but the Camera Controls are much easier.

Using the Camera Controls

The Camera Controls allow you to pan, rotate, and zoom in on the scene. These controls, shown in Figure 6-7, have an immediate impact on the scene displayed in the Document Window. By using these controls, you can control precisely which part of the scene is displayed.

Using the Camera Shortcut Icons

The top three icons in the Camera Controls let you select the right hand, face, or left hand cameras. Although these icons by default are used to switch between the face and hand cameras, these icons can be used as shortcuts for any of the preset cameras. To change the camera shortcut, simply select the camera preset that you want to use in the Select Camera icon and click on one of the shortcut icons with the Alt/Option key held down.

Enabling Camera Animation Mode

The key icon toggles animating cameras on and off. The key icon is colored red when animating is enabled. When enabled, animation keys are recorded whenever the camera is moved. This same option can be toggled using the Animating option in the Properties palette.

Using Flyaround Mode

The Flyaround button toggles on Flyaround mode, which spins the camera about the figure's center and animates the scene objects, as shown for three frames in Figure 6-8. This provides a quick view of all sides of the scene. While in Flyaround mode, you can move the cursor in the Document Window up and down to change the angle of the spinning camera. Clicking again on the Flyaround button returns the view to its previous setting. You can also access Flyaround mode using the Camera Controls pop-up menu and the Display, Camera View menu or by pressing Ctrl/Command+L.

QUICKTIP While the scene is spinning about the current figure, you can still use the Camera Controls to change the view and zoom in and out.

FIGURE 6-7
Camera Controls

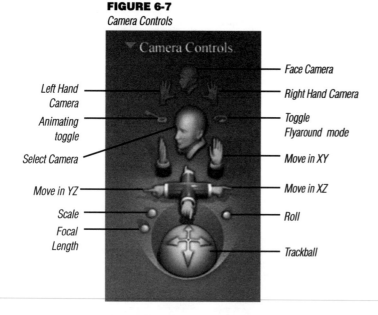

Left Hand Camera · Face Camera · Right Hand Camera · Animating toggle · Toggle Flyaround mode · Select Camera · Move in XY · Move in YZ · Move in XZ · Scale · Roll · Focal Length · Trackball

FIGURE 6-8
Flyaround mode

Moving and Rotating a Camera

The hand icons in the Camera Controls are used to move the camera view within the YZ plane, the XY plane, or XZ plane. To use these icons, just click them and drag. The view in the Document Window is updated as you drag. The sphere with arrows on it at the bottom of the Camera Controls, called the **Trackball**, is used to rotate the camera. It is used like the move icons by clicking and dragging in the direction you want to rotate the camera. You can also access the Trackball by holding down the Alt/Option key and dragging in the Document Window. The Roll button tilts the figure within the Document Window about its center. You can also change the camera's position and rotation by dragging the parameter dials in the Parameters palette.

QUICKTIP Mini-sized controls for positioning and rotating the camera view are included on the top-right corner of the Document Window.

Changing a Camera's Scale and Focal Length

The final two Camera Controls buttons to the left of the Trackball are for adjusting the camera's scale and focal length. Dragging on the Scale button changes the size of the figure within the viewpane, and dragging with the Focal Length button changes the center focus point for the camera, which results in the how close or far the figure appears from the camera.

FIGURE 6-9
Camera properties

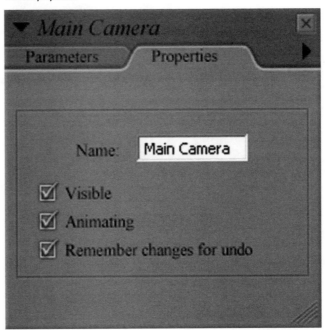

Undoing Camera Changes

Whenever a camera moves or rotates to show a different view, you can keep track of the view changes in the Undo cache so they can be undone, but frequent camera moves can quickly fill up the Undo cache, overwriting any figure posing changes that have recently been made. If you disable the Remember Changes for Undo option in the Properties palette, shown in Figure 6-9, for the selected camera, view changes aren't kept in the Undo cache.

Using Display Guides

The Display, Guides menu command includes several useful display guides that can help as you begin to move the cameras about the scene. In addition to the two guides used to indicate the relative size and proportions of the figure, the Display, Guides menu command also includes the following guides, shown and labeled in Figure 6-10:

- **Ground Plane:** Can be turned on and off. It is useful to help set the vertical alignment of objects in the scene. The Material Room can also be used to apply a unique material to the ground plane.

- **Horizon Line:** Adds a set of horizontal dashed lines across the Document Window to show where the horizon in the distance is located.

- **Vanishing Lines:** Marks the point off in the distance where all objects converge to show **perspective**. This guide is helpful for determining the amount of perspective distortion in the scene.

- **Focus Distance Guide:** Marks the point where the camera is in focus. This is used to determine the center point for the Depth of Field render effect. This point is set uniquely for each camera.

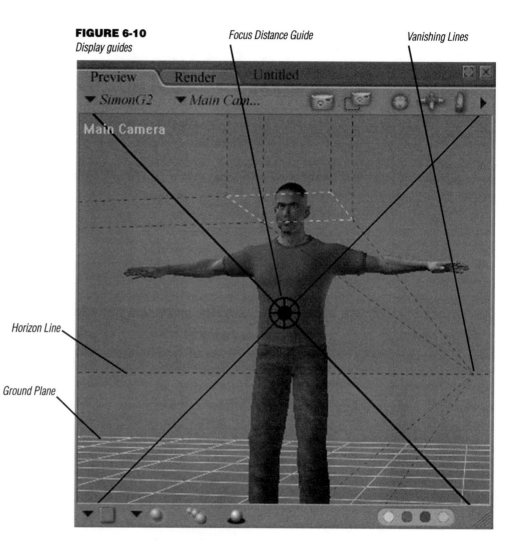

FIGURE 6-10
Display guides

Focus Distance Guide

Vanishing Lines

Horizon Line

Ground Plane

FIGURE 6-11
Camera shortcut icons

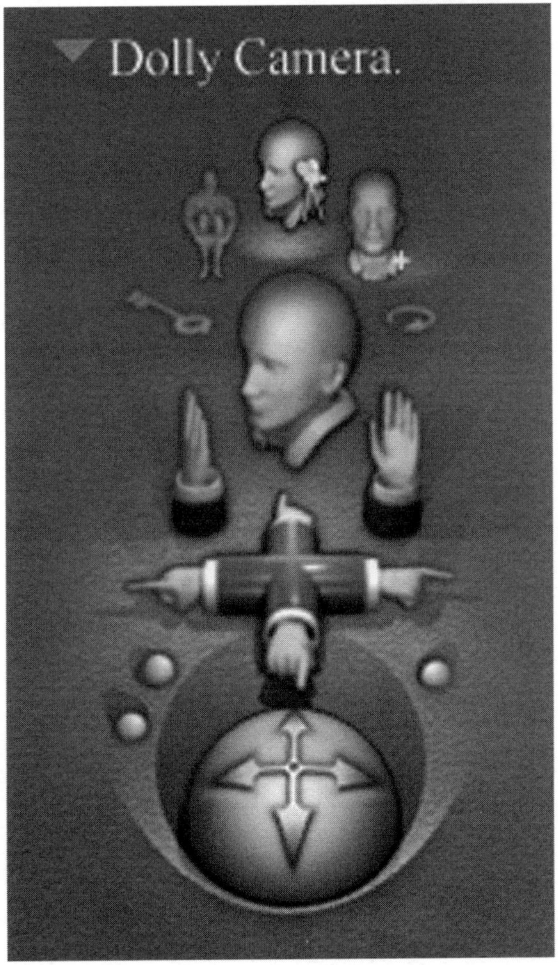

Set the Camera Shortcut Icons

1. Select the Posing camera from the drop-down list at the top of the Camera Controls.

   The Posing Camera icon appears in the Camera Controls.

2. Hold down the Alt/Option key and click on the Right Hand Cam shortcut icon.

   The Posing Camera icon takes the place of the Right Hand icon.

3. Repeat Steps 1 and 2 for the other camera shortcut icons using the Dolly and Auxiliary cameras.

   The Camera Shortcut icons now have new icons, as shown in Figure 6-11.

4. Select File, Save As and save the file as **Camera shortcut icons.pz3**.

Position the Main Camera

1. Open Poser with the default figure visible. The Main camera is selected by default.

2. Click on the Trackball and drag it to the right to change the camera's view.

3. Drag on the Move in XY hand icon to center the figure's head in the view, and then drag the Move in XZ icon to zoom in on the left side of the figure, as shown in Figure 6-12.

4. Select File, Save As and save the file as **Zoomed main camera.pz3**.

FIGURE 6-12
Zoomed Main camera

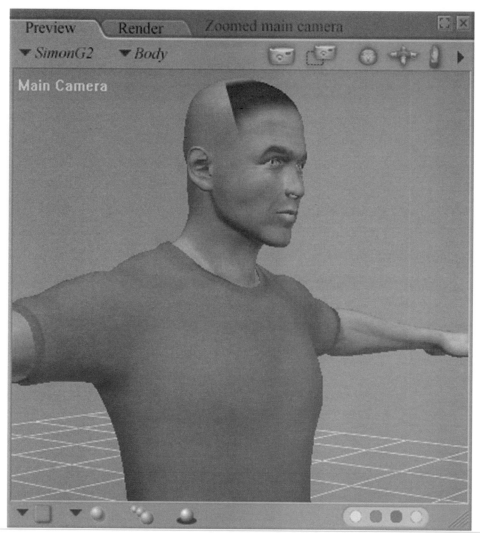

FIGURE 6-13

Positioned Posing camera

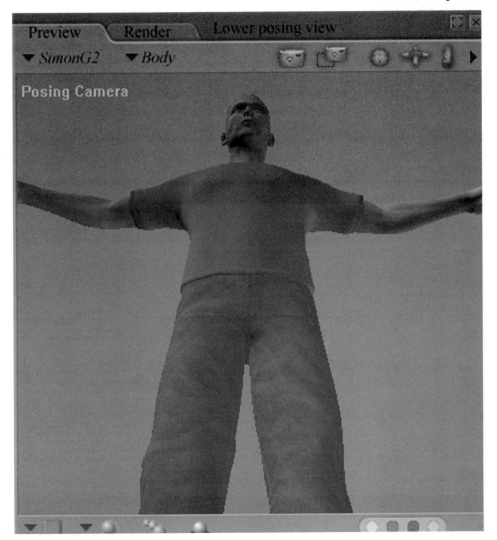

1. Open Poser with the default figure visible.

2. Select the Posing camera from the pop-up list at the top of the Camera Controls.

3. Click on the Trackball and drag it downward to change the camera's view to be below the figure.

4. Drag the Move in XZ icon to zoom in on the figure, and then drag the Move in XY icon to center the figure, as shown in Figure 6-13.

5. Select File, Save As and save the file as **Lower posing view.pz3**.

CHANGE
CAMERA PARAMETERS

What You'll Do

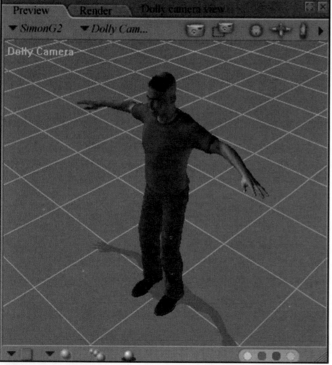

When a camera is selected from the Actor List at the top of the Document Window or the Parameters/Properties palette, you can access its parameters and properties. The parameter dials offer several additional controls that aren't available within the Camera Controls.

In this lesson, you learn what each of the various camera parameters is for.

Changing Perspective

Perspective gives the effect that the scene is receding into a converging point in the distance. The Perspective value is tied to the Focal Length value (or simply Focal in the Parameters palette). The focal length is the distance from the camera where the camera is in focus. At low Focal and Perspective values, the scene objects appear distorted, as shown in Figure 6-14. These values have no effect on orthographic cameras. The Focal Length and Perspective values can be set using the Camera Controls or the parameter dials.

> **QUICKTIP** To get a quick idea of how much perspective is in the current scene, look at how square the ground plane is.

Creating Depth of Field

A **depth of field** effect occurs when the camera is focused on a specific point in the scene and all other points closer or farther from this point appear blurry. The larger the distance from the focal point, the greater the amount of blur. The Focus Distance parameter lets you interactively set the focal point for the scene by dragging a set of crosshairs about the scene.

FIGURE 6-14
Distorted perspective

> **QUICKTIP** While you're changing the Focus Distance value, the Focal Distance Guide appears to help you position the focus point. Enable the Display, Guides, Focal Distance Guide menu to toggle this guide on.

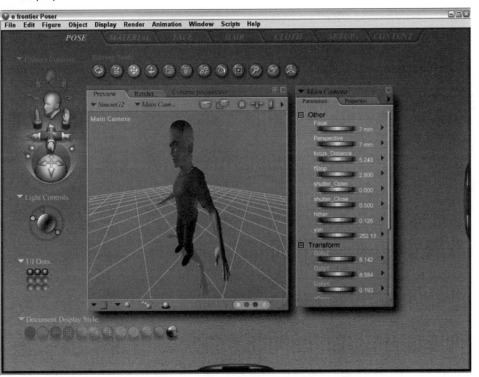

Another parameter that impacts the depth of field effect is the F-stop. This parameter sets the size of the camera's aperture. Cameras with a larger aperture let more light in when the image is captured. Setting the F-stop value to a low value causes the blurring for objects positioned away from the focal point more pronounced. Higher F-stop values reduce the blurring effect. In Figure 6-15, the image on the left uses an F-stop value of 0.4, and the image on the right uses an F-stop value of 6.4. Notice how changing the F-stop value affects the depth of field effect.

NOTE To see the depth of field effect, you must enable the Depth of Field option in the Render Settings dialog box. More on the Render Settings dialog box is covered in Chapter 16, "Rendering Scenes."

Creating a Time-Lapse Motion Blur

The Shutter Open and Shutter Close parameters can be adjusted to create a time-lapse **motion blur**. Motion blur causes objects in motion to be blurred as they move across the current frame. By leaving the camera shutter open longer, a value measured in frames, the scene motion becomes blurred as it moves. This is a good effect to use to show objects moving very fast, such as an airplane propeller or a speeding superhero. Figure 6-16 shows a ball object being moved rapidly in front of a figure. The image to the left has the shutter open for half a frame, but the image on the right has it open for two frames. The slower shutter results in a more extreme blur effect. The effect of these parameters is visible only when the Motion Blur render option in the Render Settings dialog box is enabled.

FIGURE 6-15
The F-stop value affects the intensity of the blur for the depth of field effect

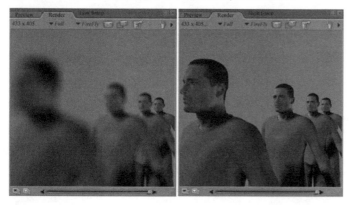

FIGURE 6-16
The number of frames the Shutter stays open affects the motion blur

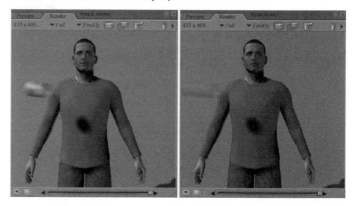

Setting Clipping Planes

A clipping plane is an imaginary plane that is parallel to the camera view and causes all objects closer than the Hither plane and farther than the Yon plane to be hidden. These planes can be used to hide certain objects in the scene for quicker rendering or to cut through an object to see its interior. Figure 6-17 shows the Hither plane slicing through the front of the default figure. The clipping planes only affect the Preview display, not the rendered scene.

NOTE The Hither and Yon clipping planes can be used only when the OpenGL view option is selected.

Using Camera Transform Parameters

The Dolly parameters have the effect of panning the camera from side to side. The Scale values cause the camera to zoom in and out of the scene, and the Orbit values cause the camera to rotate about the scene's center point. The Dolly and Posingcameras use Roll, Pitch, and Yaw

parameters instead of Orbit because their rotations are about the camera's center instead of a point in front of the camera.

Resetting Cameras

If the camera's parameters throw the camera off and you lose control of your view, you can always reset the current camera by loading the default camera setting from the Library.

FIGURE 6-17
Slicing through a figure with the Hither plane

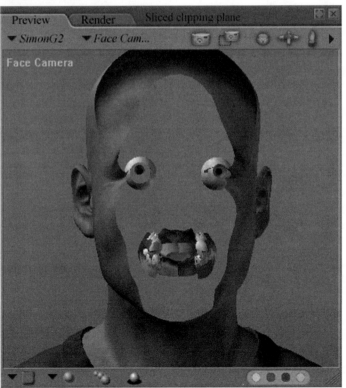

Use the Dolly Camera

1. Open Poser with the default figure visible.

2. From the Camera Controls pop-up menu, select Dolly Camera. Then, from the Actor List at the top of the Document Window, select the Cameras, Dolly Camera option.

3. Select Window, Parameter Dials to open the Parameters/Properties palette, if it isn't already open.

4. Drag the Pitch dial to –35, the Yaw dial to 45, the DollyZ to 2.0, the DollyY to 3.0, and the DollyX to 2.0.

   Notice how the Dolly camera rotates about its own center, as shown in Figure 6-18.

5. Select File, Save As and save the file as **Dolly camera view.pz3**.

Reset a Camera

1. Open Poser with the default figure visible.

2. From the Camera Controls, drag the parameter dials and the Camera Controls until nothing is visible in the Document Window.

3. Open the Library and navigate to the Camera Sets folder, and then select a nonorthogonal view and click the Apply Library Preset button.

   The camera returns to a view that you can use.

FIGURE 6-18
Dolly camera view

AIM AND
ATTACH CAMERAS

What You'll Do

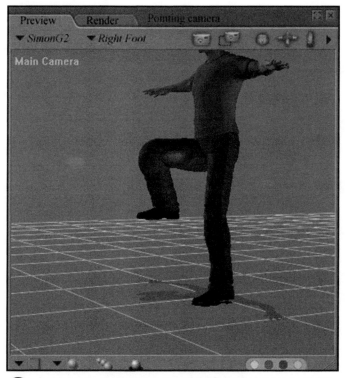

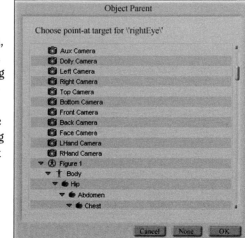

In this lesson, you learn how to use the Point At menu command to aim cameras and attach cameras to figure elements.

In addition to the many controls, parameters, and properties available for lights and cameras, there are also controls available for making cameras point at specific items and for attaching and parenting cameras to other scene items.

Pointing Cameras at Items

You can aim cameras to point at a specific scene item. This item can be any body part, prop, light, or even another camera. To point a camera at a specific item, first select the camera using the Actor List at the top of the Document Window or the Parameters/Properties palette. Then, choose Object, Point At. The Object Parent dialog box, shown in Figure 6-19, appears with a hierarchical list of the scene items. Within this dialog box, select the item that you want the camera to point at and click OK.

FIGURE 6-19
Object Parent dialog box

NOTE Even though the Object Parent dialog box is used to select the point at object, the Point At command doesn't actually parent the object as the Hierarchy Editor shows.

Once the Point At command is used, a Point At parameter appears in the Parameters palette. If you change this value to 0, the camera no longer follows the selected item. To remove the Point At feature, select the item and the Object, Point At menu command again and choose the None button in the Object Parent dialog box.

Pointing Items at the Camera

In addition to having a camera follow an item, you can also do the opposite and have an item point at the camera. For most body parts, this will cause the object to rotate at askew angles, but for the eyeballs it works quite well. Figure 6-20 shows the eyeballs of the default figure set to point at the main camera. The result is that the figure is looking directly at the camera.

Attaching Cameras to Items

You can attach cameras to scene items using Object, Change Parent. This menu command also opens the Object Parent dialog box, where you can choose an item to be the camera's parent. Once attached, the camera moves along with the attached item. Parenting a camera to a body part

and moving the figure causes the figure (or body part) to stand still while the scene and background move independently.

Using the Camera Dots

If you want to temporarily remember a specific camera setting for use during the current session, you can use the **Camera Dots** to place the current camera settings. To remember camera settings, select the Camera Dots option from the pop-up menu at the top of the Memory Dots control, as

FIGURE 6-20
Eyeballs can be set to point at the camera

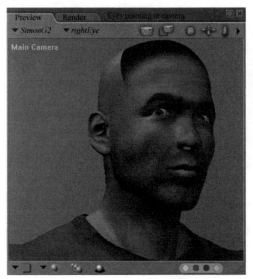

shown in Figure 6-21, or select the Edit, Memorize, Camera menu. Clicking a dot once adds the current camera to the selected dot where you can recall it at any time by clicking the dot that holds the camera settings. Holding down the Alt/Option key while clicking a Camera Dot clears the dot.

QUICKTIP Poser allows a unique set of Camera Dots for every room.

FIGURE 6-21
Camera Dots

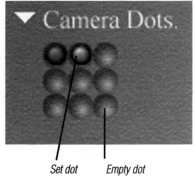

Set dot   Empty dot

1. Open Poser with the default man visible.

2. Select the Main Camera item from the Actor List at the top of the Document Window.

3. With the Main Camera item selected, choose Object, Point At.

   The Object Parent dialog box opens.

4. Select the Right Foot element in the Object Parent dialog box and click OK.

5. Select and move the camera about the Document Window.

   Notice how the camera stays focused on the foot element as it is moved about the scene, as shown in Figure 6-22.

6. Select File, Save As and save the file as **Pointing camera.pz3**.

FIGURE 6-22

Pointing main camera

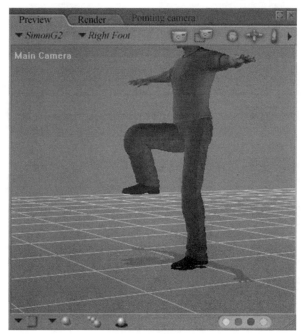

1. Open Poser with the default figure visible.
2. From the Actor List at the top of the Document Window, select the Cameras, Main Camera option.
3. With the Main Camera item selected, choose Object, Change Parent.

   The Object Parent dialog box opens.
4. Select the Left Hand element in the Change Parent dialog box and click OK.
5. Select and rotate the left arm in the Document Window.

   Notice how the camera changes as the left hand moves, as shown in Figure 6-23.
6. Select File, Save As and save the file as **Attached camera.pz3**.

FIGURE 6-23
Attached camera

CHANGE THE
BACKGROUND

What You'll Do

In this lesson, you learn how to change the Document Window background.

Adding a background image or movie can often help you as you pose a figure. Imagine loading the movie of a dancer as a background. You could them animate the dance steps by matching the figure to the background movie. You can also render background images to add a nice backdrop to your scene.

Changing the Background Color

Changing the background color is accomplished easily using the color dots found at the bottom of the Document Window. There are color dots for changing the Foreground, Background, Shadow, and Ground colors. Clicking any of these dots opens a pop-up color palette where you can select a new color.

Loading a Background Image

You load background images using the File, Import, Background Picture menu command. This makes the Open dialog box appear where you can select the image file to open as a background. The file formats that can be imported include .SGI, .BMP, .EXR, .GIF, .HDR, .JPEG, .MAC, .PCD, .PNG, .PSD, .TGA, and .TIF files.

QUICKTIP To render the scene with a transparent background so the image can be composited with other elements, use the .PNG file format.

If the Document Window is set at a resolution different than the loaded background image, a warning dialog box appears asking if you want to change the Document Window to match the image resolution. Figure 6-24 shows the Document Window with a background image loaded.

NOTE If a background image is loaded, but doesn't appear, select Display, Show Background Picture (Ctrl/Command+B) to make the background image visible.

Loading a Background Movie

In addition to static images, Poser can also load movie files as a background. Windows systems use a File, Import, AVI Footage menu command and Macintosh systems use a File, Import, QuickTime Footage menu command. Either command makes an Open dialog box appear where you can select the appropriate file to open. Figure 6-25 shows the Document Window with a background movie.

Clearing the Background

To remove the background picture or movie, use the Display, Clear Background Picture or the Display, Clear Background Footage menu commands.

FIGURE 6-24
Loaded background image

FIGURE 6-25
Loaded background movie

Using a Background Shader

If you open the Material Room, you can select the Background option from the Material List at the top of the Shader Win-dow. This opens the nodes used for the background in the Shader Window, as shown in Figure 6-26. Using these nodes, you can define a shader that is rendered along with the background image or movie. To enable the designated background shader, choose the Display, Use Background Shader Node menu command.

FIGURE 6-26

Background shader

Load a Background Picture

1. Select File, Import, Background Picture.

   The Open dialog box appears.

2. Select the Oregon coast.jpg image file and click Open.

   A warning dialog box appears stating that the Document Window is different than the image resolution. Click the No button to keep the Document Window the same size. The image appears in the background of the Document Window.

3. Open the Library and apply a walking pose to the character. Then use the Camera Controls to position the figure in the scene so he appears to be walking down the path.

4. Select the Display, Guides, Ground Plane menu to hide the ground plane. Then disable the view shadows using the Shadows toggle at the bottom of the Document Window.

   The figure meshes with the background image, as shown in Figure 6-27.

5. Select File, Save As and save the file as **Background image.pz3**.

FIGURE 6-27
Background image

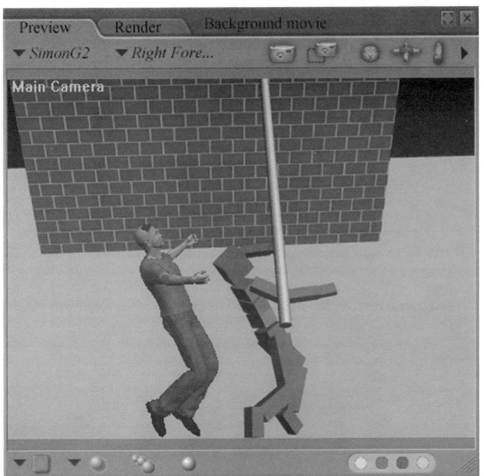

FIGURE 6-28

Background movie

1. Open Poser with the default figure visible.

2. Select File, Import, AVI Footage.

   The Open dialog box appears.

3. Select the Swinging into a wall.avi movie file and click Open.

   A warning dialog box appears stating that the width/height ratio is different than the Document Window. Click No to continue. The first frame of the movie appears in the background of the Document Window.

4. Open the Animation Controls and drag the Timeline to frame 10.

   Frame 10 of the background video is displayed.

5. Move and rotate the figure to correspond to the background video's character.

6. Select the Display, Guides, Ground Plane menu to hide the ground plane. Then disable the view shadows using the Shadows toggle at the bottom of the Document Window.

   Aligning the figure to the background video frame by frame lets you create realistic motions, as shown in Figure 6-28.

7. Select File, Save As and save the file as **Background movie.pz3**.

CHAPTER REVIEW

Chapter Summary

This chapter covered two important items used to create a scene other than a posed figure and props—cameras and backgrounds. This chapter presented each of the available preset lights and explained how to control them with the Camera Controls. It also included an in-depth look at the various camera parameters and showed how you could aim cameras with the Point At command. The various background options were also covered, including background colors, images, and movies.

What You Have Learned

In this chapter, you

- Learned about the different light types and how to access them.
- Used the various Camera Controls.
- Changed the camera shortcut items to use different cameras.
- Used Flyaround mode to quickly see the scene from all angles.
- Positioned and rotated cameras to change the scene view.
- Discovered the various camera parameters and properties.
- Attached and aimed cameras to and at objects.

- Created a new background with colors, images, materials, and movies.

Key Terms from This Chapter

- **Background image.** An image that is set to appear behind the scene.
- **Camera Dots.** An interface control used to remember and recall camera position and properties.
- **Clipping plane.** A plane positioned parallel to the camera that defines the border beyond which scene objects aren't visible.
- **Depth of field.** An optical effect that focuses the view at the focal point and gradually blurs all objects farther than the focal point.
- **Dolly.** A camera motion that moves the view closer or farther from the scene.
- **Focal length.** The distance from the camera's center where the image is in focus.
- **Flyaround mode.** A toggle mode that causes the camera to spin about the central axis of the current scene, animating its view from all angles.

- **F-stop.** A camera setting that determines the size of the aperture and that affects the intensity of the blurring for a depth of field effect.
- **Motion blur.** An optical effect that causes objects in motion to appear blurred as they move through the scene.
- **Orthographic camera.** A camera that is positioned at the end of an axis and displays the scene as a 2D plane where all dimensions are accurate. Top, Bottom, Front, Back, Left, and Right are examples of orthographic cameras.
- **Perspective.** An optical property that displays depth by having all object edges gradually converge to a point in the distance.
- **Posing camera.** A camera that stays focused on the scene's selected figure.
- **Shadow camera.** A camera that is positioned in the same location as a light.
- **Trackball.** A ball-like control within the Camera Controls that rotates the scene.
- **Vanishing lines.** Guide lines that lead from the edges of an object to the perspective converging point.

chapter 7
ADDING
SCENE LIGHTING

1. Learn basic lighting techniques.

2. Work with lights.

3. Enable shadows and ambient occlusion.

4. Set light materials.

5. Use image-based lighting.

chapter 7 ADDING
SCENE LIGHTING

After you spend time posing your figure and positioning props and cameras, you might feel you are ready to see your scene in all its glory. However, you might be disappointed if you don't have any lights in your scene. Luckily, Poser is smart enough to include and enable several lights by default. Understanding the basics of lighting design will help as you position lights within the scene.

All lights within the scene can be controlled using the Light Controls. The Light Controls let you change the position, color, number, and intensity of the scene lights. You can also change the light's parameters and properties using the parameter dials in the Parameters/Properties palette. If you don't know where to start in configuring your lights and cameras, you can look in the Library palette for several examples of lighting presets that can help you as you start out.

Poser includes several light types, including Spot, Infinite, Point, and Image-Based Lights. Lights can also be set to cast shadows. Shadows can be either ray-traced shadows with sharp edges or depth-map shadows that are more diffuse. The Properties palette also includes an option to enable ambient occlusion, which can be used in place of shadows to add depth to the scene objects. Using the Material Room, you can enable some special effects for lights, such as projecting lights. Poser also includes some specialized features that let you point lights at specific items in the scene. For example, you can point spotlights at a figure's head or hands to always keep the figure in the light during an animation.

Image-based lights provide a way to create a realistic lighting environment by wrapping a specialized image around the scene. The image that is wrapped is called a **light probe,** and it includes a broad range of light sources from a sampled environment.

Tools You'll Use

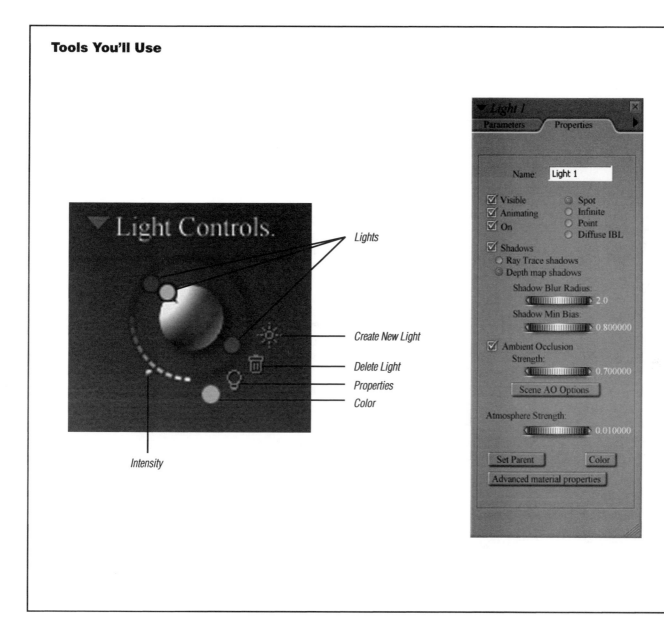

Light Controls.

Lights

Create New Light

Delete Light

Properties

Color

Intensity

Light 1

Parameters | Properties

Name: Light 1

☑ Visible   ○ Spot
☑ Animating   ○ Infinite
☑ On   ○ Point
               ○ Diffuse IBL

☑ Shadows
  ○ Ray Trace shadows
  ○ Depth map shadows

Shadow Blur Radius:
◀▥▥▥▥▥▥▥▶ 2.0

Shadow Min Bias:
◀▥▥▥▥▥▥▥▥▶ 0.800000

☑ Ambient Occlusion
Strength:
◀▥▥▥▥▥▥▥▥▥▶ 0.700000

Scene AO Options

Atmosphere Strength:
◀▥▥▥▥▥▥▥▥▶ 0.010000

Set Parent   Color

Advanced material properties

LEARN
BASIC LIGHTING TECHNIQUES

What You'll Do

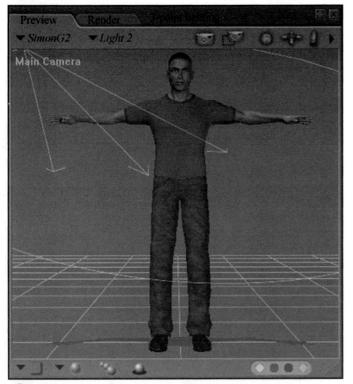

In this lesson, you practice some basic lighting techniques.

Poser's default lighting setup is good for emphasizing poses, but understanding some of the basics of lighting design can help establish the mood of your scene.

Using 3-Point Lighting

The most popular method for lighting a scene is called *3-point lighting design*. This design uses three lights—a key light, a back light, and one or more fill lights. The key light is the main light source for the scene. It is typically positioned at 45 degrees from the horizon and off to the side to shine down at an angle. The key light should also be the only light that is set to cast a shadow. It should also be the most intense light in the scene.

The back light is positioned behind the scene objects where it doesn't shine into the camera. It is used to highlight the silhouetting edge of the scene characters. The intensity of the back light should be about half the intensity of the key light.

The fill lights are positioned at ground level in front of the scene and used to highlight and add depth to the scene forms. There can be several fill lights depending on how the scene objects are positioned, but their total intensity shouldn't exceed half of the intensity of the key light. Figure 7-1 shows the default figure, first with only the key light, and then with the key and back lights, and finally with key, back, and fill lights.

Creating a Rim Light

Rim lights are used to create a silhouetting effect. They are created by positioning a light aimed at the current camera and positioning the main character of the scene between the light and the camera. The result is to highlight the outer rim of the character.

Using Underlighting

If you position the key light underneath the main figure and point it upward, you'll get an unnatural effect that casts shadows upward, much like holding a flashlight under a person's chin. This lighting technique is often used in horror films to create a sinister, evil looking character, as shown in Figure 7-2.

FIGURE 7-1

Figure lit with key, back, and fill lights (from left to right)

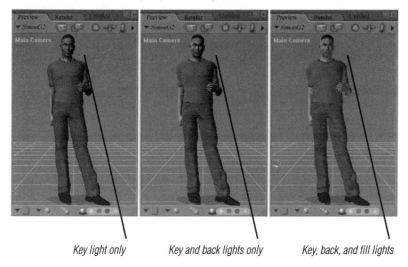

Key light only   *Key and back lights only*   *Key, back, and fill lights*

FIGURE 7-2

Figure lit with underlighting

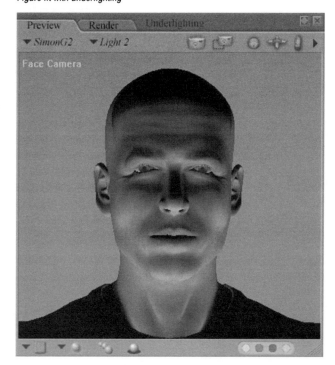

Using Light Color

Light color can dramatically change the mood of a scene. Warm colors such as yellow, orange, and red can create a feeling of warmth and excitement, but cool colors like green, blue, and purple denote a calmness and subdued mood.

Light color can also be used to establish where the scene takes place. Bright yellow lights are useful for daytime outdoor scenes, softer blue lights are good for creating moonlight, red and orange lights can create the glow of firelight, and white lights with a touch of blue are useful for simulating indoor fluorescent lights.

FIGURE 7-3

3-point lighting

Establish 3-Point Lighting

1. Open Poser with the default man visible.

2. Select the default light in front of the character and increase its intensity slightly.

3. Select the back light and drag it so it points downward on the figure from above. In the Properties palette, disable Shadows for this light.

4. Select the fill light to the side of the Light Controls and decrease its Intensity. Then disable its Shadows in the Properties palette.

The 3-point lighting design gives a good sense of depth and volume to the figure, as shown in Figure 7-3.

5. Select File, Save As and save the file as 3-point lighting.pz3.

WORK
WITH LIGHTS

What You'll Do

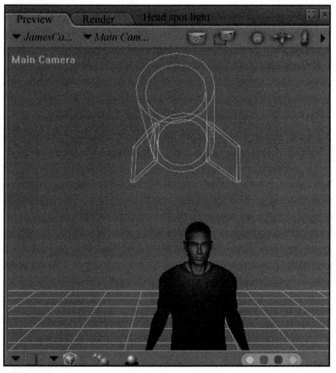

In this lesson, you learn how to work effectively with lights.

If a scene contained no lights, all scene items wouldn't be visible, but Poser has three lights that are enabled by default. You can easily add more light sources to the scene. Poser works with four light sources—**infinite lights, spotlights, point lights,** and **diffuse image-based lights** (IBLs).

Learning the Light Types

Infinite lights shine from a distance, so all its rays are parallel when they strike the scene objects. This causes all scene elements to receive an equal amount of light. Spotlights are focused, casting light only to those scene objects that are within the cone of influence; objects farther away receive less light than closer objects. Point lights cast light in all directions from a single point, such as a light bulb or a candle in a room. Diffuse image-based lights (IBL) lights define the scene lighting by building an image of the scene that holds all the lighting information.

NOTE When using point lights and diffuse IBL lights, realistic shadows can be computed only using ray tracing.

Creating New Lights

All scene lights are displayed within the Light Controls. New lights can be created by clicking the Create Light button. By default, the Create Light button creates a spotlight, but you can change the type of light using the options in the Properties palette. Poser lets you switch easily between the various light types. You can select the type of light to create if you right-click on the Create Light button and select the light type from the pop-up menu or use the Object, Create Light menu.

Using the Light Controls

The Light Controls offer a convenient way of creating and positioning lights, as well as setting light properties. To open the Light Controls, select Window, Light Controls. The Light Controls, shown in Figure 7-4, include a large sample sphere in the center that shows the lighting effects; surrounding it are three smaller circles. These smaller circles are the lights. You can change their locations by dragging them about the larger sphere. When you select a circle representing a light, controls for changing its intensity, color, and properties appear. There are also buttons for removing the selected light and creating new lights.

If you click on the title of the Light Controls, you can access a pop-up menu of options. Using these pop-up menu options, you can select a specific light, as well as create and delete lights and access the Properties palette for the selected light. There are also two positioning modes.

The default mode is Revolving. Dragging the smaller spheres in the Light Controls around the larger sphere with this mode enabled orbits the selected light about the larger sphere, thus changing its position. Dragging the smaller spheres with the Rotate mode enabled keeps the light in its current position, but rotates it about, which changes where it is aiming.

FIGURE 7-4
Light Controls

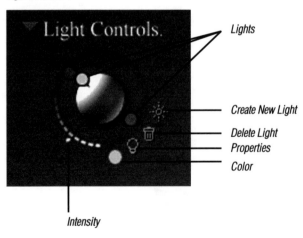

Changing Light Color

When a light is selected, you can click on the colored dot beneath the Light Controls or click on the Color button in the Properties palette to open a color selector dialog box where you can choose a different light color.

QUICKTIP When the Color Selector dialog box is open, you can select any color currently visible on the computer, whether it is within the current interface or from another application.

Selecting and Positioning Lights

You can select lights by clicking their circular icons in the Light Controls, by selecting a light from the Actor List located at the top of the Document Window, or by choosing a light from the Hierarchy Editor. When a light is selected, an indicator of the light, shown in Figure 7-5, becomes visible within the Document Window. You can position lights by dragging their circular icons with the Light Controls or by dragging their indicator in the Document Window using the Editing Tools. Each indicator in the Document Window is different depending on the light type that is selected. You also can position lights using the parameter dials found in the Parameters palette.

NOTE When the spotlight type is selected, the parameter dials include values for setting the spotlight's cone distance and angle.

FIGURE 7-5
Light indicators appear in the Document Window

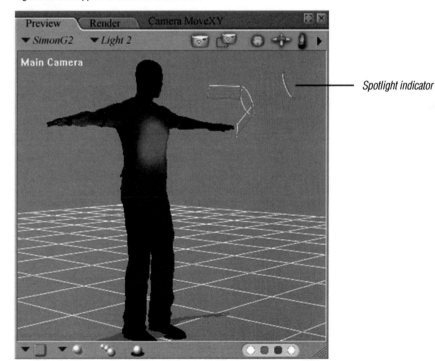

Spotlight indicator

Setting Light Properties

You can set several light properties in the Light Controls, but an extended set of properties is available in the Properties panel, as shown in Figure 7-6. The Name field lists the light's name, which is simply Light and a number by default, but you can type a new name. The Visible property makes the visual indicator of the light appear in the Document Window, the Animating property enables the light to be animated, and the On property turns the light on and off. The Properties palette also includes a set of radio buttons for selecting the light type and controls for shadows and **ambient occlusion**.

Setting Light Parameters

In addition to the settings in the Properties palette, there are several more values in the Parameters palette for controlling lights. For Spot and Point lights, you can set the Distance Start and Distance End values, which denote the distance from the light's center where the light starts to decay and the distance where the light has diminished to zero. For spotlights, you can also set Angle Start and Angle End values, which are the strength of the light at the cone's point and the strength of the light at the end of the cone.

The Parameters palette also includes settings for controlling the intensity of the enabled shadows with the Shadow parameter. A value of 0 turns off shadows, and

higher values gradually darken the shadow until a value of 100, which is maximum. The Map Size is used to specify the size of the bitmap in pixels of the shadow map. Larger shadow maps have a finer resolution but require more memory.

The Red, Green, Blue, and Intensity values set the light's color and power. These parameters work the same as the settings found in the Light Controls.

FIGURE 7-6
Light properties

Pointing Lights at Objects

Lights can also be set to point specifically at an object in the scene using the Object, Point At command. This causes the Point At dialog box, shown in Figure 7-7, to appear where you can select the point at object. Once a point at object is selected, the light continues to point at the selected object even as the light is moved throughout the scene. To remove the Point At link between an object and a light, select the Object, Point At command again and choose the None button.

Parenting Lights

Another way to control lights is to parent the lights to a scene object. This is accomplished by clicking on the Set Parent button in the Properties palette or by selecting the Object, Change Parent menu command. Once a light is parented to a scene object, it moves with the object as the object's position changes in the scene. The parented relationship is also shown in the Hierarchy Editor. To unparent a light, simply select the Universe object as its new parent.

| NOTE Only Spot and Point lights can be parented.

FIGURE 7-7
Point At dialog box

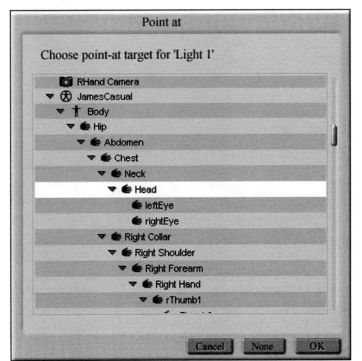

Create and Position a Spotlight

1. Open Poser with the default man visible.

2. Select each of the light circles in the Light Controls and click the Delete Light button to remove the default lights. Click OK in the Delete confirmation dialog box that appears.

3. Click the Create Light button in the Light Controls.

   A new light circle is added to the Light Controls, and a spotlight indicator appears in the Document Window.

4. Drag the light circle in the Light Controls to roughly position the new spotlight above the scene figure.

5. Drag the Move XZ control in the Camera Controls to zoom out the scene until the spotlight indicator is visible in the Document Window.

6. Select Window, Parameter Dials to open the Parameters palette, if it isn't already open, and set the Angle End value to 30.

7. Select the main spotlight object from the Actor List at the top of the Document Window.

8. Select the Object, Point At menu command.

9. In the Point At dialog box that appears, select the Head object and click the OK button.

10. Select and move the spotlight about the scene.

    The spotlight points at the head object regardless of where it is moved within the scene, as shown in Figure 7-8.

11. Select File, Save As and save the file as **Head spot light.pz3**.

FIGURE 7-8
Spotlight focused on the figure's head

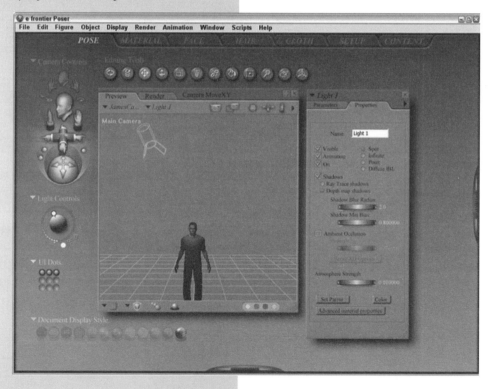

ENABLE SHADOWS
AND AMBIENT OCCLUSION

What You'll Do

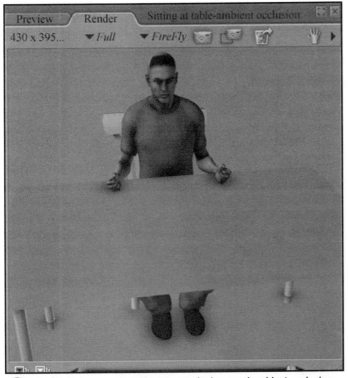

In this lesson, you learn how to set shadows and ambient occlusion

Within the Properties palette for lights are two options for enabling shadows and ambient occlusion. Shadows can add a lot to the realism of the scene, and learning the various shadowing options will give you better control over how shadows appear in the scene. Ambient occlusion is a render property that can simulate the dark corners of objects that are surrounded by walls and other objects.

Enabling Shadows

Shadows are computed when the scene is rendered, and two methods exist for creating shadows—ray trace and depth map. Ray-trace shadows have a sharp edge and are much more realistic because they are created by following each light ray as it bounces about the scene, but the drawback is that they can take a considerable amount of time to render. Depth-map shadows are blurrier, but they can be rendered very quickly.

Blurring Shadows

You can set the amount of blur that a shadow has using the Shadow Blur Radius setting. The Shadow Min Bias setting prevents the scene objects from casting shadows on themselves. Figure 7-9 shows two rendered images side by side in the Render panel with Shadow Map shadows with different Blur Radius settings. Notice how the left half of the figure has a blurry shadow and the right half is clean.

QUICKTIP If multiple lights are included in a scene, only enable shadows for one light in the scene.

Reusing Shadow Maps

If you select the Depth Map Shadows option, the Shadow Map is computed the first time you render the scene, but the shadow map can be saved and reused on subsequent renders to save time. To have Poser reuse the computed shadow map, enable the Render, Reuse Shadow Maps menu option.

To force Poser to render the shadow maps again, select the Render, Clear Shadow Maps. Shadow maps should be re-rendered whenever the scene objects move or if the lights move or change parameters.

NOTE When a light object is selected, the Parameters palette includes a Map Size value, which sets the size in pixels of the computed shadow map. Larger shadow maps take up more memory but have a finer resolution.

FIGURE 7-9
Shadows can be blurred

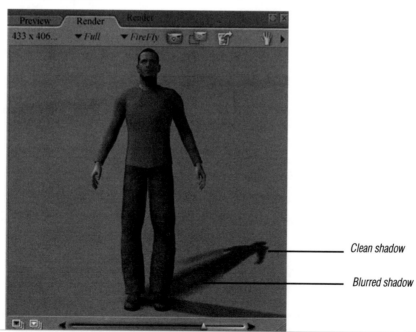

Clean shadow

Blurred shadow

Enabling Ambient Occlusion

Ambient light, as specified for the various surfaces in the Material Room, is a general lighting that lights all scene objects without radiating from a particular source. It occurs naturally by light that bounces off the surfaces of objects. Ambient light, in particular, affects shadows. *Ambient Occlusion* is an effect that diminishes ambient light from the scene, thus causing shadows to appear darker and providing more contrast for the rendered image. When an object is surrounded by walls or other objects, the amount of light that can bounce about the object is reduced, causing more shadows to appear in areas close to the obscured area.

Figure 7-10 shows a figure rendered with and without ambient occlusion.

> **CAUTION** Ambient occlusion will be rendered only if the Ray Tracing option is enabled in the Render Settings dialog box.

FIGURE 7-10
Ambient occlusion

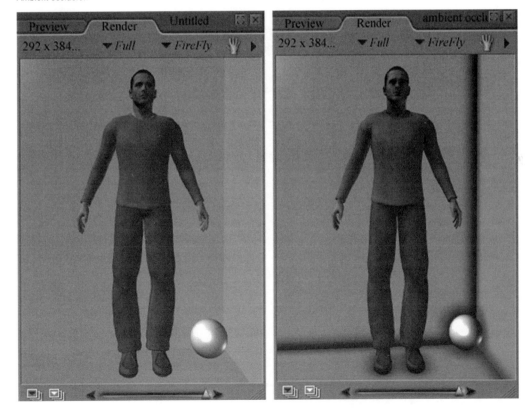

The Strength value sets how dark the ambient shadows are in the scene. In addition to the Strength value, you can open the Scene Ambient Occlusion Options dialog box, shown in Figure 7-11, using the Scene Ambient Occlusion Options button in the Properties palette. This dialog box includes three additional values—Max Distance, which defines the distance that ray-traced rays are allowed to travel; Bias, which defines where the light rays originate from; and Number of Samples, which determines how many light rays are cast into the scene. Increasing the Number of Samples will make the shadows sharper and less blurry.

CAUTION Using high Max Distance or Number of Samples values can result in a very long rendering time.

FIGURE 7-11
Scene Ambient Occlusion Options dialog box

Scene Ambient Occlusion Options

Max Distance: 0.152388

Bias: 0.002359

Num Samples: 3

Cancel   OK

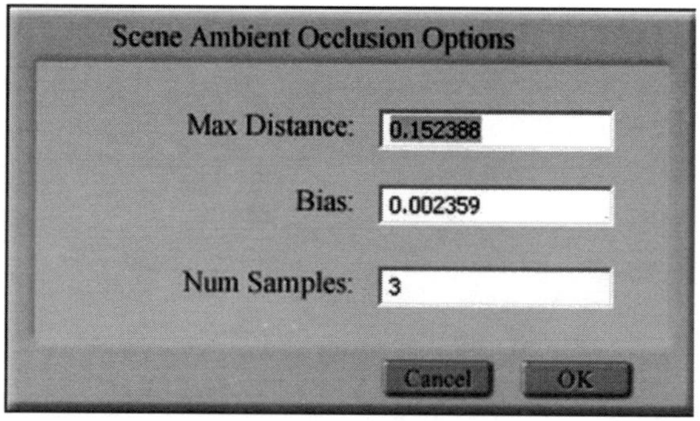

FIGURE 7-12

Rendered figure with shadow

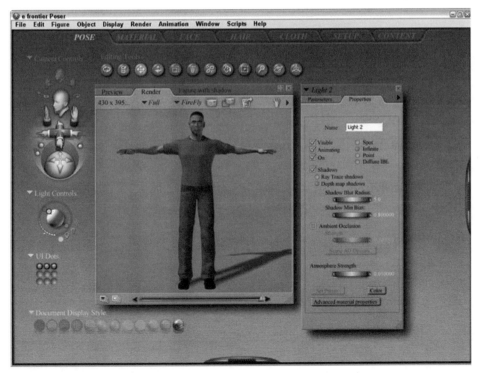

1. Open Poser with the default man visible.

2. Select Lights, Light 1 from the Actor List at the top of the Document Window.

3. Select Window, Parameter Dials to open the Parameters/Properties palette, if it isn't already open. Click the Properties tab and disable the Shadows option to turn off shadows for this light. Repeat this step for Light 3.

4. Select Light 2 and enable the Shadows option in the Properties palette. Then select the Depth Map Shadows option and set the Shadow Blur Radius to 5.0.

5. Click the Render button in the Document Window.

   The scene is rendered, and the rendered image is displayed in the Document Window with shadows, as shown in Figure 7-12.

6. Select File, Save As and save the file as **Figure with shadow.pz3**.

Enable Ambient Occlusion

1. Open the Sitting at table.pz3 file from the Chap 07 folder.

2. Select each of the lights in turn in the Actor List and disable the Shadow option in the Properties palette.

3. Select Light 2 and enable the Ambient Occlusion option. Set the Strength value to 2.5.

4. Select the Render, Render Settings menu command to open the Render Settings dialog box. Select the Manual Settings option and enable the Raytracing option. Then click the Save Settings button at the bottom of the dialog box.

5. Click the Render button 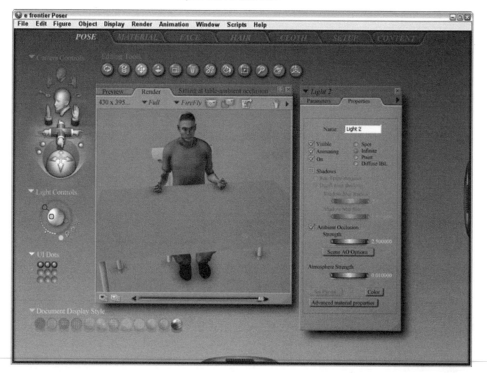 in the Document Window.

   The scene is rendered, and the rendered image is displayed in the Document Window, as shown in Figure 7-13.

6. Select File, Save As and save the file as Sitting at table-ambient occlusion.pz3.

FIGURE 7-13
Ambient occlusion shows shadows around objects close to each other

L E S S O N   4

SET
LIGHT MATERIALS

What You'll Do

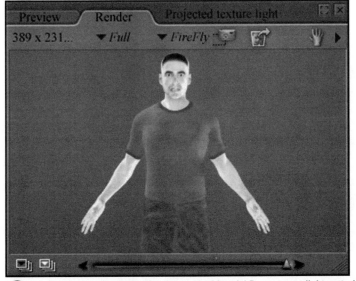

▶ In this lesson, you learn how to use the Material Room to set light materials.

If you look closely at the Properties palette when a light is selected, you'll notice that there is a button labeled Advanced Material Properties. Clicking this button opens the Advanced panel in the Material Room with the selected light's nodes visible. Although you can set a light's color and intensity in the Light Controls, the Material Room offers many more options for controlling the look of a light.

Accessing Light Material Properties

If you select a light from the Actor List in the Material Room, you can view a node listing all the light's material values in the Advanced panel of the Shader Window, as shown in Figure 7-14.

Projecting a Textured Light

If you change a light's color, the entire scene is affected by the light color, and the light color is mixed with any diffuse surface colors, but using the light material values, you can also have the light project a texture. This effect is like shining a light through a transparent image. To create such an effect, simply add a texture to the light material. You can do this in either the Simple or Advanced panels of the Material Room. Figure 7-15 shows a texture image added to a light in the Simple panel of the Material Room.

FIGURE 7-14

Light material values

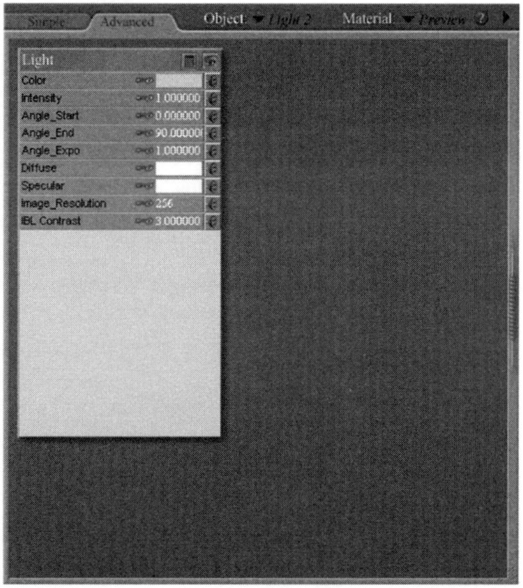

FIGURE 7-15

Light projected image

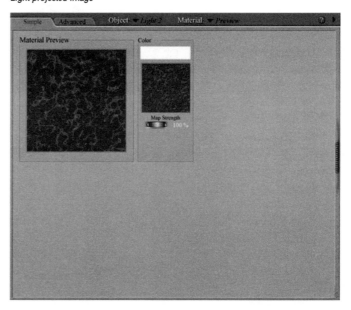

FIGURE 7-16

Projected texture light

Project a Textured Light

1. Open Poser with the default man visible.

2. Select Lights, Light 2 from the Actor List at the top of the Document Window.

3. Select Window, Parameter Dials to open the Parameters/Properties palette, if it isn't already open. Click the Diffuse IBL option to make the selected light an image-based light.

4. With the Light 2 object still selected, click the Material tab to open the Material Room.

5. Select the Simple tab in the Shader Window and click the image area under the color swatch. In the Texture Manager that opens, click the Browse button and load the Banana Husk.tif image. Then click OK.

6. From the Document Window's pop-up menu, select the Render option.

   The scene is rendered and the rendered image is displayed in the Document Window, as shown in Figure 7-16. Notice how the figure is colored using the texture image for a light source.

7. Select File, Save As and save the file as **Projected texture light.pz3**.

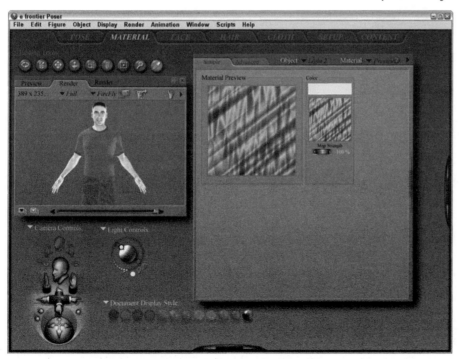

LESSON 5

USE
IMAGE-BASED LIGHTING

What You'll Do

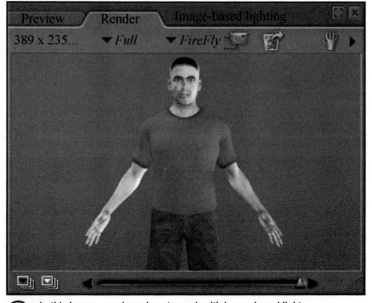

In this lesson, you learn how to work with image-based lights.

If you're using only three lights to light the scene, your results probably aren't as realistic as they could be. If you stop and take a look at the light sources that are lighting the current room, chances are that they come from multiple sources, including the sky above, an open window, light from a room down the hall, and so on. Poser provides a way to include all these sources as a way to light the scene.

Image-based lighting (IBL) uses a specific type of image, called a *light probe*, to simulate an environment's diverse set of light sources. These images are then wrapped about the scene, and its values are used to light the scene it surrounds. Several sample IBL files are included in the Library in the Lights category, as shown in Figure 7-17.

Enabling Image-Based Lights

One of the available light types is the Diffuse IBL light. This light type lets you add a loaded image or texture as the light source. The controlling shader tree can even be animated to show effects like a flashing light or a disco-ball light. The Wacros

panel includes a preset for loading textures for an IBL light.

QUICKTIP Because image-based lighting has multiple light sources, it is best to enable ambient occlusion instead of shadows.

FIGURE 7-17

The Library includes several image-based lights

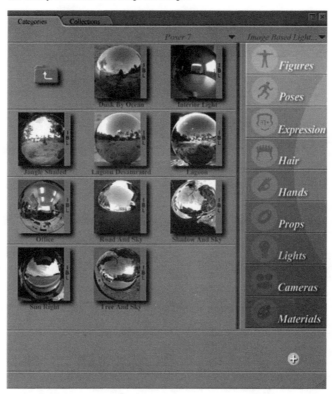

Using Light Probes

The most effective images to use for image-based lights are light probes. Light probes are created using a reflective sphere that can capture a full range of the surrounding environment. Figure 7-18 shows a sample light probe taken from the Poser Library. The warped shape of the light probe image straightens out nicely when wrapped around the current scene.

Loading HDR Image Maps

Poser can also load High Dynamic Range (HDR) images and use them as light probes. HDR images use a larger range of values to designate light values. The result is an image that is much richer in light information and perfect for image-based lighting.

NEW POSER 7 FEATURE
The ability to load HDR images as image-based lights is new to Poser 7.

FIGURE 7-18
A sample light probe

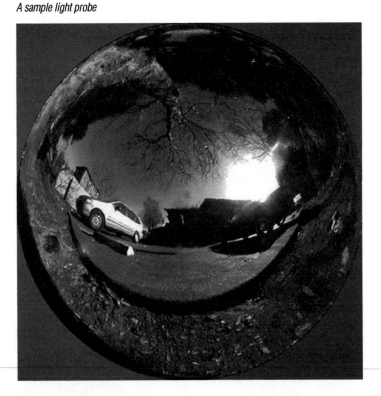

FIGURE 7-19

Image-based lighting

Enable Image-Based Lighting

1. Open Poser with the default man visible.

2. Select Lights, Light 2 from the Actor List at the top of the Document Window.

3. Select Window, Parameter Dials to open the Parameters/Properties palette, if it isn't already open. Click the Diffuse IBL option to make the selected light an image-based light.

4. Click on the Advanced Material Properties button at the bottom of the Properties palette to open the Material Room.

5. Open the Wacros panel and click the IBL button.

6. In the Texture Manager dialog box that opens, click the Browse button and locate the Light Probes folder located at Runtime/Libraries/Light/Image Based Lighting, where Poser is installed. Then select a light probe image and click the Open button.

7. The next dialog box asks if you want to activate ambient occlusion. Click the Yes button.

8. Click the Render button at the top of the Document Window.

   The light probe image is added as an image map to the shader, and the resulting render using the image-based lighting is displayed in the Document Window, as shown in Figure 7-19.

9. Select File, Save As and save the file as **Image-based lighting.pz3**.

CHAPTER REVIEW

Chapter Summary

This chapter covered how lights can be used not only to highlight the scene objects, but also to create a mood for the scene. Along the way, it covered the Light Controls and all the various light properties, including light color, intensity, shadows, and ambient occlusion. You also learned about several ways to position and point lights at objects in the scene. The chapter concluded by showing how textures can be projected into the scene using lights and how image-based lighting can be used to increase the realism of rendered images.

What You Have Learned

In this chapter, you

- Established a basic 3-point lighting design.
- Learned about the different light types.
- Used the Light Controls to create new lights, position lights, and change a light's color and intensity.
- Pointed lights at specific scene objects and parented lights.
- Learned about the different light types.
- Enabled shadows to the selected light.
- Enabled and configured ambient occlusion for a light.
- Changed light materials, including projecting textures onto the scene.
- Used image-based lighting to create a realistic lighting environment.

Key Terms from This Chapter

- **3-point lighting.** A basic lighting design that consists of a key light, back light, and fill light.
- **Ambient occlusion.** An effect that diminishes ambient light from the scene, thus causing shadows to appear darker and providing more contrast for the rendered image.
- **Back light.** A light positioned behind the scene to cast light on the edges of the scene objects.
- **Depth-map shadows.** Shadows that are calculated and the shadow information is saved in a depth map, resulting in shadows with blurred edges.
- **Fill light.** A secondary light used to fill in the gaps of the scene.
- **High Dynamic Range (HDR) images.** An image format that captures more detail about the lighting of the environment.
- **Image-based lights (IBL).** A light that illuminates the scene by deriving all light information from an image map.
- **Infinite light.** A light that simulates shining from an infinite distance so all light rays are parallel.
- **Key light.** The main light in a scene used to cast shadows.
- **Light probe.** An environment image taken of a reflective sphere that holds lighting information about the entire environment.
- **Point light.** A light that projects light rays in all directions equally.
- **Ray-trace shadows.** Shadows that are calculated using an accurate raytracing method that results in sharp edges.
- **Shadow map.** A bitmap that includes all the computed shadows for the scene. Shadow maps can be reused to speed up rendering.
- **Spotlight.** A light that projects light within a cone of influence.
- **Textured light.** A light that projects a texture map onto the scene.

chapter

8
CREATING
AND APPLYING MATERIALS

1. Learn the Material Room interface.

2. Create simple materials.

3. Create advanced materials.

4. Learn the various material nodes.

5. Use wacros.

6. Create smoothing and material groups.

7. Add atmosphere effects.

8 CREATING
AND APPLYING MATERIALS

Do you remember when television went from black and white to color? How about when computers went from black and white to color? What about PDAs? Adding colors and materials to objects adds an entirely new dimension to the scene, and the same is true with Poser figures.

After loading and posing a figure, you can add many details to the scene using materials. *Materials* are coverings used for the various elements in the scene. They can be as simple as a color, or as complex as a full texture with bumps and highlights.

You can load Poser materials, like many other facets of Poser, from the Library palette or create them by hand using the controls found in the Material Room. Within the Material Room is the **Shader Window**, which includes two different interface panels. The Simple panel includes only basic material properties such as **Diffuse Color, Highlights**, Ambient, Reflection, Bump, and **Transparency**. The Advanced panel includes an interface for compositing nodes to create multi-layered materials.

Advanced materials are created using sets of values called *nodes*, which are combined in such a way that one node controls the value of a connected node. Every node includes a Value Input and a Value Output icon that can be connected, forming a chain of values. You can create several categories of nodes, including a set for performing mathematical functions, a category to control different lighting models, and several 2D and 3D textures that can be manipulated using values.

You can enable several specific material properties, such as subsurface scattering and refraction using the scripts found in the Wacros palette.

You also can smooth or facet adjacent polygons by setting the global or local Crease Angle value. Smoothing groups can also be established using the Group Editor to define which polygons are smoothed together. To apply materials to certain sections of a figure, you can create custom **material groups** using the Grouping tool and the Group Editor.

You can use the Material Room to access several scene materials, such as lights, backgrounds, and atmospheric effects. Effects such as depth cueing and volume fog can add to the ambience of a scene.

Tools You'll Use

Texture map

Root node

Connected node

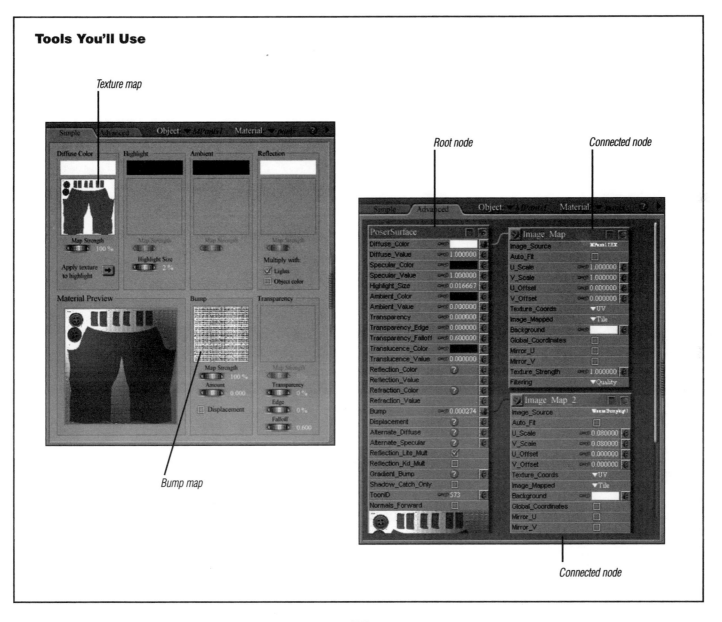

Bump map

Connected node

LEARN
THE MATERIAL ROOM INTERFACE

What You'll Do

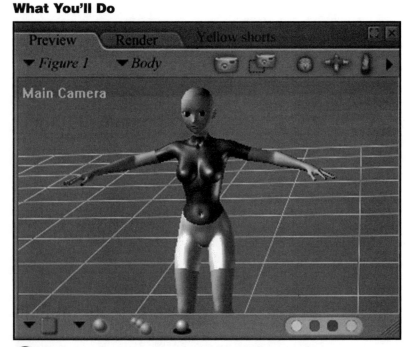

In this lesson, you learn how to use the Material Room interface.

You open the Material Room by clicking the Material tab at the top of the Poser interface or by selecting the Render, Materials menu command. This opens an interface setup that is different from the Pose Room, as shown in Figure 8-1, although it includes all of the same controls as the Pose Room, including the Document Window, the Camera and Light Controls, the Document Display Style and Editing Tools button sets. The main interface found in the Material Room is the Shader Window.

When the Material Room is opened, you can load materials from the Library. Chapter 2, "Using the Poser Library," covers using the Library palette.

> **NOTE** Some third-party vendors combine several material definitions into a single .MAT file. These .MAT files have been replaced by the newer .MC6 and .MCZ formats in Poser 6, but if you change the extension of a .MAT file to .MC6, it can be opened in Poser 7.

Using the Shader Window

The Shader Window, shown in Figure 8-2, is a large interface for creating and editing materials. The material displayed in the Shader Window is applied to the material group listed in the Material List at the top of the Shader Window. The Material List includes all the material groups for the object selected in the Object List. The Object List lets you select from the scene props, lights, the current figure, or the background or atmosphere. The top of the Shader Window also includes a help icon that opens the Room Help and a pop-up menu.

Selecting Material Groups with the Material Select Tool

In addition to the Material List located at the top of the Shader Window, you can also select material groups using the Material Select tool (which looks like an eyedropper) found among the Editing Tools buttons. When you drag this tool over the figure in the Document Window, the cursor looks like an eyedropper. Any material group that is selected automatically appears in the Material List, and its material is displayed in the Shader Window.

FIGURE 8-1

Material Room interface

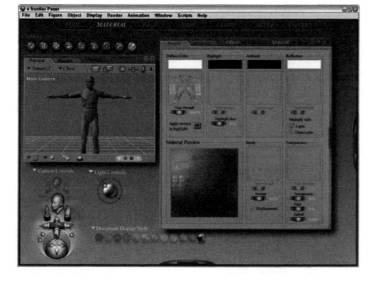

FIGURE 8-2

Shader Window

Object List   Material List   Pop-up menu

Room help

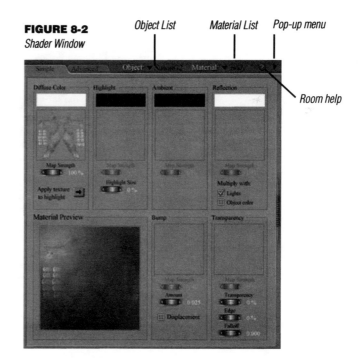

Using the Simple Material Panel

The Shader Window is divided into two separate panels, each opened with the corresponding tab. The Simple Material panel includes the most basic materials and offers a quick and easy way to quickly build and apply materials. The materials included on the Simple Material panel include Diffuse Color, Ambient, Highlight, Reflection, Bump, and Transparency along with all the controls to define and edit these properties. The panel also includes a Material Preview pane, which displays a rendered example of the designated material.

Using the Advanced Material Panel

The Advanced Material panel, shown in Figure 8-3, includes panels known as *nodes*. Each node has many material properties, and you can connect multiple nodes to create unique and diverse material types. In the top-right corner of each node are two icons that you can use to show or hide the material values and the preview pane.

FIGURE 8-3
Advanced Material panel

Show/Hide Values button

Show/Hide Preview Pane button

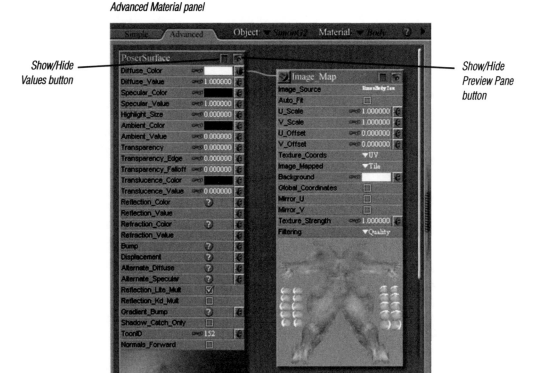

Accessing the Wacros Palette

To the right side of the Shader Window is a side window control bar. Clicking this bar opens the Wacros palette, as shown in Figure 8-4. Wacros are scripted actions that you can access to help automate the building of advanced materials, such as adding refraction and reflection to the current material and setting up toon rendering. With the User Defined button, you can access custom-created wacros. You create custom wacros by using *PoserPython*, a scripting language available within Poser. More on creating custom wacros is covered in Chapter 18, "Writing Python Scripts."

Previewing Materials

If you have selected the OpenGL Display option for the Document Window, you can preview actual shader nodes within the preview window. This is a huge help because it lets you see your advanced materials without waiting for the image to be rendered. Some effects such as bump maps cannot be previewed.

| NEW POSER 7 FEATURE
The ability to view shaders within the Document Window is new to Poser 7.

FIGURE 8-4
Wacros palette

The availability of this feature depends on the video hardware included on your computer. To check the compatibility of your hardware card and to enable the shader display in the Document Window, open the Render Settings dialog box using the Render, Render Settings menu. Then select the Preview panel, as shown in Figure 8-5.

If your video card supports hardware shading, a note will be listed in this panel, and an option to Enable Hardware Shading will be available. There is also an option to Optimize Simple Materials. If this option is selected, shaders aren't created for any simple materials in the scene. You can also set the resolution of the Preview Texture up to

4096, depending on what your graphics processor can handle.

NOTE All texture maps are square so a single value is used to specify their size. A setting of 512 creates a texture map that is 512 pixels by 512 pixels.

FIGURE 8-5

Preview panel of the Render Settings dialog box

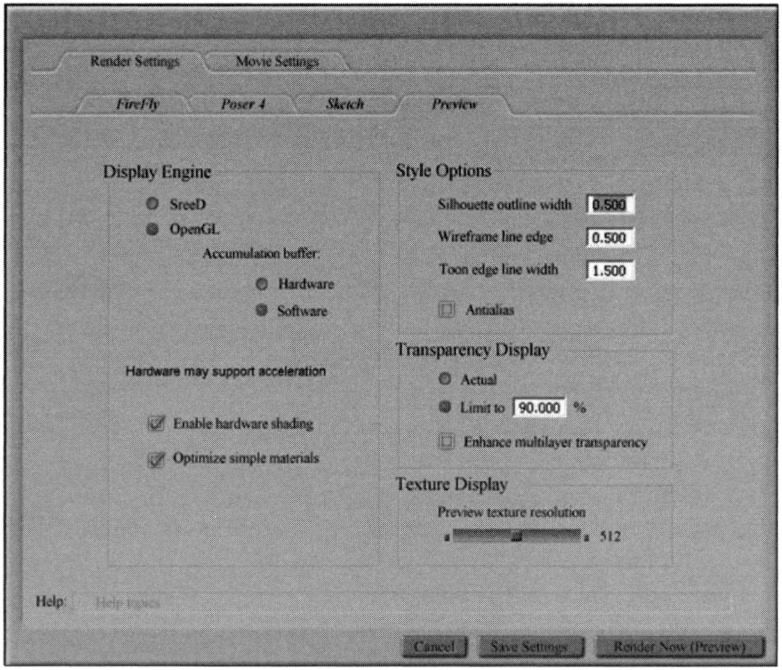

FIGURE 8-6

Simple yellow shorts

1. Load the Aiko model from the Library palette or any other figure with clothes.

2. Click the Material tab to access the Material Room.

   A new interface appears including the same controls available in the Pose Room.

3. Select the Figure 1 object from the Object List at the top of the Shader Window.

   The Select Material tool is selected by default when the Material Room is opened.

4. Click the figure's thigh element in the Document Window.

   The SkinHip material group is automatically selected in the Material List at the top of the Shader Window.

5. Click the color swatch beneath the Diffuse Color title in the Simple panel of the Shader Window and select a yellow color from the pop-up color palette.

   The Aiko figure shown in the Document Window is displayed with a yellow-colored shorts, as shown in Figure 8-6.

6. Select File, Save As and save the file as **Yellow shorts.pz3**.

CREATE
SIMPLE MATERIALS

What You'll Do

In this lesson, you learn how to create simple materials.

The Simple Material panel of the Shader Window only includes six simple material properties, but you can create an amazing variety of materials from these simple properties.

Changing Color

Directly underneath the Diffuse Color, Highlight, Ambient, and Reflection material properties in the Simple Material panel is a color swatch that sets the color for the respective property. You can change the current color by clicking this color swatch and selecting a new color from the pop-up color palette, shown in Figure 8-7. To open the standard color selector dialog box, click the icon in the upper-right corner of the pop-up color palette.

Adding Texture Maps

The open space underneath the color swatches is to hold a texture map that is loaded from the hard disk. To load a texture map, simply click the open space and the Texture Manager dialog box, shown in Figure 8-8, opens. This dialog box includes a preview of the selected image, a drop-down list containing recently loaded images, and a Browse button where you can locate new images to load. Once a texture map is loaded, you can change its brightness using the Map Strength dial. Each property that can use a texture map has a Map Strength parameter dial. This value sets how strong the texture map is. For example, a Map Strength value of 100 will cause the full texture map to be used and a Map Strength value of 0 will turn off the texture map.

FIGURE 8-7
Pop-up color palette

Open Color Selector dialog box

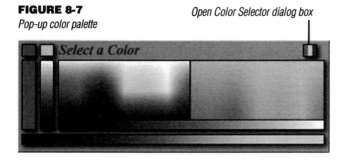

FIGURE 8-8
Texture Manager dialog box

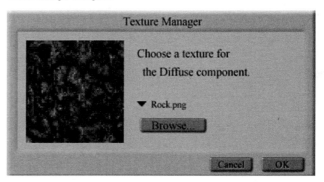

Adding Highlights

Highlights are surface areas where the reflected light is most intense. The color brightness determines the intensity of the highlights and you can also set the size of the highlights using the Highlight Size dial. Smooth shiny surfaces will have smaller, brighter highlights and rougher surfaces will have larger, fuzzier highlights because the reflected light is scattered more. If the Apply Texture to Highlight option is enabled for the Diffuse Color property, the texture map for the Diffuse Color is copied to the Highlight property and only the bright areas of the texture image receive the highlights. Figure 8-9 shows a material with a highlight.

QUICKTIP For realistic scenes, make sure the highlight color is the same as the main light color.

Using Diffuse and Ambient Colors

The Diffuse Color property sets the surface color of the material, and the Ambient property sets the color of the indirect light in the scene. These two colors are combined when used together. For example, a material with a red Diffuse Color and a blue Ambient color would appear purple.

QUICKTIP The Diffuse Color will tint any texture map that is applied to the Diffuse Color property. To avoid tinting the texture map, set the Diffuse Color to white.

FIGURE 8-9
Material with highlights

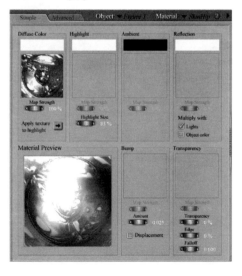

Enabling Reflections

You can use reflections to reflect an environment image off the current surface. When you click the texture map area, a selection dialog box, shown in Figure 8-10, enables you to apply the reflected texture image as a spherical map or a ray-trace reflection. A *spherical map* reflects the texture image about the selected object as if it were inside a large sphere. A *ray-trace reflection* uses a special rendering technique to follow each light ray as it bounces about the scene to create perfect reflections. More on ray tracing is covered in Chapter 16, "Rendering Scenes."

FIGURE 8-10
Choose a reflection type

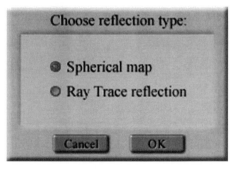

Of these two methods, the Spherical Map method renders much quicker, but the Ray Trace Reflection method results in higher quality reflections. You can multiply the reflected image with the Lights and the Object Color by enabling the options under the Reflection texture image. These options will tint the reflected image with the object color and dim the reflected image due to the direct lighting applied to the reflection. Figure 8-11 shows a rendering of a simple ball object that has a reflected material applied to it.

NOTE Reflection maps aren't visible in the Document Window. You can see them only after rendering the scene.

Adding Bump Maps

A bump map texture image adds a relief to the surface of the material. This is accomplished by making the light areas of the bump appear to be raised from the surface and the darker areas to be indented. You can use the Amount dial to set the depth of the bumps. Regardless of the Amount value, bump maps are simulated only on the object's surface without altering the actual geometry. To have a bump map change the object's geometry, you can use a displacement map. Figure 8-12 shows a simple material with a bump texture applied.

CAUTION The Amount value is measured in real-world units based on the type of units set in the Preferences dialog box. If the units are set to meters or feet, this value will be fairly small.

FIGURE 8-11

Reflective material on a sphere

FIGURE 8-12

Bump material

NOTE Early versions of Poser applied bump maps using a gradient image format with the .BUM extension. You can use the .BUM files if you add an Image Map node with the .BUM file loaded and connect it to the Gradient attribute. You'll also need to disable the Ignore Shader Trees option in the Poser 4 panel of the Render Settings dialog box.

Using Displacement Maps

You can also enable the Displacement option within the Bump attribute, which applies the texture as a displacement map. A displacement map is different from a bump it that is actually changes the geometry of the object to include the affected bumps. You can see this geometry change along the edges of the object surface, as shown in Figure 8-13, which shows a positive displacement map on the left and a

negative displacement map on the right. Displacement maps are preferred if any shadows cross the mapped object because shadows are accurately displayed for displacement maps. Bump and displacement maps typically are not visible until the scene is rendered. Displacement maps are covered in more detail in Chapter 16, "Rendering Scenes."

QUICKTIP You can set the Amount value to a negative number to make the lighter areas of the bump map indented and the darker areas raised.

Even though the Displacement option is enabled, the displacement map won't be rendered unless the Use Displacement Maps option in the Render Settings dialog box is enabled.

Using Transparency

You can use the Transparency value to make your entire material transparent. Transparency means that you can see through the material, like glass, to the objects behind it. The Edge value sets how transparent the edges of the material are, and the Falloff value causes the areas closer to the edges to become less transparent. You can also select a texture map to define the areas where the material is transparent with light areas being transparent and dark areas, opaque (or nontransparent). Figure 8-14 shows a transparent material applied to the skin material group of a figure. This creates an eerie invisible man effect. Notice how you can see the interior objects like the eyes and teeth through the semi-transparent skin.

FIGURE 8-13
Positive and negative displacement map

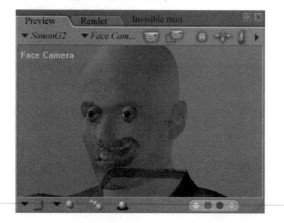

FIGURE 8-14
Transparent material

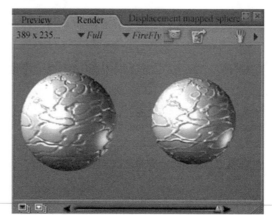

FIGURE 8-15

Simple green materials on a frog figure

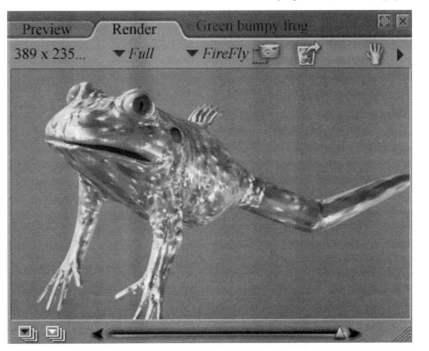

1. Open the Poser Library and locate the Frog figure in the Animals folder.

2. Click on the Material tab to open the Material Room.

3. Click on the frog's skin with the Material Select tool.

   The frog's default skin textures are displayed in the Simple material panel.

4. Click on the texture under the Diffuse Color attribute and select the None option from the Texture Manager dialog box. Then click on the Diffuse Color color swatch and choose a green color.

5. Click on the Highlight color and set it to white and set the Highlight Size to 15.

6. Click on the Bump texture and replace it with the Cells.tif texture file or another texture file. Set the Map Strength to 50% and the Amount to 0.007.

7. Select the Eyeball group from the Material List at the top of the Simple panel. Replace the texture with the None option in the Texture Manager and choose a bright yellow color. Then set the Transparency to 25.

8. In the Document Window, click on the Render button to see the resulting materials.

   The rendered frog with various simple materials is shown in Figure 8-15.

9. Select File, Save As and save the file as **Green bumpy frog.pz3**.

CREATE
ADVANCED MATERIALS

What You'll Do

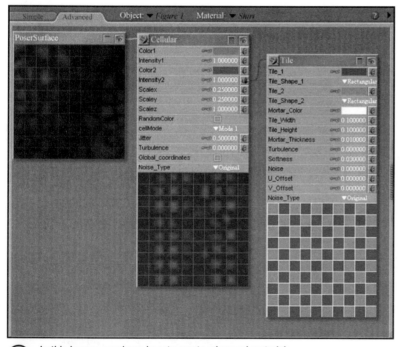

To create advanced materials, select the Advanced tab at the top of the Shader Window to open the Advanced Material panel. Within this panel, you can select and edit the various nodes, link nodes together, and create new nodes. All nodes plug into the root node that is applied to the selected object. Learning to work with material nodes is the key to creating complex materials.

In this lesson, you learn how to create advanced materials.

Selecting and Moving Nodes

The Shader Window is an open space for positioning and connecting material nodes. Click a node to select it. The selected node can be moved to a new position by dragging its title bar. You can select several nodes at the same time by holding down the Shift key and clicking on their title bars. You can also select all nodes by clicking the pop-up menu in the upper-right corner or by right-clicking in the Shader Window and choosing the Select All command.

> **QUICKTIP** To save space in the Shader Window, click the buttons in the upper-right corner of the node to hide both the value list and the preview window. Only the title bar will remain.

Viewing the Root Node

The root node is titled *PoserSurface*, as shown in Figure 8-16, and is always the final surface that is applied to the material group. The root node has no Output value. Different root nodes exist, depending on the type of item that you can create a material for. Poser includes four root nodes:

- **Material/Hair root node:** Used to define materials for figures, props, and hairstyles.

- **Light root node:** Used to define the materials applied to the selected light.

- **Background root node:** Used to define the materials applied to the scene background.

- **Atmosphere root node:** Used to define atmospheric materials, such as fog and haze.

FIGURE 8-16
Root material node

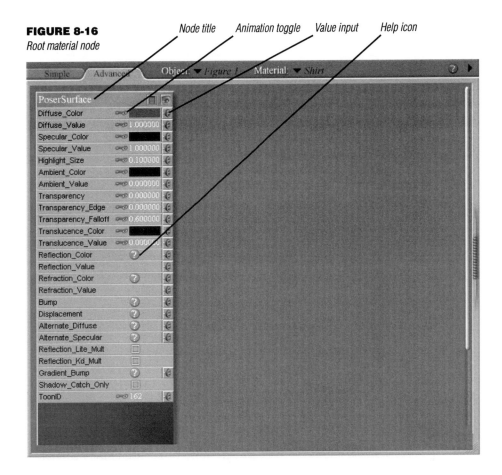

Node title   Animation toggle   Value input   Help icon

Changing Material Attribute Values

The root node includes many values that you can edit. Some of these values have color swatches, others have numeric values, and some are merely check boxes. Next to some of the attributes is a question mark button. Clicking this button opens a window providing some help with the attribute. The attributes found in the material/hair root node include the following:

- **Diffuse Color:** Defines the surface color of the object.
- **Diffuse Value:** Defines the strength of the diffuse color. A value of 0 makes the diffuse color black, whereas a value of 1 matches the defined diffuse color.
- **Specular Color:** Defines the color the highlights.
- **Specular Value:** Defines the strength of the specular color.
- **Highlight Size:** Defines how sharp or fuzzy the highlight is. Shiny surfaces have smaller, sharper highlights, and rough surfaces have larger highlights.
- **Ambient Color:** Defines the ambient color for the scene. This color shades all objects in the scene including shadows.
- **Ambient Value:** Defines the strength of the ambient color.

- **Transparency:** Defines the amount of transparency of the material. A value of 1 is fully transparent, and a value of 0 is fully opaque.
- **Transparency Edge:** Defines the amount of transparency applied to the edges of the object.
- **Transparency Falloff:** Defines how quickly the transparency fades as you approach the object edge.
- **Translucence Color:** Defines the color of light passing through a transparent object.
- **Translucence Value:** Defines the strength of the translucence.

NOTE Most of the remaining material attributes have no value, but can be connected to other nodes, such as a texture or variable node.

- **Reflection Color:** Defines a color reflected off the surface.
- **Reflection Value:** Defines the strength of the reflection color or texture.
- **Refraction Color:** Defines a color refracted or bent through a transparent surface.
- **Refraction Value:** Defines the strength of the refraction color.
- **Bump:** Defines a bump map that is applied to the material.
- **Displacement:** Defines a displacement that is applied to the material to change its geometry.

- **Alternate Diffuse:** An alternative attribute for applying diffuse colors and/or textures.
- *Alternate Specular:* An alternative attribute for applying specular highlights.
- **Reflection Lite Mult:** An option to multiply the lighting effects into the reflection map.
- **Reflection KD Mult:** An option to tint the reflection map by the diffuse color.
- **Gradient Bump:** An attribute to use gradient maps as bump maps. This attribute isn't used by the current renderer and is only included for backwards compatibility.
- **Shadow Catch Only:** An option to make all transparent surfaces appear opaque for shadows. The result is to cast a shadow onto a transparent surface such as shadow puppets on a sheet.
- **ToonID:** When rendering using the cartoon shader, each edge is outlined. By giving each separate material a different ID, multiple outlines will not be applied to a single object.
- **Normals Forward:** An option to align all the surface normals to point forward.

NOTE All values assigned in the Simple Material panel are automatically transferred to the material in the Advanced Material panel.

Animating Material Attribute Values

The values with key icons can be animated. Clicking the key icon opens a pop-up menu where you can select to enable animation mode, view the Parameter Settings dialog box for the given attribute, or open the attribute's animation graph. When animation mode is enabled, you can animate the parameter by selecting an animation frame and changing the parameter value. More on animating materials is covered in Chapter 13, "Animating Figures and Scenes."

NOTE The material attribute key icon turns green when animation mode is enabled.

Creating New Material Nodes

There are several ways to create a new material node, such as clicking a Value Input, clicking the Shader Window's pop-up menu, or right-clicking in the Shader Window. All of these methods open a pop-up menu that includes an option to Create New Node.

Figure 8-17 shows a newly created 3D texture node called Marble. This new node includes several additional values and a Value Output icon in its upper-left corner.

Connecting Material Nodes

To the right of every value is a plug socket icon, known as a Value Input. Clicking this icon opens a pop-up menu where you can create and attach a new node. You can connect any two material nodes using the Value Input and Value Output nodes. To connect two nodes, simply drag from the Value Output to the Value Input or vice versa. When connected, a light blue line (or cord) is shown connecting the two nodes, and the node with the Value Output controls the value of the node with the Value Input. For example, connecting a Marble output node to the root node's Diffuse Color value makes the marble texture appear as part of the root material, as shown in Figure 8-18. You can disconnect nodes by clicking the Value Input icon and selecting Disconnect from the pop-up menu. Each Value Input and Value Output icon can be connected to multiple different nodes.

The Shader Window pop-up menu includes commands for deleting, cutting, copying, and pasting the selected nodes. The pasted nodes are given the same name as their original with a different number attached on the end.

FIGURE 8-17
New material node

Value output

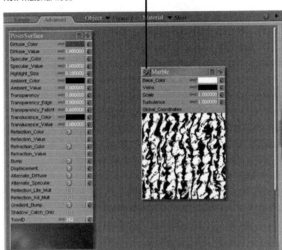

FIGURE 8-18
Two connected material nodes

Connecting node line

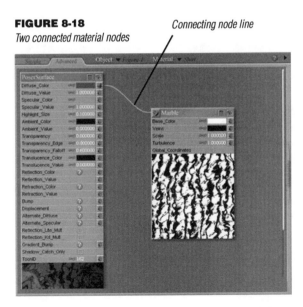

Use Texture Nodes

1. Open Poser and click the Material tab to access the Material Room.

2. Click the Advanced tab in the Shader Window.

3. Click the Value Input icon [icon] for the Diffuse Color value and select New Node, 3d Textures, Cellular from the pop-up menu.

   The Cellular material node is added to the Shader Window with a line connected to the Diffuse Color's Value Input icon.

4. Click the color swatch for the Color 1 value in the Cellular node and select a red color from the pop-up color palette. Then, click the color swatch for the Color 2 value in the Cellular node and select a blue color from the pop-up color palette. Change the Scale X and Scale Y values to 0.25.

5. Click the Value Input icon for the Intensity 2 value in the Cellular node and select New Node, 2d Textures, Tile from the pop-up menu.

   The Tile material node is added to the Shader Window with a line connected to the Cellular node's Intensity 2's Value Input icon.

6. Click the Node Preview button [icon] in the upper-right corner of both texture nodes.

   The preview pane for the Cellular node shows several red colored cells among a light blue grid pattern, as shown in Figure 8-19.

7. Select File, Save As and save the file as **Texture pattern.pz3**.

FIGURE 8-19

Texture pattern material

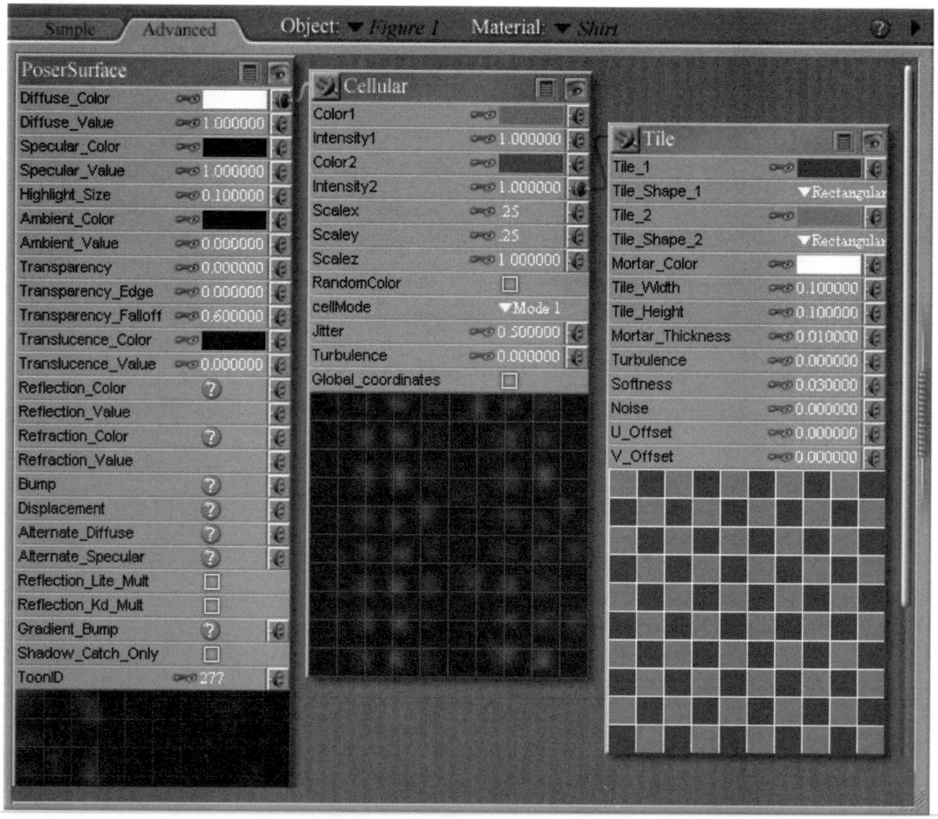

LEARN
THE VARIOUS MATERIAL NODES

What You'll Do

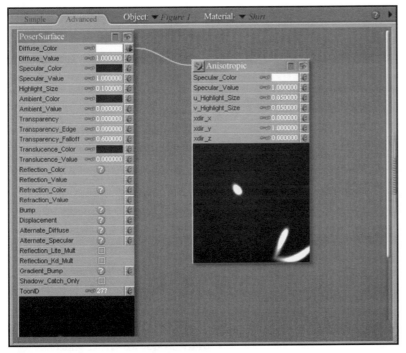

In this lesson, you discover the available material nodes.

When creating a new material node, there are several categories of nodes available, each with its own unique attributes. The available nodes are divided into the following categories:

- **Math:** Used to mathematically manipulate values such as adding, subtracting, and multiplying values together.

- **Lighting:** Used to alter the scene lighting method to change highlight shapes or to specify a certain effect, like toon shading.

- **Variables:** Used to add variable values to the material values, such as the current frame number, the dimensions of the current point, or the current pixel.

- **3D Textures:** Includes several preset 3D texture maps such as Noise, Clouds, Marble, and Granite.

- **2D Textures:** Includes several preset 2D texture maps such as Brick, Tile, and Weave. It also includes nodes for loading image files and movies.

Using Math Nodes

You can use math nodes to combine two values using several different mathematical functions. The available math nodes include

- **Blender:** Used to blend between two colors.

- **Edge Blend:** Used to blend between an Inner Color and an Outer Color, where the Inner Color faces the camera and the Outer Color faces away from the camera.

- **Component:** Used to extract Red, Green, or Blue components from a color based on the Component value where Red = 1, Green = 2, and Blue =3.

- **Math Functions:** Used to combine two values using a mathematical function. Available functions include Add, Subtract, Multiply, Divide, Sin, Cos, Tan, Sqrt, Pow, Exp, Log, Mod, Abs, Sign, Min, Max, Clamp, Ceil, Floor, Round, Step, Smoothstep, Bias, and Gain.

- **Color Math:** Includes the same mathematical functions as the Math Functions node, except it works with two colors instead of two values.

- **User Defined:** Used to define a color using numeric color values. It lets you choose from Red, Green, Blue (RGB); Hue, Saturation, Lightness (HSL); and Hue, Saturation, Value (HSV) color models.

- **Simple Color:** Lets you select a single color using the pop-up color palette.

- **Color Ramp:** Includes four colors that are used to create a gradient ramp.

- **HSV:** Defines colors using Hue, Saturation, and Value color attributes.

QUICKTIP Holding down the Alt/Option key while clicking a color swatch automatically opens the Color Selector dialog box.

Using Lighting Nodes

The Lighting nodes let you specify a very specific lighting model for the current material. For example, the Special, Hair node lets you select colors for the hair roots, hair tips, and the root's transparency. Each light node listed below includes a submenu of available nodes.

- **Specular:** Used to select from several types of highlights, each with their own shape, color, size and intensity values. The available options include Anisotropic, Phong, Glossy, Blinn, and Specular.

- **Diffuse:** Used to alter how the diffuse color is affected by the lighting. The options include Clay, Diffuse, Probe Light, and Toon.

- **Special:** Several additional specialized lighting models. The options include Skin, Velvet, Hair, and Fast Scatter.

- **Ray Trace:** Several ray-trace options used to create photo-realistic scenes. The options include Reflect, Refract, Ambient Occlusion, Gather, and Scatter.

- **Environment Map:** Includes a single option of Sphere Map for creating a reflection sphere map.

Using Variables Nodes

These nodes are used to represent specific scene values such as the current point. The available Variable nodes include

- **N:** Includes the X, Y, and Z values of the normal at the current point used to determine the polygon's orientation.

- **P:** Includes the X, Y, and Z values of the current point.

- **Frame Number:** The current frame number for animation sequences.

- **u, v:** References the texture location of the pixel currently being rendered.

- **Du, Dv:** References the change rate of the texture coordinates or how fast the rendering is progressing.

- **dPdv, dPdu:** References the change rate of the current point.

- **dNdv, dNdu:** References the change rate of the surface normals.

Using 2D and 3D Texture Nodes

The texture nodes are divided into two categories—3D and 2D. 3D textures maintain their material properties regardless of the shape of the object they are applied to, whereas 2D textures are simply images that are wrapped about the object. All of these textures are convenient because they can be selected and applied without having to load an image. The available 3D textures include

- **Fractal Sum:** Creates a fractal-based texture.

- **FBM:** Creates a texture based on multiple fractals.

- **Turbulence:** Creates another variant fractal texture.

- **Noise:** Creates a static texture useful for adding variety to materials.

- **Cellular:** Creates a texture of repeating cells.

- **Clouds:** Creates a texture that resembles clouds.

- **Spots:** Creates a texture of random spots.

- **Marble:** Creates a texture that resembles a marble rock surface.

- **Granite:** Creates a texture that resembles a granite rock surface.

- **Wood:** Creates a texture that resembles a wood grain.

- **Wave 3d:** Creates a texture of concentric circles.

Figure 8-20 shows each of the available 3D texture nodes.

FIGURE 8-20

3D texture nodes

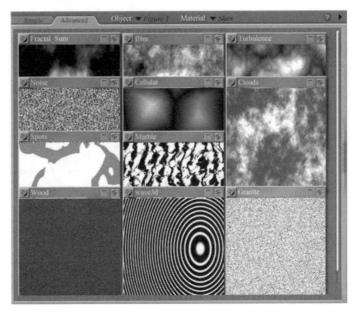

The available 2D textures include:

- **Wave 2d:** A texture map of concentric circles.

- **Image Map:** An image map loaded from the hard disk.

- **Brick:** An image map of a set of bricks.

- **Tile:** An image map of alternating checkerboard patterns.

- **Weave:** An image map of a basket weave pattern.

- **Movie:** A movie file loaded from the hard drive.

Figure 8-21 shows each of the available 2D texture nodes.

FIGURE 8-21

2D texture nodes

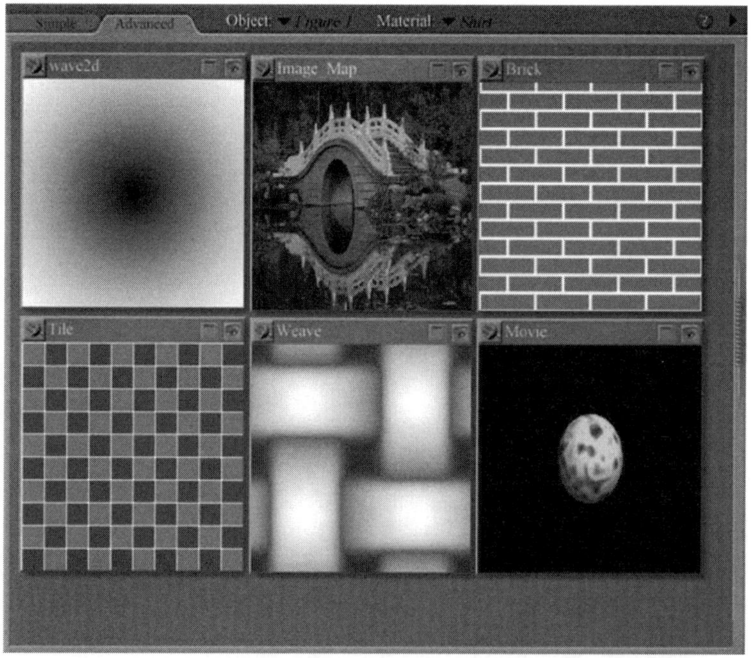

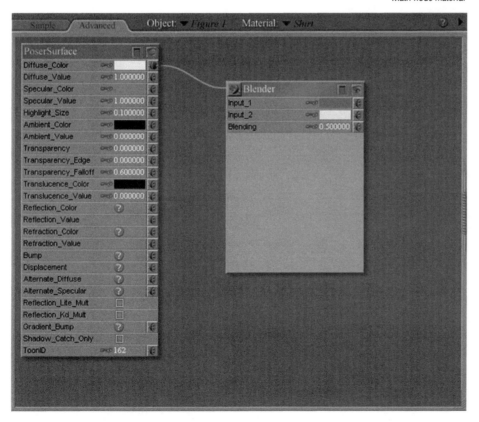

FIGURE 8-22

Math node material

1. Open Poser and click the Material tab to access the Material Room.

2. Click the Advanced tab in the Shader Window.

3. Click the Value Input icon for the Diffuse Color value and select New Node, Math, Blender from the pop-up menu.

   The Blender material node is added to the Shader Window with a line connected to the Diffuse Color's Value Input icon.

4. Click the color swatch for Input 1 in the Blender node and select a red color from the pop-up color palette. Then, click the color swatch for the Input 2 value in the Blender node and select a yellow color.

5. Click the Node Preview button in the upper-right corner of the Blender node.

   The preview pane for the Blender node shows a bright orange color created by blending together the red and yellow colors, as shown in Figure 8-22.

6. Select File, Save As and save the file as **Blended color.pz3**.

Use a Lighting Node

1. Open Poser and click the Material tab to access the Material Room.

2. Click the Advanced tab in the Shader Window.

3. Click the Value Input icon for the Diffuse Color value and select New Node, Lighting, Specular, Anisotropic from the pop-up menu.

   The Anisotropic material node is added to the Shader Window with a line connected to the Diffuse Color's Value Input icon. Anisotropic highlights are elliptical rather than circular.

4. Click the color swatch for Specular Color value in the Anisotropic node and select a gold color from the pop-up color palette.

5. Click the Node Preview button in the upper-right corner of the Anisotropic node.

   The preview pane for the Anisotropic node shows a gold-colored elliptical highlight, as shown in Figure 8-23.

6. Select File, Save As and save the file as **Anisotropic highlight.pz3**.

FIGURE 8-23

Lighting node material

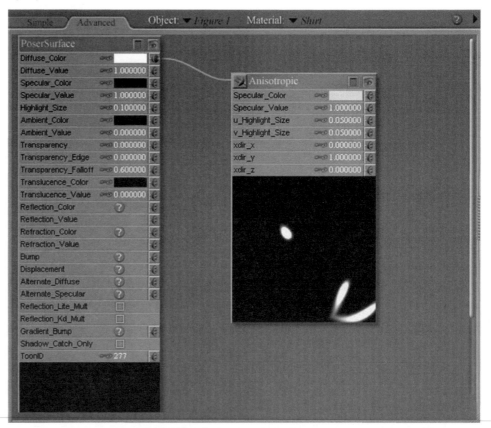

USE WACROS

What You'll Do

In this lesson, you learn how to use the scripts in the Wacros palette.

Connecting most nodes to create advanced materials is easy to do with a little experimentation, but others can be downright tricky. To help you with these trickier materials, the Wacros palette includes several predefined scripts that can quickly add and connect the nodes needed to create certain effects.

Wacros are PoserPython scripts that deal specifically with materials. They are typically used to add certain nodes needed to create a specific type of material, such as a Toon Render or a Shadow Catcher material. You can access them from the Wacros palette located to the right side of the Shader Window. Clicking a Wacros button executes the script for the current material, and Shift-clicking on a button executes the script for all the materials that are part of the current object.

Adding Reflections and Refractions

You can add reflections to a material using the Simple Materials panel, but to enable true spherical reflections and to be able to configure the reflections, you also need the Add Reflection button. This button adds several nodes to the Shader window and connects them to the Reflection Color value, as shown in Figure 8-24.

The Add Refraction wacro works in a similar manner, adding the nodes needed to create refractions through transparent surfaces. Refractions work only through transparent and semi-transparent materials.

Adding Subsurface Scattering

Subsurface scattering spreads reflected light across the surface of an object, creating the effect that the light can shine through thinner parts of the model. For example, lights shining behind a character's head will illuminate the ears as if they were translucent.

The Add Subsurface Scattering wacro adds three nodes—Edge Blend, Fastscatter, and Blinn—to the Shader window and connects them to the Alternate Diffuse and Alternate Specular values, as shown in Figure 8-25, to increase the color around the edges of the object.

FIGURE 8-24
The Add Reflection wacro

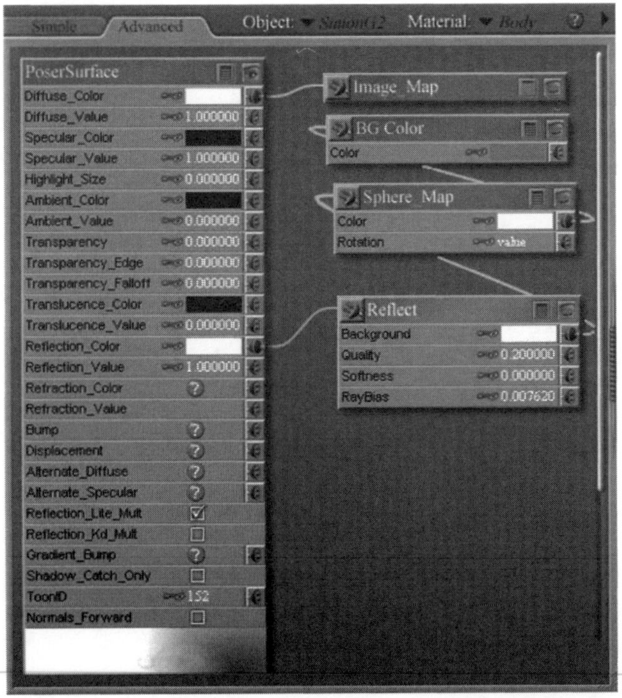

FIGURE 8-25
The Add Subsurface Scattering wacro

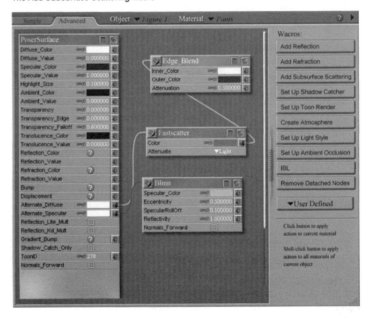

Enabling Shadow Catcher and Toon Rendering

The Shadow Catcher wacro makes the current object completely transparent, but enables the ShadowCatchOnly option, which lets it display shadows that are cast onto it. You can use this option to give shadows the ability to be expressive and positioned independent of the floor.

This wacro adds a Toon node and connects it to the Alternate Diffuse value in the root node, enabling the material to be rendered as a cartoon. It is used in conjunction with the Toon Outline render option in the Render Settings dialog box.

Using Atmosphere Presets

The Create Atmosphere button opens a simple dialog box where you can choose from four preset atmospheric effects, including Fog, Smokey, Smokey Room, and Depth Cue. After making a selection, the wacro sets up all the necessary nodes to create your selection for the Atmosphere node. More on adding Atmosphere effects to the scene is covered later in this chapter.

Defining a Light Style

This wacro can only be applied when a light object is selected in the Shader Window. It opens a simple dialog box where you can choose from three light styles, including Diffuse Only, Specular Only, and White Only. After you make a selection, the wacro changes the colors used for the Diffuse and Specular values to white and black, black and white, or both to white, depending on your selection.

Enabling Ambient Occlusion and Image-Based Lighting

The Set Up Ambient Occlusion button can only be applied when a light object is selected in the Shader Window. It sets up ambient occlusion for the selected light material by enabling the Ambient Occlusion option in the Properties palette.

> **NOTE** Ambient occlusion works only if the Ray-tracing option is enabled in the Render Settings dialog box.

The IBL button can be applied only when a light object is selected in the Shader Window. It opens the Texture Manager, where you can select the image to use for your image-based light, and it offers to enable ambient occlusion. You can learn more about image-based lighting and ambient occlusion in Chapter 7, "Adding Scene Lighting."

Removing Detached Nodes

If you've created a complex material and it includes some nodes that aren't connected to anything, you can use the Remove Detached Nodes button to quickly remove any detached nodes. Detached nodes have no effect on the material and will only take up memory.

Adding New Wacros

You can add new wacros to the Wacros palette in the same manner as you add scripts to the Python Scripts palette by clicking an open button to open a dialog box. Clicking a script button with the Alt/Option key held down clears the selected button, and clicking a Wacros button with the Ctrl/Command button held down opens the script within a text editor for editing.

> **QUICKTIP** If you place a script file in the \Runtime\Python\poserScripts\Wacros\UserDefined directory, the script will appear under the User Defined pop-up menu the next time you restart Poser.

Use the Wacros Palette

1. Open Poser with the default figure visible.

2. Click the Material tab to the open the Material Room.

3. Click the side window control to the right of the Shader Window to open the Wacros palette (if necessary).

4. Click the Set Up Toon Render button. A dialog box will appear asking if you want to have highlights on toon surfaces. Click Yes to accept this option.

   A new node is added to the Shader Window, as shown in Figure 8-26.

5. Select File, Save As and save the file as **Toon render wacro.pz3**.

FIGURE 8-26

Toon render wacro

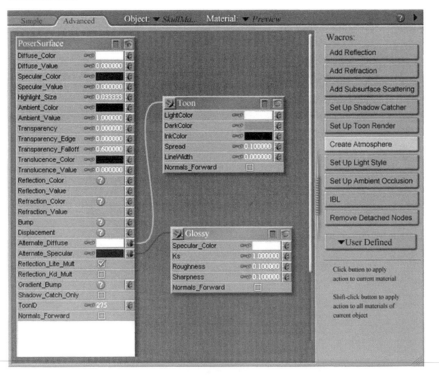

CREATE SMOOTHING
AND MATERIAL GROUPS

What You'll Do

In this lesson, you learn how to create smoothing and material groups with the Group Editor.

The Group Editor can be used to identify groups of polygons that need to have the same type of material or that need to be smoothed together. For example, consider the neckline of a figure where the shirt meets the neck. It would look funny if some of the neck polygons were colored the same as the shirt or vice versa. It would also look strange if the polygons in the shirt were smoothed with the neck. The shirt and the neck each form a separate material and smoothing groups.

Figure elements are divided into objects that align with the figure's bones to allow for easy figure posing, but the materials don't often follow these groupings. For example, the elements covered by the shirt area could include multiple elements, including the chest, abdomen, and both collars and upper arms, whereas the head as a single element can require separate material groups for the scalp, lips, cheeks, teeth, and tongue.

Setting Crease Angles

You can set smoothing at the global level using the Default Crease Angle value found in the Document panel of the General Preferences dialog box or at the local body part level using the Crease Angle value in the Properties palette, as shown in Figure 8-27.

FIGURE 8-27
Properties palette

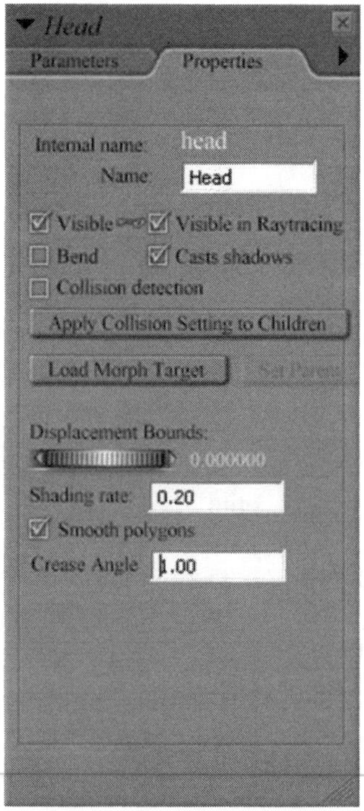

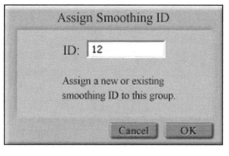

The Crease Angle is determined by computing the angle between the normal vectors of two adjacent polygons. If the angle is greater than the Crease Angle value, the edge between the two polygons is made into a crease or a hard edge. If the angle value is less than the global or local Crease Angle, the polygon faces are smoothed together.

NOTE The Crease Angle value in the Properties palette takes precedence over the global Crease Angle value.

Most Crease Angle values are between 80 to 90 degrees, which causes almost all adjacent polygons to be smoothed. If a low Crease Angle value were used, the object would appear faceted where every polygon is shown.

FIGURE 8-28
Assign Smoothing ID dialog box

Using Smoothing Groups

Even though a crease angle is set for an entire body part or object, you may want to have some hard edges across an object, such as the collar of a shirt. You can do this by defining a **smoothing group**. A smoothing group is created using the Group Editor panel.

With the Group Editor panel open, simply select all the polygons that need to be smoothed together and click the Assign Smoothing ID button. This opens the Assign Smoothing ID dialog box, shown in Figure 8-28, where you can enter a smoothing ID number. This gives each of the polygons within the smoothing group the same smoothing ID. Polygons along the border of a smoothing group have a hard edge.

Using the Grouping Tool

The Grouping Tool found in the Editing Tools opens the Group Editor panel, shown in Figure 8-29. Within this panel are buttons for creating a material group that can be recognized in the Shader Window. By dragging over polygons in the Document Window with the Grouping tool, you can select polygons as part of the group. The selected polygons are highlighted in red in the Document Window.

QUICKTIP To see the polygons clearly, select a wireframe display style from the Document Display Style control bar.

Deselecting Polygons

To remove polygons from the current selection, click the Deselect button at the top of the Group Editor and click the polygons you want to remove.

QUICKTIP You can also access the Deselect button by holding down the Ctrl/Command key.

FIGURE 8-29
Group Editor panel

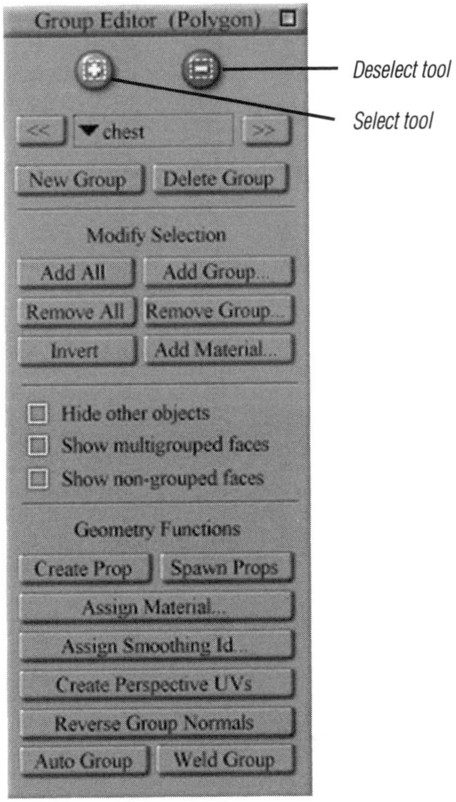

Deselect tool

Select tool

Creating a Material Group

Once all the polygons for the material group are selected, click the Assign Material button in the Group Editor. This opens the Assign Material dialog box, shown in Figure 8-30, where you can type a name for the new material group. After you click OK, you can select the new material group from the Material List in the Shader Window.

FIGURE 8-30
Assign Material dialog box

Set a Global Crease Angle

1. Open Poser and load the Kitty Robot figure, found in the CP Partners/Sanctum Art folder, from the Library.

2. Select the Edit, General Parameters menu to open the General Parameters dialog box.

3. Set the Default Crease Angle to 1.0 and click the OK button.

   The entire model becomes faceted showing each polygon in the model, as shown in Figure 8-31.

4. Select File, Save As and save the file as **Faceted robot.pz3**.

FIGURE 8-31
Faceted robot

FIGURE 8-32

Green stripe

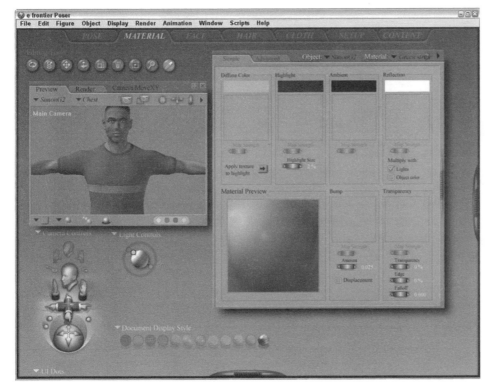

Create a Material Group

1. Open Poser and click the Material tab to access the Material Room.

2. Click the Grouping Tool button 🔲 in the Editing Tools controls.

   The Group Editor panel appears, and the figure in the Document Window goes dark.

3. Click the Hidden Line button in the Document Display Style controls.

4. Click the chest object in the middle of the Document Window.

   All the polygons that make up the chest element are highlighted in red.

5. Click the Deselect button 🔲 in the Group Editor panel and drag over the top polygons in the Document Window to remove them from the selected polygons.

6. When just a single band of polygons surround the mid-section of the figure in the Document Window, click the Assign Material button in the Group Editor panel.

   The Assign Material dialog box appears.

7. Type the name **Shirt stripe** in the Assign Material dialog box and click OK.

8. Select the Shirt stripe material group from the Material List at the top of the Shader Window and change the Diffuse Color to green.

9. Click the Smooth Shaded button in the Document Display Style controls.

   The material group is colored green, as shown in Figure 8-32.

10. Select File, Save As and save the file as **Green stripe.pz3**.

ADD
ATMOSPHERE EFFECTS

What You'll Do

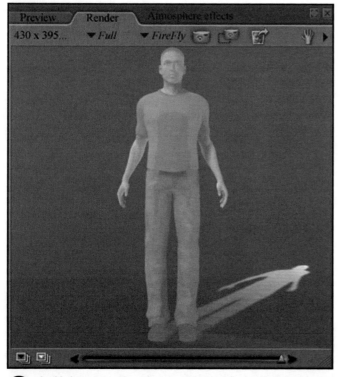

If you look in the Material List found at the top of the Shader Window in the Material Room, you'll find an Atmosphere option directly below the Background option. Selecting this option opens the Atmosphere root node in the Advanced panel of the Shader Window, as shown in Figure 8-33. Using this node, you can add depth cue and volume atmospheric effects to the rendered scene.

In this lesson, you learn how to add atmospheric effects to the scene.

CAUTION Enabling atmosphere effects can add a substantial amount of time to the rendering process.

Enabling Depth Cueing

By selecting the Depth Cue option in the root Atmosphere node, you can turn on the depth cueing atmospheric effect. This works just like the Depth Cue option in the Document Window by making objects farther away in the scene appear hazier.

Adding a Volume Effect

The volume atmospheric effect adds a fog and haze to the scene by coloring all scene objects with the designated color. When the volume effect is enabled, notice how the figure details are washed out by the fog effect. The volume effect also affects shadows.

FIGURE 8-33
Atmosphere root shader

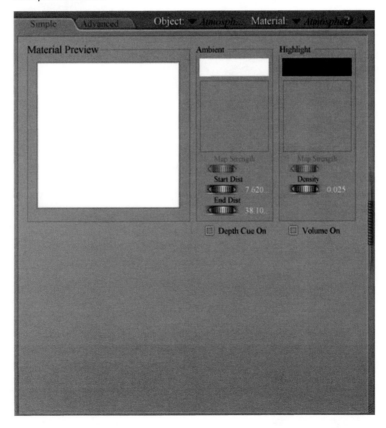

Enable Atmosphere Effects

1. Open Poser with the default figure visible.

2. Click the Material tab at the top of the interface to open the Material Room and click the Advanced tab in the Shader Window, if necessary.

3. Select the Atmosphere option from the Object List at the top of the Shader Window.

   The Atmosphere root node appears in the Shader Window.

4. Enable the Depth Cue On and Volume On values in the Atmosphere root node.

5. Click the Pose tab to move back to the Pose Room.

6. Click the Render button at the top of the Document Window.

   The scene is rendered using the atmospheric effects, as shown in Figure 8-34.

7. Select File, Save As and save the file as **Atmospheric effects.pz3**.

FIGURE 8-34
Rendered atmosphere effects

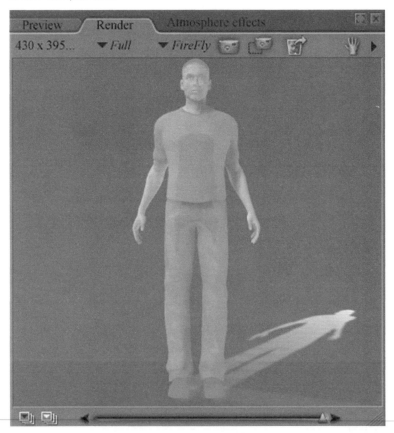

CHAPTER REVIEW

Chapter Summary

This chapter explained how materials can be used to define how the surface looks when rendered. Materials are created in the Material Room, and the Library includes an assortment of preset materials you can apply to material groups. Simple materials include properties such as color, highlight, reflection, and transparency, and you create advanced materials by connecting material nodes together within the Shader Window. Several complex material properties can be created using the Wacros palette. Finally, the chapter showed how new smoothing and material groups can be created using the Group Editor and how atmosphere effects can be added to the scene.

What You Have Learned

In this chapter, you

- Discovered the layout of the Material Room interface including the Shader Window.
- Used the Select Material tool to select a material group in the Document Window.
- Discovered how materials can be previewed in the Document Window using OpenGL.
- Learned the properties used to create simple materials, including color,

highlight, ambient, reflection, bump, and transparency.
- Added texture images to materials.
- Learned what the various root material values are used for.
- Connected material nodes together and created new material nodes.
- Reviewed a list of the available material nodes.
- Used the Wacros palette to enable specific material properties.
- Set the global and local crease angle.
- Created a new smoothing and material group using the Group Editor.
- Added depth cueing and volume atmospheric effects to the scene.

Key Terms from This Chapter

- **Ambient color.** A global pervasive light color that is applied to the entire scene.
- **Bump map.** A 2D bitmap image that adds a relief texture to the surface of an object like an orange rind.
- **Depth cueing.** An atmospheric effect that makes objects farther away in the scene appear hazier.
- **Diffuse color.** The surface color emitted by an object.
- **Displacement map.** A 2D bitmap image that controls the displacement of geometry objects.

- **Highlight.** The spot on an object where the light is reflected with the greatest intensity. Also known as a *specular* highlight.
- **Material group.** A group of selected polygons that defines a region where similar materials are applied, such as a shirt or pants group.
- **Material node.** A dialog box of material properties that can be connected to control another material value.
- **Opaque.** The opposite of transparency. When objects cannot be seen through.
- **Root node.** The top-level material node.
- **Shader Window.** An interface found in the Material Room where new custom materials can be created.
- **Smoothing group.** A group of polygons that are smoothed between adjacent polygons without any hard edges.
- **Texture map.** An 2D image file that is wrapped about a surface.
- **Transparency.** A material property that defines how easy an object is to see through, like glass.
- **Volume effect.** An atmospheric effect that colors all scene objects with the designated color, much like fog.
- **Wacro.** A custom PoserPython script used within the Shader Window to create new material types.

chapter

9 CREATING A FACE AND
FACIAL EXPRESSIONS

1. Learn the Face Room interface.

2. Create a face from photos.

3. Change texture variation.

4. Use the Face Shaping tool.

5. Add the face to the figure.

6. Work with expressions.

9 CREATING A FACE AND
FACIAL EXPRESSIONS

If you've ever wanted to place your face on a super hero's body, now is your chance. The Face Room includes several sets of controls for creating and modifying the look of the figure face. These modified faces are then applied to the figure model.

There are two ways to modify faces in the Face Room and controls to use each way. One way is to change the face texture, which can include color, shading, highlighting, beard, and so on. Another way to alter the face is to change the head's geometry by deforming the head model.

A number of parameters are available for changing the face's texture, including the ability to load custom face images. Using the Photo Lineup panes in the Face Room, you can load custom front and side view face images and map them to the head geometry for the current figure. You can

also save the existing texture map and edit it within an image-editing package.

Even more parameters are available to change the head geometry, including an interface Face Shaping tool, which lets you deform the head geometry by dragging in a separate pane. You can apply the resulting face to the current figure by simply clicking a button.

This chapter also looks at the parameters available for working with **expressions**. When the head element is selected, a number of parameter dials are available in the Parameter palette. These dials let you control the look of the Brow, Eyes, Nose, Jaw, Lips, and Tongue to create an infinite number of expressions. The parameters also include several Phonemes morphs that can simulate the facial expressions used to speak.

Tools You'll Use

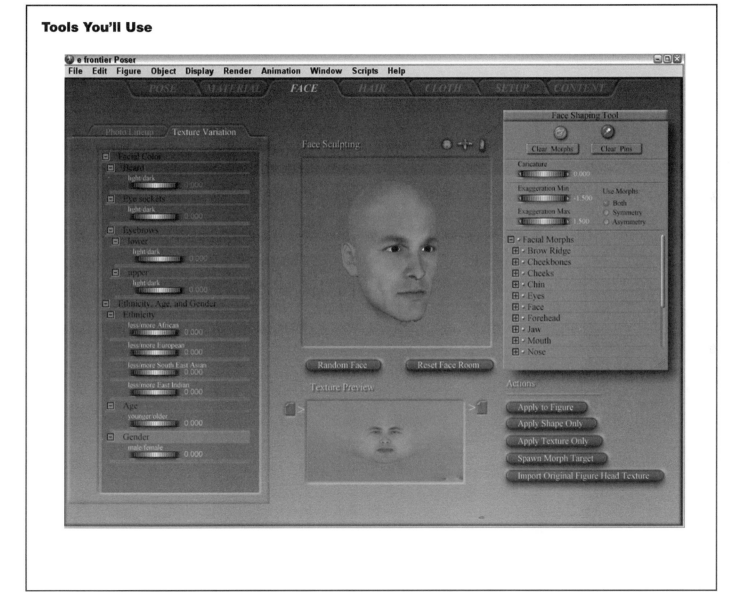

LEARN THE
FACE ROOM INTERFACE

What You'll Do

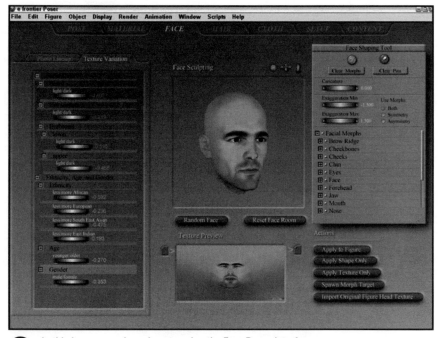

In this lesson, you learn how to using the Face Room interface.

You open the Face Room by clicking the Face tab at the top of the Poser interface. This opens an interface setup that is different from the Pose Room, as shown in Figure 9-1. The main interfaces within this room are the Photo Lineup panes, the Face Sculpting Preview pane, and the Face Shaping Tool dialog box.

CAUTION You cannot access the File, Save menu command when the Face Room is open. To save the current scene, click the Pose tab to access the Pose Room again.

Using the Photo Lineup Panel

You use the Photo Lineup panels, shown in Figure 9-2, to load custom front and side face images into the Face Room. These images can then be matched to a 3D head using a series of walkthrough steps. To the left side of the panes are several buttons used to load, remove, and manipulate the face images.

FIGURE 9-1

Face Room interface

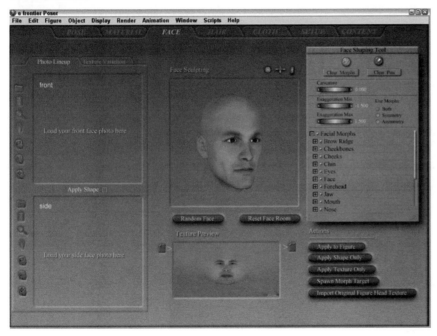

FIGURE 9-2

Photo Lineup panes

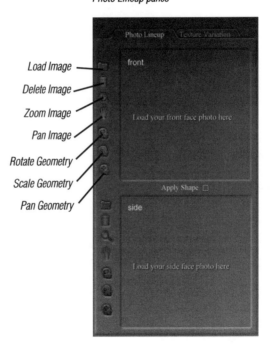

Using the Texture Variation Pane

You access the Texture Variation pane, shown in Figure 9-3, by clicking the Texture Variation tab at the top of the Photo Lineup panes. Using this pane, you can adjust the parameters of the loaded face images. The parameters contained within this pane include Facial Colors for the Beard, Eye Sockets, and Eyebrows, along with parameters to define the Ethnicity, Age, and Gender of the face.

Using the Face Sculpting Pane

The Face Sculpting pane, shown in Figure 9-4, shows a preview of the current images mapped onto 3D geometry. You can move and rotate the face within the preview pane using the three view controls at the top-right corner of the pane. The Face Sculpting pane also lets you interactively change the face's shape by dragging with the Putty and Pin tools located in the Face Shaping Tool panel or by changing the parameters located in the Face Shaping Tool panel. The Face Sculpting pane also includes Random Face and Reset Face Room buttons.

FIGURE 9-3

Texture Variation pane

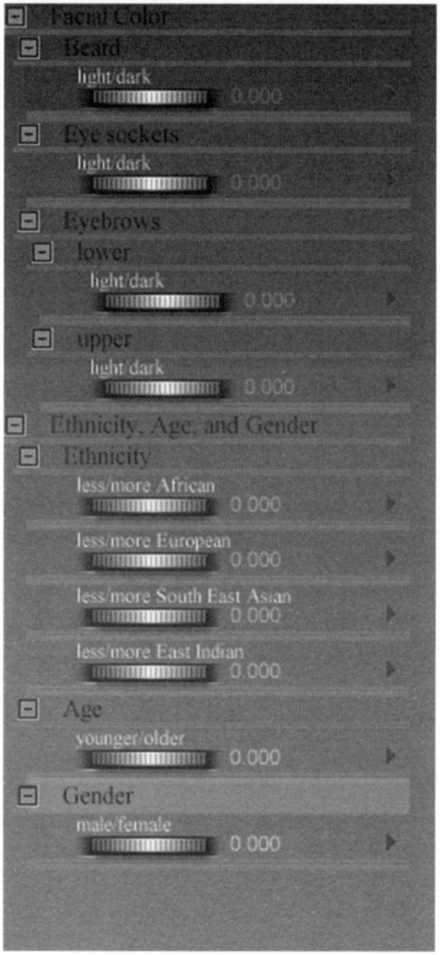

FIGURE 9-4

Face Sculpting pane

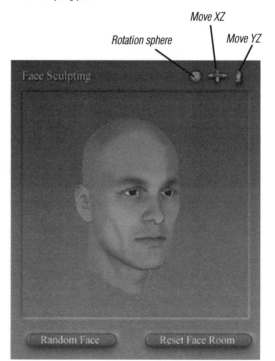

Using the Texture Preview Pane

The Texture Preview pane, shown in Figure 9-5, shows the actual 2D texture that is generated by the Face Room and is mapped onto the 3D geometry to create a completed head. Using the buttons to the left and right of the Texture Preview pane, you can load and save the texture map to the hard drive where you can edit it using an external image-editing package.

Using the Actions Buttons

You can use the Actions buttons, shown in Figure 9-6, to perform several specific tasks, such as applying the finished face to the current figure.

Using the Face Shaping Tool Panel

The Face Shaping Tool panel, shown in Figure 9-7, includes two buttons for accessing the Putty and the Pin tools. These tools alter the shape of the face in the Face Sculpting pane. The Face Shaping Tool panel also includes a long list of parameters that you can use to precisely alter almost every aspect of the face such as the brow ridge, the cheekbones, the eyes, forehead, mouth, and nose.

FIGURE 9-6
Actions buttons

FIGURE 9-7
Face Shaping Tool panel

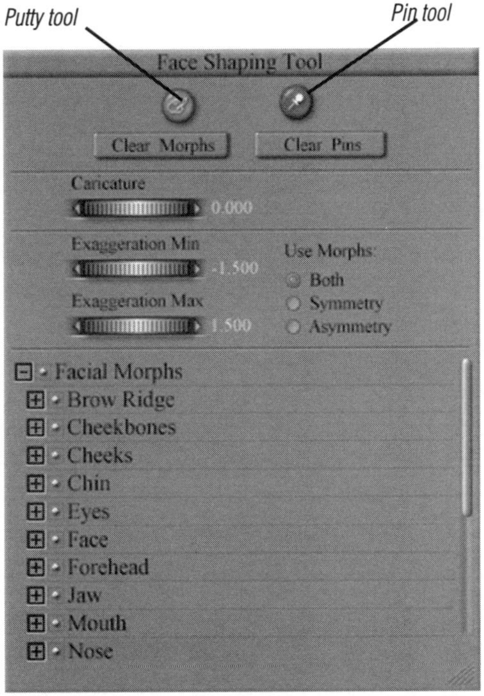

FIGURE 9-5
Texture Preview pane

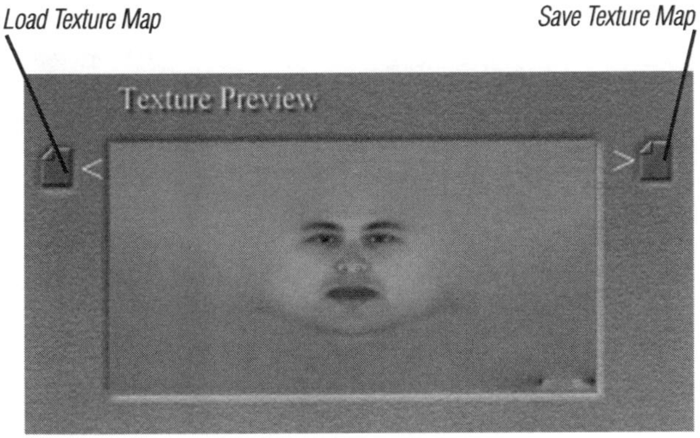

Load Texture Map   *Save Texture Map*

Access the Face Room Controls

1. Open the Poser interface with the default figure visible.

2. Click the Face tab to access the Face Room.

3. Click the Random Face button to load a random face.

   A new interface appears with a unique set of controls, as shown in Figure 9-8.

4. Click the Pose tab to access the Pose Room again.

5. Select File, Save As and save the file as **Face room.pz3**.

FIGURE 9-8

Face Room

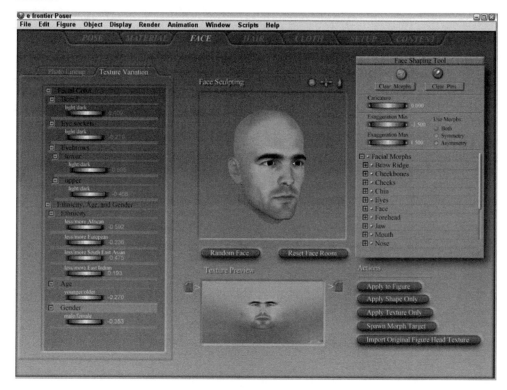

CREATE A
FACE FROM PHOTOS

What You'll Do

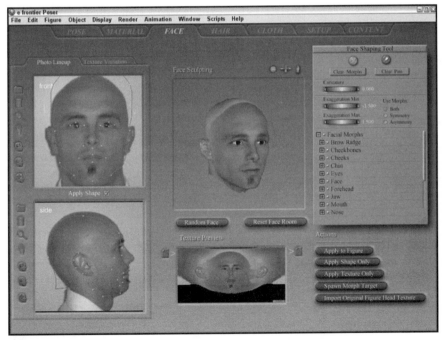

The Face Room includes the capability to create a custom face from digital photos. The needed photos are a front view and a profile view. You can map these images onto the current head element.

▶ *In this lesson, you learn how to create a custom face from loaded front and side view images.*

Preparing Face Images for Poser

If you're capturing your own digital photos for use in the Face Room, there are several guidelines that you can follow to make the process easier. Following these tips will result in a cleaner import:

- **Minimize the amount of hair.** The 3D model that the facial images are mapped to are bald; hair can be added using props or the Hair Room. If you can, shoot a subject with a bald head or have the subject pull their hair back so the ears and forehead are exposed.

- **Avoid smiles.** Although a smiling face is a joy, when capturing facial photos, try to have the subject remain expressionless. If the face is in a relaxed state, the match will be better.

- **Simplify the background.** If you capture the images in front of a plain white background, the facial features will stand out and be easier to align. Avoid shooting your facial images with a complex background. If you can't control the background, it can be removed using an image-editing package like Photoshop.

- **Eliminate shadows.** When lighting your subject, make sure the light on the subject's face is sufficient enough to eliminate all shadows cast on the background.

- **Crop images to the same size.** The Photo Lineup wizard assumes that the facial snapshots are roughly the same size and that the images are cropped to show the face in good detail. It helps to make the front and side shots the same size.

- **Pinch the facial features.** If you pull the digital images into an image-editing package, select all the front facial features and scale them down to be tighter. This compensates for the curvature of the head and better aligns the features.

- **Use a template.** Some figures include a template that unwraps the polygons applied to a figure into a template that you can use to help you identify where the seams of the texture map are located.

Loading the Front Face Image

To load a front face image, click the Load Image button to the left of the front pane in the Photo Lineup panel. This opens the Load Front Face Image dialog box to help in the alignment of the photo, shown in Figure 9-9. This panel lets you position the front image by clicking once to locate the corner of the right eye and again to locate the corner of the left lip. This dialog box also includes a Flip button that you can use to flip the image about its vertical center. After you click to locate the left corner of the lip, the image is placed in the front pane of the Photo Lineup panel. If you make a mistake, use the Delete Image button to remove the loaded image.

NOTE Only specific image formats can be loaded into the Face Room. The accepted image formats include .JPG, .PNG, .BMP, .TIF, .GIF, and .PCX.

FIGURE 9-9
Front image placement

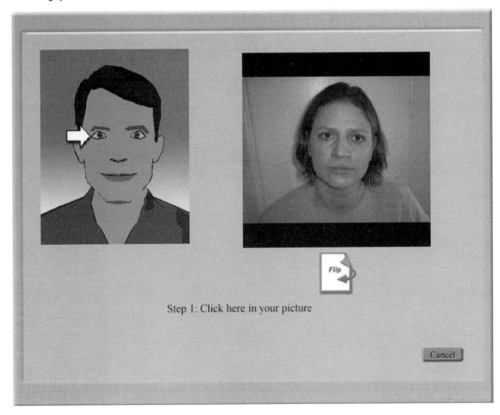

Step 1: Click here in your picture

Loading the Side Face Image

To load a side face image, click the Load Image button to the left of the side pane in the Photo Lineup panel. This opens the Load Side Face Image dialog box to help in the alignment of the photo, shown in Figure 9-10. This panel lets you position the side image by clicking once to locate the top of the right ear and again to locate the front of the chin. This dialog box also includes a Flip button that you can use to flip the image about its vertical center. After you click to locate the front of the chin, the image is placed in the side pane of the Photo Lineup panel.

FIGURE 9-10
Side image placement

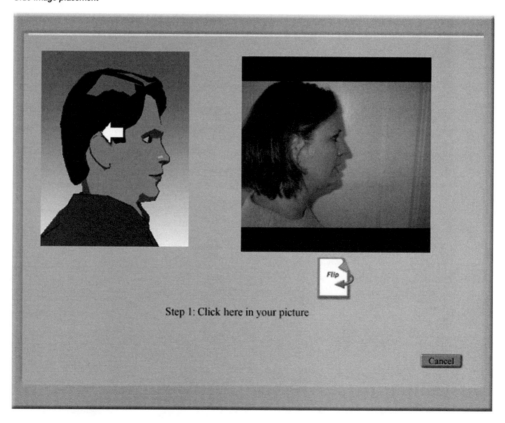

Step 1: Click here in your picture

Flip

Cancel

Aligning the Face to the Images

Once the face images are loaded into the Photo Lineup panel, a red outline of the 3D head element is projected on top of the images with green dots to mark the key features, such as the corners of the eyes, mouth, and nose. Using the Zoom and Pan Image tools to the left of the front and side panes, you can resize and move the images, and, using the Rotate, Scale, and Pan Geometry tools, you can change the outlines to match the images. For detailed work, drag the green dots to their correct location. Figure 9-11 shows the results after matching the outline points to the images.

> **NOTE** It is often easier to manipulate the photos in an image editing program than to match the figure in the Face Room.

Applying the Face Shape from Photos

Moving the alignment dots in the Photo Lineup panel not only aligns the image with the current head model, but it also defines the shape of the head model. To see the shape changes, enable the Apply Shape option located between the front and side panes. This updates the Preview window with the new head shape.

Exporting the Face Map

Once you align the face map to the face model as best you can, you can export the map using the button to the right of Texture Preview. This exported map can be edited further to clean up the mesh even more. The cleaned-up map can then be imported back into the Face Room.

FIGURE 9-11

Aligned face images

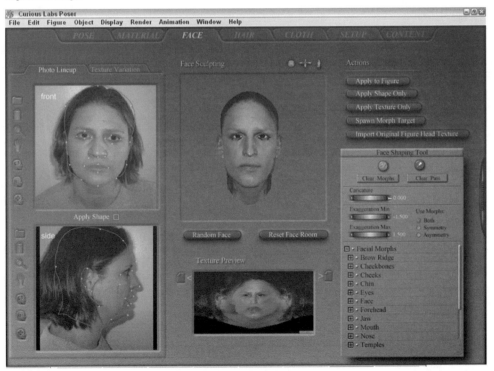

Create a Face from Photos

1. Open the Poser interface with the default figure visible.

2. Click the Face tab to access the Face Room.

3. Click the Load Image button to the left of the front pane in the Photo Lineup panel and select the Chris—front02.jpg file from the file dialog box. Click Open.

   A placement dialog box opens.

4. Click in the photo, as the placement dialog box instructs, on the corner of the right eye and at the corner of the left lips.

5. Click the Load Image button to the left of the side pane in the Photo Lineup panel and select the Chris – side01.jpg file from the file dialog box. Click Open.

6. Click in the photo, as the placement dialog box instructs, at the top of the ear and at the front of the chin.

   The placement dialog box closes automatically, and the photos appear in the Photo Lineup panel with red outlines on top of each.

7. Drag the Zoom Image tool in the front pane to show the details of the eyes and mouth photo up close.

8. Drag the Scale Geometry tool in the side pane until the outline roughly matches the image, and then select the Pan Geometry tool to align the outline with the photo.

9. Drag the green placement points in the front and side panes to align with the photos.

   The Preview pane shows the resulting face, as shown in Figure 9-12.

10. Click the Apply to Figure button, switch back to the Pose Room, select File, Save As, and save the file as **Custom photo face.pz3**.

FIGURE 9-12
Custom photo face

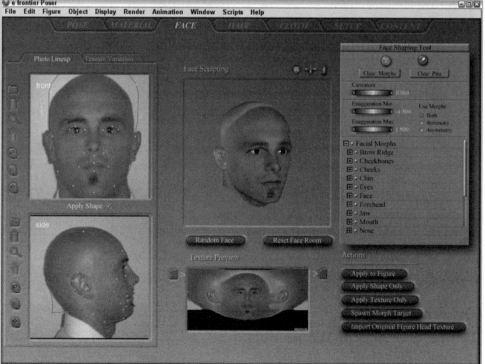

CHANGE
TEXTURE VARIATION

What You'll Do

In this lesson, you learn how to change the texture parameters for the face.

Clicking the Texture Variation tab next to the Photo Lineup tab opens a panel of options that you can use to change the texture for the current face. You can apply these texture variations to both custom loaded photos or to the default face textures. The changes are immediately visible in the Face Sculpting and Texture Preview panes.

Changing Facial Color

The Facial Color options can lighten or darken the beard, eye sockets, or upper and lower eyebrows. Positive values will darken and negative values will lighten the selected areas. Figure 9-13 shows the default face with a darkened beard and eyebrows and lightened eye sockets.

Changing Ethnicity

Within the Ethnicity, Age, and Gender options are the Ethnicity options. You can use these parameters to make the face more or less African, European, South East Asian, and East Indian. Each of these options will change the skin color in a different manner and add highlights about the face. Figure 9-14 shows the East Indian option. Notice the darker highlights about the eyebrows.

FIGURE 9-13

Darkened and lightened face features

FIGURE 9-14

Altered ethnicity

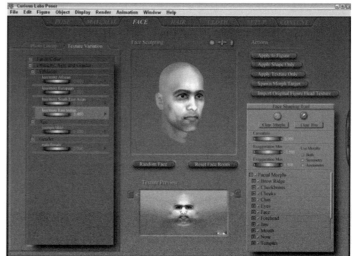

Changing Age

The Age parameter changes the highlighting on the face to display wrinkles and lighting to make the face appear younger or older. Figure 9-15 shows a face that has been aged.

Changing Gender

The final face texture option enables you to change the current face from male to female and vice versa. Female features have redder lips and lighter skin tones, whereas male faces feature darker skin tones and darker highlights around the beard and brows. Figure 9-16 shows the female features.

Randomizing the Face Map

Beneath the Face Sculpting pane is a button that you can use to randomize the face. This is accomplished by changing the values in the Texture Variation panel, but it doesn't change the shape of the 3D head model at all.

FIGURE 9-15

Aged face

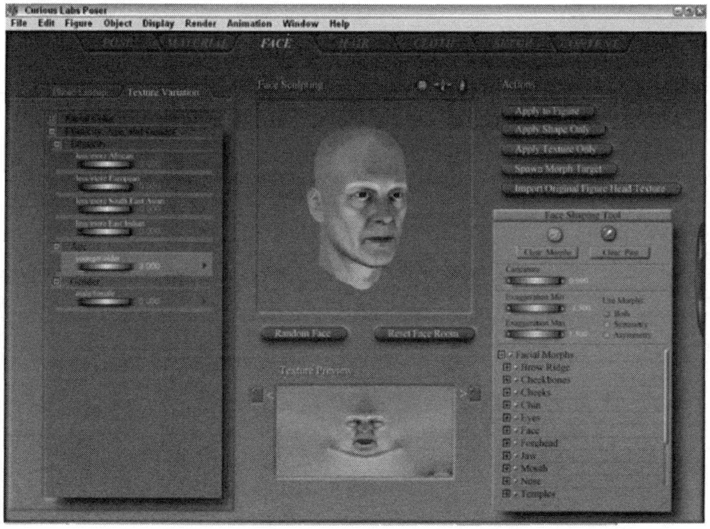

FIGURE 9-16

Female face features

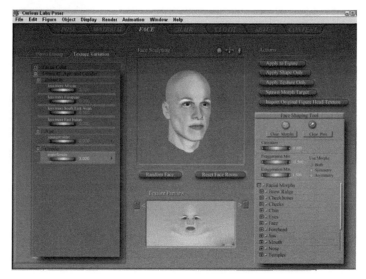

Add Texture Variation

1. Open the Poser interface with the default figure visible.

2. Click the Face tab to access the Face Room.

3. Click the Texture Variation tab to open the Texture Variation panel.

4. Open the Facial Color set of parameters and set the Beard parameter to 3.0.

5. Open the Ethnicity, Age, and Gender set of parameters and set the Less/More African parameter to 1.0 and the Age parameter to 0.5.

   The face texture is updated in the other Face Room panes, as shown in Figure 9-17.

6. Click the Apply to Figure button, switch back to the Pose Room, select File, Save As, and save the file as **Texture variation.pz3**.

FIGURE 9-17

Face texture variation

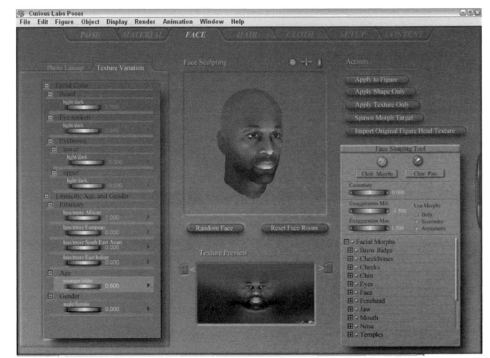

USE THE FACE
SHAPING TOOL

What You'll Do

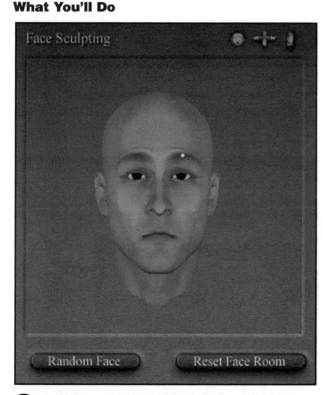

In this lesson, you learn how to use the Face Shaping tool
and parameters to distort the face's shape.

The various options found in the Texture Variation
panel change the look of the face by changing only
the texture of the face, but you can change the face
also by modifying the shape of the head model. This
is accomplished using the Face Shaping tool and
the Face Sculpting pane.

Using the Putty Tool

The Putty tool is selected by default in the Face
Shaping Tool panel. It allows you to sculpt the current face by dragging in the Face Sculpting pane.
When you first click the face, the vertex closest to
where you click is selected and appears as a green
dot. With a single vertex selected, you can drag the
vertex to a new location. When dragging a vertex,
its movement is made based on the current camera
view. You can use the camera tools in the upper-
right corner of the Face Sculpting pane to rotate,
pan, and zoom the face camera. If you make a mistake, you can remove all modifications using the
Clear Morphs button.

Pinning Vertices

As you drag a single vertex with the Putty tool, adjacent vertices and body parts are moved along with the vertex. For example, dragging a vertex in the forehead region also moves the eyebrows. If you want to keep a specific set of vertices positioned relative to each other, you can use the **Pin tool** to click the vertices that you want to remain in position. Pinned vertices are displayed as red dots, as shown in Figure 9-18. The Clear Pins button will remove all current pins.

Setting Exaggeration Limits

If you want to set a limit on how far face vertices can be deformed, you can use the Exaggeration Min and Exaggeration Max parameters to set limits to the face deformation. If you try to move a face feature that has reached its boundary, the deformation will still stop.

| **QUICKTIP** A good place to use Exaggeration limits is to prevent the face from collapsing in on itself.

Using the Caricature Parameter

The Caricature parameter emphasizes any existing deformation to a greater extent.

This is helpful for creating cartoon-like faces. Negative values can be used to de-emphasize a particular feature. Figure 9-19 shows a figure with an over-emphasized nose and chin that was created by increasing the Caricature value.

Making Symmetrical Deformations

To the right of the Exaggeration parameters are options for using morphs. When the **Symmetry** option is selected, all deformations applied to one half of the face are mirrored on the other half, but when the **Asymmetry** option is selected, you can change one side of the face from the other.

FIGURE 9-18
Pinned vertices

Pinned vertices

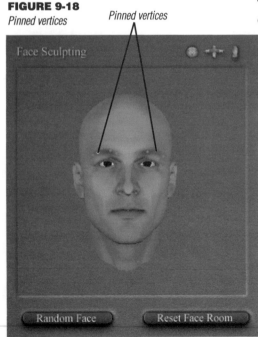

FIGURE 9-19
Caricature emphasized face

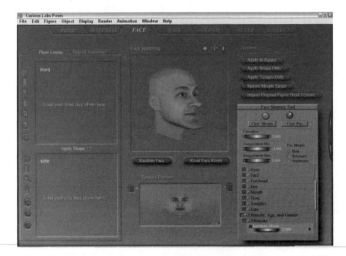

Altering Face Parameters

At the bottom of the Face Shaping Tool panel are many parameters divided into categories that you can use in conjunction with the Putty tool to deform the face shape. Each category includes several parameters, and changing these parameters provides a more focused way to deform the facial features. The available face categories and their parameters are listed in Table 9-1.

Table 9-1: Face Parameters

Category	Parameters
Brow Ridge	High/Low, Inner-Up/Down, Outer-Up/Down, Forward Axis Twist
Cheekbones	High/Low, Shallow/Pronounced, Thin/Wide, Protrusion Asymmetry
Cheeks	Concave/Convex, Round/Gaunt
Chin	Forward/Backward, Pronounced/Recessed, Retracted/Jutting, Shallow/Deep, Small/Large, Short/Tall, Thin/Wide, Chin Axis Twist, Forward Axis Twist, Transverse Shift
Eyes	Up/Down, Small/Large, Tilt Inward/Outward, Together/Apart, Height Disparity, Transverse Shift
Face	Brow-Nose-Chin Ratio, Forehead-Sellion-Nose Ratio, Light/Heavy, Round/Gaunt, Thin/Wide, Coronal Bend, Coronal Shear, Vertical Axis Twist
Forehead	Small/Large, Short/Tall, Tilt Forward/Back, Forward Axis Twist
Jaw	Retracted/Jutting, Wide/Thin, Jaw-Neck Slope High/Low, Concave/Convex
Mouth	Drawn/Pursed, Happy/Sad, High/Low, Protruding/Retracted, Tilt Up/Down, Underbite/Overbite, Mouth-Chin Distance Short/Long, Corners Transverse Shift, Forward Axis Twist, Transverse Shift, Twist and Shift
Mouth, Lips	Deflated/Inflated, Large/Small, Puckered/Retracted
Nose	Up/Down, Flat/Pointed, Short/Long, Tilt Up/Down, Frontal Axis Twist, Tip Transverse Shift, Transverse Shift, Vertical Axis Twist
Nose, Bridge	Shallow/Deep, Short/Long, Transverse Shift
Nose, Nostrils	Tilt Up/Down, Small/Large, Thin/Wide, Frontal Axis Twist, Transverse Shift
Nose, Sellion	Up/Down, Shallow/Deep, Thin/Wide, Transverse Shift
Temples	Thin/Wide
Ears	Up/Down, Back/Front, Short/Long, Thin/Wide, Vertical Shear, Forward Axis Shear
Ethnicity	Less/More African, Less/More European, Less/More South East Asian, Less/More East Indian
Age	Younger/Older
Gender	Male/Female

Use the Face Shaping Tool

1. Open the Poser interface with the default figure visible.
2. Click the Face tab to access the Face Room.
3. Drag on the Rotate control in the upper-right corner of the Face Sculpting pane until the front of the default face is visible.
4. With the Putty tool ⚙ selected, drag upward on the left eyebrow.

   Both eyebrows are moved upward together.
5. In the Face Shaping Tool panel, expand the Mouth category and set the Happy/Sad parameter to 2.0.

   The face is altered to show whimpering, as shown in Figure 9-21.
6. Click the Apply to Figure button, switch back to the Pose Room, select File, Save As and save the file as **Whimper face.pz3**.

Locking Face Parameters

To the immediate left of each parameter title is a small green dot. Clicking this green dot changes it to a lock icon, as shown in Figure 9-20. This lock icon locks the given parameter so it cannot be changed with the Putty tool.

FIGURE 9-20
Locked parameter

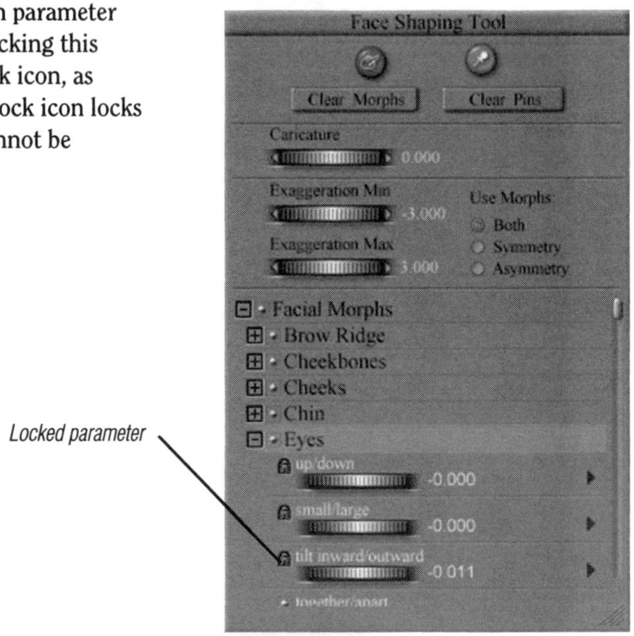

Locked parameter

FIGURE 9-21
Whimper face

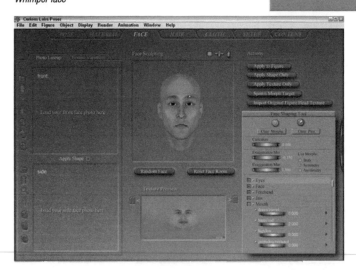

ADD THE FACE
TO THE FIGURE

What You'll Do

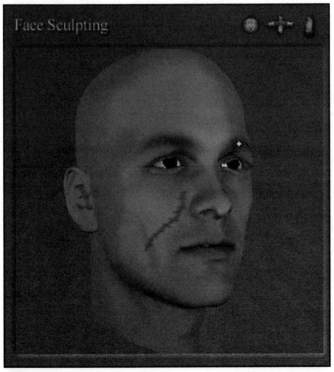

In this lesson, you learn how to apply the face to the current figure.

If you spent some time creating a perfect-looking face, you may be concerned to notice that the File, Save menu command is disabled from the Face Room, but no need to worry. To save the face (no pun intended) and the Face Room settings, you need to switch back to the Pose Room and save the current file. If you open the scene again after saving, all the Face Room settings are recalled as they were regardless of whether the face was applied to the figure or not.

CAUTION Head objects found in the Face Room are designed to fit with the figures for Poser 5, 6, and 7, but if the Face Room head is applied to other figures, they will not fit correctly.

Applying a Face to the Current Figure

To apply the current face texture and shape to the current figure, simply click the Apply to Figure button. This replaces the existing head element with the one defined in the Face Room. The Apply Shape Only button places only the new head shape onto the figure without the face texture, and the Apply Texture Only button causes only the defined texture to be placed on the current figure head, without any shape changes.

| **CAUTION** After you click the Apply to Figure or the Apply Shape Only buttons, a warning dialog box will appear stating that applying a modified head shape to an older figure model may result in unmatched polygons around the neck.

Importing the Original Figure Texture Face Map

If you want to import the existing face texture from the current figure into the Face Room, click the Import Original Figure Head Texture button. This loads the texture used by the existing figure into the Face Room, as shown in Figure 9-22.

FIGURE 9-22

Imported face texture

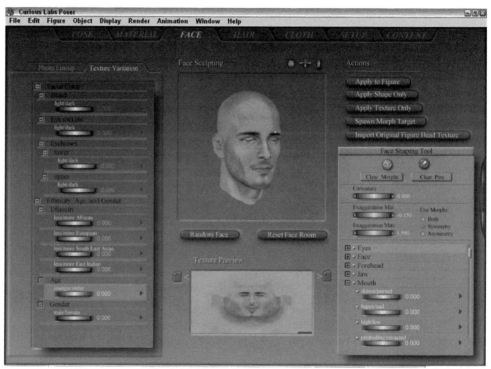

Loading and Saving Texture Maps

On either side of the Texture Preview pane are small buttons that you can use to load (the one on the left) and save (the one on the right) the existing texture map. Both of these buttons open a file dialog box where you can select the file to open or save a new file. Saved texture maps are saved to a 512 X 512–pixel image using the image format that you select. The saved texture map can then be loaded within an image-editing package such as Photoshop to be edited and reloaded into Poser.

Figure 9-23 shows the default face texture map loaded within Photoshop.

CAUTION Although you can save texture maps in Photoshop's .PSD file format, you cannot load them back into Poser using this format.

FIGURE 9-23
Texture map loaded in Photoshop

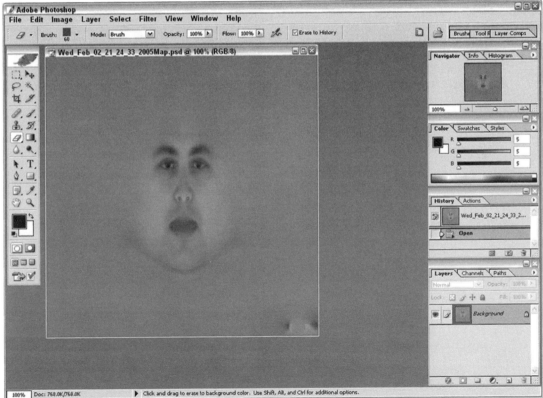

Synching Face and Body Color

When a face with a different skin color is applied to a figure, a warning dialog box appears identifying that the face and body skin colors are different and asks if you want to synchronize the two. Clicking Yes will change the body skin color to match the face.

Save, Edit, and Load a Face Texture Map

1. Open the Poser interface with the default figure visible.

2. Click the Face tab to access the Face Room.

3. Click the Save Texture button 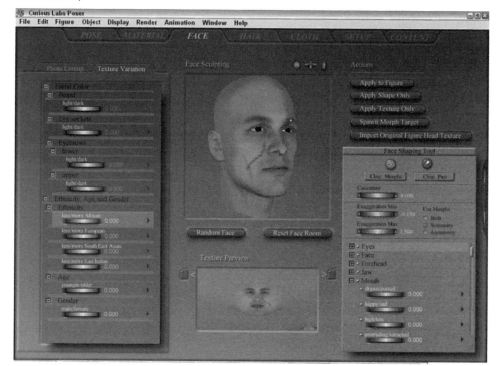 to the right of the Texture Preview pane. In the Save As dialog box, choose the .PSD file format and click Save.

4. Locate the saved texture file and open it in Photoshop.

5. Within Photoshop, edit the texture image by adding a scar to the image with the Paint Brush tool. Then save the texture file as **Texture map with scar.jpg**.

6. Back within Poser, click the Load Texture button to the left of the Texture Preview pane in the Face Room. Then locate and load the saved file.

The face is updated with the edited texture map, as shown in Figure 9-24.

7. Click the Apply to Figure button, switch back to the Pose Room, select File, Save As, and save the file as **Face with scar.pz3**.

FIGURE 9-24

Edited texture map

WORK WITH
EXPRESSIONS

What You'll Do

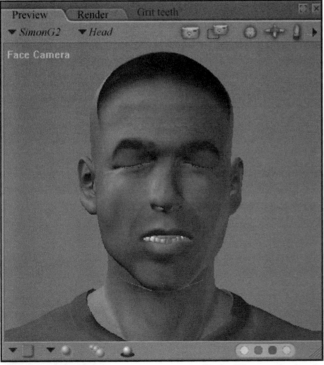

In this lesson, you learn how to work with the Library to load and save expressions.

Before leaving this chapter, you need to look closely at the thumbnails located within the Expressions category of the Library. These expressions give the character a different facial look and are different from the faces created in the Face Room. You can also make facial expressions automatically using the Talk Designer, which is covered in Chapter 15, "Lip Synching with Talk Designer."

Loading Expressions from the Library

To access the available expressions from the Library, click the Expression category and navigate to the folder containing the types of expressions you want to apply to the current figure. Within each folder are thumbnails of the various expressions. With an expression thumbnail selected, click the Change Expression button at the bottom of the Library palette. The selected expression is loaded onto the figure.

Creating a Custom Expression

When the head element is selected, the Parameters/Properties palette includes all the parameters for creating a custom expression. The available parameters for the head element for creating expressions include those listed in Table 9-2.

Table 9-2: Head Parameters

Category	Parameters
Brow	Brow Up All, Brow Up Left, Brow Up Right, Brow Up Center, Brow Furrow, Scowl, Scowl Left, Scowl Right
Eyes	Look Up, Look Down, Blink, Blink Left, Blink Right, Eyes Dilate, Eyes Up-Down, Eyes Side-Side, Eyes Smile, Eyes Wide, Eyes Worry, Wince, Lower Eye Lid Up
Nose	Nostril Flare, Nose Wrinkle
Jaw	Jaw Shift Left, Jaw Shift Right, Mouth Open
Lips	Smile, Smile Full, Smile Grin, Smile Left, Smile Right, Smile Thin, Smile Teeth, Smile Small, Snarl, Snarl Left, Snarl Right, Lip orner Depressors, Lip Lower Depressor, Lip Upper Raiser, Lip Stretch, Lip Stretch Left, Lip Stretch Right, Pucker
Tongue	Tongue Out, Tongue Roll, Tongue Tip Up-Down, Tongue Curl Up-Down
Phonemes	Mouth A, Mouth CH, Mouth E, Mouth F, Mouth TH, Mouth O, Mouth M, Mouth P, Mouth R, Mouth U, Mouth W, Tongue L,

NEW POSER 7 FEATURE The default Poser 7 figure includes several additional face morph targets.

FIGURE 9-25
Random expression loaded from the Library

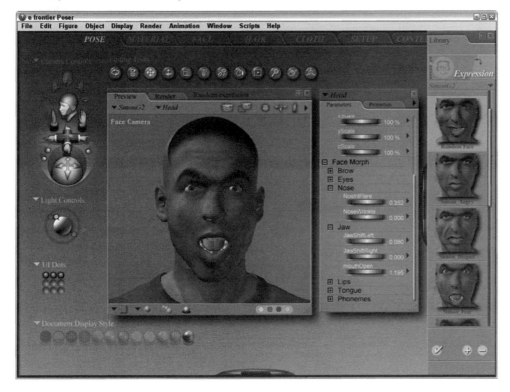

1. Open Poser with the default man visible.

2. Select the Face Camera from the Camera Controls.

3. Click the side control to the right of the interface to open the Library palette or select Window, Libraries.

4. Click the Expression category at the top of the Library palette and navigate to the James folder.

5. Select the Random Face thumbnail and click the Replace Expression button at the bottom of the Library palette.

   The expression you see will likely vary from the figure. A new expression is generated every time the Random Face expression is applied. The selected expression is loaded into the Shader Window, as shown in Figure 9-25.

6. Select File, Save As and save the file as **Random expression.pz3**.

Save a Material to the Library

1. Open Poser with the default man visible.

2. Select the Face Camera from the Camera Controls.

3. Select the head element in the Document Window and select Window, Parameter Dials to open the Parameters/Properties palette (if necessary).

4. Expand the Eyes category in the Parameters palette and set the Blink parameter to 1.0. Then expand the Phonemes category and set the Mouth A parameter to 0.5.

   The new expression is shown in Figure 9-26.

5. Select File, Save As and save the file as **Grit teeth.pz3**.

FIGURE 9-26

New expression

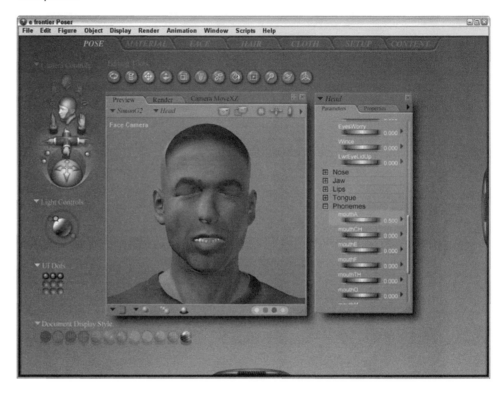

CHAPTER REVIEW

Chapter Summary

This chapter covers all the features found in the Face Room, including the capability to create a face from loaded images. Using the parameters found in the Texture Variation panel, you can change the texture for the current face or using the Face Shaping tool, and you can deform the geometry of the actual head model. You can then apply the resulting face directly to the figure. This chapter also covered facial expressions that are possible using the Face Morph values available in the Parameters palette.

What You Have Learned

In this chapter, you:

- Discovered the layout of the Face Room interface, including the Face Shaping Tool panel.
- Loaded and positioned front and side face images to create a custom face.
- Changed the texture parameters, including facial color, ethnicity, age, and gender.
- Interactively deformed the face model using the Putty and Pin tools.

- Changed the face shape using the parameters found in the Face Shaping Tool panel.
- Applied the finished face to the current figure.
- Saved and loaded texture maps for editing in an external image-editing package.
- Loaded expressions from the Library and saved expressions back to the Library.
- Saved and loaded texture maps for editing in an external image-editing package.

Key Terms from This Chapter

- **Caricature.** A silly drawing of a face that overemphasizes a person's prominent features such as a large nose, big ears, or a small mouth.
- **Ethnicity.** The facial features that are inherent to a unique ethnic group, such as African-Americans, Europeans, and Asians.
- **Expression.** When the face features are saved in a unique position to show different emotions.

- **Face shape.** The underlying 3D geometry that the texture is mapped on in order to create the face.
- **Face texture map.** An image that is wrapped about the head model to show details.
- **Phonemes.** Facial expressions that occur when different speaking sounds are made.
- **Pin tool.** A tool used to prevent vertices from moving out of position.
- **Putty tool.** A tool used to sculpt the shape of a face.
- **Sellion.** That part of the nose that extends from its tip up between the eyes.
- **Symmetry.** A property of faces that makes all features on one side of the face the same as features on the opposite side.
- **Temples.** The portion of the face that lies between the ears and the eyes.

chapter 10
ADDING HAIR

1. Learn the Hair Room interface.

2. Grow hair.

3. Style hair.

4. Use hair dynamics.

5. Change hair material.

chapter 10 ADDING HAIR

Unless you're partial to bald heads, nothing can add more to the details of your figure than a nice head of hair. However, a bad hairstyle can detract quite a bit from your figure. Another tricky part of working with hair is that it can add significantly to the complexity of your scene, which increases file size and update and render times; but the power made possible by the Poser Hair Room is definitely worth it.

Poser offers two ways to add hair to your figures. The first is using prop-based hair that can be loaded from the Library. This hair is loaded as a prop and is designed to fit perfectly on certain figures. Prop hair can be moved and positioned just like other props in the scene. Some prop hair can be conformed to the figure. The second method for adding hair deals with strand-based hair and can only be manipulated in the Hair Room.

The Hair Room includes a robust interface for adding hair to your figures, allowing you to add hair anywhere to the figure using a hair group and selected using the Group Editor. Once a hair group is defined, you can grow **guide hairs**, which are sim-

ply a representation of the full set of hair. With guide hairs in place, you can control their length and relative position.

Poser's styling tools let you control hair parameters, such as **hair density**, root and tip width, **clumpiness**, and **kinkiness**. In addition to these parameters, the **Hair Style Tool** panel includes tools for selecting individual hairs or groups of hair and interactively applying transformations, curls, and twisting.

You can also define dynamic parameters that are used to compute the position and motion of hairs through all animated frames. These dynamic parameters include gravity, **springiness**, and **stiffness**, and can even include collision detection. In addition to gravity, you can add wind force to the simulation using the Wind Force deformer to blow the hair about.

Finally, you can use the Material Room to change the material values used to shade the hair. By manipulating these values, you can change the hair's color, softness, and highlights.

Tools You'll Use

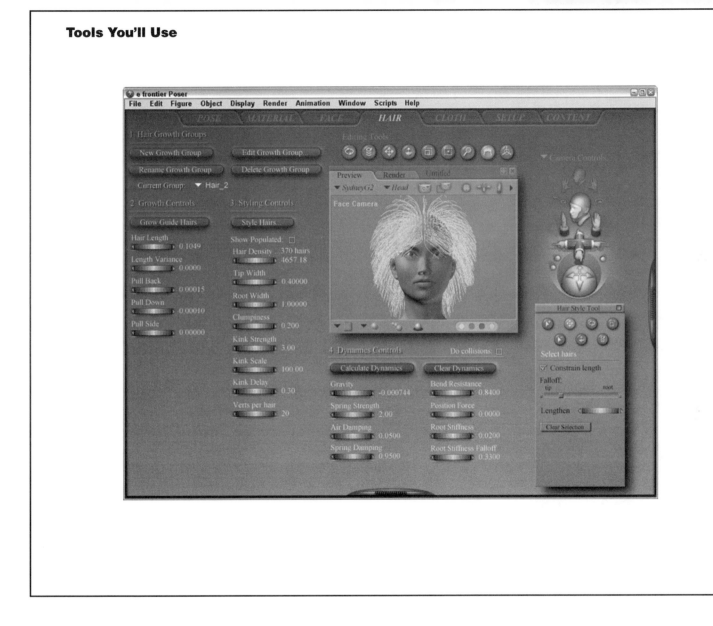

LEARN THE
HAIR ROOM INTERFACE

What You'll Do

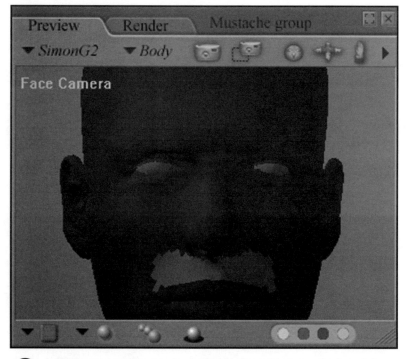

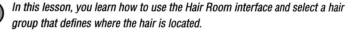

In this lesson, you learn how to use the Hair Room interface and select a hair group that defines where the hair is located.

You open the Hair Room by clicking the Hair tab at the top of the Poser interface. This opens an interface setup that is different from the Pose Room, as shown in Figure 10-1, although it includes all of the same controls as the Pose Room, including the Document Window, the Camera and Light controls, and the Display Styles and Editing Tools button sets. The Hair Room interface also includes four additional sets of buttons that are used to group, create, style, and move hair.

Using the Hair Controls

When the Hair Room is first opened, only the New Growth Group button in the **Hair Growth Groups** set of controls is enabled. Before you can set any hair properties, you must create a hair growth group. This allows you to select, name, and create several different areas where hair is located. Once you create a hair growth group, the parameters in the Hair Growth controls become active. The remaining two sets of parameters—the Styling Controls and Dynamics Controls—only become active once you click the Grow Guide Hairs button.

Accessing the Hair Style Tool

Within the Editing Tools is a special tool that is only available within the Hair Room.

The Hair Style tool opens a panel, shown in Figure 10-2, where you can style individual selections of hair. Each of the tools available on the Hair Style Tool panel is explained in the Hair Styling lesson to follow.

FIGURE 10-1
Hair Room interface

FIGURE 10-2
Hair Style Tool panel

Specifying Hair Location

The first step in adding hair to a figure is to select the figure polygons where the hair will be located. Each separate occurrence of hair is grouped and named. You create groups using the Group Editor.

Creating a Hair Growth Group

You use the four buttons located in the Hair Growth Groups controls to create and manage separate groups of hair. To create a hair growth group, click the New Growth Group button. This opens a simple dialog box where you can give the growth group a name. The default name is *Hair* followed by a sequential number. Each new growth group is added to the Current Group list where you can select the current group. You can rename the current growth group by clicking the Rename Growth Group button. This makes the same naming dialog box appear.

Selecting a Hair Growth Group

You can add new polygons to the group by clicking polygons or dragging an outline over the polygons to select in the Document Window with the Select Polygons tool. All polygons that are selected with the

Select Polygons tool are highlighted in red. You can remove polygons from the current group with the Deselect Polygons tool. The Add All button adds all polygons that belong to the body part listed in the Actor List at the top of the Document Window, and the Remove All button removes all polygons. The Invert button inverts the selection for the current body part.

> **QUICKTIP** Holding down the Ctrl/Command key with the Select Polygons tool selected lets you remove polygons from the selection and vice versa.

Deleting Hair Growth Groups

You can delete the current hair growth group by clicking the Delete Growth Group button. This button causes a confirmation dialog box to appear asking if you are sure that you want to delete the current growth group.

Editing Hair Growth Groups

If you click the Edit Growth Group button, the Group Editor, shown in Figure 10-3, opens with the current growth group listed as the current group. When the Group Editor is opened, the figure appears dark gray.

FIGURE 10-3
Group Editor

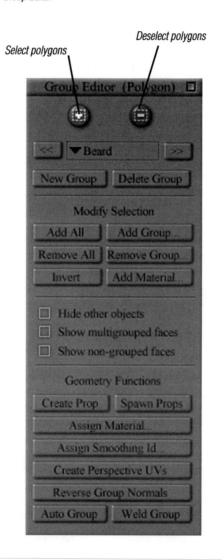

Select polygons

Deselect polygons

FIGURE 10-4

Mustache group

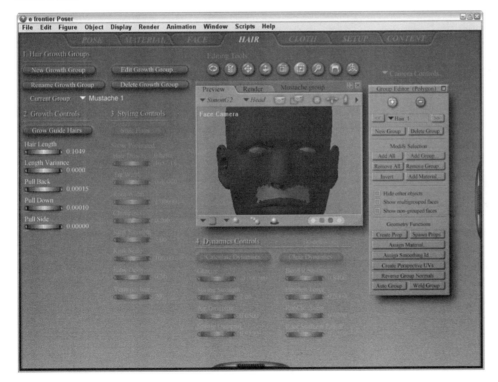

1. Open Poser with the default man visible.

2. Click the Hair tab at the top of the interface to open the Hair Room.

3. Select the Head element in the Document Window, and then click the New Growth Group button and name the new group **Mustache**. Click OK.

   The new growth group name appears in the Current Group list.

4. Select the Face Camera 🗿 from the Camera tools to zoom in on the face in the Document Window.

5. Click the Edit Growth Group button to open the Group Editor panel.

6. Select the Head element from the Actor List at the top of the Document Window.

7. With the Select Polygons tool 🗿 selected in the Group Editor panel, drag over the polygons between the nose and mouth in the Document Window.

   The selected polygons are highlighted in red, as shown in Figure 10-4.

8. Select File, Save As and save the file as **Mustache group.pz3**.

GROW
HAIR

What You'll Do

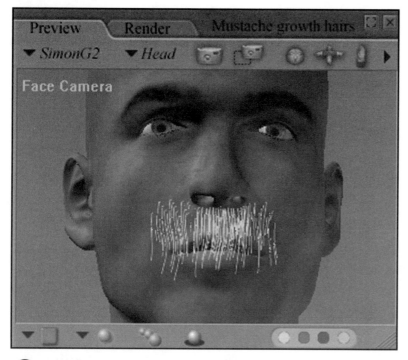

 In this lesson, you learn how to grow guide hairs and set the hair's length and initial position.

After you define a hair growth group, the buttons in the Growth Controls become active. These buttons let you grow guide hairs and define the hair's initial parameters.

Growing Guide Hairs

Clicking the Grow Guide Hairs button will add hairs to the selected hair group and these hairs become visible in the Document Window, as shown in Figure 10-5. Don't be alarmed if the new hairs stick straight out or if they appear to be too thin; you can relax and thicken them during the styling phase.

Setting Hair Length

Once the guide hairs are visible (or even before they are visible), you can change their length using the Hair Length parameter. If you change the Hair Length parameter after the guide hairs have been created, the hairs displayed in the Document Window will change as the parameter is changed.

Setting Hair Variance

The Length Variance parameter changes the range of different hair lengths that are possible. Setting this value to 0.0 results in a hairstyle where every hair strand is equal in length. Increasing this value causes the hair to become more wild, messy, and shaggy, as shown in Figure 10-6.

FIGURE 10-5
Guide hairs

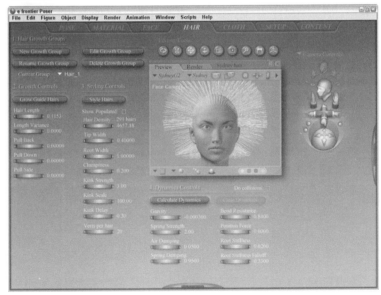

FIGURE 10-6
Messy hair

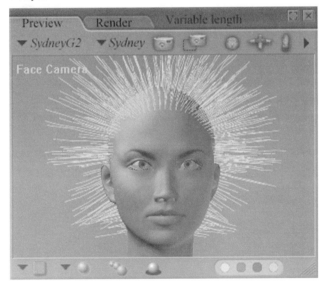

Moving Hair

Although most of the hair movement is accomplished during the styling phase, you can use the Pull Back, Pull Down, and Pull Side parameters to move all the hairs a given direction. You can set these parameters to positive and negative values. The Pull Back parameter can move hairs towards the back of the head, as shown in Figure 10-7, or forward with a negative value.

The Pull Down parameter can move the hairs vertically straight up with a negative value, as shown in Figure 10-8, or straight down with a positive value.

FIGURE 10-7
Hair pulled back

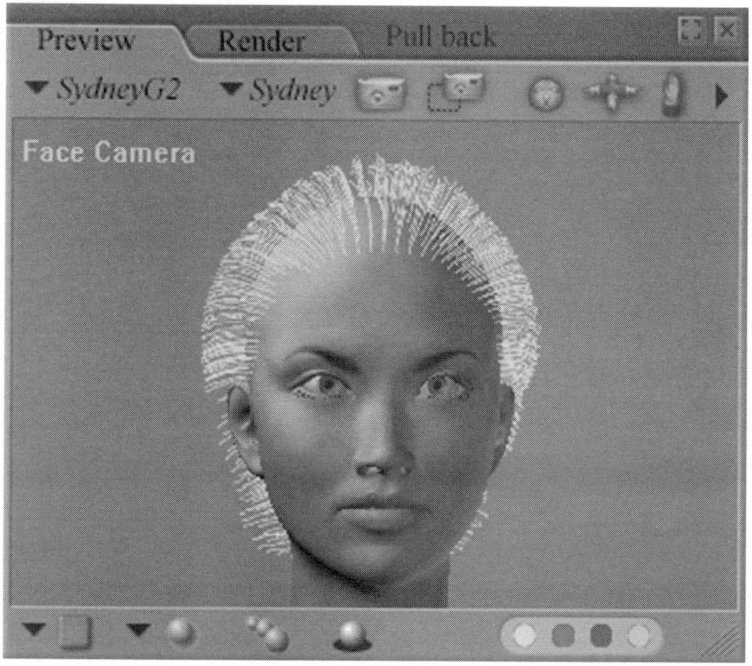

FIGURE 10-8
Hair straight up

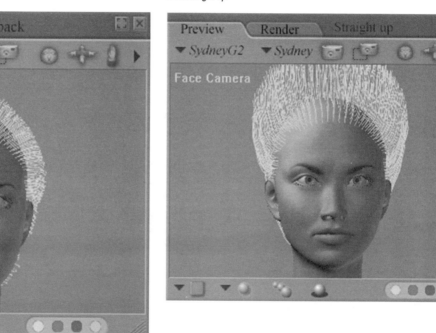

The Pull Side parameter will move the hairs to the figure's left with a negative value and to the figure's right with a positive value, as shown in Figure 10-9.

QUICKTIP The parameters in the Growth Controls section provide an effective way to accomplish major hair styling. The Styling Controls can then be used for minor improvements.

Using Hair on Props

Hair groups aren't limited to only figure elements; you can also create and add hair to prop objects. Figure 10-10 shows a hair growth group added to the chair prop.

FIGURE 10-9
Hair pulled to the side

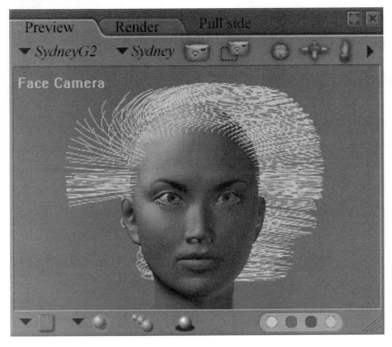

FIGURE 10-10
Hair applied to a prop

Create Guide Hairs

1. Select File, Open and open the Mustache group.pz3 file.

2. Click the Hair tab at the top of the interface to open the Hair Room.

3. Click the Head element in the Document Window and select the Mustache group from the Current Group controls.

4. Click the Grow Guide Hairs button.

   Several long hairs are displayed for the mustache group in the Document Window.

5. Set the Hair Length parameter to 0.0183, the Length Variance, Pull Back, and Pull Side parameters to 0.0, and the Pull Down parameter to 0.0015.

6. Select the Texture Shaded button in the Display Style controls.

   The short guide hairs are displayed in the Document Window, as shown in Figure 10-11.

7. Select File, Save As and save the file as **Mustache guide hairs.pz3**.

FIGURE 10-11
Mustache guide hairs

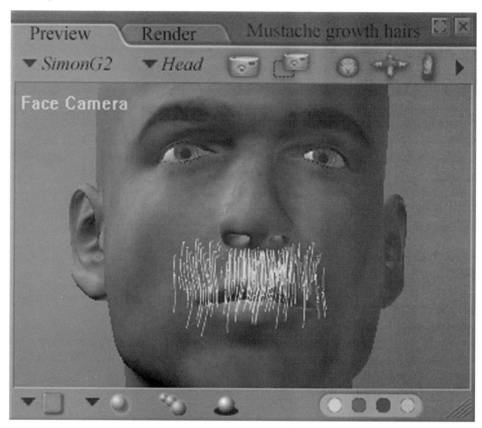

STYLE HAIR

What You'll Do

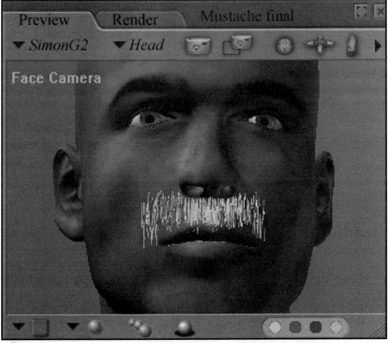

In this lesson, you learn how to style hair using parameters and the Hair Style Tool panel.

Once you add the guide hairs to the hair growth group, you can style them collectively using the parameters found in the Styling Controls. For further modification, you can use the Hair Style tool to select and individually style and change single hairs or groups of hair.

Setting Hair Density

At the top of the Styling Controls is a Show Populated option. When this option is enabled, all designated hairs are shown in the Document Window, but when this option is disabled, only a sampling of the total number of hairs are displayed. If the hairstyle includes a large number of hairs, updating the Document Window may take some time. This option offers a way to speed up the refresh rate of the Document Window. The total number of hairs is displayed directly beneath the Show Populated option. You can change the total number of hairs using the Hair Density parameter. Figure 10-12 shows a figure with a full head of hair.

CAUTION Adding hairs to a figure will greatly increase its total size and will also increase the time needed to render the scene.

FIGURE 10-12
Dense hair

Using Hairstyle Parameters

Beneath the Hair Density parameter are several additional style parameters. These parameters are applied to all hairs within the current hair group, and you can use them to customize the look of the hair. The additional hairstyle parameters include the following:

- **Tip Width:** Defines the width of the hair at its tip.

- **Root Width:** Defines the width of the hair at its root. For normal hair, the Root Width value is typically greater than the Tip Width value. Hairs with equal Root and Tip Width values are more coarse and stringy.

- **Clumpiness:** Causes hair strands to group together into clumps like dreadlocks. You can set this to a negative value to make hair more feather-like.

- **Kink Strength:** Defines how wavy and curly the hair is. Figure 10-13 shows some hair with a fairly high Kink Strength value.

- **Kink Scale:** Defines the size of the wave and curl applied to the hair. This value can range between 1 and 1000.

> **QUICKTIP** If you increase the Kink Strength value and nothing happens, check to make sure that the Kink Scale value isn't set to 0.

- **Kink Delay:** Defines the point along the hair length from the **hair root** where the wave and curl begins. This value can range from 0 for hair that curls at the root to 1.0 for hairs that curl at the tip. Figure 10-14 shows some hair with the Kink Scale and Kink Delay values set to their maximum values.

- **Verts Per Hair:** Defines the number of vertices used to represent each strand of hair. This value can range from 4 for straight hairs to 100 for smooth hair. The default of 20 is enough for most hairstyles.

> **CAUTION** Increasing this value above the default of 20 can increase the render time significantly.

FIGURE 10-13
Kinky hair

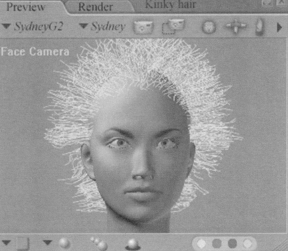

FIGURE 10-14
Curls at hair tips

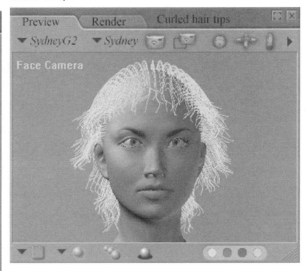

Using the Hair Style Tool

You can open the Hair Style Tool panel, shown in Figure 10-15, by clicking the Style Hairs button in the Styling Controls or by selecting the Hair Style tool from the Editing Tools. When the Hair Style Tool panel first opens, only the Select Hairs button is enabled.

Selecting Hairs

With the Select Hairs tool selected, you can select a single hair or a group of hairs in the Document Window by clicking them or by dragging an outline around the hairs that you want to select. A single vertex at the end of each selected hair is highlighted when the hair is selected. Once some hairs are selected, the other tools in the Hair Style Tool panel become available. You can deselect hairs using the Deselect Hairs tool, or you can drop the entire selection by clicking the Clear Selection button.

QUICKTIP Holding down the Ctrl/Command key with the Select Hair tool selected lets you remove hairs from the selection, whereas holding down the Ctrl/Command key with the Deselect Hair tool selected lets you add hairs to the selection.

Styling Selected Hairs

The various styling tools included in the Hair Style Tool panel let you translate, rotate, scale, and twist the selected hairs. The direction of the hair movement depends on the current camera. The Constrain Length option causes all selected hairs to remain the same length, and the Falloff setting controls whether the tool's effect is applied to the root, tip, or somewhere in between. The Lengthen parameter dial can lengthen or shorten the selected hairs. Figure 10-16 shows a female figure with some curls added to the tips of the hair with the Rotate tool.

FIGURE 10-15
Hair Style Tool panel

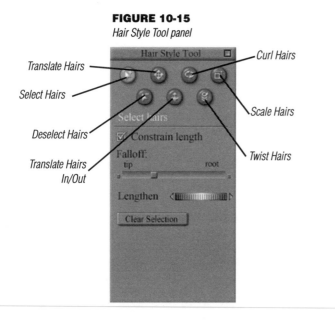

Translate Hairs
Select Hairs
Deselect Hairs
Translate Hairs In/Out
Curl Hairs
Scale Hairs
Twist Hairs

FIGURE 10-16
Curled hair

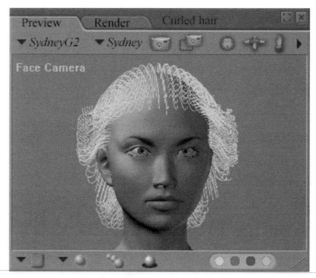

FIGURE 10-17

Mustache final

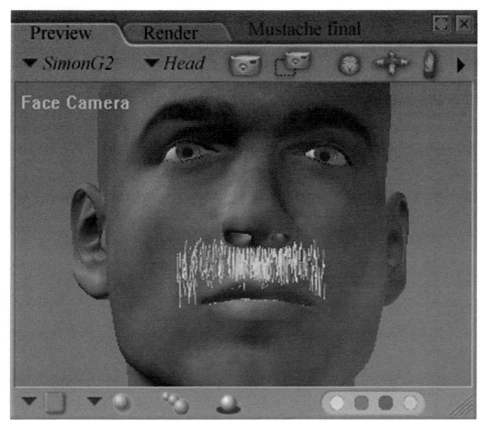

1. Select File, Open and open the Mustache guide hairs.pz3 file.

2. Click the Hair tab at the top of the interface to open the Hair Room.

3. Click the Head element in the Document Window and select the Mustache group from the Current Group controls.

4. In the Styling Controls, enable the Show Populated option.

   Many additional hairs are displayed for the mustache group in the Document Window.

5. Click the Hair Density parameter and set it to 100. Set the Clumpiness to 0.0, the Kink Strength to 2.0, the Kink Scale to 100, and the Kink Delay to 0.5.

6. Click the Style Hairs button and drag over the hairs that cover the lips to select them. Then disable the Constrain Length option and drag the Length parameter dial to the left to shorten the selected hairs.

   The mustache hairs in the Document Window are clearly visible, as shown in Figure 10-17.

7. Select File, Save As and save the file as **Mustache final.pz3**.

Use the Hair Style Tool

1. Open Poser with the default man visible.

2. Click the Hair tab at the top of the interface to open the Hair Room.

3. Select the Head element in the Document Window, then click the New Growth Group button and name the new group **Hair_1**. Click OK.

4. Select the Face Camera from the Camera Controls to zoom in on the face in the Document Window.

5. Click the Edit Growth Group button to open the Group Editor panel.

6. Drag over the top half of the skull in the Document Window with the Select Polygons tool. Then, drag on the rotate sphere in the Camera Controls to make the side of the head visible and drag over the side of the head above the ear. Repeat for the back and opposite side of the head until the entire area where hair belongs on the head is selected. If you make a mistake, you can remove polygons with the Deselect Polygons tool.

7. Once the hair group is selected, close the Group Editor and click the Grow Guide Hairs button.

   Some sample guide hairs are displayed for the current hair group.

8. Set the Hair Length parameter to 0.2, the Pull Down parameter to .0002, and the Hair Density parameter to 2000. Enable the Show Populated option.

9. Click the Style Hairs button to open the Hair Style Tool panel.

10. Drag the rotate sphere in the Camera tools until the side of the head is visible. Drag over the hairs located at the back of the neck with the Select Hairs tool to select them.

    The vertices at the hair tips are displayed as yellow dots for the selected hairs.

11. Drag the Lengthen parameter dial to right in the Hair Style Tool panel to lengthen the hairs.

12. Drag the rotate sphere in the Camera Controls until the back of the head is visible. Select the Scale Hairs tool and drag in the Document Window to the left to pull the hairs at the back of the neck in towards the midline of the head.

13. Drag the rotate sphere in the Camera Controls until the front side of the head is visible again.

    The hairstyle is displayed in the Document Window, as shown in Figure 10-18.

14. Select File, Save As and save the file as **Mullet hair.pz3**.

FIGURE 10-18
Mullet hair

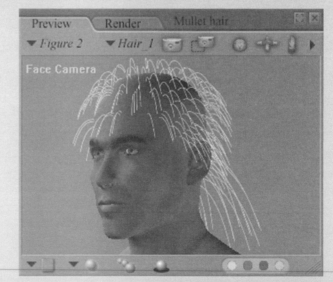

USE
HAIR DYNAMICS

What You'll Do

 In this lesson, you learn how to use hair dynamics.

In real life, hair doesn't just stick up in the air unless you use a lot of styling gel. Another way to position hair is to define the hair properties with the **Dynamics Controls** parameters and let the software calculate where the hair should fall for every animated frame using gravity, collisions, and **damping**.

Defining Hair's Dynamic Parameters

The dynamic parameters are used to define how the hair reacts to the motion of the body part to which it is attached. These parameters define how springy, stiff, and resistant to bending the hairs are. The available dynamic parameters for hair include

- Gravity: Defines the strength of the gravity force that acts on the hair. A negative Gravity value pulls hair towards the ground, and a positive value pushes it away from the ground.

- Spring Strength: Defines how springy hair reacts to motion. Hair with a high Spring Strength value will bounce in response to motion.

- Air Damping: Defines how resistant the hair is to the air. Hair with a low Air Damping value won't be affected by wind as much as hair with a higher Air Damping value.

- Spring Damping: Defines how quickly springy hair quits bouncing. Hair with high Spring Strength and low Spring Damping values will bounce longer than hair with a higher Spring Damping value.

- Bend Resistance: Defines the hair's ability to resist folding in on itself.

- Position Force: Causes hair to stay in its place and defy the hair dynamics.

This value, like hairspray, keeps each hair separated.

- Root Stiffness: Defines how stiff the hair is at its root and how quickly the hair roots move with the head.

- Root Stiffness Falloff: Defines how far the root stiffness carries up the length of the hair. A value of 0.0 causes the entire hair to maintain the same Root Stiffness value, and a value of 1.0 makes the hair less stiff immediately beyond the root.

> **NOTE** Some dynamic objects, such as wind, can add an additional force to the dynamics of hair. More on using these dynamic objects is covered in Chapter 14, "Morphing Figures and Using Deformers."

Enabling Collisions

The Do Collisions option in the Dynamics Controls enables collisions to be calculated as part of the dynamic simulation. This computes whether the hair collides with other polygons, such as props, ears, hands, and the like. Enabling collisions can add to the time required to compute the hair dynamics.

> **NOTE** If the Do Collisions option is enabled, the dynamic hair will take much longer to compute.

Calculating Dynamics

Once you set the dynamics parameters, you can click the Calculated Dynamics button. This computes the position and movement of each hair for every animation frame. A simple progress dialog box, shown in Figure 10-19, appears when the calculations are initiated. This dialog box includes a Cancel button that you can use to cancel the calculations at any time. The Clear Dynamics button removes all saved dynamics calculations.

FIGURE 10-19
Calculate Dynamics process dialog box

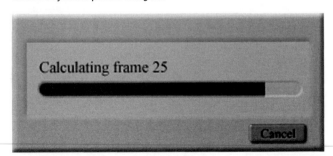

FIGURE 10-20

Dynamic hair

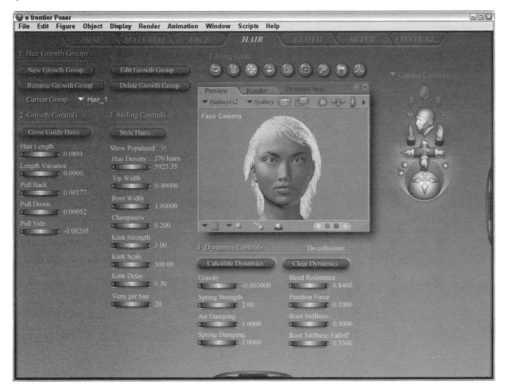

1. Select File, Open and open the Dense hair.pz3 file.

2. Click the Hair tab at the top of the interface to open the Hair Room.

3. Click the Head element in the Document Window and select the Hair_1 group from the Current Group controls.

4. In the Dynamics Controls, enable the Do Collisions option.

5. Click the Gravity parameter and set it to –0.003. Set the Spring Strength to 2.0 and the Air and Spring Damping to 1.0. Then set the Position Force and Root Stiffness to 0.1.

   Setting the Air and Spring Damping values to a high positive value will act to resist the effects of gravity on the hair, and the Spring Strength value will make the hair spring slightly as it reaches its top position. The Position Force and Root Stiffness values act together like hairspray to make the hair stay in its general position.

6. Click the Calculate Dynamics button.

   A progress dialog box appears and lists each frame as it is calculated. At the completion of the calculations, the resulting hair for the current frame is displayed, as shown in Figure 10-20.

7. Select File, Save As and save the file as **Dynamic hair.pz3**.

CHANGE
HAIR MATERIAL

What You'll Do

 In this lesson, you learn how to change the hair's material values.

Selecting the hair group in the Material Room lets you change the material used to shade the hair, including its root color, tip color, highlights, and root softness.

Viewing Hair Material

To view the material used to shade hair, open the Material Room and select the hair group from the Props menu in the Object List at the top of the Shader Window. This will make the hair material visible in the Advanced panel of the Shader Window, as shown in Figure 10-21.

FIGURE 10-21

Hair material in the Shader Window

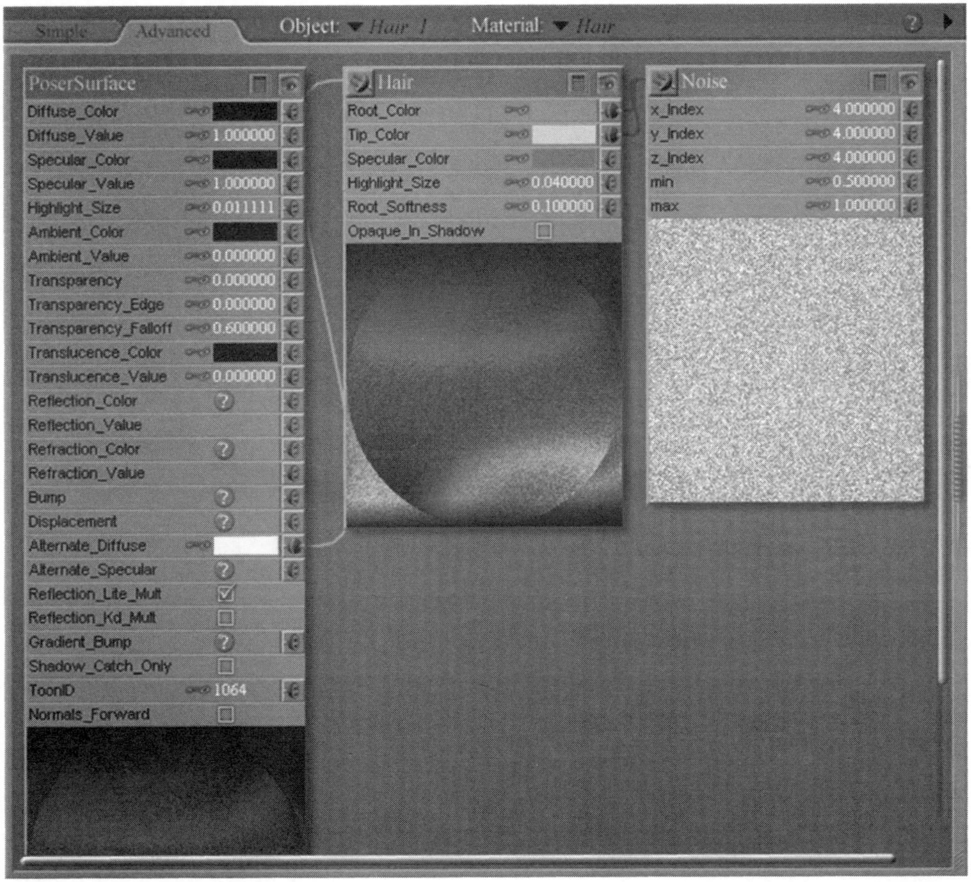

Change Hair Color

1. Select File, Open and open the Dynamic hair.pz3 file.

2. Click the Hair tab to access the Hair Room.

3. Select the Props, Hair_1 option from the Object List at the top of the Shader Window.

4. Click the Material tab at the top of the interface to open the Material Room.

5. Click the Advanced tab to open the Advanced panel in the Shader Window.

6. Click the color swatch for the Root Color value and select a dark red color. Then, click the color swatch for the Tip Color value and select a light red color.

   Changing the hair color won't change the color in the Document Window, but it will be visible when the scene is rendered.

7. Click the Render button [icon] in the Document Window.

   The hair for the figure is rendered with red hair, as shown in Figure 10-22.

8. Select File, Save As and save the file as **Red hair.pz3**.

Setting Hair Material Properties

With the hair group selected, the Shader Window includes a specific node that includes several unique material properties, including

- **Root Color:** Defines the hair color at the hair root.

- **Tip Color:** Defines the hair color at the hair tip.

- **Specular Color:** Defines the color used for specular highlights.

- **Highlight Size:** Defines how big the highlights are that reflect off the hair.

- **Root Softness:** Defines the transparency of the hair at its roots.

- **Opaque in Shadow:** Causes hair to be fully visible without any transparency when the hair is in shadow.

The Hair node should always be connected into the Alternate Diffuse attribute.

QUICKTIP Keeping the Opaque in Shadow option enabled drastically reduces render time for scenes that include hair. It also allows you to use a reduced hair density value.

FIGURE 10-22
Red hair

CHAPTER REVIEW

Chapter Summary

This chapter covered all the features found in the Hair Room, including the capabilities to define hair groups, to grow guide hairs, and to set their length. Styling hair is made possible with the Styling Controls and the Hair Style Tool panel. You can also define the dynamics parameters used to compute the hair simulation. Finally, you can also change the material used to shade the hair.

What You Have Learned

In this chapter, you:

- Discovered the layout of the Hair Room interface, including the Hair Style Tool panel.

- Learned how to load preset hairstyles into the current scene.

- Created unique hair groups using the Group Editor.

- Grew guide hairs and set the hair length and position.

- Styled hair using parameters and the Hair Style Tool panel.

- Defined the dynamic properties of hair and calculated the hair's dynamic positions.

- Changed the hair's material parameters in the Material Room.

Key Terms from This Chapter

- **Clumpiness.** The tendency of hair to clump together into groups.

- **Damping.** The tendency of an object to resist bouncing after being set in motion. The opposite of springiness.

- **Dynamics.** The study of the motions of connected objects.

- **Guide hairs.** A sampling of hairs that show where the full set of hair will be located.

- **Hair density.** The total number of hairs for a given hair group.

- **Hair growth group.** A grouped selection of polygons that define where the hair is to be located.

- **Hair root.** The end of the hair nearest the figure.

- **Hair Style tool.** A tool that is used to style individual hairs or groups of selected hairs.

- **Hair tip.** The end of the hair farthest away from the figure.

- **Kinkiness.** The amount of curl in each hair.

- **Springiness.** The tendency of an object to bounce after being set in motion.

- **Stiffness.** A property that makes hairs resist motion.

chapter

11

WORKING WITH
DYNAMIC CLOTH

1. Create a cloth simulation.

2. Create cloth.

3. Create cloth groups.

4. Simulate cloth dynamics.

chapter 11 WORKING WITH
DYNAMIC CLOTH

Many of the early Poser images featured many naked figures or figures with tight spandex. This was because adding realistic cloth with its folds and smooth flowing surfaces was difficult. The later versions of Poser now include the Cloth Room, where you can simulate the movement and **draping** of cloth, and you'll never need to wash it or send it to the dry cleaners.

Just like hair, Poser offers two ways to apply clothing to the figure. The first method is to apply prop clothes. These clothes are typically custom made to fit a specific figure, as well as conformed to fit the figure exactly and to match the figure's pose as it changes. A detailed discussion of conforming clothes is found in Chapter 5, "Dealing with Props."

The second method uses dynamic cloth that can be simulated to flow and interact with the figure and other scene props using the Cloth Room. Clothing and various props can be made into dynamic cloth in the Cloth Room. Dynamic cloth can have a wide range of parameters for

defining how the cloth folds on itself, how dense the cloth is, its **friction** parameters, how it is affected by the air, and how stretchy the cloth is. Using these parameters, you can define any type of cloth, from soft fine silks to hard coarse leather.

You can also select which scene objects the cloth collides with. By enabling **collisions** between the cloth and the figure, you can realistically drape cloth over the figure or over other scene objects.

You can also divide cloth into groups using the Group Editor. Each group can have its own defined parameters, making it possible to simulate a single cloth object made from several different types of material.

Calculating a simulation actually creates animation keys for the cloth interacting with the figure and other scene objects.

Dynamic cloth objects can be made to react to external forces, such as wind. You can learn more about the Wind Deformer in Chapter 14, "Morphing Figures and Using Deformers."

Tools You'll Use

Draped cloth

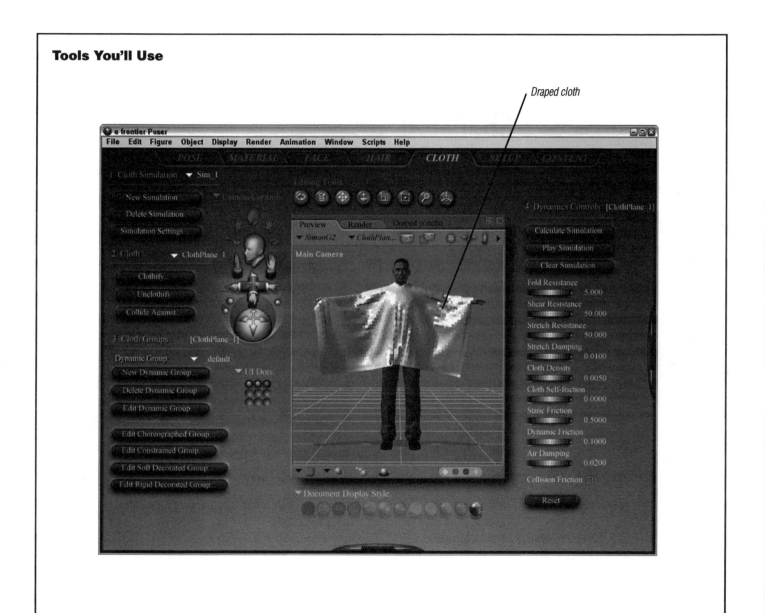

CREATE A
CLOTH SIMULATION

What You'll Do

Simulation Settings

Simulation Name: Flag_Sim

Simulation Range

Start frame: 1   Steps per frame
End frame: 30   ◀▦▦▦▦▦▦▶ 2.000

Additional Cloth Collision Options

☑ Object vertex against cloth polygon   [Default is cloth vertex against
☐ Object polygon against cloth polygon   object polygon]
☐ Cloth self-collision

Cloth Draping

Drape frames: 5

Cancel   OK

▶ *In this lesson, you learn how to create a new cloth simulation.*

The first step in creating dynamic cloth effects is to create a simulation. A single Poser scene can include several different cloth simulations to control, for example, a figure's coat and a flag they are holding. By separating each cloth effect into a separate simulation, you can control which effects are included with the current animation.

You can open the Cloth Room by clicking the Cloth tab at the top of the Poser interface. This opens an interface setup that is different from the Pose Room, as shown in Figure 11-1, although it includes all of the same controls as the Pose Room, including the Document Window, the Camera and Light Controls, the Document Display Style and Editing Tools button sets. The Cloth Room interface also includes four additional sets of buttons that are used to group, load, and dynamically simulate the motion of cloth objects.

Using the Cloth Controls

When you first open the Cloth Room, only the New Simulation button in the **Cloth Simulation** set of controls is enabled. Before any cloth properties can be set, you must add a clothing prop to the scene. Once you create a new simulation, the Clothify button in the Cloth controls becomes active. The remaining two sets of controls only become active once you select an object using the Clothify button.

Creating and Naming a New Simulation

To create a new simulation, click the New Simulation button in the Cloth Simulation controls of the Cloth Room. This opens the Simulation Settings dialog box, shown in Figure 11-2. Using this dialog box, you can name the current simulation. All current simulations are listed in the drop-down list menu next to the Cloth Simulation controls title. The default simulation names are Sim_1, Sim_2, and so on.

NOTE A single file can include multiple simulations, but each simulation will add a lot of time to simulation computations. Each cloth item can only be added to a single simulation.

FIGURE 11-1

Cloth Room interface

FIGURE 11-2

Simulation Settings dialog box

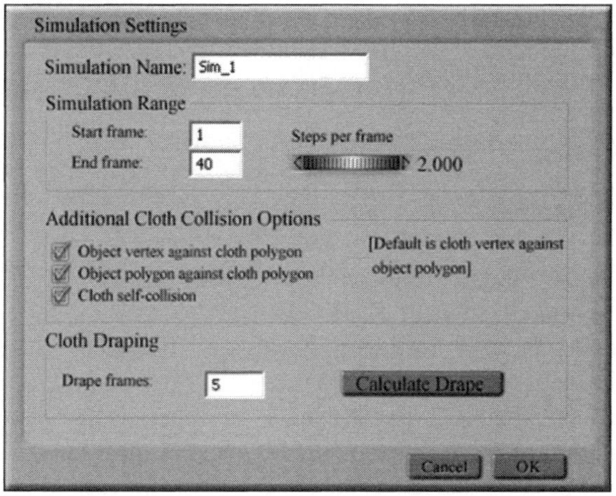

Setting Simulation Range

The Simulation Settings dialog box includes settings for controlling the precise range for the simulation using the Start and End Frame values. All animation frames prior to the Start Frame will display the cloth in its starting position, and all frames that follow the End Frame display the cloth in its final position. You can use Steps Per Frame option to change how often the cloth simulation is calculated. A Steps Per Frame setting of 1 computes the cloth's position only once for every frame, and a Steps Per Frame setting of 2 computes the cloth's position twice every frame. Higher Step size values will result in a smoother simulation, but it will require much longer to compute the simulation.

Setting Collision Options

Collisions between the cloth object, the figure and the other scene forces are the reactions that determine the cloth's dynamic motion. By default, these collisions are determined by watching the position of the cloth vertices relative to the scene polygon faces, but you can enable several additional collision checks in the Simulation Settings dialog box for more accurate collisions.

CAUTION Enabling any of these additional collision options substantially increases the simulation computation time.

The additional collision options include the following

- Object Vertex against Cloth Polygon: This option is opposite of the default, but will help prevent having figure objects, such as hands, penetrate the center of the cloth.

- Object Polygon against Cloth Polygon: This option will help prevent large flat figure areas, such as the chest, penetrate the cloth when the two are placed parallel to each other.

- Cloth Self-Collision: This option keeps the cloth from folding in on itself by detecting when the cloth object intersects with itself.

Using Cloth Draping

When a cloth object is added to the scene, it is probably stiff and doesn't fit with its surroundings. You could manually place the cloth object to a more realistic setting, but it is easier to let the simulation do it for you using the Drape settings. The Drape Frames setting in the Simulation Settings dialog box lets you set the number of frames that are allowed to let the cloth settle into the scene. Once these frames are completed, the cloth's draped position is used as the starting point for the simulation. The Calculate Drape button lets you initiate the drape computations immediately.

Changing Simulation Settings

After clicking OK, the Simulation Settings dialog box closes, and the simulation is added to the current list of simulations. The Clothify button also becomes active for selecting the cloth object. If you want to revisit the simulation settings, you can click the Simulation Settings button to open the dialog box again.

Deleting Simulations

The current simulation is listed in the drop-down list at the top of the Cloth Simulation controls. To delete this current simulation, click the Delete Simulation button, and a confirmation dialog box appears asking if you really want to delete the current simulation.

FIGURE 11-3

New simulation settings

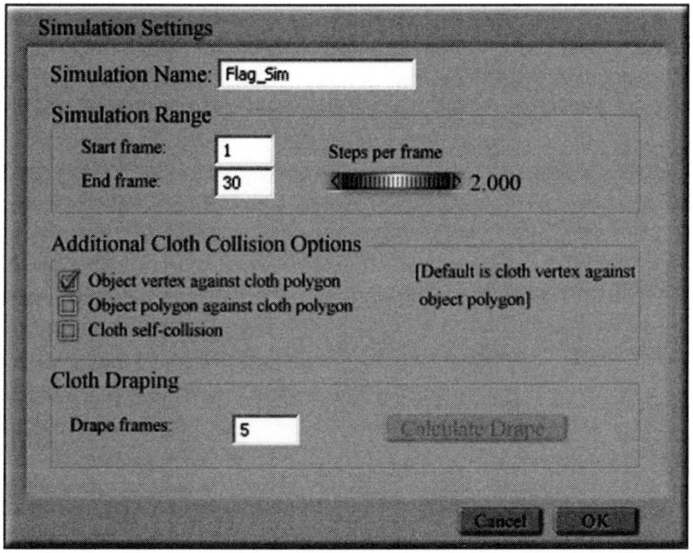

Simulation Settings

Simulation Name: Flag_Sim

Simulation Range

Start frame:	1	Steps per frame
End frame:	30	◄▮▮▮▮▮▮▮▮▮▮▮▮► 2.000

Additional Cloth Collision Options

☑ Object vertex against cloth polygon   [Default is cloth vertex against
☐ Object polygon against cloth polygon   object polygon]
☐ Cloth self-collision

Cloth Draping

Drape frames: 5   Calculate Drape

Cancel   OK

Create a New Simulation

1. Open Poser with the default man visible.
2. Click the Cloth tab at the top of the interface to open the Cloth Room.
3. Click the New Simulation button at the top of the Cloth Simulation set of controls.

   The Simulation Settings dialog box opens.
4. Change the name of the simulation to **Flag_Sim** and enable the Object Vertex Against Cloth Polygon option, as shown in Figure 11-3. Click OK.
5. Select File, Save As and save the file as **New simulation.pz3**.

CREATE
CLOTH

What You'll Do

In this lesson, you learn how to convert clothing and prop objects into cloth objects.

The Cloth controls in the Cloth Room include buttons for creating cloth objects and for specifying which objects should be computed as collide objects. Any prop object, and even body parts, can be made into a cloth object using the Clothify button.

| **CAUTION** Conforming clothes are typically applied as a figure and not a prop and cannot be turned into cloth objects.

Using Primitives for Cloth

Within the Props category of the Library is a subfolder named Primitives that includes a collection of standard 3D objects, such as a sphere, cube, cone, and cylinder. There is also an object labeled as a Hi-Res Square. By selecting, scaling, and clothifying these various objects, you can create an assortment of towels, blankets, scarves, shawls, and flags. The Hi-Res Square prop object actually shows up in the Actor List named Cloth Plane.

QUICKTIP You can also import and use external objects as cloth objects. Make sure that the imported objects have a fairly high resolution so the deformations can be accurately represented.

Using Clothify

Once you've created a simulation, the Clothify button becomes active. Clicking this button opens the Clothify dialog box,

shown in Figure 11-4, where you can select the object to make into cloth. The current object selected in the Document Window is shown in the Clothify dialog box by default, but you can select any loaded body part or prop from the drop-down list.

QUICKTIP Tight-fitting clothes like underwear and bikinis do not benefit from dynamic simulations.

Removing Clothify

All clothified objects are listed in the drop-down list next to the Cloth controls title. You can change the current cloth object back into a normal object using the Unclothify button.

Enabling Collisions

When a simulation is calculated, the cloth object will fall under the weight of gravity straight to the ground plane unless you

select an object to collide with the cloth. Clicking the Collide Against button opens the Cloth Collision Objects dialog box, shown in Figure 11-5. At the top of the Cloth Collision Objects dialog box is a list of all the objects that the cloth will collide with. Clicking the Add/Remove button opens the Select Objects dialog box, shown in Figure 11-6, where you can select collision objects by selecting specific objects.

FIGURE 11-6
Select Objects dialog box

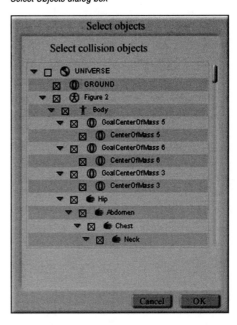

Figure 11-4
Clothify dialog box

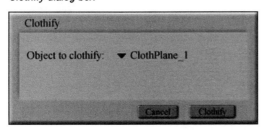

FIGURE 11-5
Cloth Collision Objects dialog box

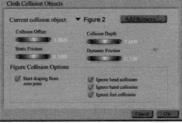

Setting Collision Options

If multiple specific objects are enabled as collision objects, each selection can have its own collision settings. To change the settings for the collision object listed at the top of the Cloth Collision Objects dialog box, drag the parameter dial or click and type a new value in the value field. The available collision parameters and options include

- **Collision Offset:** The offset value provides some space between the cloth image and the object that it is colliding with in order to prevent the object from intersecting with the cloth. You might be tempted to set this value to 0 so the cloth lies directly on the body part, but as the simulation progresses, some portions of the cloth may push through the various body parts. Leaving the offset set between 1 and 1.5 will help prevent this.

- **Collision Depth:** The depth value defines how close the cloth vertices must be to the object polygons in order to be detected as a collision. Setting this value higher will prevent the skin from poking through the cloth item.

- **Static Friction:** This parameter defines the friction between the cloth and the colliding object to start the objects moving. For example, silk and hard plastic would have a very low Static Friction value because it would take very little force to start the two objects moving, whereas leather and denim would have a higher Static Friction value because a larger force would be required to start moving the two objects relative to one another.

- **Dynamic Friction:** This parameter defines the friction between the cloth and colliding object to keep the objects that are already moving in motion relative to one another. For example, a quilt moving over a rocky surface would have a fairly high Dynamic Friction value and would stop moving quickly, but a piece of ice on a smooth steel bar would continue sliding for some distance, thus having a low Dynamic Friction value.

- **Start Draping from Zero Pose:** When conforming clothes are applied to a figure and the figure's pose is changed, the clothes will follow the figure's form, but they will be offset slightly. To make the cloth object drape over the figure for the new pose, enable this option.

- **Ignore Head, Hand and Feet, Collisions:** When you slip on a shirt, you scrunch your hands together to slide your arm into the sleeve. In Poser, you can simply disable hand collisions from the simulation. The same can be done for the head and feet.

QUICKTIP Another way to handle skin poking through clothing is to select and hide the body part that is poking through the clothing. For conforming prop clothing and dynamic cloth, this works quite well.

Create Cloth

1. Choose File, Open and select and open the New simulation.pz3 file.

2. Click the side control to the right of the interface to open the Library palette or select Window, Libraries.

3. lick the Props category at the top of the Library palette and navigate to the Primitives folder.

4. Select the Square Hi-Res thumbnail and click the Add New Item button at the bottom of the Library palette.

The square object appears under the figure in the Document Window.

5. With the Translate/Pull Tool selected in the Editing Tools, drag the square object up above the figure's head.

6. Click the Cloth tab at the top of the interface to open the Cloth Room.

7. With the square object still selected, click the Clothify button. In the Clothify dialog box, click the Clothify button.

8. Click the Collide Against button to open the Cloth Collision Objects dialog box. Click the Add/Remove button and select the James Casual object in the Select Ojbects dialog box. Then scroll down through the hierarchy list, deselect the Neck, Head, and Eye objects, and click OK.

9. In the Cloth Collision Objects dialog box, enable the Ignore Head Collisions option and click OK.

10. Click the Calculate Simulation button.

A progress dialog box appears, and every frame for the simulation is calculated. The result is that the square object acts like a blanket that covers the head of the figure, as shown in Figure 11-7.

11. Select File, Save As and save the file as **Draped poncho.pz3**.

FIGURE 11-7

Poncho around neck

Use Figure Clothes

1. Open Poser with the default man visible.

2. Locate the SydneyG2 figure in the Library and replace the default figure with her. Then locate the red_dress clothing item in the Poser 6/Jessi Clothing folder of the Props category and add it to the scene.

   The knees poke through the dress when it is first added to the scene.

3. Click the Cloth tab at the top of the interface to open the Cloth Room. Click on the New Simulation button and click the OK button to accept the default settings.

4. With the dress prop object still selected, click the Clothify button. In the Clothify dialog box, click the Clothify button.

5. Click the Collide Against button to open the Cloth Collision Objects dialog box. Click the Add/Remove button and select the SimonG2 object in the Select Objects dialog box and click OK.

6. Click on the Simulation Settings button and set the Drape Frames to 5. Click the Calculate Drape button.

   The dress is draped to cover the knees that are poking through.

7. Open the Animation Controls, and then drag the Timeline marker to frame 10. Then select and drag the left foot forward and click the Add Key Frames button to create a motion of the leg coming forward.

8. Click the Calculate Simulation button.

   A progress dialog box appears, and every frame for the simulation is calculated. The result is that the dress object drapes over the moving leg, as shown in Figure 11-8.

9. Select File, Save As and save the file as **Cloth dress.pz3**.

FIGURE 11-8
Dress that moves with the body

CREATE
CLOTH GROUPS

What You'll Do

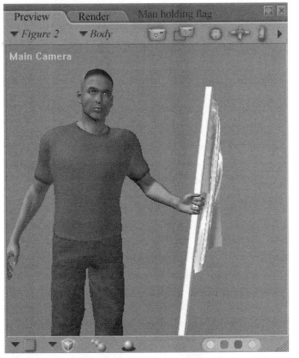

In this lesson, you learn how to specify different cloth groups.

You can divide created cloth objects into groups that act differently, as needed. You can do this to represent different types of material, to animate the cloth itself, or to constrain a portion of the cloth so it doesn't move at all. You create cloth groups using the Group Editor, except cloth groups use vertices instead of polygons to define the group.

Creating a Dynamic Cloth Group

When a cloth object is created, all vertices belong to a single group labeled *default*. This default group is a dynamic type group, which means that it is included in the simulation calculations using the dynamics parameters set in the Dynamics Controls. A single cloth object can include several dynamic groups. To create a new dynamic group, click the New Dynamic Group button and type the group's name in the simple dialog box that appears. All created cloth groups are listed in the drop-down list at the top of the Cloth Groups controls. You can delete the selected group by clicking the Delete Dynamic Group button.

Editing a Dynamic Cloth Group

Clicking the Edit Dynamic Group button opens the Group Editor in Vertex selection mode, as shown in Figure 11-9, and darkens all objects in the Document Window. Using the Select Vertices tool in the Group Editor, you can select which vertices are included in the current dynamic group. The Deselect Vertices tool can be used to remove vertices from the current selection.

QUICKTIP You can also access the Deselect Vertices tool when the Select Vertices tool is selected by holding down the Ctrl/Command key and vice versa.

FIGURE 11-9
Group Editor in Vertex mode

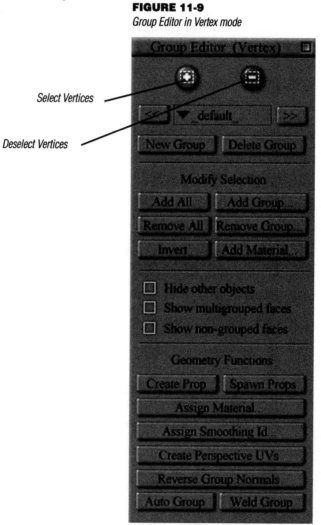

Select Vertices

Deselect Vertices

Using Other Cloth Groups

In addition to the dynamic cloth groups, a cloth object can also include several other cloth groups. Each cloth object can only include one of each of these other groups, so their names cannot be changed. Also, each vertex can only be added to a single group, so adding a vertex to one of these groups will remove it from its current group. The other available groups include the following:

- **Choreographed Group:** The Choreographed cloth group is a set of vertices that can be animated as a group using keyframes. This group is useful if you want to animate the motion of a separate piece of clothing, such as a scarf being blown away where you want to control its motion precisely.

- **Constrained Group:** The Constrained cloth group are those objects that are constrained to not be moved by the dynamic simulation, but constrained vertices can still move with the body part directly underneath it. This group is good for simulating the corner of coat getting stuck on a fence.

- **Soft Decorated Group:** The Soft Decorated cloth group is used to remove objects that have small flexible details, such as shirt pockets and fringe lace, from the simulation while still allowing the detail to move with the cloth. The Soft differs from the Rigid group in that it can flex and bend, while the Rigid group remains solid.

- **Rigid Decorated Group:** The Rigid Decorated cloth group is used to remove objects that have small solid details such as buttons and belt buckles from the simulated while still allowing the detail to move with the cloth. The rigid group remains solid and is inflexible.

Clicking the Edit button for any of these other groups opens the Group Editor where you can select the vertices that are part of the group.

Create Cloth Groups

1. Choose File, Open and open the Man holding flag.pz3 file.

2. Click the Cloth tab at the top of the interface to open the Cloth Room.

3. Click the New Simulation button at the top of the Cloth Simulation set of controls.

4. Change the name of the simulation to **Flag** and click OK.

5. With the flag object selected, click the Clothify button. In the Clothify dialog box, click the Clothify button.

6. Click the Collide Against button to open the Cloth Collision Objects dialog box. Click the Add/Remove button and select the Cyl_1 object in the Select Objects dialog box. Then click OK, once to close the Select Objects dialog box and again to close the Cloth Collision Objects dialog box.

7. Click the Edit Choreographed Group button.

   The Group Editor appears with the Select Vertices tool 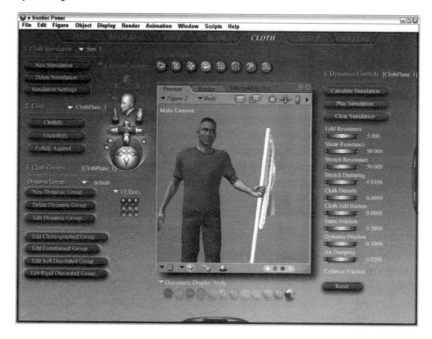 *enabled.*

8. Drag over all the vertices on the left side of the flag where it connects with the pole. Then close the Group Editor.

9. Click the Calculate Simulation button.

   A progress dialog box appears, and every frame for the simulation is calculated. The result is that the flag object falls limp under the effect of gravity, as shown in Figure 11-10.

10. Select File, Save As and save the file as **Dynamic flag.pz3**.

FIGURE 11-10
Dynamic flag

SIMULATE
CLOTH DYNAMICS

What You'll Do

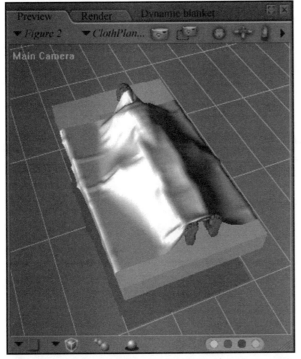

In this lesson, you learn how to set cloth parameters and calculate the simulation.

The final step is to define the cloth parameters for each dynamic group and to calculate the simulation. The controls to accomplish this final step are found in the Dynamics Controls.

Setting Cloth Parameters

For each dynamic group, you can set the parameters found in the Dynamics Controls. These parameters define how the cloth moves during the simulation. The cloth parameters can be reset to their default values at any time by clicking the Reset button located below all the parameter dials. The available cloth parameters include the following:

- Fold Resistance: This parameter value defines how resistant the current cloth group is to folding. Low values act like a thin scarf that easily folds on itself, and higher values act like rigid plastic that doesn't easily fold on itself.

- Shear Resistance: This parameter value defines how resistant the current cloth group is to shearing the surface against itself. Low values allow one edge of the cloth to easily move, while the other end is stationary. It can also be thought of as the cloth's ability to hold its shape. A silk scarf has a low Shear Resistance as it falls into a clump when dropped. A cotton sweatshirt would have a medium Shear Resistance value because it somewhat maintains it shape, and a leather belt has a high Shear Resistance.

- **Stretch Resistance:** This parameter value defines how resistant the current cloth group is to stretching. Low values allow the cloth to stretch a great deal, such as a rubber band, and high values prevent the cloth from stretching, like denim or burlap. Socks tend to have a lower Stretch Resistance, which means they can be pulled over the foot, but coats and caps tend to have a higher Stretch Resistance; they don't stretch.

- **Stretch Damping:** This parameter value defines how quickly the stretching of the cloth fades. A high value causes the stretching to quickly stop, such as a cotton t-shirt, and a low value lets the stretching continue for a longer period of time, such as spandex. Suspenders have a very low Stretch Resistance value, thus enabling them to stretch relatively easily, but also a high Stretch Damping value, causing them to rebound quickly.

- **Cloth Density:** This parameter value defines how heavy the cloth is per unit area. Low values are light cloth items, like a silk scarf, and high values are much heavier, like leather or denim. Cloth groups with a higher density will be more affected by gravity, friction, and collisions.

- **Cloth Self-Friction:** This parameter value defines how much friction the cloth has when rubbed against itself.

Low values allow the cloth to easily move across its own surface, again like silk, but high values cannot be easily rubbed together, like denim. Velcro has a very high Cloth Self-Friction value that prevents it from moving against itself.

- **Static Friction:** This parameter value defines how much force is required to begin to move cloth over an object. Low values require little force to begin to slide across the surface of another object, such as an ice cube on a plastic plane, but high values require a substantial amount of force to start moving, such as wood on sandpaper.

- **Dynamic Friction:** This parameter value is similar to Static Friction, except it defines the amount of force required to keep a moving object in motion. Low values, again like ice on plastic, require very little force to keep the ice moving across the surface, but high values like wood on sandpaper require quite a bit of force to keep the surfaces moving.

NOTE The Static and Dynamic Friction settings can be set in the Cloth Properties section or in the Cloth Collision Objects dialog box. The Collision Friction option lets you set which friction values are used.

- **Air Damping:** This parameter value defines how much the cloth group is

affected by air currents, such as wind. Low values allow the cloth to move easily when blown by the wind, like a flag, but high values aren't impacted by air currents as much, such as the flag pole.

- **Collision Friction:** This option disables the Static and Dynamic Friction parameter values when enabled and uses the Static and Dynamic Friction values set in the Cloth Collision Objects dialog box instead.

Calculating the Simulation

Clicking the Calculate Simulation button starts the calculation process, and a progress dialog box, shown in Figure 11-11, appears that gives details on the progress of the calculations. The calculations can be cancelled at any time using the Cancel button.

Viewing the Simulation

The Play Simulation button plays back all the calculated frames for the simulation in the Document Window.

FIGURE 11-11
Simulation calculation progress dialog box

Clearing the Simulation

The Clear Simulation button removes all the calculated simulation keys, but it doesn't change any of your current collision, group, or parameter settings.

FIGURE 11-12
Dynamic blanket

1. Choose File, Open and open the Man in bed.pz3 file.

2. Click the Cloth tab at the top of the interface to open the Cloth Room.

3. Click the New Simulation button at the top of the Cloth Simulation set of controls.

4. Change the name of the simulation to **Blanket**, enable the Object Vertex against Cloth Polygon option, and click OK.

5. With the blanket object selected, click the Clothify button. In the Clothify dialog box, click the Clothify button.

6. Click the Collide Against button to open the Cloth Collision Objects dialog box. Click the Add/Remove button and select the Figure 11 and box_1 objects in the Select Objects dialog box. Then click OK, once to close the Select Objects dialog box and again to close the Cloth Collision Objects dialog box.

7. With the default dynamic cloth group selected, set the Fold Resistance parameter to 10, the Cloth Density parameter to 0.01, and the Cloth Self-Friction parameter to 0.1.

8. Click the Calculate Simulation button.

   A progress dialog box appears, and every frame for the simulation is calculated. The result is that the blanket object falls under the effect of gravity and covers the man's figure, as shown in Figure 11-12.

9. Select File, Save As and save the file as **Dynamic blanket.pz3**.

CHAPTER REVIEW

Chapter Summary

This chapter covers all the features found in the Cloth Room, including the ability to create new cloth simulations, convert clothing and prop objects into cloth objects, enable collisions, define cloth groups, set cloth parameters, and calculate the simulation. The resulting cloth simulations can create realistic interactions between cloth and the various scene objects.

What You Have Learned

In this chapter, you:

- Created and named a new cloth simulation.
- Set the initial draping of a cloth object.
- Created cloth objects from clothing and prop objects.
- Enabled collisions between the current cloth object and other scene objects.
- Created new dynamic cloth groups and other cloth groups for choreographing and constraining cloth vertices using the Group Editor.
- Learned and set the various cloth parameters.
- Calculated a cloth simulation for a given range of frames.

Key Terms from This Chapter

- **Air Damping.** A cloth parameter value that defines how much the cloth group is affected by air currents, such as wind.
- **Choreographed group.** A set of cloth vertices that can be animated as a group using keyframes.
- **Cloth Density.** A cloth parameter value that defines how heavy the cloth is per unit area.
- **Cloth Self-Friction.** A cloth parameter value that defines how much friction the cloth has when rubbed against itself.
- **Cloth simulation.** The process of calculating the position and motion of a cloth object as it is moved by forces and collides with various scene objects.
- **Clothify.** The process of converting a prop object into a cloth object.
- **Collision.** An event that occurs when a vertex of a cloth object intersects with the polygon face of a scene object.
- **Constrained group.** A cloth group of vertices that are constrained to not be moved by the dynamic simulation.
- **Draping.** The process of letting a cloth object fall to rest about a scene object.
- **Dynamic Friction.** A cloth parameter

value that is similar to Static Friction, except it defines the amount of force required to keep a moving object in motion.
- **Fold Resistance.** A cloth parameter value that defines how resistant the current cloth group is to folding.
- **Friction.** A force that resists the movement of one object over another.
- **Rigid Decorated group.** A cloth group that is removed from the dynamic simulation that remains solid and is inflexible.
- **Shear Resistance.** A cloth parameter value that defines how resistant the current cloth group is to shearing the surface against itself.
- **Soft Decorated group.** A cloth group that is removed from the dynamic simulation that can still flex and bend.
- **Simulation range.** The number of frames that are included in the simulation marked by Start and End Frames.
- **Static Friction.** A cloth parameter value that defines how much force is required to begin to move cloth over an object.
- **Stretch Damping.** A cloth parameter value that defines how quickly the stretching of the cloth fades.
- **Stretch Resistance.** A cloth parameter value that defines how resistant the current cloth group is to stretching.

chapter 12
RIGGING A FIGURE
WITH BONES

1. Access and edit existing bone structures.

2. Create and name bones.

3. Group body parts.

4. Use Inverse Kinematics.

5. Use the Joint Editor.

chapter 12 RIGGING A FIGURE
WITH BONES

When posing the various body parts in the Pose Room, you may wonder how the arm knows to bend at the elbow. The answer lies in the invisible bone structure that exists underneath the body mesh. This underlying bone structure is called the *figure rig,* and the process of creating a skeleton and connecting it to the actual model is called **rigging**.

If you open the Setup Room, the bone structure becomes visible and can be edited. The Setup Room is identical to the Pose Room, except that the **bone objects** are visible. Now let's all sing together, "The knee bone is connected to the shin bone."

You can also use the Setup Room to add a new bone structure to custom figures that are imported, allowing them to be posed also. You create and manipulate new bones using the **Bone Creation** tool or you can load an existing bone structure from a Library figure and edit it to match the new figure.

Once you add new bones to a figure, you can position them using the Editing Tools and the Joint Editor dialog box so that the connection between bones are located within the figure's **joint**. You can also set limits for the joints to control how the bones move so the elbow or knee joints don't move backwards.

After positioning the bones so their joints are in the right location, you can select geometry groups to move with each bone using the Group Editor.

The final step is to establish any Inverse Kinematic chains, such as for the limbs, so the hands can be placed to control the rest of the arm.

To control exactly which objects are moved, twisted along with the movement of the joint, you can use the Joint Editor. The Joint Editor can also make muscles bulge along with the joint movement.

Tools You'll Use

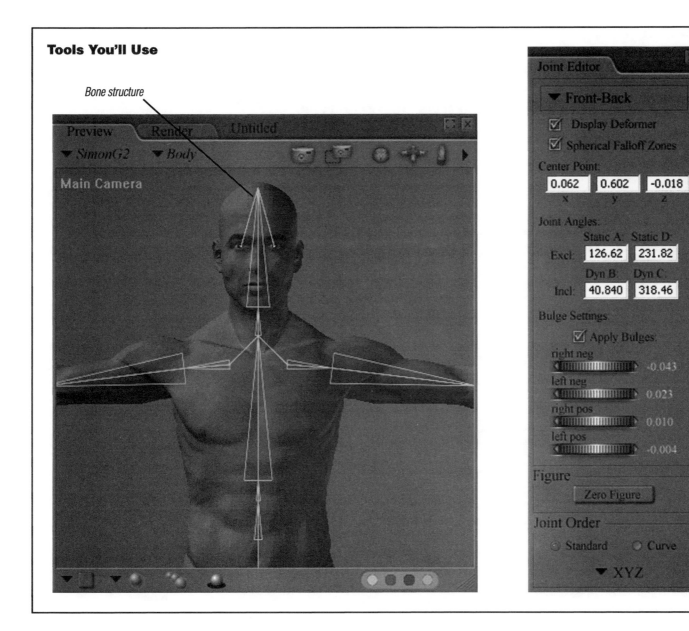

Bone structure

Preview | Render | Untitled

▼ SimonG2 ▼ Body

Main Camera

Joint Editor

▼ **Front-Back**

☑ Display Deformer
☑ Spherical Falloff Zones

Center Point:

| 0.062 | 0.602 | -0.018 |
| x | y | z |

Joint Angles:

| | Static A: | Static D: |
| Excl: | 126.62 | 231.82 |

| | Dyn B: | Dyn C: |
| Incl: | 40.840 | 318.46 |

Bulge Settings:

☑ Apply Bulges:

right neg
〈▥▥▥▥▥▥▥▥▥▥〉 -0.043

left neg
〈▥▥▥▥▥▥▥▥▥▥〉 0.023

right pos
〈▥▥▥▥▥▥▥▥▥▥〉 0.010

left pos
〈▥▥▥▥▥▥▥▥▥▥〉 -0.004

Figure

Zero Figure

Joint Order

◉ Standard   ○ Curve

▼ XYZ

ACCESS AND EDIT
EXISTING BONE STRUCTURES

What You'll Do

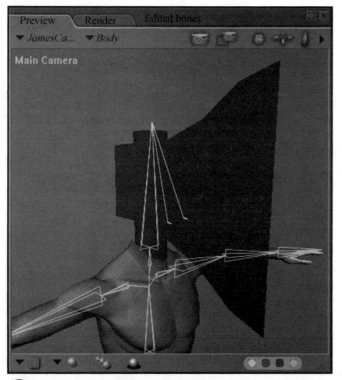

▶ In this lesson, you learn how to access bone structures in the Setup Room and edit those structures.

When the Setup Room is opened, the figure's bones are displayed on top of the current figure, as shown in Figure 12-1. The bones appear as a linked set of triangle objects.

> **NOTE** When the Setup Room is opened, a warning dialog box appears reminding you that if the figure has any morph targets, then changing the bone's grouping could mess up the morph targets.

> **NOTE** If you select the File, Save menu command while the Setup Room is open, Poser will automatically switch back to the Pose Room.

Selecting Bones

When you move the cursor over the top of the various bones in the Document Window, each bone becomes highlighted and clicking the highlighted bone selects it. The selected bone turns red.

> **NOTE** Regardless of the current figure pose, the figure in the Setup Room is displayed with its arms outstretched. This pose makes it easier to position bones.

Editing Bones

Within the Setup Room, you can move, rotate, or scale the selected bone using the Editing Tools. You can also change the bone's position and orientation using the parameter dials. Moving a bone also moves all the children bones under the existing bone.

CAUTION Moving existing bone groups away from their grouped geometry can radically distort the figure.

Changing Bone Endpoints

If you move the mouse over the start or end point of a bone, the cursor will change to a circular shape. Clicking and dragging with this circular-shaped cursor moves just the end point while leaving the opposite end point in place. This provides an easy way to extend and position bones. Moving end points works with any of the selected editing tools.

Making Symmetrical Changes

You also can take advantage of the Figure, Symmetry command options to copy the bone positions between the right and left sides of the current figure. Using these commands, you can copy the left side to the right side, the right side to the left side, swap the two sides, or adjust just the arms or legs.

QUICKTIP You can also use the Joint Editor to position bones.

FIGURE 12-1

Setup Room

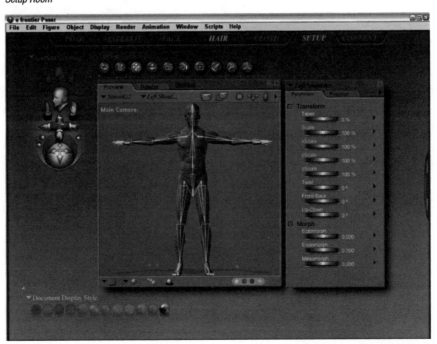

1. Choose File, Open and open the Hatchet head.pz3 file.

   This file includes the default man figure whose head has been replaced with a hatchet object.

2. Select the Face Camera 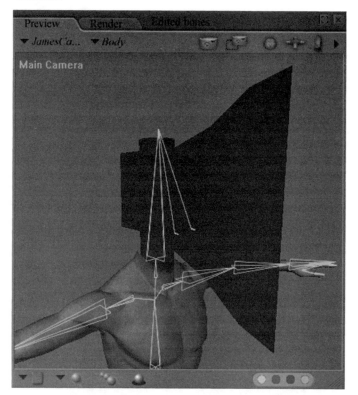 from the Camera Controls.

3. Click the Setup tab to open the Setup Room. A warning dialog box will appear stating that morph targets may become unusable. Click OK to continue.

   A set of bones is displayed on top of the current figure.

4. Click the top bone that controls the head to select it.

   The selected bone turns red to show it is selected.

5. Move the cursor over the top end point of the selected bone. When the cursor changes to a circular cursor, drag the bone end point upward until the bone covers the entire ball object, as shown in Figure 12-2.

6. Select File, Save As and save the file as **Edited bones.pz3**.

FIGURE 12-2
Edited bones

CREATE
AND NAME BONES

What You'll Do

In this lesson, you learn how to load a skeleton onto an imported figure and create new bone sets.

Figures included in the Poser Library have a detailed bone structure already included, and editing them isn't required unless you drastically change the figure's geometry. The more likely place to use the Setup Room features is to endow an imported figure with a bone structure.

Importing Figure Geometry

Figures created in an external 3D package can be imported into Poser using the File, Import menu command. Poser can import 3D objects saved in the QuickDraw (.3DMF), 3d Studio (.3DS), .DXF, Wavefront (.OBJ), and Lightwave (.LWO) formats. Imported objects appear in Poser as props. If you select the imported prop and then open the Setup Room, a warning dialog box appears informing you that the selected prop object will be converted into a figure.

QUICKTIP If the default figure gets in the way of the imported figure, you can select and hide the default figure using the Figure, Hide Figure menu command or simply delete the figure.

Loading an Existing Skeleton from the Library

If you load a figure from the Library into Poser while the Setup Room is open, the figure's skeleton will be loaded. You can then edit this skeleton to fit the new figure. This can be a huge time-saver if the skeleton is close enough to the new figure. Figure 12-3 shows a simple ball prop that has been added to the scene and the skeleton for a figure has been added from the Library.

FIGURE 12-3
Loaded skeleton

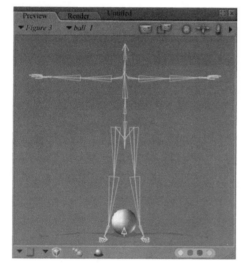

Using the Bone Creation Tool

If an existing skeleton can't be found to load into the new figure, you can create a new skeleton using the Bone Creation tool. This tool is found with the Editing Tools within the Setup Room. You create new bones by dragging from the bone's base to its tip. You can create multiple bones in succession by continuing to drag with the Bone Creation tool. Each new bone that is created becomes a child to the previous bone, and all the bones together create a *bone chain*. Figure 12-4 shows five bones that were created in order using the Bone Creation tool.

FIGURE 12-4
New bone chain

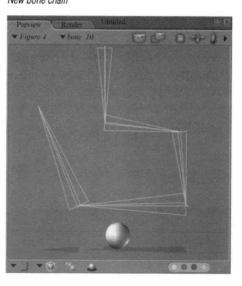

Deleting Bones

If you create a bone that you want to remove, simply select the bone and press the Delete key. A confirmation dialog box will appear asking if you are sure that you want to delete the object. If one of the center bones of a chain is deleted, the bones on either end are reoriented to make up for the deleted bone.

Naming Bones

Each newly created bone is given a default name, which exists of the word *Bone* followed by a number. This name is listed and can be changed in the Name text field located in the Properties panel of the Parameters/Properties palette. The internal name is used to match the bone to a geometry group name.

> **QUICKTIP** The default name doesn't describe the bone's location. For clarity when working with bones, change the name to something meaningful, like Left_upper_arm_bone.

Attaching a Bone to an Existing Bone

Using the Bone Creation tool is great for creating skeletons for snakes and worms that have all their bones connected in one long head-to-tail line, but to create a human skeleton, you'll need to branch bones so that two separate bone chains can be connected to the hip bone. If you select a bone and drag with the Bone Creation tool, the new bone will be attached to the end of the selected bone.

Two other ways to attach the selected bone to another bone are to click the Set Parent button in the Properties panel or to select the Object, Change Parent menu command. Both of these methods will open a hierarchical list of scene objects where you can select the bone's new parent. Figure 12-5 shows a set of bones that splits into two chains.

FIGURE 12-5
Split bone chains

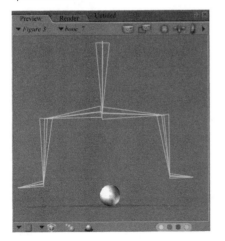

Load a Skeleton

1. Open Poser with the default man visible.

2. Select File, Import, Wavefront OBJ. In the Prop Import Options dialog box, deselect the Centered option, enable the Place on Floor option, and then click OK. Then, select and import the Simple figure.obj file.

   The simple figure object is imported as a prop.

3. With the imported figure selected, click the Setup tab at the top of the interface to open the Setup Room and click OK in the warning dialog box that appears.

   The Setup Room appears with only the imported figure visible.

4. Click the side control to the right of the interface to open the Library palette or select Window, Libraries.

5. Click the Figures category at the top of the Library palette and navigate to the Additional Figures folder. Select the Mannequin thumbnail and click the Replace Figure button at the bottom of the Library palette.

   The skeleton for the Mannequin figure is loaded into the Setup Room.

6. Select the hip bone and drag the entire skeleton until it is aligned with the simple figure.

7. Position the cursor over the shoulder joint until it turns into a circle icon, and then drag the arm into position to match the simple figure. Repeat this step for the opposite shoulder.

8. Drag the upper leg joints into position, then select the Rotate tool from the Editing tools and rotate the leg bones until they are aligned with the simple figure. Then scale the leg bones with the Scale tool to fit within the simple figure.

   After repositioning the loaded bones, each of the bones is located within the simple figure, as shown in Figure 12-6.

9. Select File, Save As and save the file as **Simple figure with loaded skeleton**.

FIGURE 12-6
Simple figure with loaded skeleton

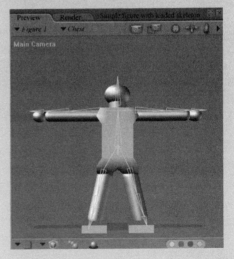

Create a New Skeleton

1. Open Poser with the default man visible.

2. Select File, Import, Wavefront OBJ. In the Prop Import Options dialog box, deselect the Centered option, enable the Place on Floor option, and then click OK. Then, select and import the Mushroom.obj file.

   The mushroom object is imported as a prop.

3. Select the default figure and choose Figure, Hide Figure or disable the Visible option in the Properties palette.

4. With the mushroom object selected, click the Setup tab at the top of the interface to open the Setup Room and click OK in the warning dialog box that appears.

   The Setup Room appears with only the mushroom object visible.

5. Select the Bone Creation tool  from the Editing Tools, and then click at the base of the mushroom object and drag about a third of the way up the mushroom top. Then click and drag two more times to create three connected bones for the mushroom stem.

6. At the top of the mushroom, continue the chain of bones by making two additional bones down the right side of the mushroom.

7. Click the top bone in the mushroom stem to select it and drag to create two more bones along the left side of the mushroom.

8. Open the Properties panel, select the first new bone, and name it **Stem1** by typing the new name in the Name and the Internal Name text fields. Continue to select and name the remaining bones in the stem. Then name the bones along the top of the mushroom, **Top right1**, and so on.

   The completed custom skeleton for the mushroom object is shown in Figure 12-7.

9. Select File, Save As and save the file as **Mushroom skeleton.pz3**.

FIGURE 12-7
Custom mushroom skeleton

GROUP
BODY PARTS

What You'll Do

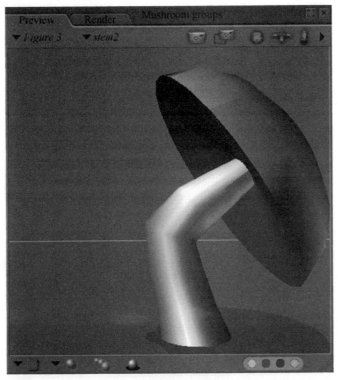

▶ *In this lesson, you learn how to group body parts for each bone.*

In order to make the figure's body parts move with the bones, you'll need to group each of the various body parts together using the Group Editor. This body part group should have the same name as the bone's internal name.

Grouping Body Parts

To group the body parts together, click the Grouping tool in the Editing Tools to open the Group Editor, shown in Figure 12-8. If you click the Previous Group and Next Group buttons, you can scroll through the existing bones. Once a bone name is selected, you can drag in the Document Window with the Select Polygon tool to add polygons to that bone's group or remove polygons from the current group with the Deselect Polygons tool. Holding down the Ctrl/Command key will switch to the opposite tool.

QUICKTIP Be sure to check on the back side of the figure for polygons to add to the group.

Group Body Parts

1. Choose File, Open and open the Mushroom skeleton.pz3 file.

   This file includes the imported mushroom figure with the bones created in the last example.

2. With the mushroom object selected, click the Setup tab at the top of the interface to open the Setup Room.

3. Click the Grouping tool 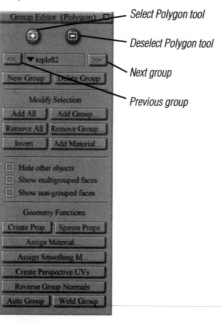 in the Editing Tools controls to open the Group Editor.

4. Click the Next Group button >> in the Group Editor until the Stem1 group is listed as the current group. Then drag in the Document Window to select the polygons surrounding the Stem1 bone.

   The selected polygons are highlighted red.

5. Rotate the Document Window by dragging on the small Rotate sphere icon at the top-right corner of the Document Window to rotate the view to the side of the mushroom and select the side polygons that surround the Stem1 bone. Continue to rotate the view and to select polygons around the entire figure.

6. Repeat Steps 4 and 5 for the remaining bones. Click the Show Non-Grouped Faces option in the Group Editor to see if there are any polygons that haven't been assigned to a group.

7. Click the Pose tab to switch back to the Pose Room and drag on the top of the stem to see how the mushroom bends.

   The mushroom bends by moving the underlying bones, as shown in Figure 12-9.

8. Select File, Save As and save the file as **Mushroom groups.pz3**.

Viewing Orphan Polygons

If you switch to a different room by clicking one of the tabs at the top of the interface, a warning dialog box will appear if any polygons exist that haven't been assigned to a group. These orphan polygons will be left behind in the Document Window as the figure is moved and posed. To prevent this problem, you need to make sure that every figure polygon is assigned to a group. If you want to see which polygons still aren't part of a group, click the Show Non-Grouped Faces option in the Group Editor. All polygons that aren't part of a group are highlighted in red.

FIGURE 12-8
Group Editor

Select Polygon tool

Deselect Polygon tool

Next group

Previous group

Matching Body Part Groups to Bones

If you import a figure with its own set of groups, you'll need to make sure that the name of each bone matches the body part group. If the names match, moving the bone in the Pose Room will move the body part correctly.

FIGURE 12-9
Mushroom with groups

USE
INVERSE KINEMATICS

What You'll Do

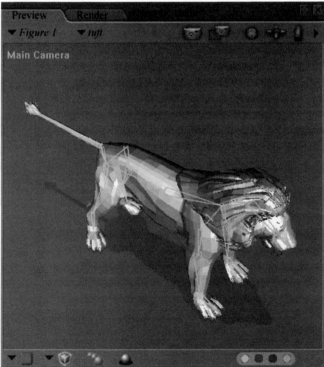

In this lesson, you learn how to create a new IK chain.

Kinematics is the physics behind the movement of linked objects. Bone structures are a good example of a set of linked objects that can be defined using kinematic solutions. For example, because the shoulder is connected to the arm bones, which are connected to the hand, you can use kinematic equations to determine the position of the hand as the shoulder moves. Inverse Kinematics works backwards by solving the shoulder's position as the hand is moved.

The benefit of Inverse Kinematics is that it is often easier to animate characters by placing their hands and feet than placing their hips and shoulders. For example, imagine a character walking across the floor and reaching for a door handle. To animate this sequence by moving only the upper thigh and upper arm bones would be difficult, but with Inverse Kinematics enabled, you can position the feet for the steps and the hand for the door handle, and the remaining body parts just follow.

Working with Inverse Kinematics

When Poser first loads, select the default figure's Left Thigh object and try to move it with the Translate/Pull tool. The upper thigh element might twist a little, but because it is part of the IK chain, it won't move out of place unless the end of the IK chain, the foot, is moved.

Now try disabling IK and moving the upper thigh element again. This time the upper thigh moves easily and the foot moves along with it. The trick is to learn when to use IK and when to disable it.

QUICKTIP You should enable and use IK if you need to place the end of an IK chain, such as a hand or a foot, in a specific location, but for general body movement and poses, you can disable IK.

In order for Inverse Kinematics to work, you need to select a parent object (the root object) and one of its children objects (the goal object) connected in a chain. All the bones between these two selected bones are collectively called an IK chain. You can select IK chains by using the Hierarchy Editor. This dialog box is opened with the Window, Hierarchy Editor menu command. All IK chains for the current figure are displayed at the bottom of the Hierarchy Editor, shown in Figure 12-10.

FIGURE 12-10
Hierarchy Editor

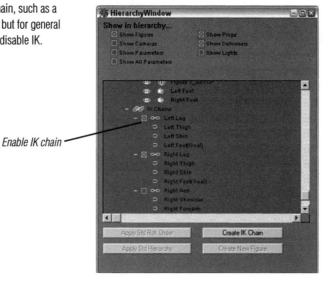

Enable IK chain

Viewing IK Chains

All existing IK chains are listed at the bottom of the Hierarchy Editor, as shown in Figure 12-11. Each IK chain lists all the elements included in the chain from root to end element, called the *goal*. To the left of each IK chain is a check box that you can use to enable and disable the selected IK chain.

FIGURE 12-11
IK chains in the Hierarchy Editor

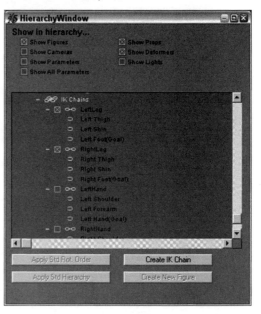

Creating New IK Chains

You can create new IK chains using the Hierarchy Editor. These new IK chains can be created for manually imported characters, for new types of figures, such as the tail of an animal, or to add an attached prop to an existing IK chain. To create an IK chain, select the IK Chains title in the Hierarchy Editor to make the Create IK Chain button active. Clicking the Create IK Chain button opens a dialog box where you can give the new IK chain a name. The newly named IK chain appears at the bottom of the Hierarchy Editor. You can then drag and drop elements of the chain onto the new chain name. The first element under the new IK Chain title is the root element, and the last one is the goal. The goal element is marked with the word *goal* is parentheses.

> **NOTE** Newly created IK chains are also listed in the Figure, Use Inverse Kinematics menu command.

Enabling Inverse Kinematics

Inverse Kinematics can only be enabled for a set of connected body parts referred to as a kinematic chain. For Poser, you can enable Inverse Kinematics (IK) for four kinematic chains—right and left arms and legs. IK is enabled by default for the legs, but not for the arms. You can enable or disable IK using the Figure, Use Inverse Kinematics menu command. When enabled, a small check mark appears next to the menu.

Using the Chain Break Tool

IK chains aren't the only elements that have control over other body parts. Actually, almost all body parts are connected and can influence one another. If you drag an arm element far enough, the torso will move along with it, but you can use the **Chain Break tool** (L) to prevent the movement of connected elements.

If you select the Chain Break tool, several chain break icons appear on the figure in the Document Window, as shown in Figure 12-12. These icons mark body parts that are prevented from moving with adjacent elements. By default, the head, hip, right,

and left buttock elements have a chain break icon on them. This means that the head moves independently of the torso, and the torso moves independently of the legs.

If you click an element with the Chain Break tool, you can place or remove these icons. For example, if you click the right and left collar elements, moving the arms will have no effect on the torso.

> **CAUTION** The chain break icon for the hip cannot be removed.

FIGURE 12-12
Default chain break icons

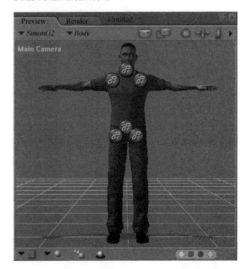

1. Select File, Open and open the Lion.pz3 file.

   This file includes a loaded lion figure.

2. Select Window, Hierarchy Editor to open the Hierarchy Editor.

3. Scroll to the bottom of the Hierarchy Editor and select the IK Chains title. Then, click the Create IK Chain button at the bottom of the dialog box.

4. In the Set Name dialog box that appears, type the name, **Tail**, and click OK

5. Scroll back up in the Hierarchy Editor and select and drag the Tail 1, Tail 2, Tail 3, Tail 4, and Tuft elements and drop them on the newly created Tail IK Chain title.

6. Reorder the tail elements so they appear in order with the Tuft element designated as the goal.

7. Click the square box to the left of the Tail title ⊠ ∞ Tail to enable the IK chain. Then, select and move the tuft element.

   As the tuft element is moved, the other members of the IK chain are also moved, as shown in Figure 12-13.

8. Select File, Save As and save the file as **New IK chain.pz3**.

FIGURE 12-13
New tail IK chain

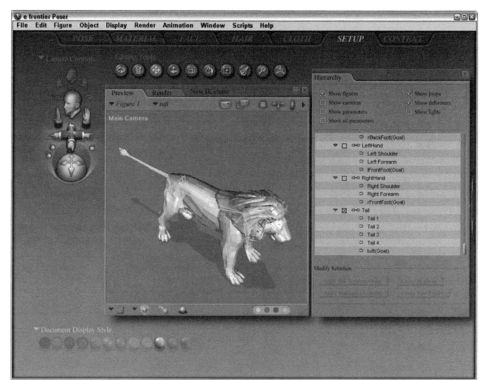

FIGURE 12-14

Chain break applied to right collar

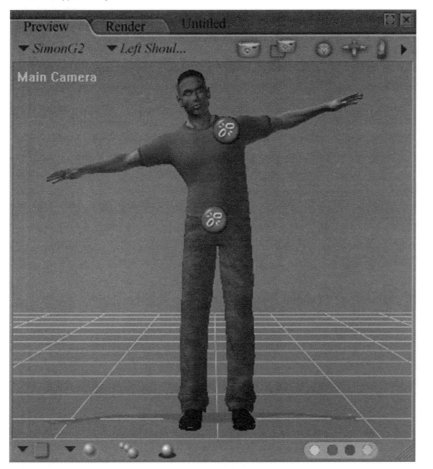

1. Open Poser with the default figure visible.

2. Select Window, Editing Tools to make the Editing Tools buttons visible, if necessary.

3. Select and pull the right upper arm element away from the center of the figure.

Notice how the torso moves with the arm element.

4. Select the Chain Break tool 🔘 from the Editing Tools (or press the L key) and click the left collar element.

A chain break icon is placed in the center of the element, as shown in Figure 12-14.

5. Select the Translate/Pull tool from the Editing Tools (or press the T key) and drag the left upper arm.

With the chain break icon placed on the left collar element, the torso remains fixed as you move the left upper arm.

6. Select File, Save As and save the file as **Chain break figure.pz3**.

Create an IK Chain

1. Select File, Open and open the Mushroom groups.pz3 file.

2. Select Window, Hierarchy Editor to open the Hierarchy Editor.

3. Scroll to the bottom of the Hierarchy Editor and select the IK Chains title. Then, click the Create IK Chain button at the bottom of the dialog box.

4. In the Set Name dialog box that appears, accept the name New IK Chain, and click OK.

5. Scroll to the list of mushroom bones in the Hierarchy Editor and select and drag the Stem1, Stem2, and Stem3 elements and drop them on the newly created IK Chain title.

6. Reorder the stem elements so they appear in order with the Stem3 element designated as the goal.

7. Click the square box to the left of the new IK chain title 🔲 ⭕-⭕ New IK Chain to enable the IK chain. Then, select and move the top element in the Pose Room.

   As the top of the mushroom is moved, the stem bones of the IK chain are also moved, as shown in Figure 12-15.

8. Select File, Save As and save the file as **Mushroom with IK chain.pz3**.

FIGURE 12-15
Mushroom with IK chain

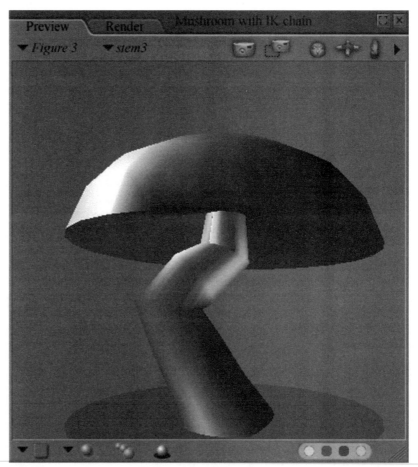

USE THE
JOINT EDITOR

What You'll Do

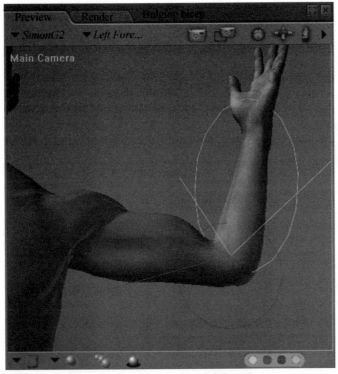

 In this lesson, you learn how to use the Joint Editor.

The most critical bone position for effective figures is the location of the joint found at the base of the bone. This joint controls how the body parts bend when the angle between adjacent bones is reduced. To precisely control the location of the joint and to define how the joint bends and twists, you can use the Joint Editor, shown in Figure 12-16. You open this panel by using the Window, Joint Editor menu command. The Joint Editor includes several sets of controls, and you can switch between these sets using the drop-down menu at the top of the editor.

FIGURE 12-16
Joint Editor

Zeroing the Figure

The Zero Figure button in the Joint Editor sets the rotation value of all joints to zero, thus causing the figure to assume its default pose with arms outstretched.

Centering the Joint

The Center set of controls displays the dimensions for the center point and the end point (if the bone doesn't include a child). The center point is the point about which the bone rotates. The panel also includes the orientation values for the center point. The Align button automatically aligns the center point to the nearest body part. When this option is selected, the center point is displayed as a green set of axes crossing where the center point is located, as shown for the shoulder joint in Figure 12-17. Moving the cursor over the center point lets you drag it to a new location.

Setting Twist Angles

The Twist option in the Joint Editor lets you set the Twist Start and Twist End values for determining the twist that the joint allows as the joint is moved. When this option is selected, the twist values are displayed as red and green lines in the Document Window.

Using Inclusion and Exclusion Angles

For the Front-Back, Side-Side, Up-Down, and Bend options, you can specify an inclusion angle (shown in green) and an exclusion angle (shown in red). All polygons within the inclusion angle are affected by the movement of the joint, and all polygons within the exclusion angle are not affected by the joint movement. Figure 12-18 shows the inclusion and exclusion angles for the Side-Side option. Notice how the inclusion angle includes all the polygons from the neck up, and the exclusion angle prevents any change for the polygons below the neck.

FIGURE 12-17
Center point

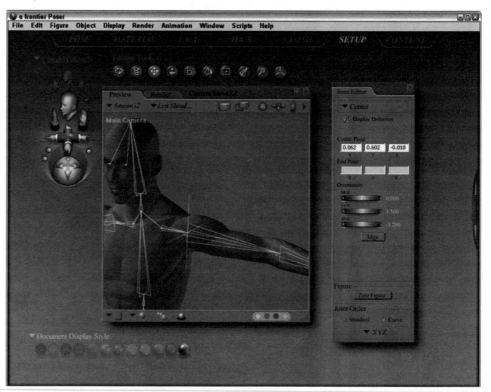

Bulging Muscles

Also within the Joint Editor panel for the Front-Back, Up-Down, and Bend options are the Bulge settings. By enabling bulges, you can set how much the muscle within the Inclusion area bulges (with a positive value) or pinches (with a negative value).

Setting Scale Values

The Scale options let you set the Scale values for the adjacent joints so that when one body part is scaled, the adjacent parts are scaled along with it. This can be used to prevent discontinuities to the figure. For example, when scaling the abdomen, you'll also want to scale the lower part of the chest. The Scaling values include High End, High Start, Low End, and Low Start.

FIGURE 12-18

Inclusion and exclusion angles

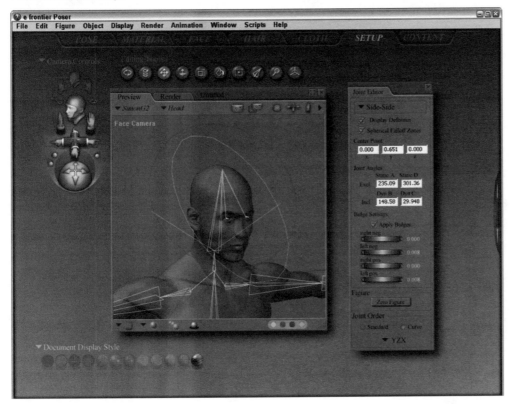

Make Bulging Muscles

1. Open Poser with the default man visible.

2. Choose Window, Joint Editor to open the Joint Editor.

3. Select the left forearm element and choose the Bend option from the top drop-down list.

4. Click the Zero Figure button in the Joint Editor.

   The figure is displayed in its default position with arms outstretched.

5. Select the View Magnifier tool from the Editing Tools and drag over the entire left arm in the Document Window to expand the view.

6. Select the Twist tool in the Editing Tools and drag on the upper arm to twist the entire arm until the palm is facing upward.

7. With the left forearm selected, enable the Apply Bulges option in the Joint Editor and set the Left Negative bulge value to 0.15.

8. Select the Rotate tool from the Editing Tools and drag the forearm element upward.

   As the forearm is brought towards the head, the bicep muscle bulges, as shown in Figure 12-19.

9. Select File, Save As and save the file as **Bulging bicep.pz3**.

FIGURE 12-19

Bulging bicep

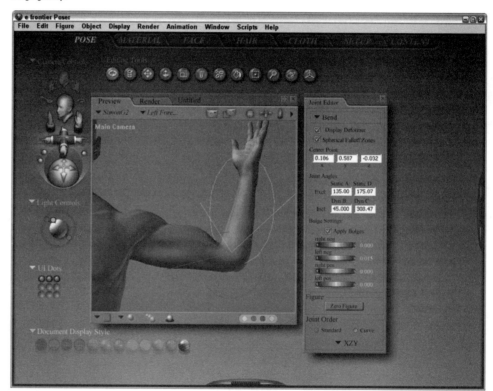

CHAPTER REVIEW

Chapter Summary

This chapter covered all the features found in the Setup Room, including the capability to edit bones used to pose the various body parts. The chapter also covered loading a skeleton onto an imported figure and creating a new set of bones, grouping body parts for each bone, and creating Inverse Kinematics chains. The Joint Editor was also covered as a way to make muscles bulge.

What You Have Learned

In this chapter, you

- Discovered the layout of the Setup Room and learned how to select bones.
- Edited bones using the Editing Tools.
- Loaded an existing skeleton onto an imported figure using the Library.
- Created a new set of bones using the Bone Creation tool.
- Grouped body parts for each bone using the Group Editor.
- Created a new IK chain to enable child objects to control parent objects using the Hierarchy Editor.
- Defined the joint settings using the Joint Editor.

Key Terms from This Chapter

- **Body part group.** A set of polygons that shares the same name as the bone that is controlling it.
- **Bone.** An invisible object that exists beneath the surface of the figure and defines how the attached body part moves as the bone is moved.
- **Bone Creation tool.** A tool used to create and place new bones.
- **Bulge.** The process of increasing a muscle's size as a joint's angle is decreased.
- **Joint.** The base of a bone that marks the position between two bones where the body parts bend.
- **Joint Editor.** A palette used to position and define the attributes of each bone and its relationship to the figure.
- **IK chain.** A set of hierarchically linked bones that are enabled using Inverse Kinematics, including root and goal objects.
- **Inclusion and exclusion angles.** Angles used to mark the polygons that are affected and unaffected by the joint's movement.

- **Inverse Kinematics.** A method for enabling child objects to control their parents.
- **Orphan polygons.** All polygons that don't belong to a group.
- **Rig.** The underlying bone skeleton used to control the position of the figure's body parts.
- **Rigging.** The process of creating a bone skeleton and connecting it to the figure's model.
- **Skeleton.** A hierarchy of bones arranged to match the figure it controls.

chapter 13
ANIMATING
FIGURES AND SCENES

1. Work with keyframes.

2. Use the Animation Palette.

3. Edit animation graphs.

4. Use animation layers.

5. Define an animation set.

6. Create a walk path.

13 ANIMATING
FIGURES AND SCENES

Posing figures is great, but with the animation features, you can make the scene come alive and allow your characters to walk and talk. Museum statues are fine, but isn't a walking, breathing figure more interesting? Animation sequences that you create in Poser can be exported to the .AVI or QuickTime video formats.

The simplest way to animate scene objects is to create keyframes for separate poses at the beginning and end of the motion. Poser can then calculate all the intermediate positions automatically by interpolating between the two poses. These keyframes are created using the Animation Controls bar at the bottom of the interface. These controls let you move through the different animation frames and keys and play the resulting animation.

You can open the Animation Palette to view all the keys for the scene. This palette also lets you move, slide, and edit the existing

keys to align them between the different animation objects. The Animation Palette keeps track of all the various animated objects and lets you move, copy, and synch keys between different scene elements.

You can also animate every parameter, and the parameter values are shown as a graph over time. Using the parameter graph interface, you can change the interpolation method, which defines the shape of the parameter graph over time.

The Animation Palette also includes a panel for specifying animation layers. Layers can be turned on and off and blended together. Animation sets can be used to save specific motions to be reused. Another way to automate an animation cycle is with the Walk Designer. This interface lets you animate a character's walking cycle, including the swinging of arms, twisting of the body, and the placing of steps one over another using several unique styles.

Tools You'll Use

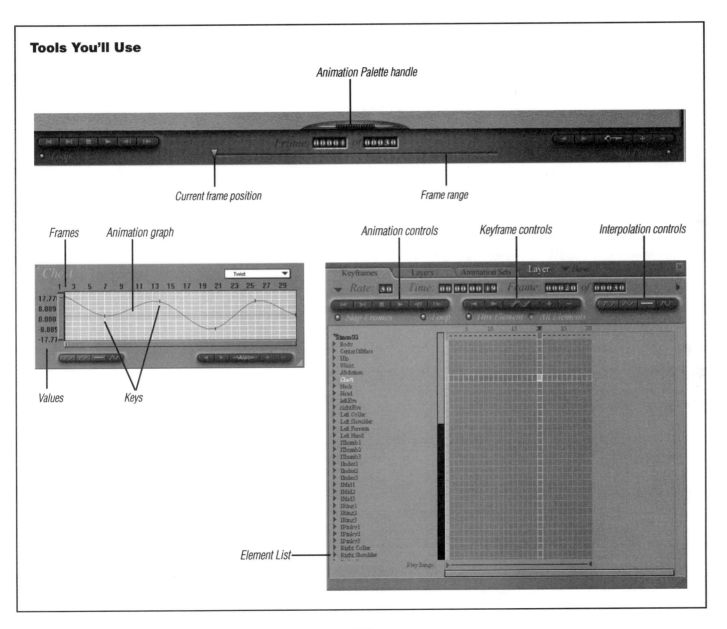

Animation Palette handle

Current frame position

Frame range

Frames

Animation graph

Animation controls

Keyframe controls

Interpolation controls

Values

Keys

Element List

WORK WITH
KEYFRAMES

What You'll Do

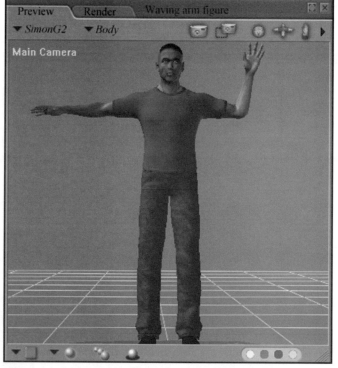

 In this lesson, you learn how to animate using keyframes.

Two main interface controls exist for working with animations. The Animation Controls at the bottom of the Poser interface offer a simple way to quickly work with animation frames and keys and the Animation Palette includes a more in-depth look at all the different animation settings.

Opening the Animation Controls

Clicking the palette handle at the bottom of the Poser window expands the Animation Controls, shown in Figure 13-1, into the interface. This set of controls includes buttons for moving between the various frames and keys. Two text fields show the current and end frame values. You can change the current frame by dragging the Timeline control positioned under the two frame values.

Moving Between Frames

The buttons on the left side of the Animation Controls bar are used to move between the different frames. The First and End Frame buttons will jump to the start or to the end of the current set of frames. The Play button cycles through all the frames from the first to the last. If the Loop option is enabled, the animation continues to play until the Stop button is pressed. The Step Forward and Step Back buttons will move forward or back a single frame with each click. You can also move through the frames by dragging the Timeline to the right or the left. To jump to a specific frame, type the frame number in the Current Frame field.

QUICKTIP The default tracking for the Document Window is set to Fast, which displays the figure as a set of boxes when the animation is played back. To see the actual figure, set the tracking at the bottom of the Document Window to Full.

Setting the Total Number of Frames

The total number of frames is also known as the *animation range*. You can change the animation range by typing a new number in the End Frame text field of the Animation Controls. If you enter a smaller number, a warning dialog box appears informing you that some frames will be deleted.

Creating Keyframes

Keyframes are simply frames that are designated as the beginning or ending position of an animated object. To create a figure keyframe, drag the Timeline slider to a different frame, move the figure, and click the Add Key Frames button in the Animation Controls. Once you create a keyframe, you can see the figure move between its original and final positions by clicking the Play button.

FIGURE 13-1

Animation Controls

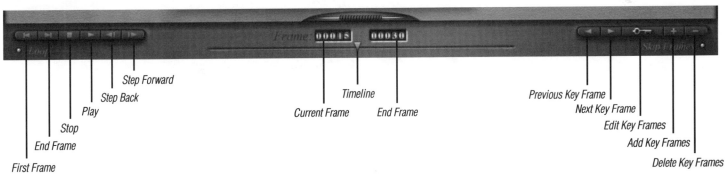

Animate with Keyframes

1. Open Poser with the default figure visible.
2. Click the side bar control at the bottom of the interface or select Window, Animation Controls.
3. Click the Animate On button  in the Camera Controls to enable the auto-animating feature.
4. Drag the Timeline to frame 10 in the Animation Controls and rotate the left arm into the waving position.
5. Drag the Timeline to frame 15 and move the forearm to the left, and then set the Timeline to frame 20 and move the forearm to the right. Then move the forearm back and forth again for frames 25 and 30.
6. Click the Play button and enable the Loop option in the Animation Controls to see the resulting animation multiple times.

   The animation is displayed in the Document Window, as shown in Figure 13-2.

7. Select File, Save As and save the file as **Waving arm figure.pz3**.

Moving Between Keyframes

As you add several keyframes to an animation sequence, you can then use the Previous and Next Key Frame buttons to move between the available keyframes. You can delete the current keyframe using the Delete Key Frames button. Clicking the Edit Key Frames button opens the Animation Palette. The Skip Frames option located below the Delete Key Frames button allows the program to skip frames as the animation sequence is being replayed in order to maintain a consistent frame rate.

FIGURE 13-2
Animated waving figure

Automatically Recording Keys

Clicking the key icon located in the Camera Controls turns on the auto-animating feature. When enabled, keys are automatically created for the current frame any time an object is moved within the Document Window.

NOTE The key icon in the Camera Controls is highlighted in red when enabled, and the key icon in the Properties palette is highlighted in green when enabled.

USE THE
ANIMATION PALETTE

What You'll Do

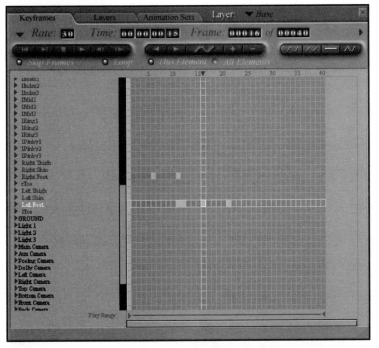

The Animation Palette, shown in Figure 13-3, is an interface that you can use to see all the keys for the entire scene at once. This makes it convenient for matching the beginning and end keys for different elements. You open the Animation Palette by clicking the Edit Key Frames button in the Animation Controls. You can also open the Animation Palette by using the Window, Animation Palette menu command.

In this lesson, you learn how to use the Animation Palette to work with keys.

Setting the Frame Rate

At the top of the Animation Palette is a value labeled Rate. This value sets the rate at which frames are played per second. Movies run at a frame rate of 24 frames per second, and computer animation typically runs at a rate of 30 frames per second for smooth animation. Half speed rates of 12 frames per second are common on the Web, but they can appear jittery. To the left of the Rate field is a pop-up menu where you can select from several preset frame rates.

Using the Animation Palette Interface

By default, the Animation Palette displays key position by frame number, but if you're trying to synch the animation with a sound track, viewing running time instead of frame numbers is helpful. The Time field at the top of the Animation Palette displays the current time in the format: hours, minutes, seconds, frames. Selecting the Display Time Code option from the Options pop-up menu displays running time labels across the top of the object rows.

Along the left side of the Animation Palette is a list of all the available scene elements, including figures, props, lights, and cameras. Clicking the small arrow icon to the left of the element title expands the element to reveal its sub-elements (such as body parts), which can also be expanded to reveal the element's parameters. Notice that the Ground element has been expanded to reveal its parameters in Figure 13-4.

FIGURE 13-3

Animation Palette

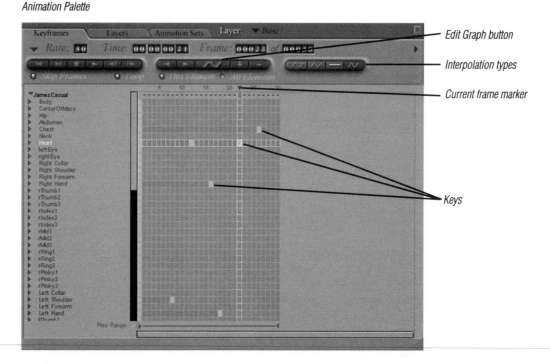

— Edit Graph button

— Interpolation types

— Current frame marker

— Keys

QUICKTIP The selected element in the Animation Palette appears highlighted in white, and the same element is selected in the Document Window.

Along the bottom of the grid cells is a green line that indicates the Play Range. By dragging the icon on either end of this green line, you can limit which portions of the animation are played in the Document Window when the Play button is clicked.

Viewing and Selecting Keys

The Animation Palette includes a list of all scene objects to the left and a table of key cells to the right. All keys created with the Animation Controls are displayed when the Animation Palette is opened. Each key is marked in a color that corresponds to its **interpolation type**, with green for spline-based interpolation, orange for linear interpolation, gray for constant interpolation,

and a diagonal line for spline breaks. The actual keys appear brighter, and the interpolated frames are the same color, only darker.

The table within the Animation Palette grid provides at a glance the available keys and lets you edit the keys by dragging them left or right. At the top of the Animation Palette are the same controls for moving between frames and keys as found in the Animation Controls bar.

FIGURE 13-4
Element parameters

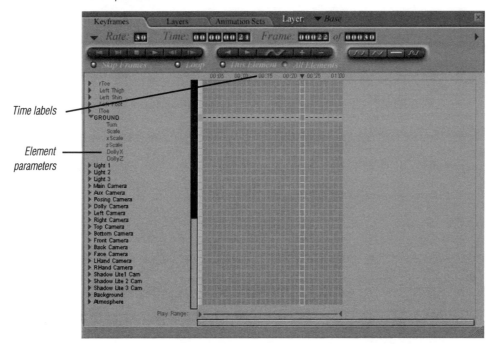

Time labels

Element parameters

You can select a single key simply by clicking it. This will highlight the entire row (representing the element or parameter) and column (representing the frame or time) that the key belongs to. You can select multiple consecutive keys at once by holding down the Shift key while clicking each grid cell. A white box surrounds all keys in the current selection. Figure 13-5 shows multiple keys selected at once.

Creating and Deleting Keys

If you click a grid cell that isn't a key, you can set a key by clicking the Add Key Frames button at the top of the Animation Palette. If the This Element option is selected, a single key is created, but if the All Elements option is selected, keys are set for the entire column. To delete a selected key, click the Delete Key Frames button or

press the Delete key. Figure 13-6 shows a column of keys created with the All Elements option.

CAUTION If the Animation Palette doesn't have focus, pressing the Delete key will delete the current figure, not the selected key.

FIGURE 13-5
Multiple keys selected

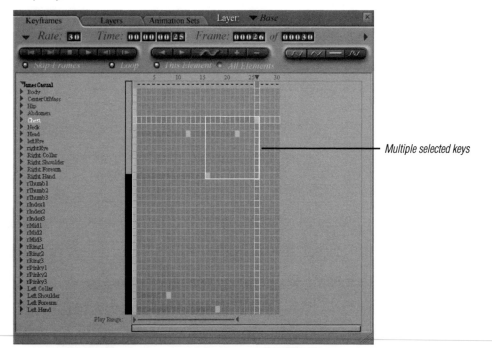

Multiple selected keys

Sliding and Copying Keys

If you click and drag on the selected key or keys, you can slide the keys to the left or to the right. This is useful when you want to synch two keys to start together. You can copy selected keyframes with the Edit, Copy menu command or by pressing Ctrl/Command+C. Similarly, you can paste keyframes to a different location with the Edit, Paste menu command or by pressing Ctrl/Command+V. You can also copy keys horizontally by dragging them with the Alt/Option key held down.

FIGURE 13-6

A column of keys

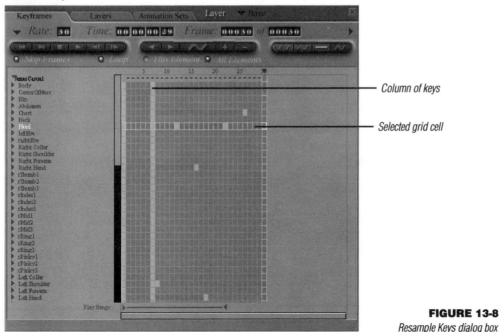

Column of keys

Selected grid cell

| **QUICKTIP** Copying the starting key to the end key for looping elements will ensure that the motion is smooth.

Retiming Keys

If you've created an animation that runs a little long or a little too short, you can use the Animation, Retime Animation menu command to scale a range a keys. This command opens the Retime Animation dialog box, shown in Figure 13-7, where you can select a set of source frames and a set of destination frames.

| **QUICKTIP** If you set the destination frames to be different than the source frames, you can copy entire blocks of keys to another part of the animation.

Resampling Keys

The Animation, Resample Key Frames menu command opens the Resample Keys dialog box, shown in Figure 13-8. Using this dialog box, you can automatically have Poser reduce and set keys at regular frames for the current element, the current figure, or for everything using the Make Key Frame every given number of frames or using the Analyze Curvature option. This is helpful for optimizing dynamic simulations that create a key for every frame.

FIGURE 13-7

Retime Animation dialog box

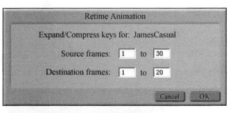

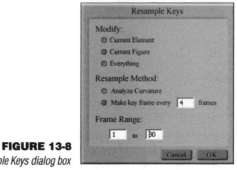

FIGURE 13-8

Resample Keys dialog box

Use the Animation Palette

1. Open Poser with the default figure visible.

2. Click the side bar control at the bottom of the interface or select Window, Animation Controls.

3. Click the Animate On button in the Camera Controls to enable the auto-animating feature. Then select the From Left camera from the Camera Controls pop-up menu.

4. Drag the Timeline to frame 10 in the Animation Controls and move the right foot object up and forward in the Document Window.

5. Click the Edit Key Frames button 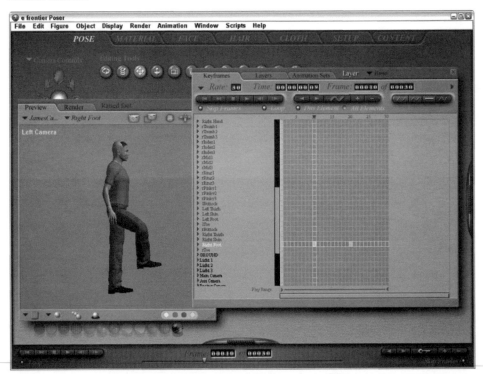 in the Animation Controls.

   The Animation Palette opens.

6. Scroll the Element List at the left of the Animation Palette until the Right Foot object and its keys are visible.

7. Click the key for the Right Foot at Frame 1 and, with the Alt/Option key held down, drag the key to the right to frame 20.

8. Click the Play button and enable the Loop option in the Animation Controls to see the resulting animation.

   The figure's right leg raises and is lowered to its original position. Figure 13-9 shows the figure with a raised foot along with the Animation Palette.

9. Select File, Save As and save the file as **Raised foot.pz3**.

FIGURE 13-9

Animated raised foot

FIGURE 13-10

Marching figure

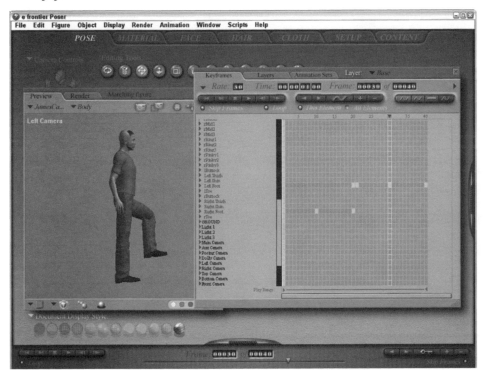

1. Choose File, Open and open the Raised foot.pz3 file.

2. Select Window, Animation Palette.

3. Enter the number **40** in the End Frame field at the top of the Animation Palette.

   Ten more frames are added to the end of the current animation.

4. Hold down the Shift key and drag over the first 20 frames for the Right Foot element to select all the keys for the right foot. Then select Edit, Copy or press the Ctrl/ Command+C keys.

5. Select the Left Foot element from the Element List to the left in the Animation Palette and select the grid cell for frame 21. Then select Edit, Paste or press the Ctrl/Command+V keys.

   The keys for the right foot have now been copied to the left foot.

6. Click the grid cell at frame 1 for the Left Foot element and drag it to the right to frame 20.

7. Click the Play button and enable the Loop option in the Animation Controls to see the resulting animation.

   The figure's right leg raises and is lowered to its original position, followed by the left foot being raised and lowered. Figure 13-10 shows the figure with a raised foot along with the Animation Palette.

8. Select File, Save As and save the file as **Marching figure.pz3**.

Scale Animation Keys

1. Choose File, Open and open the Marching figure.pz3 file.

2. Select Window, Animation Palette.

3. Select Animation, Retime Animation.

   The Retime Animation dialog box appears.

4. In the Retime Animation dialog box, set the Source Frames to 1 and 40 and the Destination Frames to 1 and 20 and click OK.

   The keys in the Animation Palette are compressed from 40 frames down to 20 frames, as shown in Figure 13-11.

5. Select File, Save As and save the file as **Double time.pz3**.

FIGURE 13-11

Marching figure double time

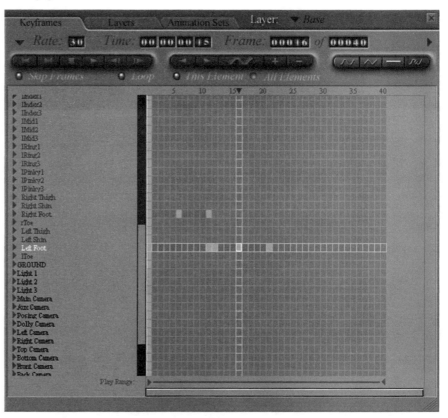

EDIT
ANIMATION GRAPHS

What You'll Do

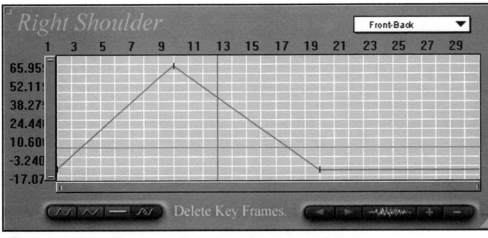

Right Shoulder

Front-Back

Delete Key Frames.

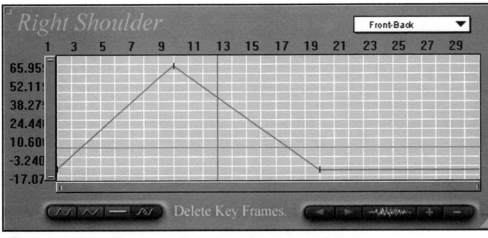 In this lesson, you learn how to edit object movement using animation graphs.

When you set keyframes to animate an object, such as raising an arm, the motion of the arm is set to gradually rise a little with each successive frame in a linear manner. But if you want the arm to quickly rise half the way and then slowly rise the rest of the way, you can use an animation graph to precisely control how the object moves over time. By changing the graph shape, you can change the resulting animation.

Accessing Animation Graphs

The easiest way to access an animation graph is to click the Edit Graph button in the Animation Palette. The animation graphs also provide a way to animate parameters throughout Poser. Another way to access animation graphs is by clicking the pop-up menu icon located to the right of each parameter value in the Parameters/Properties palette; you can select the Graph option to make an animation graph appear for the selected parameter.

Using the Animation Graph Interface

Animation graphs display a graph of the parameter value (the vertical set of numbers on the left) per frame (the horizontal set of numbers along the top of the graph), as shown in Figure 13-12. The green vertical line marks the current frame, and you can drag this line left and right to move through the available frames. The drop-down list in the upper-right corner lists all the available parameters for the selected

element. The lower-left buttons are the interpolation options that change the curve's shape, and the lower-right buttons are used to move between keys, toggle the sound display, and create and delete keys. Loading a sound file is covered in Chapter 15, "Lip Synching with Talk Designer."

QUICKTIP Click anywhere within the graph to move the current frame line.

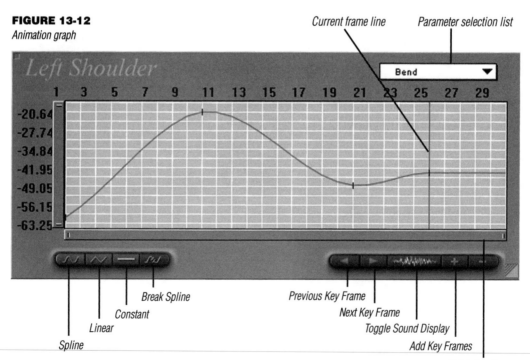

FIGURE 13-12
Animation graph

Current frame line

Parameter selection list

Break Spline

Constant

Linear

Spline

Previous Key Frame

Next Key Frame

Toggle Sound Display

Add Key Frames

Delete Key Frames

Scaling the Graph View

If the graph in the Animation Graph dialog box is too large to show the exact keys you want to work with, you can scale the graph along its values axis or along its frames axis by dragging on either end of the bar at the left and bottom of the graph area. Figure 13-13 shows a graph that has been scaled along each axis.

Adding, Moving, and Deleting Keys

Along each graph, the keys are marked as small vertical lines. Clicking the Add Key Frames button will add a new key on the graph for the current frame, which is marked by the thin vertical green line. If you move the cursor over the top of an existing key, it will change to an up-down arrow, allowing you to change the key's value by dragging it up and down. If you position the current frame marker over an existing key and click the Delete Key Frames button, the key is deleted and the curve shape changes.

Selecting and Sliding Graph Segments

To select a portion of the graph, simply drag over the portion of the curve that you want to select. The selected area is highlighted in black, as shown in Figure 13-14. Moving the cursor over the selected portion changes the cursor to side-to-side arrows, allowing you to drag the selected curve segments and any keys within the selected area left or right.

FIGURE 13-13

Scaled animation graph

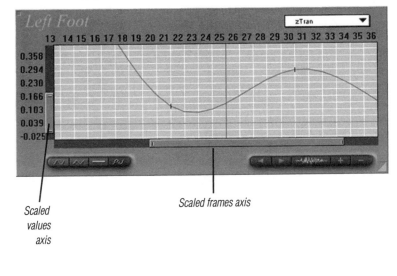

Scaled values axis

Scaled frames axis

FIGURE 13-14

Selected graph segment

Graph key   Selected graph area

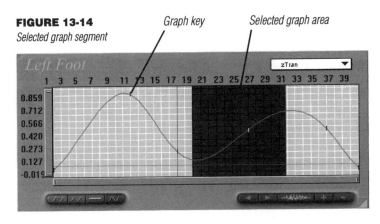

Changing the Curve's Shape

You can use the four interpolation buttons to change the shape of the graph's curve for the selected area. The default interpolation is Spline, which creates a smooth, round curve between all keys. This option is good for most animations involving figures. The Linear interpolation option makes the lines between each key a straight segment, as shown in Figure 13-15, resulting in a very rigid motion good for animating machines and robots. The Constant interpolation

option keeps the same value until the next key to form a step-like graph, shown in Figure 13-16. The final interpolation method is the Break Spline option, which adds a break at each key so that you can use the different interpolation methods between keys.

Using the Visibility Channel

For each figure and element in the scene, you can make the Visible property animatable. To do this, simply enable the small key icon next to the Visible property in the Para-

meters/Properties palette, as shown in Figure 13-17. The key turns green when enabled and is outlined when disabled. Once the property is enabled, an additional parameter dial appears in the Parameters palette named Visible. This parameter can be accessed in the Animation Graph palette. By setting keys for the Visible parameter, you can make objects slowly disappear and reappear over time. A value of 1 makes the object visible, and a value of 0 makes the object invisible.

NEW POSER 7 FEATURE

The ability to animate visibility is new to Poser 7.

FIGURE 13-15
Linear interpolation

FIGURE 13-17
The Visible property

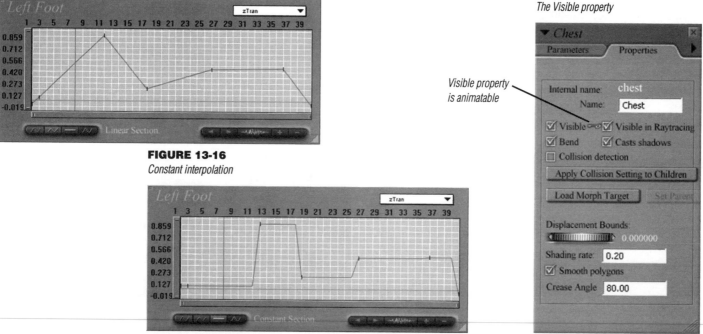

Visible property
is animatable

FIGURE 13-16
Constant interpolation

FIGURE 13-18

Animated raised arm

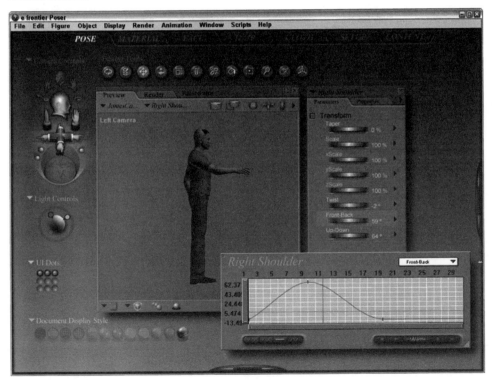

1. Open Poser with the default figure visible.

2. Select the Right Shoulder element in the Document Window and choose the From Left option from the Camera Controls pop-up menu.

3. Select Window, Parameter Dials to open the Parameters/Properties palette (if necessary).

4. Select the Graph option from the pop-up menu for the Front-Back parameter.

   The Animation Graph panel opens.

5. Click in the graph area at frame 10 and click the Add Key Frames button to add a new key. Move the cursor over the new key and drag it upward off the top of the graph. Then drag the Values Axis bar to the left of the graph area to rescale the graph. Keep dragging the key until its value is around 65.

6. Click in the graph area at frame 20 and click the Add Key Frames button to add a new key. Move the cursor over the new key and drag it downward until its value is around –12.0.

7. Drag the current frame marker back and forth in the graph panel.

   Dragging the current frame marker back and forth will move the arm in the Document Window up and down, as shown in Figure 13-18.

8. Select File, Save As and save the file as **Raised arm.pz3**.

Change the Curve's Shape

1. Choose File, Open and open the Raised arm.pz3 file.

2. Select the Right Shoulder element in the Document Window.

3. Select Window, Parameter Dials to open the Parameters/Properties palette (if necessary).

4. Select the Graph option from the pop-up menu for the Front-Back parameter.

   The Animation Graph panel opens.

5. Drag over the graph for the first 20 frames to select the area.

   The selected graph area turns black.

6. Click the Linear Interpolation button 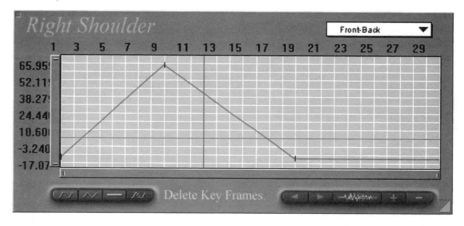 at the bottom of the animation graph panel.

   The graph segments are changed from a curve to straight lines, as shown in Figure 13-19, and the motion of the arms becomes more mechanical.

7. Select File, Save As and save the file as **Linear raised arm.pz3**.

FIGURE 13-19

Linear interpolation

Make a Figure Slowly Disappear

1. Open Poser with the default figure visible.

2. Select the Body element in the Actor List at the top of the Document Window.

3. Open the Parameters/Properties palette with the Window, Parameter Dials menus (if necessary).

4. In the Properties palette, click on the key icon to make the Visible property animatable.

   The key icon turns green.

5. Click on the Parameters tab to access the Parameters panel.

   The Visible parameter is now available.

6. Click on the menu option arrow to the right of the Visible parameter and choose the Graph option.

   The animation graph for the Body, Visible property is displayed.

7. With frame 1 selected, click on the Add Key Frame button to add a key at frame 1. Then, drag the current frame marker to frame 10 and click the Add Key Frame button again.

8. Drag both ends of the vertical scale bar and pull them towards the middle of the Values axis. Then drag the key at frame 10 downward.

   The key at frame 1 is set to 1 and the key at frame 10 is set to 0.

9. Drag from the middle of the graph over both keys and click the Spline Section button.

   The line between the two keys now gradually changes, as shown in Figure 13-20.

10. Select File, Save As and save the file as **Disappearing figure.pz3**.

FIGURE 13-20

Figure set to slowly disappear

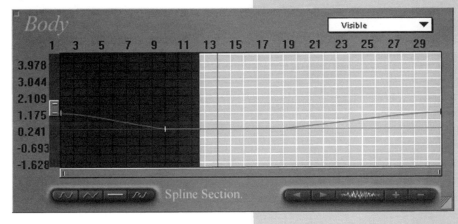

USE
ANIMATION LAYERS

What You'll Do

▶ In this lesson, you learn how to divide animation sequences using animation layers.

At the top of the Animation Palette is a Layers tab. If you click on this tab, you'll open the Animation Layers panel, shown in Figure 13-21, where you can separate specific animation sequences into layers, thus giving you more control over the resulting animation.

There are several different ways that animation layers can be used. One way is to separate several different sequences onto different layers. Then, by turning the various layers on and off, you can show several different options without having to load new files every time.

Another common way to use animation layers is to blend the sequences together to create new and interesting motions with a minimal amount of work. For example, it is fairly easy to animate a single body part, such as the arm moving to the side, but in real life, more complex motions exist. These complex motions can be created by blending together several isolated motions, such as moving the arm, twisting the torso, and rotating the shoulder.

NEW POSER 7 FEATURE

Animation layers are new to Poser 7.

Setting the Base Layer

The bottom layer is called the base layer, and it contains the entire range of frames. The base layer must always exist and cannot be deleted or renamed. The base layer always starts at frame 1, but you can change the end frame, which changes the range for the entire animation.

Creating a New Layer

You can add new layers to the panel by clicking on the New button. New layers are simply named "Layer" with a number. You can rename the layer using the Layer Name field. New layers are always placed on top of the existing layers, but you can reorganize them as needed.

QUICKTIP You should always give new layers a unique name to easily identify them as you add more layers.

Selecting Layers and Range

Only one layer can be selected at a time, and the current selection is highlighted in cyan. Once selected, you can change any of the layer's parameters in the left portion of the panel. You can also change the layer's horizontal alignment (if the layer's range is smaller than the base layer) by dragging the layer to the left or the right. You can delete the selected layer by clicking the Delete button at the top of the palette.

Enabling and Disabling Layers

Directly beneath the Layer Name field is an option to Include in Playback. This option lets you enable and disable layers.

Setting Blend Frames

For the selected layer, the Blend In and Blend Out Frames setting can be used to cause the layer's motion to gradually be added and removed from the overall animation. This is helpful if the layer includes a quick, jerking motion.

FIGURE 13-21
Animation Layers panel

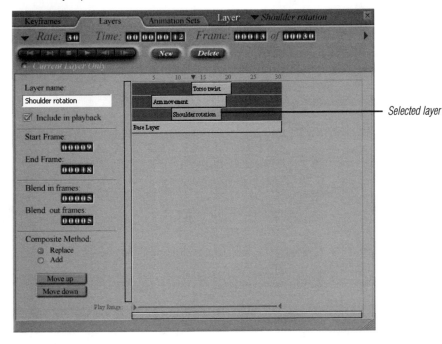

Selected layer

Changing Composite Method

The Composite Method options are used to determine how the various animation layers are combined. These options are used only if two overlapping layers affect the same body parts. For example, if the middle layer rotates the head and the top layer moves the feet, the Composite Method will have no impact. However, if both layers rotate the head, the Replace option causes the top layer motion to completely replace the middle layer's motion and, if the Add option is selected, the head motions on both layers are combined.

Changing a Layer's Position

Because the Replace Composite Method option relies on the layer's position, you can use the Move Up and Move Down buttons to change the selected layer's position relative to the other layers. No layer can be moved below the base layer.

Use Animation Layers

1. Open Poser with the default figure visible.

2. Open the Animation Controls at the bottom of the interface and click on the Edit Key Frames button to open the Animation Palette.

3. Click on the Layers tab to access the Layers panel. Then click on the New button to create a new layer. Rename the new layer **Run cycle.**

4. Open the Library palette and select the Poses category. Then, navigate to the Walk Designer folder and select and apply the G2M Run motion data.

   This motion is a loop that makes the character run over 30 frames.

5. Back in the Layers panel, click on the New button again to create a new layer. Rename the new layer **Relay handoff**. Set the start and end frames for this new layer to 10 and 20.

6. Drag the Timeline marker to frame 10 and click the Add Key Frames button in the Animation Controls. Then drag the Timeline marker to frame 15. In the Document Window, select and pull the right forearm object forward, as shown in Figure 13-22, as if the figure were handing off a baton.

FIGURE 13-22
Figure leaning forward to hand a baton

7. Within the Layers panel of the Animation Palette, select the Run cycle layer and disable the Include in Playback option. Then click the Play button.

   The animation of just the handoff is displayed.

8. Click the Stop button and enable the Include in Playback option again for the Run cycle layer. Then step through the animation one frame at a time.

Notice that the figure makes an abrupt pulling back of the arm motion at frame 15.

9. With the Relay handoff layer selected, set the Blend Out value to 6 and step through the animation again.

   This time the figure motion is more fluid and blended. Figure 13-23 shows the Animation palette.

10. Select File, Save As and save the file as **Relay handoff.pz3**.

FIGURE 13-23
Animation can be divided into layers

DEFINE AN
ANIMATION SET

What You'll Do

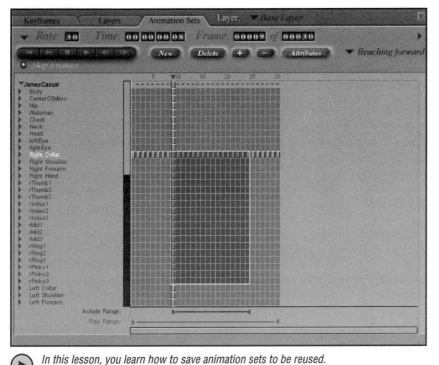

Animation sets can be defined using the Animation Sets panel of the Animation-Palette, as shown in Figure 13-24. Once defined, these animation sets can be recalled and applied to another figure. This provides a way to reuse animations.

▶ *In this lesson, you learn how to save animation sets to be reused.*

Creating a New Animation Set

To create a new animation set, simply click on the New button at the top of the palette. This opens a dialog box where you can name the new set. The new name then appears in the pop-up menu to the right of the palette.

Adding Keys to a New Animation Set

To add keys to a new animation set, drag over the range in the Animation Palette and click the Add Selection button. This highlights the selected keys in red. Keys can also be removed from the set using the Remove Selection button.

NOTE The Attributes button is reserved for use with Python scripts.

FIGURE 13-24
The Animation Sets panel of the Animation Palette

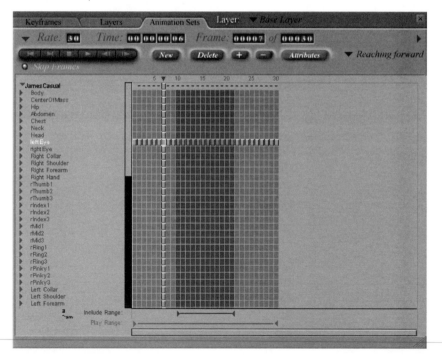

FIGURE 13-25

Saved animation set

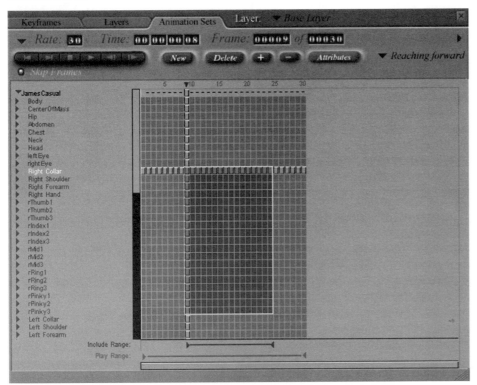

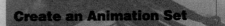
1. Open Poser with the default figure visible.

2. Select the Window, Animation Palette menu command.

   The Animation Palette opens.

3. Select the Animation Sets tab to access the Animation Sets panel. Click on the New button and name the set **Reaching forward**.

4. Drag over a set of keys in the Animation Palette and click the Add Selection button.

   The keys belonging to the animation set are displayed in red, as shown in Figure 13-25.

5. Select File, Save As and save the file as **Animation set.pz3**.

CREATE A
WALK PATH

What You'll Do

▶ *In this lesson, you learn how to animate a walk cycle using the Walk Designer.*

Once you've learned to create manual keyframes, try to create the keys to make a figure walk realistically across the floor. Although the keys involved in making a figure walk might seem rather simple, it is actually quite difficult to realistically create a walk cycle using manual keyframes. Poser includes an interface called the Walk Designer that can automatically create a walk cycle for the current figure.

Creating a Walk Path

Before you can use the Walk Designer, you need to create a *walk path*, which tells the current figure where to walk. To create a walk path, select the Figure, Create Walk Path menu command and the default walk path appears in the scene extending from the default figure, as shown in Figure 13-26. You can select this path from the Props submenu in the Actor List. It is called Path_1.

Editing a Walk Path

Along the walk path are several control points that look like simple dots. By dragging these control points, you can edit the shape of the walk path. If you click the walk path, you can add new control points to the walk path. You can delete control points by holding down the Alt/Option key and clicking the control point.

QUICKTIP It is often easiest to edit the walk path from the Top view.

Using the Walk Designer

Once you create a walk path, you can use the Walk Designer, shown in Figure 13-27, to set the parameters for the walk cycle. You open the Walk Designer dialog box by using the Window, Walk Designer menu command. To the left of the Walk Designer dialog box is a preview pane that will show a preview of the current walk settings when you click the Walk button. The 3/4, Side, Front, and Top options change the view in the preview pane, and the Figure Type button lets you open a different character file.

FIGURE 13-26

Default walk path

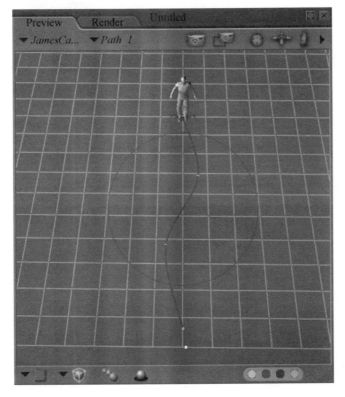

FIGURE 13-27

Walk Designer dialog box

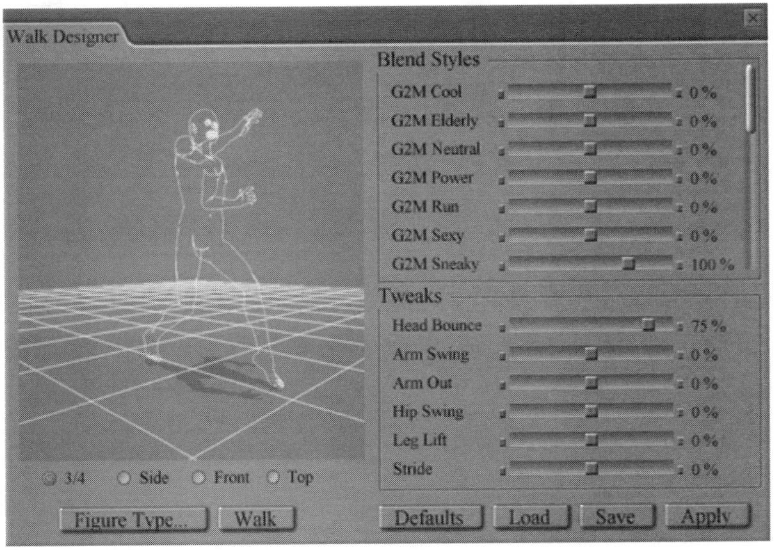

Editing the Walk Cycle

You can use all of the settings in the Blend Styles and Tweaks sections to customize the look of your walk. The Blend Styles settings control the different types of walks, such as power walk, run, sexy walk, shuffle, sneak, and strut. The Tweaks settings control how the head, arms, hips, and stride are set. The Defaults button resets all settings to their original positions.

Saving and Loading Custom Walks

If you create a custom walk cycle that you want to remember, you can use the Save button. The Save button opens a file dialog box where you can save the custom walk cycle. Walk cycles are saved as files with the .PWK extension. You can reload these files into the Walk Designer using the Load button.

FIGURE 13-28

Apply Walk dialog box

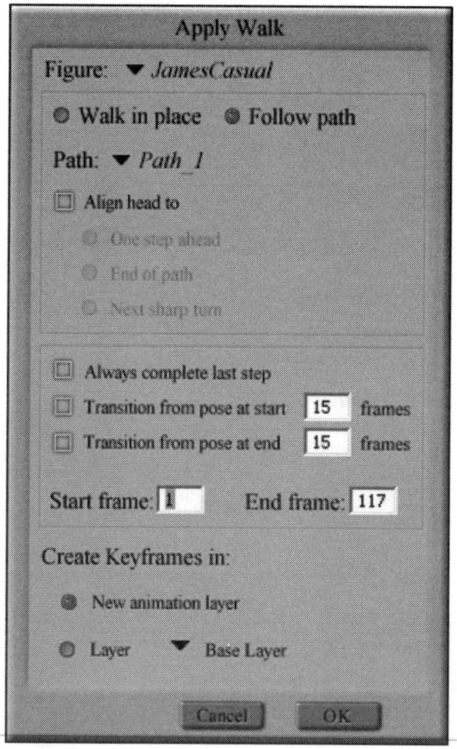

Applying a Custom Walk

After previewing your walk cycle, you can apply the finished settings to the current figure by clicking the Apply button. This opens the Apply Walk dialog box, shown in Figure 13-28. Using this dialog box, you can select which figure to apply the walk cycle to and which walk path to use. You can also select how the head is aligned, how the final steps are handled, and the total number of frames to use for the entire walk cycle. After applying the walk cycle, click the Play button in the Animation Controls to see the figure walk.

1. Open Poser with the default figure visible.

2. Select Figure, Create Walk Path.

   A walk path is added to the scene in front of the figure.

3. Drag on the Move XZ Plane to zoom out of the view and the Rotate sphere until the entire walk path is visible.

4. Drag the walk path's control points to edit the path so it winds back and forth.

5. Select Window, Walk Designer.

   The Walk Designer dialog box opens.

6. In the Walk Designer dialog box, set the G2M Sneaky setting to 100 and the Head Bounce to 75. Then click the Walk button to see a preview of the walk cycle.

7. Click the Apply button and in the Apply Walk dialog box, select the Align Head option and choose the Next Sharp Turn. Click OK.

8. Click the Play button and enable the Loop option in the Animation Controls to see the resulting animation.

   The sneaky walk cycle is applied to the figure, as shown in Figure 13-29.

9. Select File, Save As and save the file as **Sneaky figure.pz3**.

FIGURE 13-29

Sneaky walk cycle

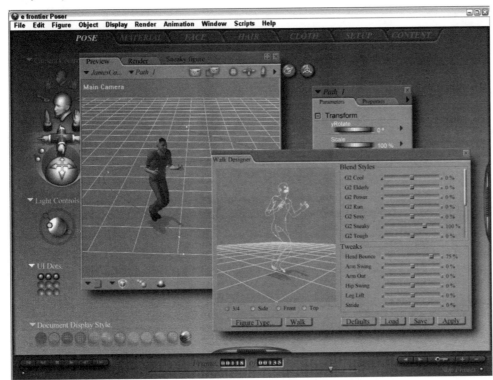

CHAPTER REVIEW

Chapter Summary

This chapter covered all the animation features found in Poser that enable you to animate using keyframes created using the Animation Controls. Once you create keys, you can use the Animation Palette to move and synch keys between different elements and view and manipulate the keys' motion using the animation graphs. You can also use the Animation Palette to divide an animation into several layers. You can save final animation files as movies using the Movie Settings panel. For creating walk cycles, the Walk Designer lets you create and use unique styles.

What You Have Learned

In this chapter, you

- Opened the Animation Controls and used them to create keyframes.

- Changed the total number of frames in an animation.

- Used the Animation Palette to create, move, scale, and edit keys for the entire scene.

- Used the Animation menu to retime and resample ranges of keys.

- Used the animation graphs to define the interpolation method used to define the shape of the curve between keys.

- Animated the visibility of objects.

- Used animation layers to divide, organize, and blend complex motions.

- Saved animation sets for reuse.

- Created a walk path and used the Walk Designer to add a walk cycle to the figure.

Key Terms from This Chapter

- **Animation layer.** An interface for dividing an animation sequence into several different sections. Layers can be combined to create complex motions from simple isolated motions.

- **Animation set.** A specific animation sequence that is named and saved to be reused on another figure.

- **Base layer.** The bottom-most layer that cannot be deleted or reduced in size.

- **Frame rate.** The rate at which frames of an animation sequence are displayed. Higher frame rates result in smoother motion, but require more memory.

- **Interpolation.** A calculation process used to determine the intermediate position of objects between two keyframes.

- **Keyframe.** A defined state of an object at one point during an animation sequence that is used to interpolate motion.

- **Loop.** A setting that causes an animation to play over and over.

- **Resampling.** The process of reducing the total number of keys required to create a motion.

- **Retiming.** The process of scaling animation keys so the relative spacing between adjacent keys remains constant.

- **Walk cycle.** A repeating set of frames that animate a figure walking.

- **Waveform.** A visual display of a sound showing its volume per time.

chapter 14

MORPHING FIGURES
AND USING DEFORMERS

1. Morph figures.

2. Create morph targets.

3. Use a magnet deformer.

4. Add a wave deformer.

5. Add a wind force deformer.

14 MORPHING FIGURES
AND USING DEFORMERS

Morphing is accomplished by interpolating the movement of an object's vertices between two set states, called *morph targets*. The result is a smooth, fluid motion that is similar to the way skin moves. It is especially good at animating facial expressions, such as expressions associated with talking.

Before you can make a morph target, you have to deform the vertices of the original object and move them from their original positions. Once the vertices have been moved, you can save a morph target. You can then use the parameter dials to move between the original state and the deformed morph target.

There are several ways to deform an object's vertices. One method is to use the Morphing tool to drag the vertices; you can

also use one of the deformer tools that are available. To deform the surface of an object, you can use the magnet and wave deformers to actually pull vertices away from a body part. You can turn these deformations into morph targets that appear in the Parameters palette.

You can also define dynamics parameters that are used to compute the position and motions of hairs through all animated frames. These dynamics parameters include gravity, springiness, and stiffness, and can even include collision detection. In addition to gravity, you can add wind force to the simulation using the wind force deformer.

Tools You'll Use

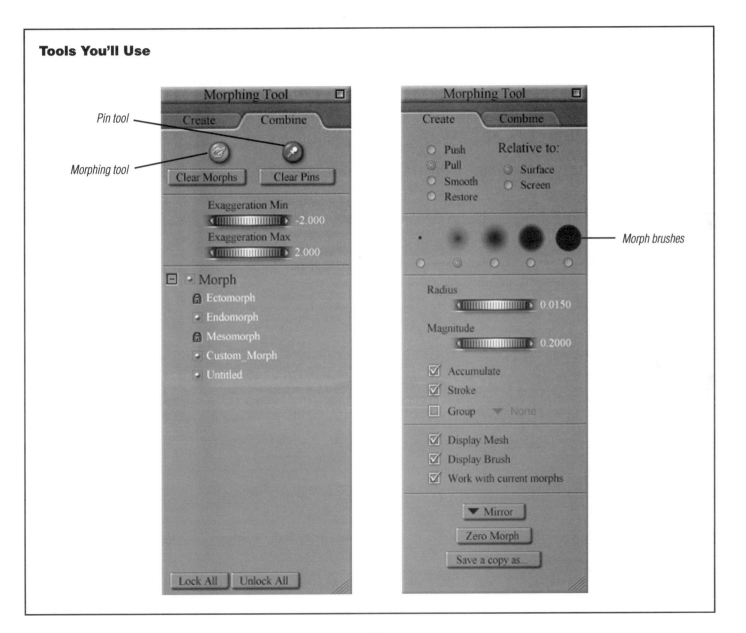

Pin tool

Morphing tool

Morph brushes

MORPH
FIGURES

What You'll Do

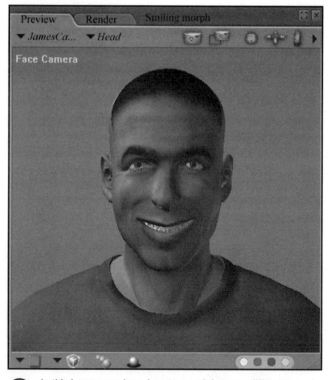

Morphing is a process where an object changes its shape and form over time. 3D morphing takes place between objects that have the same number of vertices so that each vertex knows exactly where to move to. Each morph state is known as a *morph target*.

By creating several morph targets, you can animate subtle changes, such as having the face smile or make an expression. Because the animation is based on the available morph targets, the motion flows smoothly and multiple targets can be used one after another to create complex expressions.

Using Pre-Defined Morph Targets

Most of the figures in the Poser Library have several morph targets already defined. These show up as parameters in the Parameters palette. For example, the Simon G2 figure has full-body morphs for setting the body's shape. Figure 14-1 shows the default Simon figure with the Meso-morph value increased.

Using the Morphing Tool

The Morphing tool can directly deform an element with a morph target applied to it by moving its vertices. Selecting the Morphing tool opens the Morphing Tool panel for the selected object and displays all the available morph targets that you can work with. Figure 14-2 shows the Morphing Tool panel for the body object, which includes morph targets for deforming the body's musculature.

Moving and Pinning Vertices

At the top of the Morphing Tool panel are two buttons. The Putty button lets you drag to move vertices for the selected morphs, and the Pin button lets you click to set vertices that will not move. The Clear Morphs button removes any morph editing done with the Putty tool, and the Clear Pins button removes any placed pins.

Setting Morph Limits

The Exaggeration Min and Max dials are used to control the limits of the morph. Clicking the small button to the left of each morph will toggle a lock on the morph. Locked morphs have a small lock icon displayed next to their name. If you want to lock or unlock all the morphs within the Morphing Tool panel, you can click on the Lock All or Unlock All buttons at the bottom of the palette.

FIGURE 14-1
Mesomorph pre-defined morph parameter

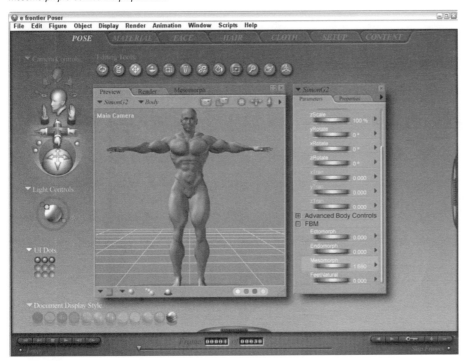

FIGURE 14-2
Morphing Tool panel

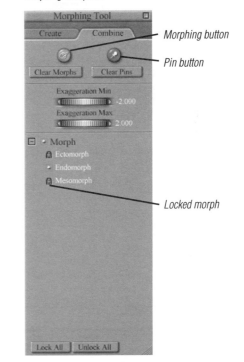

Use the Morphing Tool

1. Open Poser with the default figure visible.

2. Select Window, Editing Tools to make the Editing Tools buttons visible, if necessary.

3. Select the head object in the Document Window and choose the Face camera in the Camera Controls.

4. Select the Morphing tool 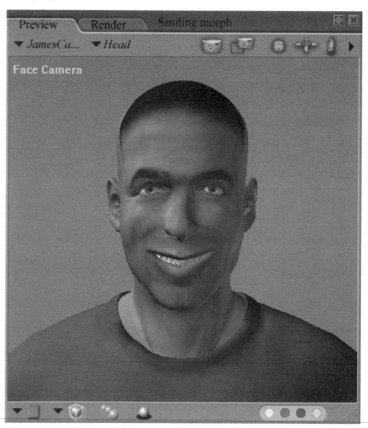 from the Editing Tools.

   The Morphing Tool panel opens with all available morphs listed.

5. Click the small button 🔒 Morph to the left of the Nose and Eyes sections in the Morphing Tool panel to lock them.

6. Click above and to the side of the mouth and drag with the Morphing tool.

   The mouth morphs into a smile, as shown in Figure 14-3.

7. Select File, Save As and save the file as **Smiling morph.pz3**.

FIGURE 14-3
Smiling morph

CREATE
MORPH TARGETS

What You'll Do

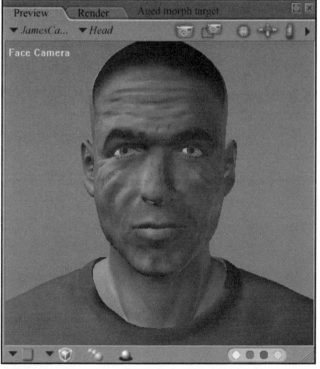

In this lesson, you learn how to create morph targets.

Once a figure is deformed using the Morphing tool, you can use the Create panel, shown in Figure 14-4, to create and save the deformed object as a morph target.

NEW POSER 7 FEATURE
The Create panel of the Morphing tool is new to Poser 7.

FIGURE 14-4
Create panel of the Morphing tool

Creating a Morph Target

Once the surface of an object is deformed, you can use the deformation to create a new morph target. Morph targets appear within the Parameters palette as a new named parameter. Dragging the parameter dial changes the deformation between the full deformation amount (with a value of 1.0) to an inverted deformation (with a value of −1.0). Morph targets provide an easy way to create subtle surface changes, and they can be animated.

Within the Create panel are several methods for deforming the morph. They include

- **Push.** Causes the vertices to be pushed inward towards the center of the object.
- **Pull.** Causes the vertices to be pulled outward away from the center of the object.
- **Smooth.** Causes a general smoothing over the entire surface, thus eliminating any extreme peaks or valleys.
- **Restore.** Causes the vertices to gradually return to their original location.

The position the vertices are moved as you drag over them and the move can be based relative to the Surface of the object, or relative to the Screen. You can also choose the Brush size and Feathering options using the Presets or with the Radius and Magnitude parameters.

The Accumulate option stacks the changes on top of one another so that more painting yields more of a change. The Stroke option lets the vertices move only one magnitude value for each time you drag over the vertices. You can also select the group that the changes are applied to. This helps prevent changing the wrong sections.

FIGURE 14-5
Brush size is displayed

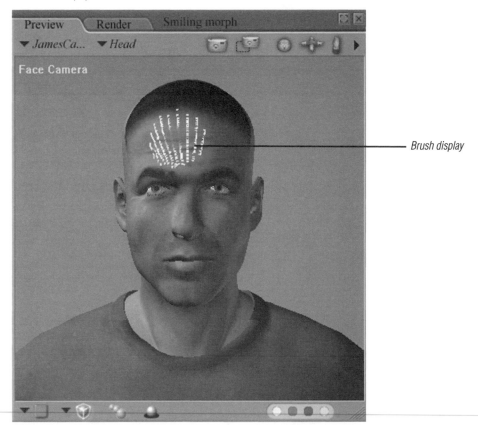

Brush display

The Display Mesh option shows the original mesh under the morph changes. The Display Brush option shows the brush as a cursor over the surface of the object, as shown in Figure 14-5. This option provides some feedback about the size of the current brush. The brush also displays a gradient showing the areas where the effect is at maximum and how the brush's power falls off with distance. The hard edge brush doesn't have a gradient.

The Mirror option includes selections for defining the symmetry axis. When enabled, any changes on one side of the object are mirrored to the opposite side automatically. This is a great way to make sure that changes on either side of the face or body are symmetrical. Zero Morph resets the vertices to their original position.

Saving a Morph Target

The Save a Copy As button in the Create panel opens a dialog box where you can name the new morph target. This new target is then added to the Parameters palette where you can test out the changes.

Spawning a New Morph Target

With a deformation set to its maximum value, you can create a new morph target using the Object, Spawn Morph Target menu command. This command opens a simple dialog box where you can name the morph target. This name appears in the Parameters palette for the selected object. Figure 14-6 shows a new morph target created for a serious condition called Chipmunk cheeks caused by stuffing nuts in your cheeks.

Deleting Morph Targets

To delete a morph target, open the Hierarchy Editor, locate and select the morph target, and press the Delete key. Morph targets will be visible when the Show Parameters option is enabled. The morph target will be located

under its object. You can also delete the morph target using the Delete Morph command in the pop-up menu to the right of the parameter.

Creating Full-Body Morphs

If your figure includes several morphs that you want to include together in a single morph target, such as a figure flexing all his arm muscles, you can create full-body morph targets using the Figure, Create

FIGURE 14-6
Chubby cheeks morph target

Full Body Morph menu command. This command makes a simple dialog box appear where you can name the morph target. The morph target appears in the Parameters palette when the Body actor is selected.

Splitting Morph Targets

You can split an existing morph target into its right and left halves using the Split Morph option in the pop-up menu. This creates two new parameter dials labeled right and left with the original name.

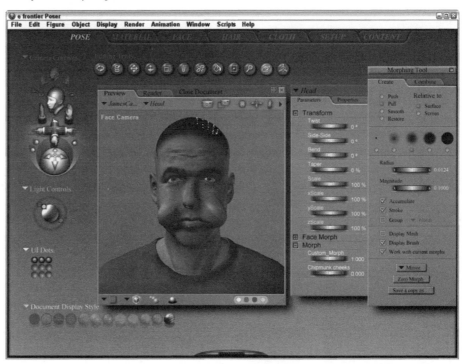

Create a Morph Target

1. Open Poser with the default figure visible.

2. In the Camera Controls, switch to the Face Camera to get a close up on the head.

3. Select the Morphing tool in the Editing Tools and click on the Create panel. Choose the Push mode and the smallest brush. Then enable the Display Brush option.

4. Drag the brush over the forehead to add some deep creases. Then drag around the edges of the mouth and to the side of the nose, concentrating on the left side of the face.

5. Once the left side of the face looks good, choose the Mirror, +x to −x option to apply the wrinkles to the opposite side of the face.

   The wrinkles add some age to the figure, as shown in Figure 14-7.

6. Click on the Save a Copy As button and name the morph target **Wrinkles**.

   The wrinkles parameter dial appears in the Parameters palette.

7. Select File, Save As and save the file as **Aged morph target.pz3**.

FIGURE 14-7

Aged face

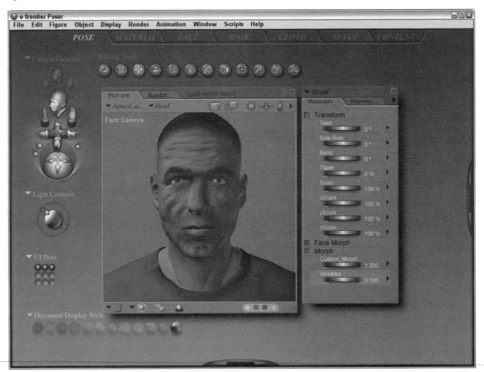

FIGURE 14-8

Now, only half the face has aged.

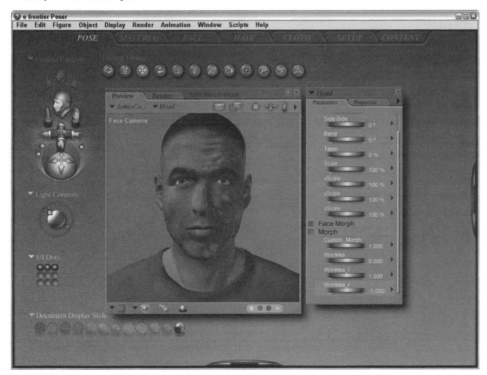

1. Choose File, Open and open the Aged morph target.pz3 file.

2. Open the Parameters palette and select the Split Morph option from the pop-up menu to the right of the Wrinkles parameter dial.

   Two new parameters, one for the left side of the face and one for the right side of the face, are added to the Parameters palette.

3. Set the Wrinkles_Left dial value to 1.0 and the Wrinkles_Right dial value to −1.0.

   The causes only half of the face to be wrinkled, as shown in Figure 14-8.

4. Select File, Save As and save the file as **Split morph target.pz3**.

USE A
MAGNET DEFORMER

What You'll Do

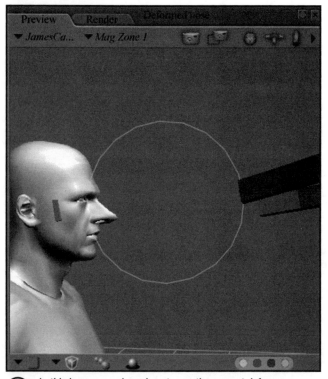

In this lesson, you learn how to use the magnet deformer.

The Editing Tools limit the editing that you can do to the individual body parts, but they cannot change the surface of objects to bulge muscles or stretch the body's skin. To deform the skin in this manner, you can use several specialized objects called *deformers*.

Learning the Deformer Types

There are three deformer objects and they are all available in the Object menu. The three deformers are:

- **Magnet:** Used to pull vertices away from an object.

- **Wave:** Used to deform surface vertices in a wave pattern.

- **Wind Force:** Used to add a wind force to the scene that is used by the hair and cloth simulations.

Creating a Magnet Deformer

You can add the magnet deformer to the scene using the Object, Create Magnet menu command. The magnet deformer can only be applied when the body part that you want to deform is selected. It cannot be used on a figure. The magnet deformer consists of three separate parts—the magnet object, its base, and the magnet zone. You can move, rotate, and scale each of these parts using the standard Editing Tools.

Using the Magnet Parts

The magnet base and the magnet object set the amount of pull that's applied to deform the body parts. The farther away these two parts are, the stronger the deformation. The magnet zone defines the area that can be deformed by the magnet deformer. Figure 14-9 shows an example of the magnet deformer in action. The magnet base is positioned at the side of the head and the magnet object is positioned away from the head, thus causing all vertices within the magnet zone to be attracted towards the magnet object. But the magnet zone limits only the ear to be deformed.

FIGURE 14-9
Magnet deformer

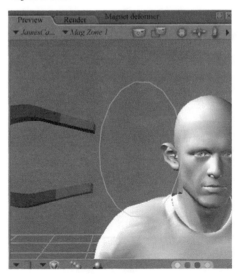

QUICKTIP You can hide deformers from the scene using the Display, Deformers, Hide All menu command and make them visible again with the Display, Deformers, Show All or the Display, Deformers, Current Selection Only menu commands.

Deforming Additional Elements

Initially, only the part that is selected when the magnet is created is deformed. However, you can add more elements to be deformed by the same magnet object by clicking the Add Element to Deform button in the Properties palette when the magnet object is selected. This button opens a Choose Actor List that displays all the available scene elements in a hierarchical list. Select the additional element you want to deform and click OK. The additional element will be deformed only if it is within the magnet zone.

FIGURE 14-10
Magnet Zone Falloff curve

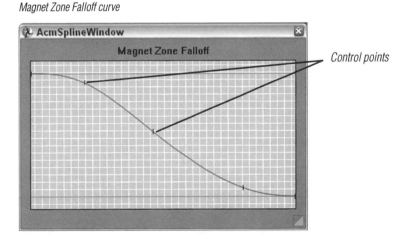

QUICKTIP Once you create a morph target, you can delete the deformer objects without affecting the morph target.

Setting Magnet Zone Falloff

When deforming muscles, you'll want a nice smooth bulge instead of a sharp pointy one. You can control the shape of the vertices that are deformed using a Falloff graph. To open the Magnet Zone Falloff curve, select the magnet zone object and click the Edit Falloff Graph button in the Properties palette. The Magnet Zone Falloff curve, shown in Figure 14-10, displays the falloff curve. You can edit this curve by dragging its control points, which are small vertical lines on the curve. To create a new control point, just click the curve where you want the new control point to be.

Control points

1. Open Poser with the default figure visible.

2. Select the Face camera  and rotate it with the Rotate sphere so the side of the head is visible.

3. Select the head object in the Document Window and choose Object, Create Magnet.

   The magnet object, the magnet base, and the magnet zone are all added to the scene.

4. Select the Rotate tool from the Editing Tools and rotate the magnet base so it is positioned at the base of the figure's nose. Select the Translate/Pull tool and move the magnet zone so only the nose is within it. Then, move the magnet object away from the head.

   The nose is deformed and extended from the face, as shown in Figure 14-11.

5. Select File, Save As and save the file as **Deformed nose.pz3**.

FIGURE 14-11
Deformed nose

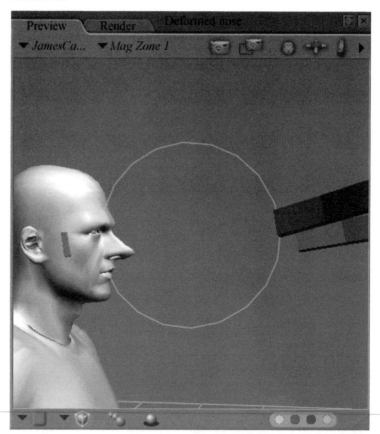

ADD A
WAVE DEFORMER

What You'll Do

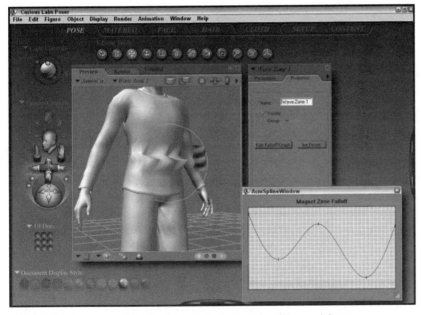

In this lesson, you learn how to deform objects using the wave deformer.

Creating a Wave Deformer

You can add the wave deformer to the scene using the Object, Create Wave menu command. It deforms objects using wave patterns. The wave deformer consists of two separate parts—the wave object and the wave zone. You can move, rotate, and scale both of these parts using the standard Editing Tools. The wave object includes options in the Properties palette for applying the deformation in a Radial direction using concentric circles or a Directional option for creating linear waves. You can also select to deform the vertices in the direction of the wave deformer or along the object's normal vectors. Figure 14-12 shows a wave deformer applied to a figure's arm.

Deforming Additional Elements

Initially, only the part that is selected when the wave is created is deformed. However, you can add more elements to be deformed by the same wave object by clicking the Add Element to Deform button in the Proper-ties palette when the wave object is selected. This button opens a Choose Actor List that displays all the available scene elements in a hierarchical list. Select the additional element you want to deform and click OK. The additional element will be deformed only if it is within the wave zone.

Setting Wave Zone Falloff

The wave deformer includes the same Falloff curve that you can select and edit using the Edit Falloff Graph button in the Properties palette.

FIGURE 14-12
Wave deformer

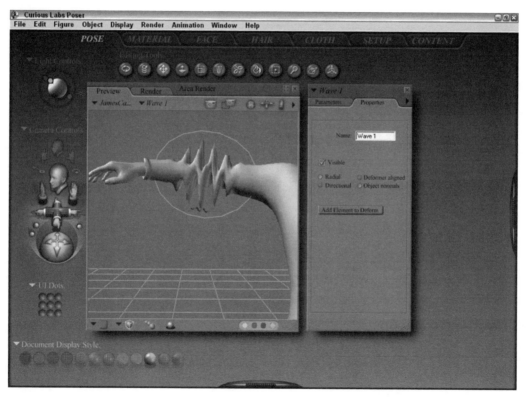

FIGURE 14-13
Wavy stomach

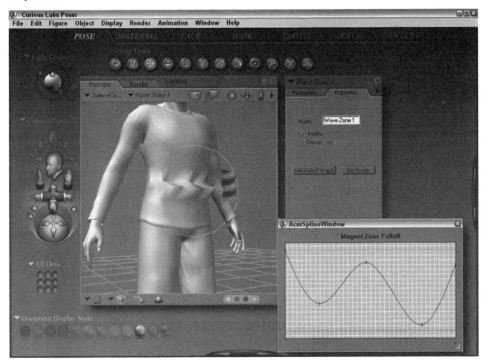

1. Open Poser with the default figure visible.

2. Drag on the Move XZ Plane control in the Camera Controls to zoom in on the stomach region and rotate the view with the Rotate sphere.

3. Select the Abdomen object in the Document Window and choose Object, Create Wave.

   The wave object and the wave zone are added to the scene.

4. Use the Rotate and Translate tools from the Editing Tools and move and rotate the wave base so it is vertically positioned in front of the stomach. Select the Translate/Pull tool and move the magnet zone so only the front of the stomach is within the zone.

5. Select the wave zone object and click the Edit Falloff Graph button in the Properties palette to open the Falloff graph. Click at the center of the curve to add a new control point and drag the control points to create a wavy pattern.

   The stomach is deformed with a wave pattern, as shown in Figure 14-13.

6. Select File, Save As and save the file as **Wavy stomach.pz3**.

ADD A
WIND FORCE DEFORMER

What You'll Do

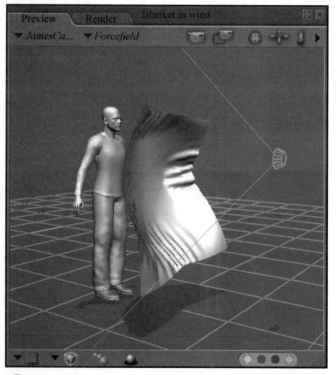

In this lesson, you learn how to add wind with the wind force deformer object.

Hair simulations include the force of gravity by default, but you can also add a directional wind force to the simulation using the Object, Create Wind Force menu command.

Positioning the Forcefield

When the wind force deformer is added to the scene, it is represented by a simple indicator that has two diagonal lines projecting from it, as shown in Figure 14-14. You can position and orient the wind indicator anywhere in the scene using the standard Editing Tools; the diagonal lines denote the direction of the wind from the center of the indicator outward towards the diagonal lines.

Changing the Forcefield's Parameters

When the wind force deformer is selected, several parameters are available in the Parameters/Properties palette, including the following:

- **Amplitude:** Sets the strength of the wind force.

- **Spread Angle:** Sets the angle for the diagonal lines, which is the area where the wind has influence.

- **Range:** Sets how far the wind force is projected.

- **Turbulence:** Sets the amount of variability applied to the wind.

The wind only affects hair that is within the Spread Angle and Range parameters.

NOTE You can also use wind force deformers to deform dynamic cloth and hair.

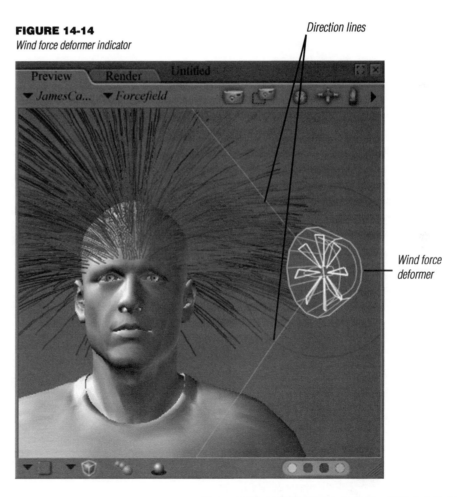

FIGURE 14-14
Wind force deformer indicator

Direction lines

Wind force deformer

Add a Wind Force Deformer to Hair

1. Choose File, Open and open the Hair in wind.pz3 file.

2. Click the Hair tab at the top of the interface to open the Hair Room.

3. Select the Object, Create Wind Force menu command to add a wind force deformer to the scene.

   The deformer appears at the scene origin.

4. Drag the deformer object with the Translate/Pull tool and the Rotate tool to position and orient the deformer in front and to the side of the figure's face so the direction lines are pointing towards the figure's head.

5. Select the Face camera from the Camera Controls.

6. Select the Window, Parameter Dials menu command to open the Parameters/Properties palette. With the deformer selected, set the Amplitude to 10, the Spread Angle to 15, the Range to 1.0, and the Turbulence to 1.0.

7. Select the hair object and click the Calculate Dynamics button.

   A progress dialog box appears, and every frame for the simulation is calculated. The result is that the hair is blown towards the back of the head, as shown in Figure 14-15.

8. Select File, Save As and save the file as **Blown hair.pz3**.

FIGURE 14-15

Blown hair

1. Choose File, Open and open the Cloth in wind.pz3 file.
2. Click the Cloth tab at the top of the interface to open the Cloth Room.
3. Select the Object, Create Wind Force menu command to add a wind force deformer to the scene.

   The deformer appears at the scene origin.
4. Drag the deformer object with the Translate/Pull tool and position it in front of the cloth object so the direction lines are pointing towards the cloth object.
5. Select the Window, Parameter Dials menu command to open the Parameters palette. With the deformer selected, set the Amplitude to 10, the Range to 2, and the Turbulence to 1.0.
6. Click the Calculate Simulation button.

   A progress dialog box appears, and every frame for the simulation is calculated. The result is that the cloth object is blown towards the default figure, as shown in Figure 14-16.
7. Select File, Save As and save the file as **Blanket in wind.pz3**.

FIGURE 14-16

Blanket in the wind

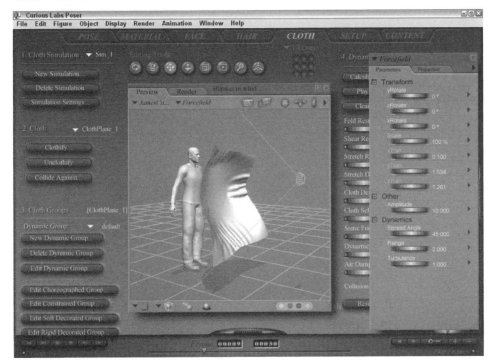

CHAPTER REVIEW

Chapter Summary

This chapter covered morphing and deforming the object to create full-body morphs. Morph targets are created by deforming an object. These deformations can be created using the Morphing tool and by using deformers. There are three available deformers in Poser: magnet, wave, and wind. You can add wind forces to the scene to interact with hair using the wind force deformer.

What You Have Learned

In this chapter, you

- Used pre-defined morph targets found in the Parameters palette.

- Created new morph targets for the Parameters palette.

- Deformed object surfaces using the Morphing tool.

- Used the Create panel to save new morph targets.

- Used the magnet and wave deformers to deform the element surfaces.

- Added wind to the simulation using a wind force deformer.

Key Terms from This Chapter

- **Deformer.** An object used to deform the surface of body parts by moving vertices.

- **Magnet.** A deformer used to pull vertices away from an object.

- **Morph target.** A custom parameter that defines an object deformation that appears as a parameter in the Parameters palette.

- **Wave.** A deformer used to deform surface vertices in a wave pattern.

- **Wind Force.** A deformer used to add a wind force to the scene that is used by the hair and cloth simulations.

chapter 15

LIP SYNCHING
WITH TALK DESIGNER

1. Use the Talk Designer interface.

2. Work with sound.

15 LIP SYNCHING
WITH TALK DESIGNER

Animating a character as it speaks can be one of the trickier animation tasks, but the entire process can be automated using Poser's Talk Designer. This interface works for facial animation in the same way that walking and running can be animated using the Walk Designer.

The Talk Designer lets you load a sound file used to synchronize with the animation. You can also load an external **Viseme Map** file that defines the facial shapes used to create speech sounds. Once loaded, Poser will detect the various speech sounds in the sound file and match them to the facial morph targets. The results make the figure speak in synch with the sound file.

The Talk Designer can also be used to control the head motions of your figures, including their eye blink rate and several emotional tweaks, in order to give your figure more life. The emotions that can be represented by dragging the Talk Designer sliders include anger, disgust, fear, joy, sadness, and surprise.

If you look closely in the Animation Graph dialog box, you'll notice a Toggle Sound Display button. If a sound is loaded into a scene using the File, Import, Sound menu, then the sound waveform can be made visible in the animation graph making it easy to synchronize the sound with the figure's keys. This feature works independently of the Talk Designer and can be used to add sound effects to the scene.

Tools You'll Use

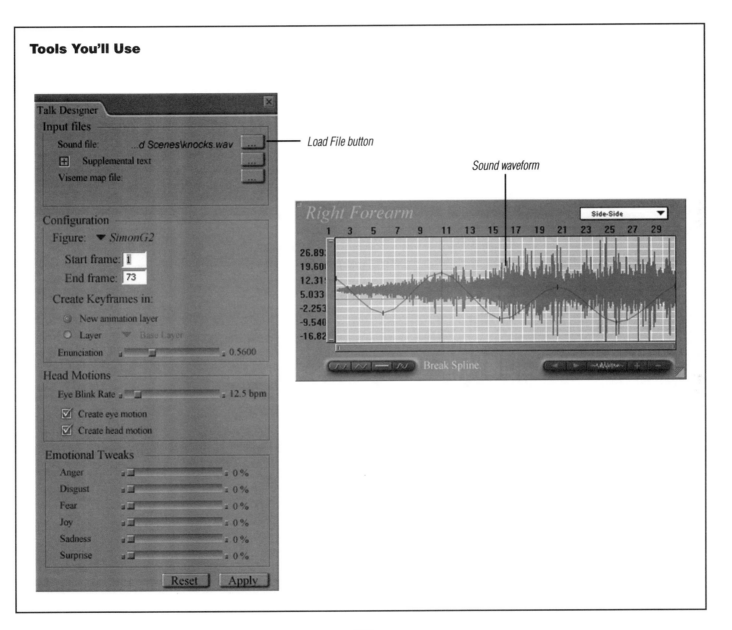

Load File button

Sound waveform

USE THE TALK
DESIGNER INTERFACE

What You'll Do

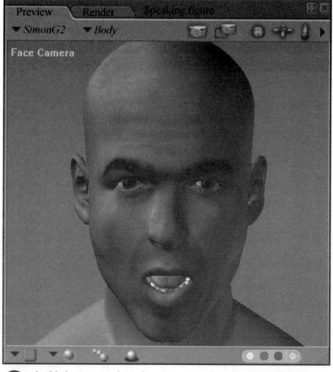

▶ In this lesson, you learn how to open and work with the Talk Designer.

You open the Talk Designer, shown in Figure 15-1, using the Window, Talk Designer menu command. This interface lets you load sound files, configure the interface, and set any head motions and emotional tweaks.

NEW POSER 7 FEATURE
The Talk Designer interface is a new feature in Poser 7.

Loading a Sound File

Sound files can be loaded directly into the Talk Designer using the Load Files button located at the top of the interface. You can also load sound files into the Talk Designer using the File, Import, LipSync Audio menu. This loads and opens the Talk Designer in one action. The file types that can be loaded into the Talk Designer include .WAV files for Windows computers and .AIFF files for Macintosh computers.

CAUTION Talk Designer has trouble with some 8-bit and 32-bit sound files. 16-bit sound files load without problems.

FIGURE 15-1

Talk Designer palette

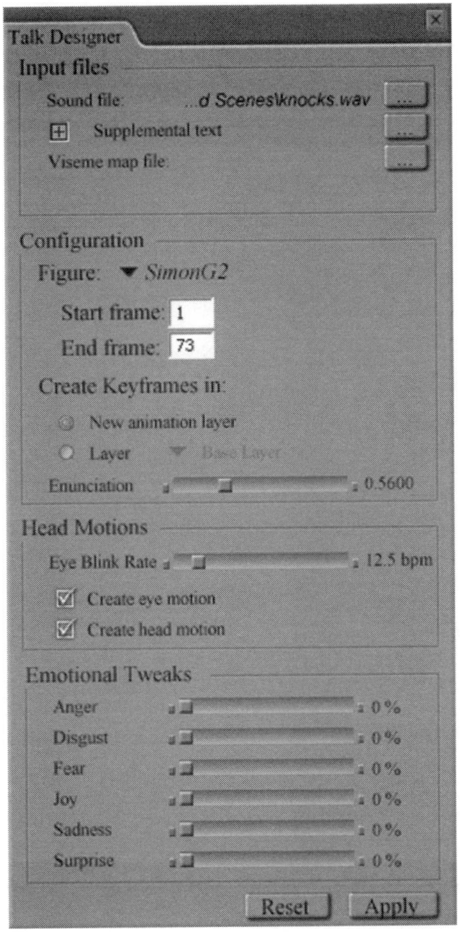

Loading a Supplemental Text File

To better identify various words in a speech, you can load or enter the text that is spoken in the sound file into the Supplemental Text area. If you click the Load File button, you can load a text file that includes the spoken words, or you can click directly on the plus icon to the left of the Supplemental Text label. A text area, shown in Figure 15-2, then opens where you can type the text directly.

FIGURE 15-2

Supplemental text area

Selecting a Viseme Map File

When a figure makes phonemes, which are the various sounds of speech, such as Ah, Oh, Ch, Em, and so on, the face has a shape (or a morph target) associated with the sound. For example, when a figure makes an Oh phoneme, the mouth is open and the lips are pulled in to create an O shape, as shown in Figure 15-3.

FIGURE 15-3

Oh phoneme sound

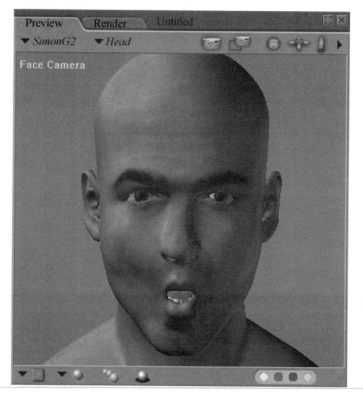

Most of the Library figures included in Poser 7 include phonemes morph targets by default. You can look for these facial morph targets by selecting the Head element and opening up the Parameters palette. If the figure includes these morph targets, there will be parameter dials under the Face Morph, Phonemes section of the Parameters palette. The common phonemes for default figures include A, CH, E,

FIGURE 15-4

The Phonemes section of the Parameters palette

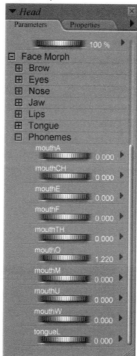

F, TH, O, M, U, W and L, as shown in Figure 15-4. The Viseme Map file relates each morph target to its corresponding phoneme. The default Viseme Map files are located in the LipSync folder where Poser is installed. If you apply the matching Viseme Map for the loaded figure from the LipSync folder, Talk Designer works fine.

CAUTION Using Talk Designer with a Viseme Map that doesn't match the current figure yields unexpected results.

Loading an External Viseme Map File

If the figure that you're using doesn't have any defined phoneme morph targets, you can check with the figure's creator to see if they have facial morph targets and a corresponding external Viseme Map file for the figure. The Viseme Map file is an .XML file that matches the various sounds to their corresponding phoneme morph targets. If you get one of these external Viseme Maps, you can load it into the Talk Designer using the Load File button to the right of the Viseme Map File label.

Configuring the Talk Designer

In the Configuration section of the Talk Designer, you can select the figure that will be doing the speaking. You can also specify the start and end frames for the animation. If you load a sound file, the end frame will automatically be set to correspond with the end of the sound file based on the length of the sound file and the frame rate.

The Create Keyframes In options let you save the animation keyframes that the Talk Designer generates to a New Animation Layer or to an existing layer. If you don't plan on using layers, you can simply select to use the base layer.

QUICKTIP It is a good idea to save the Talk Designer keyframes to a new animation layer so they don't affect any existing animations.

The facial shapes created by the Talk Designer can be subtle or exaggerated, depending on the intensity of the corresponding sound file; but by using the Enunciation slider, you can select to increase or decrease how exaggerated the facial movements are.

Setting the Blink Rate

If you speak with someone for a period of time, you might notice that all people generally blink their eyes at a rate of roughly 12.5 times a minute. Using the Eye Blink Rate, you can set this rate to be more or less than this average. A Blink Rate of 0 could be used to represent a serious focused persona, whereas a really high blink rate could simu

FIGURE 15-5
A figure blinking

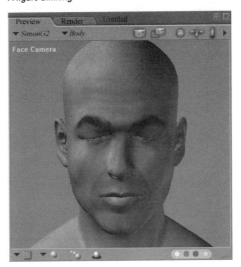

late a nervous twitch. Figure 15-5 shows a figure in the middle of a blink.

Enabling Eye and Head Motion

In addition to blinking, most people will also move their eyes about the scene as they speak. It is also common for people to naturally move their head about as they converse. Both of these patterns can be duplicated using the Create Eye Motion and Create Head Motion options. Figure 15-6 shows the eyes looking slightly off to the left as the figure speaks.

FIGURE 15-6
Eye movement during speech

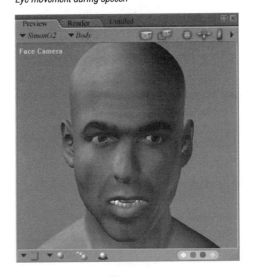

Adding Emotions

The Emotional Tweaks settings let you change the emotion that the figure uses while speaking. The six available emotions are anger, disgust, fear, joy, sadness, and surprise. You can create even more emotions by combining these sliders to different extents. Figure 15-7 shows a look created by combining anger and disgust.

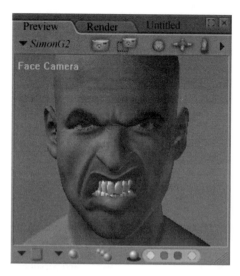

FIGURE 15-7

Anger and disgust

Animating Speech

Once you've loaded a sound file and have configured the Talk Designer, you can animate the spoken sound file using the Apply button. After the keyframes are generated, you can drag the Timeline in the Animation Controls to see the resulting animation sequence.

Animate a Figure Talking

1. Open Poser with the default figure visible and change the camera to focus on the head.

2. Select the Window, Talk Designer menu to open the Talk Designer palette.

3. Click on the Sound file Load File button and locate the Bye Bye Now.wav file and load it.

   When the sound file loads, the end frame is automatically set to coincide with the length of the sound file.

4. In the Supplemental Text area, type in the words that the sound file repeats.

5. Click on the Load File button for the Viseme Map file and locate the SimonG2Viseme-Map.xml file from the LipSync folder where Poser is installed.

6. Keep the Eye Blink Rate set to 12.5 and enable both the Create Eye Motion and the Create Head Motion options. Click the Apply button.

7. Click the Play button and enable the Loop option in the Animation Controls to see the resulting animation.

   The keyframes needed to make the figure speak are added to the scene, as shown in Figure 15-8.

8. Select File, Save As and save the file as **Speaking figure.pz3**.

FIGURE 15-8

Speaking figure

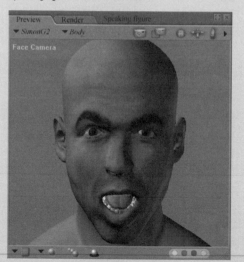

WORK WITH
SOUND

What You'll Do

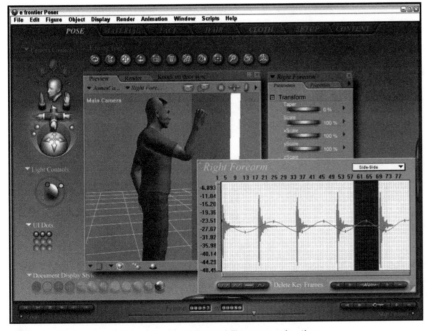

In this lesson, you learn how to add sound files to an animation.

Animations typically include sound, and Poser can import sound to be used within an animation. You can use the Animation Graph panel to synch animation keys to sound tracks, and then export completed animations to the .AVI or QuickTime movie formats.

Loading Sound Files

You can load a single sound file into Poser using the File, Import, Sound menu command. This command opens a file dialog box where you can import a .WAV file. The loaded sound file begins at frame 1 of the animation and continues for as many frames as it can, based on the frame rate. More coverage of importing content is presented in Chapter 4, "Working with Files and Accessing Content Paradise."

Synching Motion to Sound

You can view sound files in the Animation Graph panel by enabling the Toggle Sound Display button. The waveform for the imported sound appears in blue behind the animation graph, as shown in Figure 15-9. By moving the keys within the Animation Graph panel, you can synch the figure's motion to the imported sound file.

NOTE When a sound file is imported, the Sound Range is shown at the bottom of the grid cells in the Animation Palette.

Muting Sound

To mute the imported sound, simply select the Animation, Mute Sound menu command. This command is a toggle option that you can enable and disable.

Clearing Sound

To remove the imported sound, select the Animation, Clear Sound menu command.

FIGURE 15-9
Imported sound display

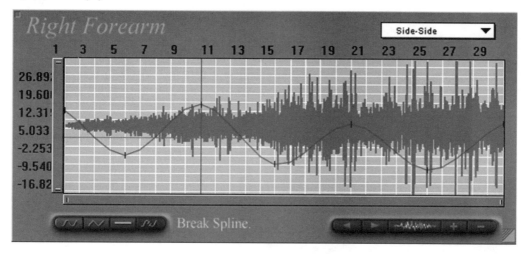

FIGURE 15-10
Synched knock on door

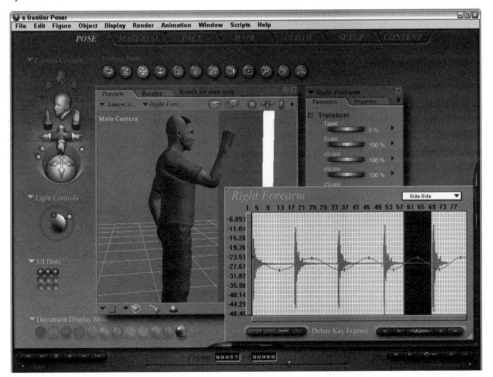

1. Choose File, Open and open the Knock on door.pz3 file.

   This file includes the default figure animated knocking on a door object using his right forearm.

2. Select the Right Forearm element in the Document Window.

3. Select Window, Parameter Dials to open the Parameter/Properties palette, if necessary.

4. Select the Graph option from the pop-up menu for the Bend parameter.

5. Select File, Import, Sound. Locate and load the knocks.wav file.

   The sound waveform appears in the back of the Animation Graph panel.

6. Drag over each of the keys and move them in the Animation Graph panel until they are aligned with the sound waveforms.

   The bottom of each curve corresponds to the hand hitting the door and should be aligned with the sound volume, whereas the top of the curve corresponds to the hand being away from the door and should be in between each sound wave, as shown in Figure 15-10.

7. Click the Play button and enable the Loop option in the Animation Controls to see the resulting animation.

8. Select File, Save As and save the file as **Knock on door sync.pz3**.

CHAPTER REVIEW

Chapter Summary

This chapter covered an impressive new feature included in Poser 7. The Talk Designer makes it possible to load a sound file and have the figure automatically detect and animate the keyframes needed to make the character speak. The Talk Designer also includes controls for setting the exaggeration of the facial morph targets, the blink rate, and facial emotions like anger, disgust, and surprise. The chapter also showed how imported sounds can be synched with scene animations.

What You Have Learned

In this chapter, you

- Opened and learned the controls of the Talk Designer interface.

- Loaded a sound file into Talk Designer.

- Added supplemental text to help Poser better match the facial morphs to the sound file.

- Loaded an external Viseme Map file.

- Configured Talk Designer to set the start and end frames and to set which animation layer the keyframes are saved.

- Set the blink rate and eye and head motion.

- Added emotions to your figure.

- Loaded and synched a sound file with an animation sequence.

Key Terms from This Chapter

- AIFF file. An audio format common on Macintosh computers.

- Phoneme. A set of common distinct sounds and the face motions required to create them. Phonemes in Poser include A, CH, E, F, TH, O, M, U, W, and L.

- Supplemental text. Text typed in to the Text Designer that matches the words in the sound file.

- Talk Designer. An interface used to automatically generate facial motions that are synched with a sound file.

- Viseme map. An XML-based file that defines the facial morph targets used to create the various phonemes.

- WAV file. An audio format common on Windows computers.

- Waveform. A visual display of a sound showing its volume per time.

chapter **16** **RENDERING** SCENES

1. Render images.

2. Access render settings.

3. Use the Sketch Designer.

4. Set render dimensions.

5. Render animations.

6. Use rendering effects.

465

16 RENDERING SCENES

The real purpose behind using Poser isn't to have fun manipulating figures, adding materials, or creating hairstyles. The real reason for using Poser is to create amazing images and animations, which is where the rendering process comes in.

Rendering is the final step that calculates all the various lights, geometries, materials, and simulations to create the final image or series of images for an animation. As part of the rendering process, there are several additional features that you can access, such as displacement maps, **antialiasing, motion blur,** and toon rendering. These processes are only possible during the final render.

A key decision in the rendering process involves weighing the image quality verses the time it takes to render an image. In the Render Settings dialog box are many options that you can enable to improve the quality of the final image, but enabling all the best quality options adds a lot of time to the rendering process. For quick preview renders, you'll want to disable

some of these features. In addition to the render settings, the Render Dimensions dialog box is used to set the size of the final rendered image.

The Render panel of the Document Window is where the rendered image appears. Using this panel, you can render the entire scene or just a specific area. You can open the current rendered image in a separate window or save the image. The Comparison slider at the bottom of the Render panel lets you compare two images by dragging the slider back and forth.

The main renderer available in Poser is the **FireFly rendering engine.** It also includes options to render the scene as a realistic photograph using advanced techniques, such as ray tracing or to render the scene as a cartoon using the Sketch Designer.

The Render Settings dialog box can also be used to render animations to the .AVI, .MOV or Flash formats.

Tools You'll Use

Available renderers

Render Quality slider

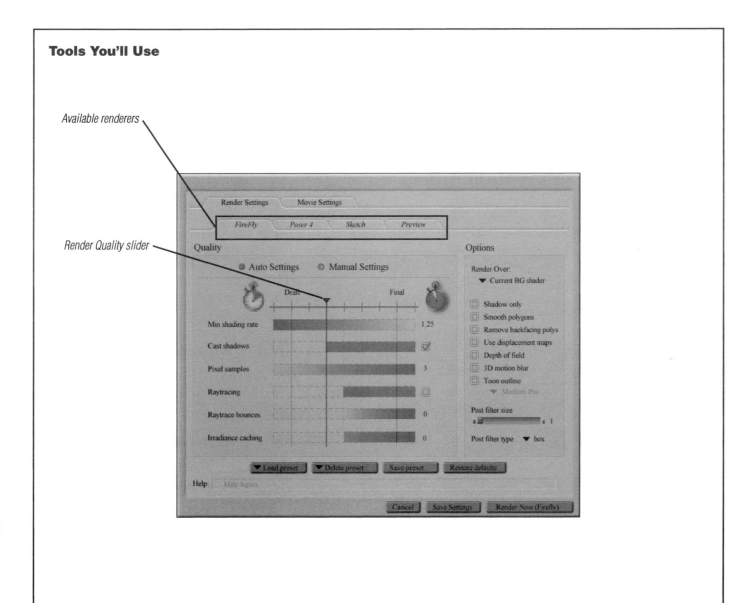

RENDER
IMAGES

What You'll Do

 In this lesson, you learn how to render images in the Render panel.

The previous chapters have pretty much focused on the Preview pane of the Document Window, but another pane exists—the Render panel. Using this panel, you can quickly render the current scene to check its look.

Quality versus Speed

The Display Style control has a number of different options for rendering the current scene in the Document Window, and the order of these options isn't random. The Display Style options are ordered by the quickest rendering method on the left (Silhouette) and the slowest on the right (Texture Shaded).

There is a direct correlation also between the speed of a rendered image and its quality. Textures, for example, add a lot of detail to a model, but they come at the cost of rendering speed and memory. You can see the relationship between render quality and speed in the Render Settings dialog box. Using the Auto Settings, you can drag the settings between Draft (fast render and low quality) and Final (slow render and high quality).

Using the Render Panel

You can open the Render panel, shown in Figure 16-1, by clicking the Render tab at the top of the Document Window. Controls along the top edge of the Render panel let you select the image resolution, select the renderer, initiate a rendering, render an area, open a new render window, and pan the current window. The panel also includes a pop-up menu of additional commands. Along the bottom of the Render panel are controls for comparing two images.

Setting the Document Window Image Resolution

The current image resolution of the Render panel is displayed at the top left. You can change these dimensions by dragging on the lower-right corner of the panel to resize it. You can set the drop-down list to the right of the resolution dimensions to render the current panel at Full, Half, or Quarter size. Figure 16-2 shows the current scene at quarter size. Clicking the Maximize Window button in the upper-right

corner will increase the size of the Render panel to fill the available space, as shown in Figure 16-3. Clicking the Maximize button again returns the Render panel to its default size.

QUICKTIP In addition to the Render panel, you can set the resolution of the render image to any size using the Render, Render Dimensions dialog box.

Close Window button
Maximize Window button

FIGURE 16-3
Maximized render panel

FIGURE 16-1
Render panel

Current renderer
Render button
Pop-up menu
Pan window

Render dimensions
Render size

FIGURE 16-2
Quarter-sized render

Selecting a Render Engine

Poser supports several rendering engines and each has its advantages. You can select which render engine renders the current scene from the Renderer drop-down list at the top of the Render panel. The available render engines include

- **FireFly:** A powerful render engine with a number of advanced features for creating realistic images.

- **Poser 4:** The render engine included with the previous versions of Poser. It offers good performance and is quick.

- **Sketch:** Renders the scene using various sketch styles defined in the Sketch Designer interface.

- **Preview:** The same render engine used to display the scene in the Preview panel. This option is the quickest rendering option.

Initiating a Render

The Render button in the Render panel starts the rendering cycle. This opens a progress dialog box that tracks the progress of the rendering process. When finished, the rendered image appears in the Render panel. If you want to check only a portion of the scene, you can click the Render Area button and drag over the area in the Render panel that you want to render, and only that selected portion will be rendered. Figure 16-4 shows the Render panel with only a small area rendered.

NOTE The Render and Render Area buttons are available in the Preview panel and also as menu commands in the Render menu. The keyboard shortcut for the Render command is Ctrl/Command+R, and the shortcut for the Render Area command is Alt+Ctrl+N (Option+Command+N on the Mac).

FIGURE 16-4
Area render

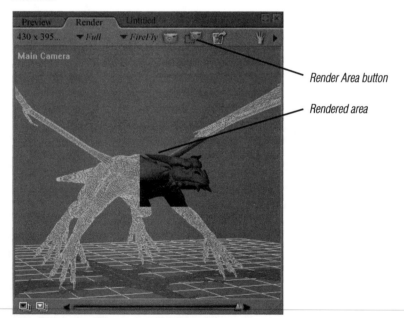

Render Area button

Rendered area

Saving a Rendered Window

If you want to save the current rendered image, you can select the Export Image option from the Document Window's pop-up menu to open the Save As dialog box. You can also save the current rendered image using the File, Export, Image menu command. You can save the rendered image as a .JPEG, .TGA, Windows Bitmap (.BMP), .PNG, .TIF, or Photoshop (.PSD) file.

NOTE Rendered images are saved to a Poser-RenderCache folder for immediate recall. You can clear this cache by deleting all the files in this folder. If you lose a rendered image, you can salvage the image from this folder also. The Render panel of the Preferences dialog box lets you set the maximum number of cached renders to keep.

If you want to keep the current rendered image around and render a new image, click the New Render Window button and the current rendered image will be opened within a separate window, as shown in Figure 16-5. When you close this window, a dialog box asks if you want to save the image. If you select to save the rendered image, a Save dialog box opens.

FIGURE 16-5
New Render window

Panning the Rendered Window

The Pan Window icon lets you pan the current rendered image if the panel is sized to be smaller than the current rendered image. To use this tool, just click the icon and drag to move the image within the panel.

Comparing Rendered Images

At the bottom-left corner of the Render panel are two icons for selecting right and left images. Each image that is rendered in the Render panel is saved with a time stamp in the right and left image icons at the bottom left. By selecting different images for the left and right, you can drag the Comparison slider to switch between the two selected images. This offers a great way to check subtle differences between rendered images. Figure 16-6 shows the Render panel when a preview rendered image and a FireFly rendered image are compared.

FIGURE 16-6
Comparing rendered images

Comparison slider

Select right image

Select left image

Setting Render Preferences

The General Preferences dialog box includes a Render panel, shown in Figure 16-7, that includes several key rendering settings. The Adaptive Bucket Size option lets Poser set the size of the chunks used to render individual processes. The Adaption Threshold sets the limit for the bucket sizes. Smaller threshold values result in larger buckets. The Memory Limit Buffer lets you specify the amount of memory to leave untouched. If the system runs out of memory, the render request will quit. In the Render Process section, you can select the Number of Threads used to complete the current render job. Specifying multiple threads can take advantage of multiple-processor or multi-core systems. The Separate Process option lets you decouple the application and render the job into separate processes. For large render jobs, this option can significantly decrease the render time because it allows the memory to be better managed by each process. However, if you are doing draft or small-area renders, enabling this option will not have any impact.

NEW POSER 7 FEATURE

Support for multiple threads and the ability to separate render processes are new to Poser 7.

QUICKTIP If you have a multi-processor system, set the number of threads to 4, but if you have a single processor system, keep the number of threads set to 1.

The Max Cached Renders value sets the number of cached rendered images that are stored in the PoserRenderCache folder. The higher this number, the more hard drive space is used, but the more rendered images are saved.

FIGURE 16-7

Render panel of the Preferences dialog box

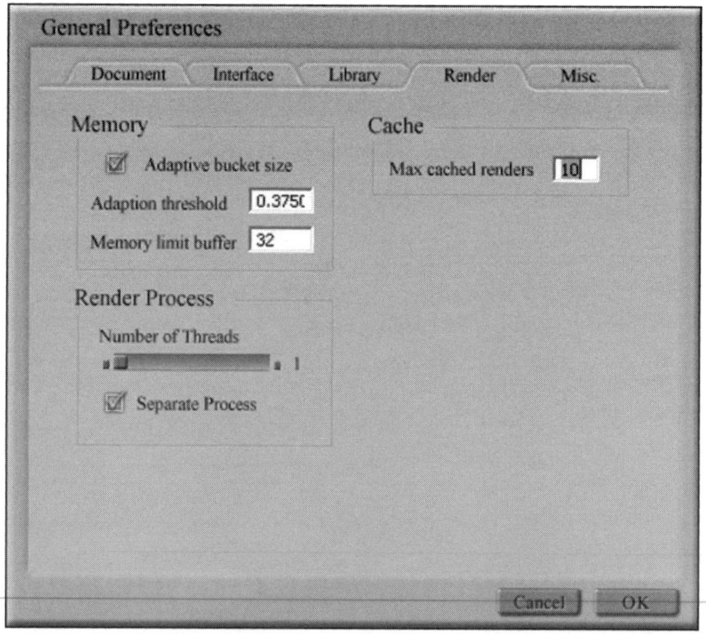

Generating Wireframe Renders

The Document Style options are actually quite versatile, and you may find a project where you'll want to render the scene using one of these styles. For example, you want to render your scene as a wireframe with the background and shadows. To do this, you simply need to select the Preview renderer and click the Render button. This will render the scene using the selected Document Style, as shown for the wireframe dragon in Figure 16-8.

FIGURE 16-8

Rendered image with wireframes

Printing from Poser

If you've created and rendered the perfect scene, you can send the image to the printer to create a hardcopy of the masterpiece using the File, Print menu. Be aware that this menu will only print the scene contained in the Preview panel. To print the rendered image, you need to export the image and print it from another application. Images are always printed by default using the full page while maintaining the image's aspect ratio.

FIGURE 16-9

Rendered image

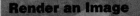

Render an Image

1. Choose File, Open and open the Aiko running.pz3 file.

2. Click the Render tab in the Document Window to open the Render panel.

3. Select the Full resolution option and choose the FireFly renderer (if necessary).

4. Click the Render button at the top of the Render panel.

    A progress dialog box appears showing the progress of the rendering. When the rendering is completed, the final image is shown in the Render panel, as shown in Figure 16-9.

Compare Images

1. With the Aiko running.pz3 file still open, change the renderer to Sketch using the Select Renderer drop-down list at the top of the Render panel.

2. Click the Render tab to render the scene with this renderer.

3. Select the most recent image from the Load Left Image list  in the lower-left corner of the Render panel and the second most recent image from the Load Right Image list . Then drag the Comparison slider to the middle.

   Half of each image is shown in the Render panel, as shown in Figure 16-10.

FIGURE 16-10

Comparing images

1. Choose File, Open and open the Aiko running.pz3 file.

2. Select the Cartoon with Lines style from the Document Style control bar.

3. Click on the Render tab in the Document Window to access the Render panel. Then select the Preview renderer.

4. Click the Render tab to render the scene with this renderer.

   The scene is rendered with the selected style, as shown in Figure 16-11.

FIGURE 16-11
Preview render

LESSON 2

ACCESS
RENDER SETTINGS

What You'll Do

In this lesson, you learn how to use the Render Settings dialog box.

Clicking the Render button will render the scene using the default render options, but you can change the render options using the Render Settings dialog box. The Render, Render Settings menu command opens the Render Settings dialog box. This dialog box is split into four panels, one for each available render engine, and you can select them using the tabs at the top of the dialog box.

QUICKTIP You can access the Render Settings dialog box also from the Document Window's pop-up menu.

Automatically Setting the FireFly Render Engine

The default panel includes settings for the default FireFly render engine, shown in Figure 16-12. At the top of the panel are two options for auto settings and manual settings. The Auto Settings option provides a simple slider control that you can use to shift the quality of the rendered image between a quick render at draft quality and a long render at final quality. For each position along the slider, the setting values are displayed.

Manually Setting the FireFly Render Engine

The Manual Settings option in the FireFly panel of the Render Settings dialog box, shown in Figure 16-13, includes all the same settings as the Auto Settings option, except you can change them manually using controls. The Acquire from Auto button copies all the auto settings to the manual controls for a good place to start. The following manual settings are available for the FireFly render engine:

FIGURE 16-12

FireFly panel in the Render Settings dialog box

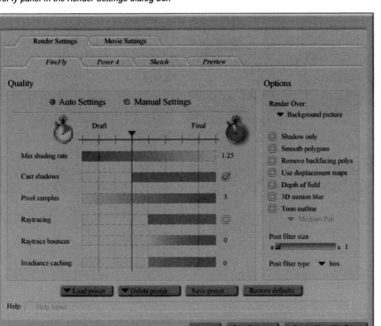

- **Cast Shadows:** Renders shadows for the scene for all figures and props that have their Cast Shadows property enabled and for all lights that have their Shadows property enabled.

- **Raytracing:** Causes the FireFly render engine to use raytracing computations to render the scene. Raytracing calculates the scene by casting light rays into the scene and following these light rays as they bounce off objects. The results are accurately rendered shadows, reflections, and materials, but enabling this option can really slow down the renderer.

- **Raytrace Bounces:** The number of times light rays are allowed to bounce about the scene during a ray-tracing calculation. Higher bounces take more time but produce better results.

- **Irradiance Caching:** Enables a memory cache that stores values for the amount of light arriving on a certain surface area. The Irradiance Caching value is actually a quality setting. Lower values result in more caching for faster renders and higher values result in higher-quality images, but require that the irradiance values be re-computed for the entire scene. An Irradiance Caching value of 0 can significantly reduce the time required to compute an ambient occlusion image, but risks being less accurate as the cached data may no longer be valid.

NOTE The Raytracing option in the Render Settings dialog box needs to be enabled to render ambient occlusion. You can see an example of ambient occlusions in Chapter 7, "Adding Scene Lighting."

- **Pixel Samples:** Determines the amount of samples that are taken for each pixel to determine its accurate color during an antialiasing pass. The higher the pixel samples, the more accurate the color at each pixel.

- **Min Shading Rate:** This value is used to divide each polygon into sections. Each section is then sampled, and the sections are averaged to determine the pixel's color. Lower values yield better results, but increase the render time. This setting is a global shading rate for all objects in the scene, but you can use the Shading Rate value in the Properties palette to set this value differently for individual objects. The object's Shading Rate value overrides any global setting.

- **Max Bucket Size:** Sets the size of the pixel area to be rendered at one time. The FireFly render engine will render the entire scene a block at a time. Large bucket values require more memory to process them.

- **Min Displacement Bounds:** The Min Displacement Bounds is set by Poser automatically in order to reduce the chance of cracks or holes appearing in the geometry. Small values result in quicker renders, but run a greater risk of having cracks appearing.

NEW POSER 7 FEATURE

Although the Texture Filtering option has been removed from the Render Settings dialog box, it is included in the render process to improve the image quality. It can now be set on individual textures. Irradiance caching is also new to Poser 7.

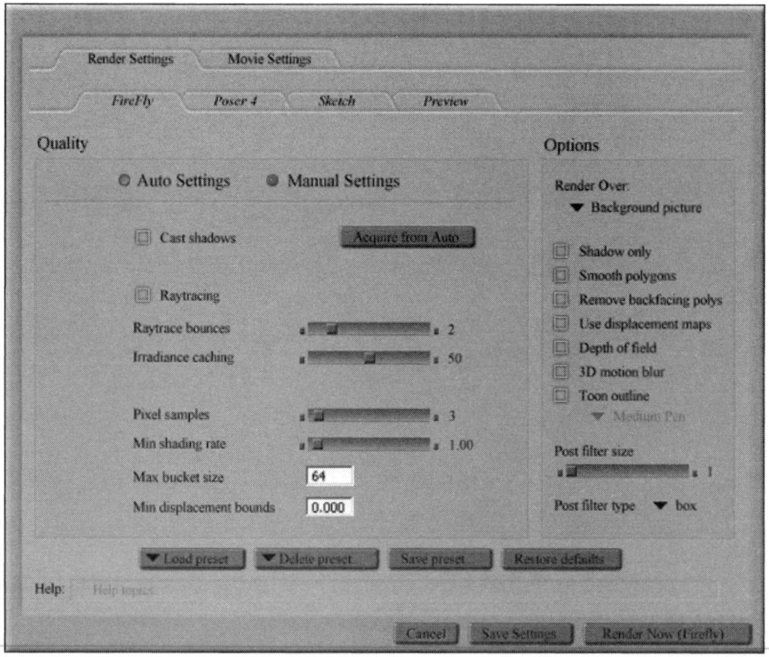

FIGURE 16-13
Manual settings for the FireFly panel in the Render Settings dialog box

Setting the FireFly Render Options

On the right side of the FireFly panel in the Render Settings dialog box are several options for the FireFly render engine. You can use these options to change how images are rendered and to add special effects. The available render options include the following:

- **Render Over:** Sets the background that is used for the rendered image. The options available in the drop-down list include Background Color, Black, Background Picture, and Current Background Shader.

- **Shadow Only:** Renders only the scene shadows.

- **Smooth Polygons:** Adds an additional smoothing pass to the geometry objects in the scene, smoothing hard edges.

- **Remove Backfacing Polygons:** Causes all polygons that are facing away from the camera to be ignored. This can speed up the rendering time.

- **Use Displacement Maps:** Enables displacement maps to be used to render the scene. Displacement maps change the actual geometry of objects when used.

- **Depth of Field:** Adds a depth of field effect to the scene. This effect focuses the camera at the center of the scene and gradually blurs all objects that are located at a distance from the center focal point.

- **3D Motion Blur:** Adds a motion blur effect to the scene. This effect blurs moving objects in the scene, depending on how fast they are moving.

- **Toon Outline:** Adds an outline to the toon rendered image. When enabled, you can choose the outline width to be thin, medium, or thick and the style to be pen, pencil, or marker.

- **Post Filter Size:** Sets the size of the area used to take samples. These samples are averaged to determine the pixel color. You can also select the filter type to be Box, Gaussian, or Sinc. The Box filter type looks at all samples equally, the Gaussian weighs the center samples more, and the Sinc option uses a sine wave to determine the sample's weight.

Loading and Saving FireFly Render Settings

Clicking the Save Preset button opens a simple dialog box where you can name the current render settings. This name then appears in the Load Presets list along with the Draft and Production options. The Delete Presets button includes a list where you can delete the current presets. At the bottom of the Render Settings dialog box is another Save Settings button. Clicking this button saves the current settings so they are retained when the dialog box is reopened.

NOTE The Save and Load Preset buttons are only available for the FireFly panel, but the Save Settings button saves the current settings for all panels.

Setting the Poser 4 Render Options

The Poser 4 tab in the Render Settings dialog box opens the Poser 4 panel, shown in Figure 16-14. This render engine doesn't include all the advanced features as in the FireFly render engine, but it renders quickly and accurately and is a good choice for preview renders. The Poser 4 render engine options include Anti-alias, Use Bump Maps, Use Texture Maps, Cast Shadows, and Ignore Shader Trees. The Ignore Shader Trees option will disable most materials.

Setting the Sketch Render Options

The Sketch tab in the Render Settings dialog box opens the Sketch panel, shown in Figure 16-15. This render engine offers you the capability to render the scene to look like it was drawn freehand with a pen, pencil, or set of markers. The Sketch panel includes several thumbnails of styles, or you can select a style from the Sketch Preset drop-down list. The Sketch Designer button opens the Sketch Designer, where you can define a custom style.

FIGURE 16-14

Poser 4 panel in the Render Settings dialog box

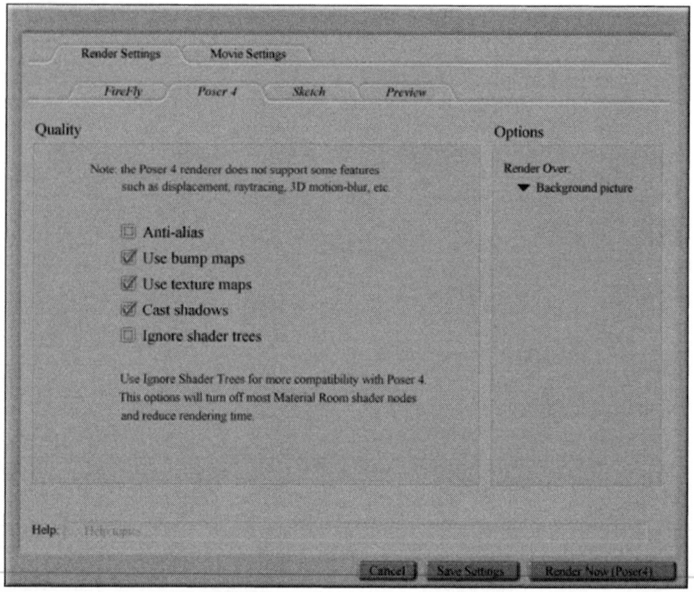

FIGURE 16-15

Sketch panel in the Render Settings dialog box

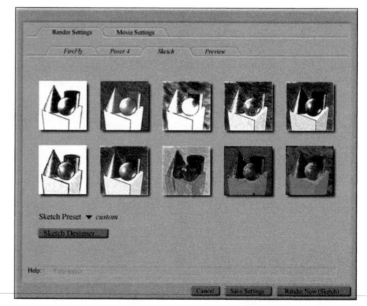

Setting the Preview Render Options

The Preview tab in the Render Settings dialog box opens the Preview panel, shown in Figure 16-16. This render engine sets the render options for the Document Window's Preview panel.

You can set the Display Engine to SreeD or OpenGL using an Accumulation Buffer in Hardware or Software. The SreeD option is a software rendering option, and OpenGL can take advantage of video card hardware to display preview renders much quicker. Poser will automatically detect and use the OpenGL option if your video card supports it.

QUICKTIP You can also set the Display Engine setting by right-clicking on the Document Window and selecting either SreeD or OpenGL.

QUICKTIP If the Document Window display is having trouble, try downloading and installing the latest OpenGL driver for your video card.

If the OpenGL option is selected, you can select to enable Hardware Shading for your materials and textures. This makes the designated materials visible in the Preview panel, which can eliminate the need to test render your images to check the applied materials. You can also control the size of the textures used to display your material previews up to 4096 by 4096 pixels.

FIGURE 16-16

Preview panel in the Render Settings dialog box

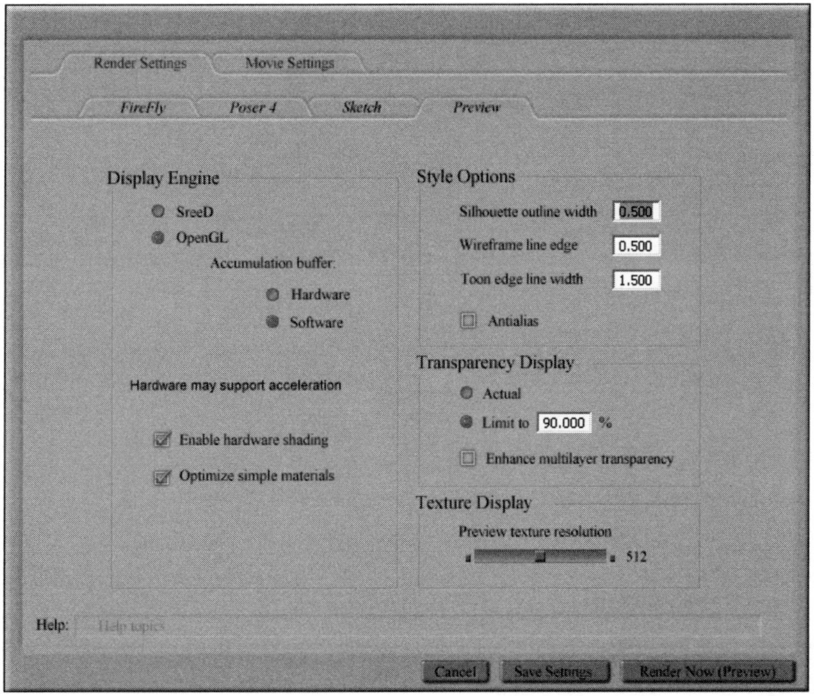

CAUTION Displaying hardware shaders is only possible if your video card supports hardware shaders in OpenGL. If your video card doesn't support this, a note, "Hardware shading not supported" will appear in the Preview panel of the Render Settings dialog box.

NEW POSER 7 FEATURE
The ability to preview hardware shaders is new to Poser 7.

The Style Options let you set the width of the silhouette outline, the wireframe line edge, and the toon edge line width. The Antialias option eliminates jagged edges by smoothing the lines between color boundaries.

You can set the Transparency Display to Actual or to be limited. If an object's transparency is set to 100%, it will be invisible in the scene, but the Limit To option makes sure that all objects are visible.

Change Rendering Settings

1. Choose File, Open and open the Aiko running.pz3 file.

2. Select Render, Render Settings to open the Render Settings dialog box.

3. In the FireFly panel, click the Auto Settings option and drag the Quality slider to Draft.

4. Click the Render Now button at the bottom-right side of the dialog box.

   A progress dialog box appears showing the progress of the rendering. When the rendering is completed, the final image is shown in the Render panel.

5. Open the Render Settings dialog box again, drag the Quality slider to Final, and click the Render Now button.

6. Select the most recent image from the Load Left Image list in the lower-left corner of the Render panel and the second most recent image from the Load Right Image list. Then drag the Comparison slider to the middle.

FIGURE 16-17
Final render of Aiko compared with the draft

Dragging the Comparison slider lets you see the difference between the Draft and Final settings, as shown in Figure 16-17.

Notice how rough the character looks on the right verses the final render on the left.

Final render

Dividing line

Draft render

USE THE
SKETCH DESIGNER

What You'll Do

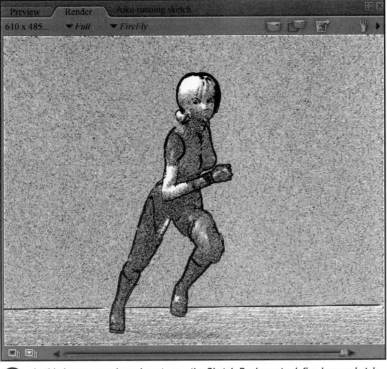

In this lesson, you learn how to use the Sketch Designer to define how a sketch rendering looks.

You can create and modify sketch presets using the Sketch Designer. You open this interface, shown in Figure 16-18, by using the Window, Sketch Designer menu command or by clicking the Sketch Designer button on the Sketch tab in the Render Settings dialog box.

Loading a Sketch Preset

Beneath the Preview pane in the Sketch Designer is a Load Preset button. This button provides access to the saved sketch presets, including Caterpillar, Colored Pencil, Colored, Dark Clouds, JacksonP BG, Loose Sketch, Pastel, Pencil and Ink, Psychedelic, Scratch Board, Scratchy, Silky, Stretch Default, Sketchy, Smoothy, Soft Charcoal, and Stroked BG. Selecting any of these presets applies the preset and updates the Preview pane.

Saving a Sketch Preset

Clicking the Save Preset button opens a simple dialog box where you can name the current sketch settings. This name then appears in the Load Presets list along with the other options. The Delete Presets button includes a list where you can delete the current presets. Next to the Save Presets button is the Restore Defaults button. You can use this button to change all the current settings back to their default states.

Changing Objects, Backgrounds, and Edges

The right portion of the Sketch Designer includes settings for defining all the sketch settings. You can use these settings to control the look of the scene objects, the scene background, or the edges using the different panels. The parameters are the same for each panel. The sketch parameters include Density, Line Length, Min Width, Max Width, Lo Brightness, Hi Brightness, Stroke Head, Stroke Tail, Line Random, Color Random, Opacity, Cross Hatch, Total Angle, and Color Cutoff.

FIGURE 16-18

Sketch Designer

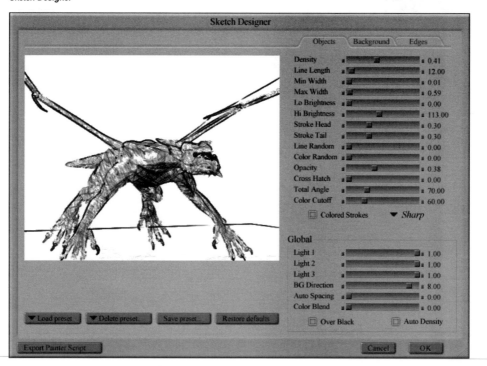

Sketching in Color and Using Brushes

The Colored Strokes option causes the sketches to be drawn in color. Next to the Colored Strokes option is a drop-down list that contains several brush types that you can use to sketch the scene. The available brushes include Sharp, Bristle, Very Soft, Soft, Less Soft, and Slanted.

Setting Global Parameters

Below the sketch parameters are a set of global parameters, including settings for each of the lights, the background direction, auto spacing, and color blend. The Over Black option causes the sketch to be drawn on a black background with white strokes, as shown in Figure 16-19. The Auto Density option sets the density for each stroke based on the scene instead of using the Density parameter. Figure 16-20 shows the default scene with the Auto Density option enabled.

Exporting Painter Scripts

The Export Painter Script button opens a file dialog box where you can save the sketch definitions to a script that Corel's Painter can read and use. The exported script is saved with the .TXT extension. This provides a way to reproduce your sketch results in a 2D software package.

FIGURE 16-19
Over Black option

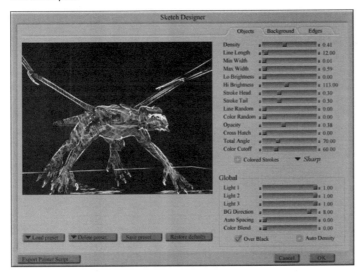

FIGURE 16-20
Auto Density option

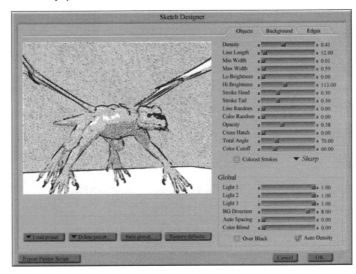

Use the Sketch Designer

1. Choose File, Open and open the Aiko running.pz3 file.

2. Select Window, Sketch Designer to open the Sketch Designer dialog box.

3. Click the Load Preset button and select the Soft Charcoal option.

4. Click the Auto Density option in the Global section and click OK.

5. Select Render, Render Settings to open the Render Settings dialog box.

6. Click the Sketch tab at the top of the Render Settings dialog box.

   The Sketch Preset is set to Custom to indicate that a custom setting has been created in the Sketch Designer.

7. Click the Render Now button at the bottom-right side of the dialog box.

   A progress dialog box appears showing the progress of the rendering. When the rendering is completed, the final image is shown in the Render panel, as shown in Figure 16-21.

8. Select File, Save As and save the file as **Aiko running sketch.pz3**.

FIGURE 16-21
Sketch render of Aiko running

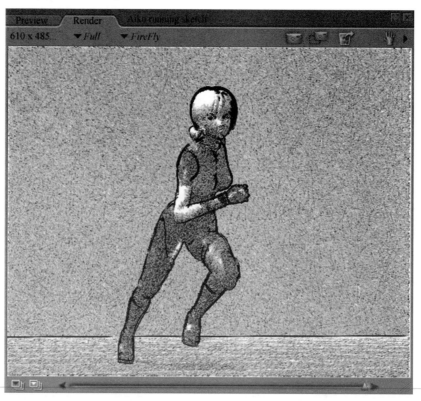

SET
RENDER DIMENSIONS

What You'll Do

 In this lesson, you learn how to set the exact size of the render image.

The default render size is the determined by the size of the Render panel, but you aren't stuck with this size. The Render, Render Dimensions menu command opens a dialog box, shown in Figure 16-22, where you can set the exact dimensions of the render image.

Using the Render Dimensions Dialog Box

The Render Dimensions dialog box includes three options—to match the preview window, to fit the image in the preview window, or to render to exact resolution. If you select the Fit in Preview Window option, an image of the size of the Document Window obeying the aspect ratio specified through width and height is placed within the Render panel.

FIGURE 16-22
Render Dimensions dialog box

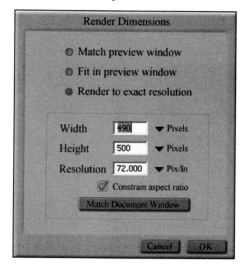

Using Exact Dimensions

Selecting the Render to Exact Resolution option in the Render Dimensions dialog box lets you enter the width and height dimensions for the render image, which can be specified using pixels, inches, or centimeters. You can also specify the resolution, which is the number of pixels per inch or pixels per centimeter. The Constrain Aspect Ratio option causes the ratio of height to width to be maintained. Clicking the Match Document Window button automatically sets the Width and Height values to the current size of the Render panel. If the render image is larger than the Render panel, you can pan about the image using the Pan Window tool in the upper-right corner of the Render panel.

QUICKTIP For computer images, a resolution setting of 72 pixels per inch is enough, but for images that will be printed, use a resolution setting of 300 pixels per inch or higher. Higher resolution settings result in larger files.

Displaying Production Frames

When a render dimension is established, you can select to view the edges of these dimension settings using the Display, Production Frame menu command. The area in the Document Window outside of the render dimensions is dimmed, as shown in Figure 16-23. The options are Image Output Size, Animation Output Size, and Off.

FIGURE 16-23
Production frame

FIGURE 16-24

Exact render dimensions

1. Choose File, Open and open the Aiko running.pz3 file.

2. Deselect the Constrain Aspect Ratio option, if necessary, then select Render, Render Dimensions to open the Render Dimensions dialog box.

3. Select the Render to Exact Resolution option and set the dimensions to 640 pixels by 480 pixels. Click OK.

4. Click the Render button at the top of the Render panel.

   A progress dialog box appears showing the progress of the rendering. When the rendering is completed, the final image is shown in the Render panel, as shown in Figure 16-24. The image is larger than the Render panel, so you can use the Pan Window tool to move the image within the Render panel.

LESSON 5

RENDER
ANIMATIONS

What You'll Do

 In this lesson, you learn how to render an animation.

The Render panel is used to render an image, but the Movie Settings panel of the Render Settings dialog box includes all the options for rendering animations. You can open this panel directly using the Animation, Make Movie menu command.

Making a Movie

You can save completed animations to a movie format using the Animation, Make Movie menu command. This opens the Movie Settings panel, shown in Figure 16-25. The Movie Settings panel lets you select the format, the renderer, the resolution, and the time span.

Using Animation Settings

The available formats are Image Files (which renders each frame a separate image), .AVI, and Flash. The Renderer options include Firefly, Poser 4, Preview, and Sketch. The Resolution options let you set the Width and Height of the rendered movie, or you can select Full, Half, Quarter, or Preview Size from the pop-up menu. The Time Span lets you set the frames that are included in the movie and whether all frames are included, the Frame Rate, or only every Nth frame. The Save Settings button will save the current settings for

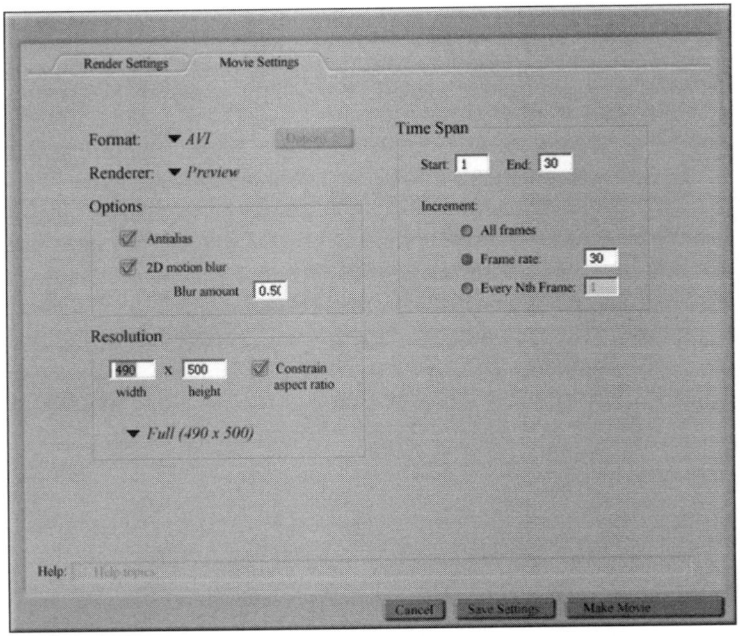

FIGURE 16-25
Movie Settings panel

next time the panel is opened, and the Make Movie button opens a file dialog box where you can save the movie file.

| **NOTE** You can play back any saved movie file using the Animation, Play Movie File menu command.

Setting Movie Options

The Options section in the Movie Settings panel includes two options—Antialias and 2D Motion Blur. The Antialias option smoothes the edges of lines by gradually changing the colors between the line and the background. This removes the jagged edges that are common in computer

images. The 2D Motion Blur option makes objects in motion blurred to show the effect of speed. The faster the object, the more blurred it becomes. Enabling either of these options increases the render time.

Creating a Flash/SWF Movie

When you select the Flash format, the Options button becomes active. Clicking the Options button opens the Flash Export dialog box, shown in Figure 16-26. This dialog box lets you select which lines are drawn, the line width, the number of colors, and the custom or auto colors.

| **CAUTION** Flash animations have a limit of 253 colors.

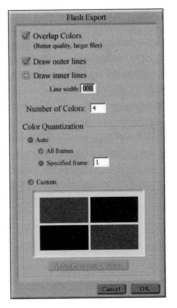

FIGURE 16-26
Flash Export dialog box

Make a Movie

1. Choose File, Open and open the Aiko running animated.pz3 file.

2. Select Animation, Make Movie.

   The Movie Settings panel opens.

3. Select the AVI option (or the MOV option for Macintosh) from the Format drop-down list, select Preview as the Renderer, select the Full resolution and All Frames. Then click the Make Movie button.

4. In the Enter Movie File Name dialog box that appears, name the movie file **Aiko running.avi**. Click Save.

5. A Video Compression dialog box appears. Click OK to accept the default settings.

   The rendering proceeds and the file are saved using the designated file name. When finished, the default media player opens and plays the file, as shown in Figure 16-27.

FIGURE 16-27
Rendered animation in Media Player

FIGURE 16-28

Rendered Flash animation in a Web browser

1. Choose File, Open and open the Knock on door sync.pz3 file.

2. Select Animation, Make Movie.

   The Movie Settings panel opens.

3. Select the Flash option from the Format drop-down list, select Preview as the renderer, set the resolution Width to 320, enable the Constrain Aspect Ratio option, select the Full resolution and All Frames. Then click the Make Movie button.

4. In the Enter Movie File Name dialog box that appears, name the movie file **Aik running.swf**. Click Save.

   The rendering proceeds and the file is saved using the designated file name. When finished, the Flash file can be viewed within a Web browser, as shown in Figure 16-28.

USE
RENDERING EFFECTS

What You'll Do

In this lesson, you learn how to enable several render effects.

The FireFly rendering engine includes several rendering options that can improve the look and add realism to the final image and/or animation. Each of these options can be enabled in the FireFly panel of the Render Settings dialog box.

Rendering Shadows Only

The Shadow Only option will render the shadows on a white background. This lets you edit the shadows independently and composite them within an image-editing package. Figure 16-29 shows a rendered image with the Shadows Only option enabled. Notice how some shadows exist on the figure itself.

Using Displacement Maps

You can add displacement maps to materials in the Material Room, but they aren't displayed until the scene is rendered. The Render Settings dialog box includes an option that must be enabled for displacement maps to be rendered. Displacement maps are different from bump maps in that they actually change the geometry of the object they are applied to. Figure 16-30 shows a grid image applied to the shirt material group of a figure.

FIGURE 16-29
Shadows only

Creating a Depth of Field Effect

A depth of field effect focuses the camera on objects at the front of the scene, and all objects at a distance are gradually blurred. The blurring is stronger the farther from the front of the scene an object is. The exact location where the camera is focused is controlled by the camera's Focal Length value, and the strength of the blur is determined by the camera's FStop value. This effect is only visible when the scene is rendered with the Depth of Field option in the Render Settings dialog box enabled. Figure 16-31 shows a line of figures with this

FIGURE 16-30
Displacement map

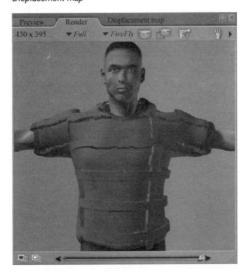

effect enabled. You can see more depth of field examples in Chapter 6, "Establishing a Scene—Cameras and Backgrounds."

QUICKTIP To see where the camera is focused, you can enable the Display, Guides, Focal Distance Guide menu command.

FIGURE 16-31
Depth of field

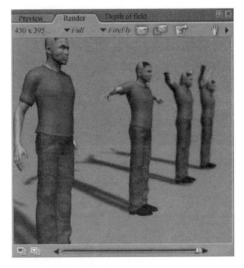

Using Motion Blur

A motion blur effect causes objects that are moving quickly through the scene to be rendered blurry. This creates the illusion of speed. Motion Blur can be computed in two ways—in 2D and in 3D. 2D motion blur can be done to the image in the Preview panel using the Render, MotionBlur Document menu command. This command is intended as a quick way to check the motion blur effect without having to render the full scene. Figure 16-32 shows a figure with an animated arm moving up and down. Using the 2D Motion Blur command, the arm is displayed as a blur. You create 3D motion blur by rendering the scene with the Motion Blur option in the Render Settings dialog box enabled. Figure 16-33

shows the same figure rendered with motion blur in the Render panel.

Testing Antialiasing

Antialiasing is a process that removes any jagged edges that occur along the edges of the figure. This is accomplished by smoothing the lines so contrast isn't so sharp. Antialiasing takes place during the rendering process, but you can also apply an antialiasing filter to the current Preview image using the Render, Antialias Document menu command.

Rendering Cartoons

The Toon Outline option in the Render Settings dialog box adds an outline around the

outside of the figure during the rendering process. This outline can be Thin, Medium or Thick using Pen, Pencil, or Markers. This option works well when the figure's materials have the Toon Shader applied to them. If the Toon Shader isn't applied, the rendered image will look realistic with an odd outline surrounding it. Figure 16-34 shows a figure rendered using the Toon Outline option and the Toon Shader applied to its material groups. You can quickly apply the default Toon Shader to material groups using the Set Up Toon Render wacro.

> **QUICKTIP** If you set the ToonID value to be the same for all body parts, the outline will not appear in between adjacent parts.

FIGURE 16-32
2D motion blur

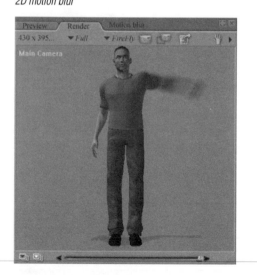

FIGURE 16-33
3D motion blur

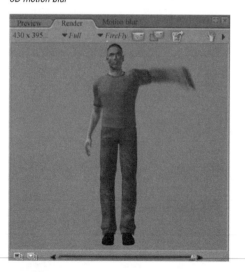

FIGURE 16-34
Cartoon render

FIGURE 16-35

Rendered displacement map

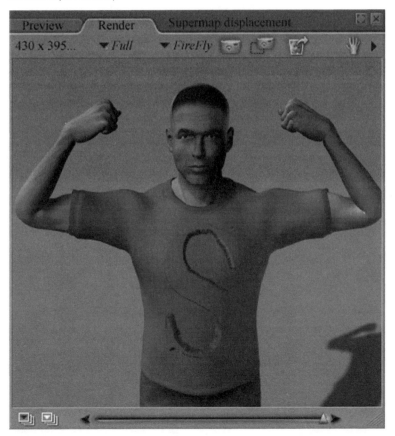

1. Choose File, Open and open the Supermap.pz3 file.

2. Click the Material tab at the top of the interface to open the Material Room and select the Simple tab to access the Simple panel.

3. Click the chest in the Document Window to select the shirt material group.

4. Click the open space under the Bump property to open the Texture Manager dialog box. Click the Browse button, and then locate and select the Capital S.tif image. Click OK.

5. Under the Bump property, select the Displacement option and set the Amount value to 0.025.

6. Switch back to the Pose Room, select the Render, Render Settings menu command to open the Render Settings dialog box, enable the Use Displacement Maps option, and then click the Render Now button.

   The rendering proceeds, and the resulting image is displayed in the Render panel, as shown in Figure 16-35.

7. Select File, Save As and save the file as **Supermap displacement.pz3**.

Use Motion Blur

1. Choose File, Open and open the Aiko running animated.pz3 file.

2. Drag the Time Slider in the Animation Controls to frame 24.

3. Select the Render, Render Settings menu command to open the Render Settings dialog box. Enable the 3D Motion Blur option and click the Render Now button.

   The rendering proceeds, and the resulting image is displayed in the Render panel, as shown in Figure 16-36. Notice how the arms are moving faster than the body and are blurred more.

FIGURE 16-36
3D motion blur

Render a Cartoon

1. Choose File, Open and open the Smile.pz3 file.

2. Click the Material tab at the top of the interface to open the Material Room and select the Advanced tab to access the Advanced panel.

3. Click the head element in the Document Window to select the head material group.

4. Click the Set Up Toon Render wacro button. A dialog box appears asking if you want highlights. Click the Yes button.

5. Click the Neck element to select and repeat Step 4 for this element. Then set the ToonID value for the Neck element to be equal to the Head object.

6. Switch back to the Pose Room, and then select the Render, Render Settings menu command to open the Render Settings dialog box. Enable the Toon Outline option, select the Thin Pen option, and click the Render Now button.

   The rendering proceeds, and the resulting image is displayed in the Render panel, as shown in Figure 16-37.

7. Select File, Save As and save the file as **Cartoon smile.pz3.**

FIGURE 16-37
Cartoon rendered image

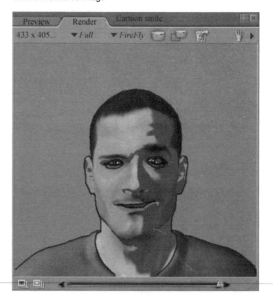

CHAPTER REVIEW

Chapter Summary

This chapter covered rendering the current scene using the Render panel. It also explained the various render settings that are available in the Render Settings dialog box, including rendering using the FireFly, Poser 4, Sketch, and Preview render engines. You can use the Sketch Designer to customize your sketch parameters when rendering a scene. The Render Dimensions dialog box can set the exact dimensions of the rendered image. The Movie Settings panel in the Render Settings dialog box lets you render animation sequences. Finally, the chapter looked at the various render options available for the FireFly renderer.

What You Have Learned

In this chapter, you

- Used the Render panel to render scene images.
- Saved rendered images to the hard drive.
- Compared rendered images in the Render panel.
- Rendered wireframe objects.

- Automatically and manually set the various render settings for the Fire-Fly render engine.
- Used the Poser 4, Sketch, and Preview render engines to render the scene.
- Loaded a sketch preset and used it to render the scene.
- Set the exact dimensions of the rendered image using the Render Dimensions dialog box.
- Accessed the Movie Settings panel to render animations.
- Used the various render options, including Shadows Only, Displacement Maps, Motion Blur, and Toon Rendering.

Key Terms from This Chapter

- **Antialiasing.** A process of smoothing rendered edges in order to remove any jagged edges.
- **FireFly render engine.** The default rendering method for rendering images in Poser. This engine includes many advanced features, such as antialiasing, motion blur, and texture filtering.

- **Irradiance caching.** The feature that caches lighting details into a buffer to decrease the render time for ambient occlusion scenes.
- **Motion blur.** A rendering option that blurs objects moving quickly in the scene.
- **Raytracing.** A rendering method that calculates the scene by casting light rays into the scene and following these light rays as they bounce off objects. The results are accurately rendered shadows, reflections, and materials.
- **Render.** The process of calculating the final look of all scene geometries, lights, materials, and textures into a final image.
- **Sketch Designer.** An interface used to define brush strokes that are used to render a scene using the Sketch render engine.
- **Texture filtering.** A process applied to 2D texture images to help avoid aliasing, moire patterns, and dropouts. It is also used to optimize performance when reading from a texture cache.

USING POSER
WITH OTHER SOFTWARE

1. Use Poser with other e frontier products.

2. Use Poser with 3D packages.

3. Retouch images in Photoshop.

USING POSER WITH
OTHER SOFTWARE

Poser is designed to work with figures and includes features for posing, editing, animating, and rendering, but there are many other 3D and graphics packages that include features that Poser can't do well. Luckily, you can export Poser figures and scenes to these other packages, where you can work on them before returning to Poser. Learning to expand your arsenal of tools helps you to improve your ability to create interesting and unique-looking scenes.

Of all the available external 3D packages, the first place to look is within e frontier's vaults. e frontier offers many different products besides Poser, and these packages are designed to work hand and hand with Poser. No sibling rivalry here. Some of the e frontier packages like Virtual Fashion extend the feature set in Poser and others like Manga Studio take the Poser figures into a different realm.

Outside of e frontier, the next group of software to look into are the various popular 3D packages. These packages let you build custom content that can be imported and used in Poser, or you can import the Poser content into these packages for animation and rendering. Although there are a lot of different 3D packages, this chapter focuses on using the key professional level tools, including 3ds Max, Maya, Softimage XSI, and Lightwave.

In addition to 3D packages, several other image-editing packages, such as Photoshop, are also very helpful for creating textures and backgrounds, and they can also be used to fix problems with a rendered image. It is often quicker and easier to fix problems in Photoshop than to take the time to re-render a scene. Photoshop also has several unique filters and features that can enhance rendered images.

Tools You'll Use

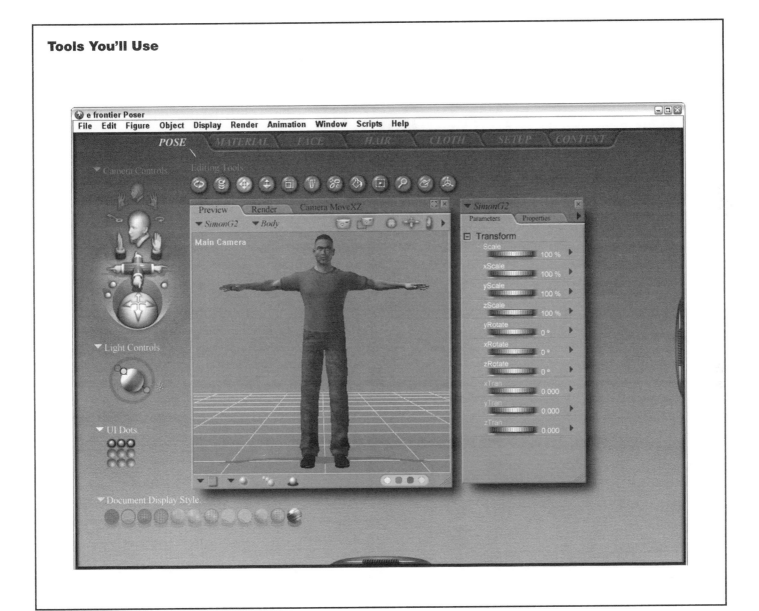

USE POSER WITH
OTHER E FRONTIER PRODUCTS

What You'll Do

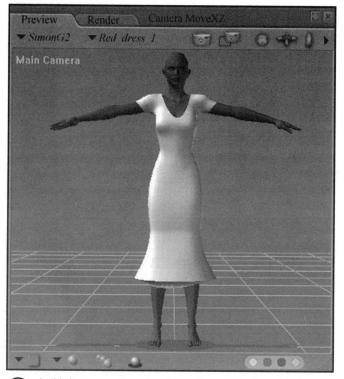

In this lesson, you learn how to use Poser with other e frontier products.

e frontier has several products that it offers. Some of these packages are designed to work closely with Poser such as Virtual Fashion, and others can be used to create Poser content like Shade. Still others are used to create unique files like Manga Studio, but allow Poser figures to be used with them.

Using Poser with Virtual Fashion

Virtual Fashion is an excellent tool if you are looking for a way to dress up your figures. It lets you create custom-designed clothes that can be exported and used directly in Poser. It even includes several Poser models as virtual models, including James and Jessi.

The software lets you create clothes in a way that is similar to real clothing designers. When you open a project, one of the Poser models is visible and covered in cloth. You can then stretch or flare out the draped cloth and cut away sections that you don't need to create a custom design, as shown in Figure 17-1. Once the shape of the design is complete, you can apply a unique fabric to the clothes. The available fabrics don't deal with Air Damping or Friction values, but are common types of cloth such as Wool, Denim, Fur, Leather, and so on.

Once the clothes shape is defined and a fabric is selected, you can go to the Fitting Room and drape the clothes over the loaded model to see how it fits. Virtual Fashion also includes a Material Editor, where you can create and modify material properties to create new types of fabrics. There is also a virtual PhotoStudio, as shown in Figure 17-2, where you can see the designed clothes set in a studio or on the runway with various lighting configurations.

In the Fitting Room is a button where you can export the custom clothes to a directory where Poser can read them. If you add the included Runtime folder to Poser, you can access Virtual Fashion's clothes directly from the Poser Library. Because the clothes are exported as props using the .PP2 format, they can be imported and used by Poser's Cloth Room to make them dynamic.

Creating Poser Content with Shade

Shade is a powerful 3D modeling and rendering package with many advanced features. It is unique in how it integrates with Poser. Shade includes a module called PoserFusion, shown in Figure 17-3, that lets you open and work with Poser figures without having to go through the export/import headache.

FIGURE 17-1

Clothes can be cut to fit a figure in Virtual Fashion

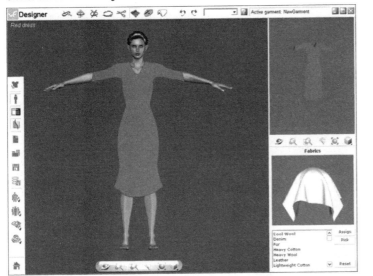

FIGURE 17-2

Clothes can be lighted in the PhotoStudio

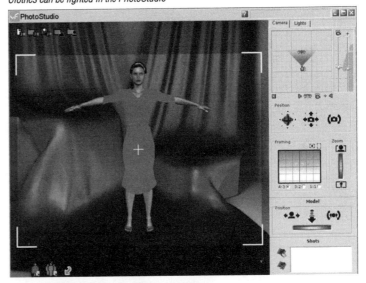

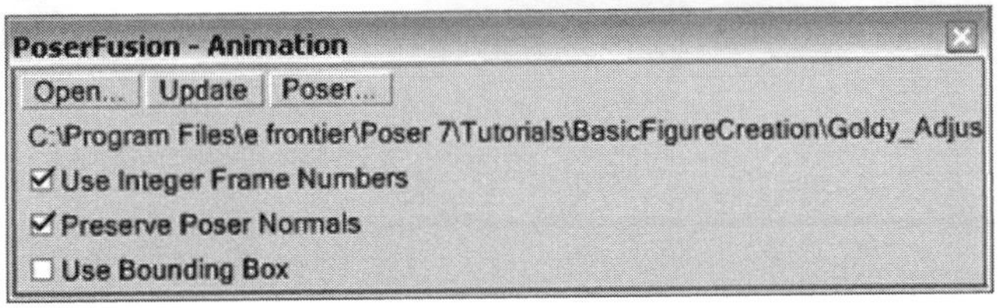

FIGURE 17-3

PoserFusion is a feature that allows Poser and Shade to work closely together

Using the PowerFusion module, a Poser figure saved in the .PZ3 file format can be opened directly into the current scene, as shown in Figure 17-4. Shade can also import and export .OBJ files if you want to export the Poser morph targets.

NOTE When Poser figures are placed in a Shade scene using PoserFusion, dynamic hair and cloth and morph targets are not supported.

Using Poser with Manga Studio

Not all products interact with Poser via importing. Some packages, such as Manga Studio, benefit from Poser's ability to quickly and accurately pose characters. These characters with their poses can be exported from Poser and imported into products like Manga Studio where the characters are ready to be placed within a Manga comic frame.

Manga Studio, shown in Figure 17-5, can import a variety of image formats and can even import 3D objects using the .DXF, Lightwave (.LWO, .LWS), and Wavefront (.OBJ) formats. 3D characters are recognized as human figures with parent-child relationships intact. Manga Studio even lets you manipulate the 3D human figure by changing its pose in simplified ways.

FIGURE 17-4

Poser figures can be placed in Shade scenes without importing

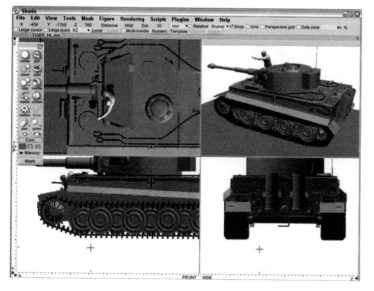

FIGURE 17-5

Manga Studio can import images and 3D human figures using the .LWS format

Use Virtual Fashion Clothes in Poser

1. Open Virtual Fashion and click the Designer link from the home page.

2. Click on the New Project button and select a new project using the Jessi model with the Skirt garment mold. Click the OK button.

   Jessi is displayed with cloth surrounding her. You can change the shape of the clothing lines that are displayed using the Straight, Flare, and Curve options in the lower-right corner.

FIGURE 17-6
Jessi with a Virtual Fashion dress

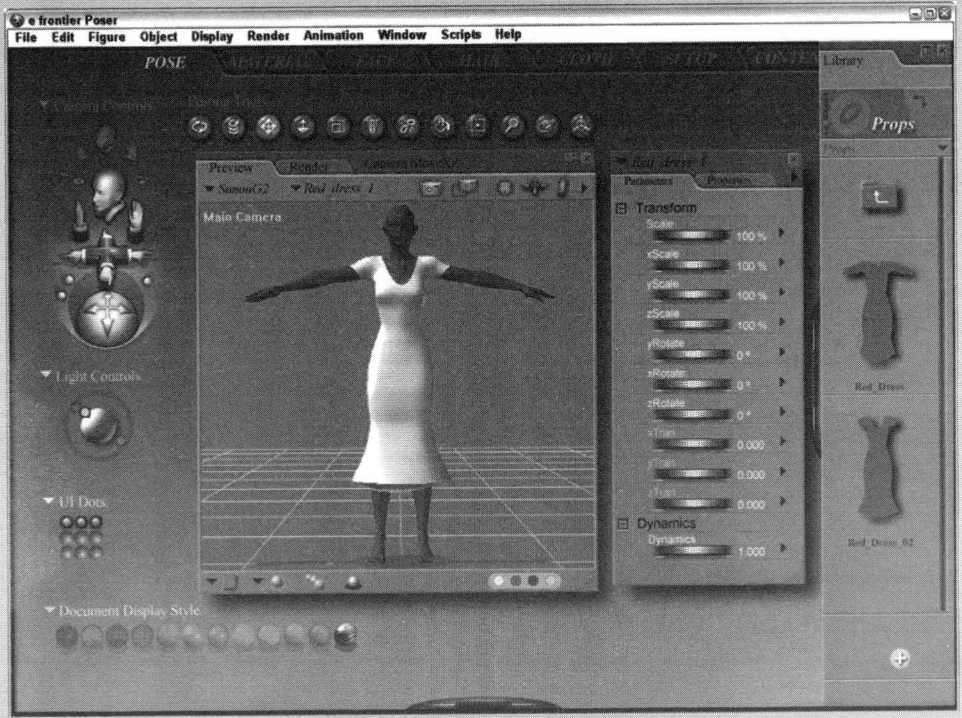

3. Select the clothing lines just under the knee and flare it out. Then select the Cutter mode and draw lines at the dress hem, the neckline, and at each arm and click the Cut tool to make a cut. Then select the Delete Element button and remove the unneeded section.

4. Click on the Fabric mode and select and assign the Lightweight Cotton fabric.

5. Click on the Fitting Room button and click on the Export Project button. In the file dialog box that opens, name the project **Red dress 02** and click the OK button.

The dress is exported to the MyPoserProjects folder where Virtual Fashion is installed.

6. Start Poser and open the Library palette. Navigate to the root folder and select the Add New Runtime option from the pop-up menu. Locate the Virtual Fashion/Runtime folder where the program is installed and add the new runtime.

A new folder is added to the Poser Library palette containing Poses, Props, and Materials. The exported clothes are found in the Props category.

7. Select the Poses category in the Library and apply the T-pose figure to the default figure.

Clothes are exported from Virtual Fashion with the clothes positioned in the T-pose, so you must select this pose before you apply clothes. You can then change the pose after the clothes have been applied to the figure.

8. Select the Props category and choose and apply the Red dress 02 thumbnail to the scene figure.

After draping the clothes using the Cloth Room, the Virtual Fashion dress is shown in Figure 17-6. You can learn more about using the Cloth Room in Chapter 11, "Working with Dynamic Cloth."

9. Select File, Save As and save the file as **Virtual Fashion dress.pz3**.

Load Poser Figure in Shade

1. Start Shade and select the View, PoserFusion menu.

   The PoserFusion module opens.

2. Click on the Poser button to see where the Poser application is located.

   Once the Poser application is located, you can use PoserFusion to open Poser .PZ3 files.

CAUTION PoserFusion in Shade 8 currently doesn't work with Poser 7. Watch for an upgrade.

3. Click the Open button and locate a Poser file saved in the .PZ3 or .PZZ format.

   The Poser file is loaded into the current Shade scene, as shown in Figure 17-7.

FIGURE 17-7
Poser figures can be loaded directly into Shade

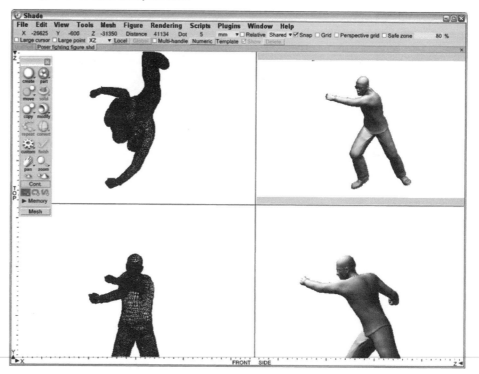

Layer Properties

Properties | 3DLT
Operation | Display | Rendering

- Camera
- SimonG2.obj

Move
X Axis:	☑	🔘	0.000 ▶
Y Axis:	☑	🔘	0.000 ▶
Z Axis:	☑	🔘	0.000 ▶
Distance:		🔘	-30.103 ▶

Rotate
X Axis:		🔘	0.000 ▶
Y Axis:		🔘	0.000 ▶
Z Axis:		🔘	0.000 ▶

Size and Perspective
Size:	☑	🔘	0.000 ▶
Perspective:		🔘	45 ▶

Motion Settings

[Preview]

☑ Show Page Image

[OK] [Cancel]

FIGURE 17-8

The 3DLT panel of the Layer Properties palette includes controls for positioning the imported figure

Import Poser Figure in Manga Studio

1. Start Poser and pose the figure for the Manga page. Then use the File, Export, Wavefront OBJ menu and save the exported figure.

2. Start Manga Studio and open a new page.

3. Select the File, 3DLT Import menu command. Click on the Open button and locate the exported Poser figure.

The Layer Properties palette with the 3DLT panel, shown in Figure 17-8, opens. Using the various Open, Rotate, and Size controls, you can set the imported figure's size, orientation, and position. After closing the Layer Properties palette, the imported figure is displayed in the selected shading method, as shown in Figure 17-9.

FIGURE 17-9

Poser figures can be added to a Manga page

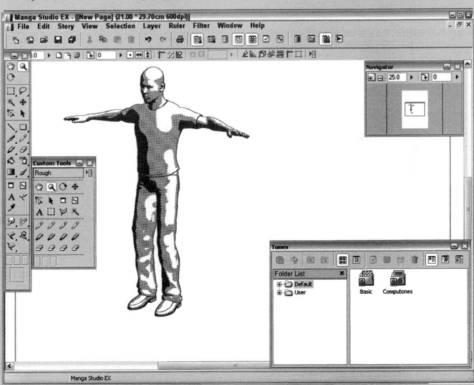

USE POSER
WITH 3D PACKAGES

What You'll Do

In this lesson, you learn how to use Poser with other 3D packages.

The mechanism for using Poser content with other 3D packages is to import and export the content. There are several 3D formats that Poser supports including .3ds, .DXF, .LWO and .OBJ. You can learn more about these formats in Chapter 4, "Working with Files and Accessing Content Paradise."

Creating Models in 3ds Max for Use in Poser

Although Poser supports the .3ds format, it actually isn't the best format to use when exchanging files between 3ds Max and Poser. The .3ds format pre-dates 3ds Max and is the format used when 3d Studio was a DOS version. Current installations of 3ds Max use the .MAX file format, and Autodesk is moving towards the Filmbox (.FBX) format; but sadly Poser doesn't support either of these formats.

CAUTION The .3ds file format has a maximum limit of 65,000 polygons.

The best available format for moving data between 3ds Max and Poser is the Wavefront .OBJ format. The .OBJ format splits the geometry information into a separate file from the material textures. OBJ materials are saved as separate .MTL files. The OBJ Exporter in 3ds Max, shown in Figure 17-10, includes options to separate the model into groups by objects or materials. If the model has any maps, you'll need to enable the Texture Coordinates option. Smooth Groups can also be exported. However, if you want to save the materials, you'll need to export them separately using the Wavefront Material format. If both the .OBJ and the .MTL files are contained in the same folder when they're imported into Poser, the materials will show up in Poser.

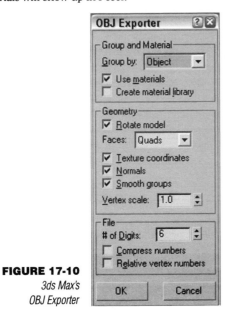

FIGURE 17-10

*3ds Max's
OBJ Exporter*

Creating Models in Maya for Use in Poser

Maya uses its own file format for saving its content using the Maya Binary (.MB) extension, but it can also export its 3D content using several different 3D formats. However, the short list available in the default version of Maya doesn't include any formats that are in common with Poser. Maya does support importing content into Maya using the Wavefront .OBJ format. Like 3ds Max, Maya is a strong supporter of the Filmbox (.FBX) format.

Even though there aren't any common formats between Maya and Poser, the extensible design of Maya makes it easy to install plug-in modules. A plug-in for exporting Maya content using the .OBJ format is available, but you'll need to make it active. The name of the Maya plug-in is objExport.cpp. You can make it active using the Window, Settings/ Preferences, Plug-in Manager menu command. Other plug-ins that allow Maya content to be exported as other formats such as .LWO are common on the Web. Once these scripts are installed, you'll be able to export Maya content to Poser.

CAUTION Maya can export content to the DXF_FBX format. Although these files have the .DXF extension, they aren't compatible with Poser.

If you can find the right script, the best format for exporting content to and from Maya is also the Wavefront .OBJ format, but you need to make sure that your models are converted to polygons before exporting them. Although Maya can work with NURBS and Subdivision Surfaces, only polygons can be imported into Poser.

Creating Models in Other 3D Packages for Use in Poser

Two other popular 3D modeling packages include Lightwave and Softimage XSI. Lightwave can export content to the .OBJ and .LWO formats, but the .LWO format obviously works the best. The best format for content in Softimage XSI is also the .OBJ format.

For all other 3D packages, look first for the .OBJ format and if it isn't available, try the 3DS or .LWO formats, but try to avoid using the .DXF format. This format is older and unstable for most products, except for CAD packages such as AutoCAD.

Import 3ds Max Content into Poser

1. Start 3ds Max and load a piece of content, such as a birdbath, as shown in Figure 17-11. Select the File, Export menu. Select a folder and name the file to be exported. Choose the Wavefront OBJ option from the File Type drop-down list and click the Export button.

   The OBJ Exported dialog box appears.

2. In the OBJ Exporter dialog box, select the Group by Object option and enable the Use Materials, Texture Coordinates, Normals, and Smooth Groups options. Then click the OK button.

   The file is exported and saved.

3. With the same object selected, choose the File, Export menu again, change the File Type to Wavefront Material (.MTL) and name the .MTL file the same as the .OBJ file. In the MTL Export dialog box that appears, enable the Export Maps option.

4. Start Poser and select the File, Import, Wavefront OBJ menu. Select the Centered and Place on Floor option in the Import Options dialog box. Then locate and open the birdbath file.

   The birdbath object is imported into Poser, as shown in Figure 17-12. If you select the various groups in the Material Room, you'll see that the material groups are intact with different materials applied.

FIGURE 17-11
A birdbath in 3ds Max

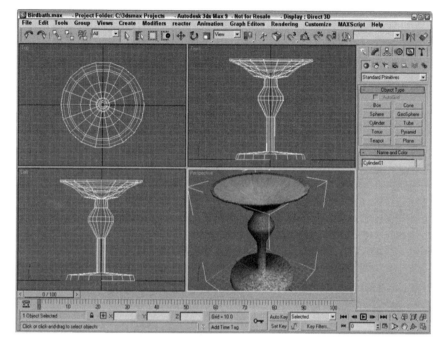

FIGURE 17-12
The birdbath imported into Poser

FIGURE 17-13

A bunch of daisies in Maya

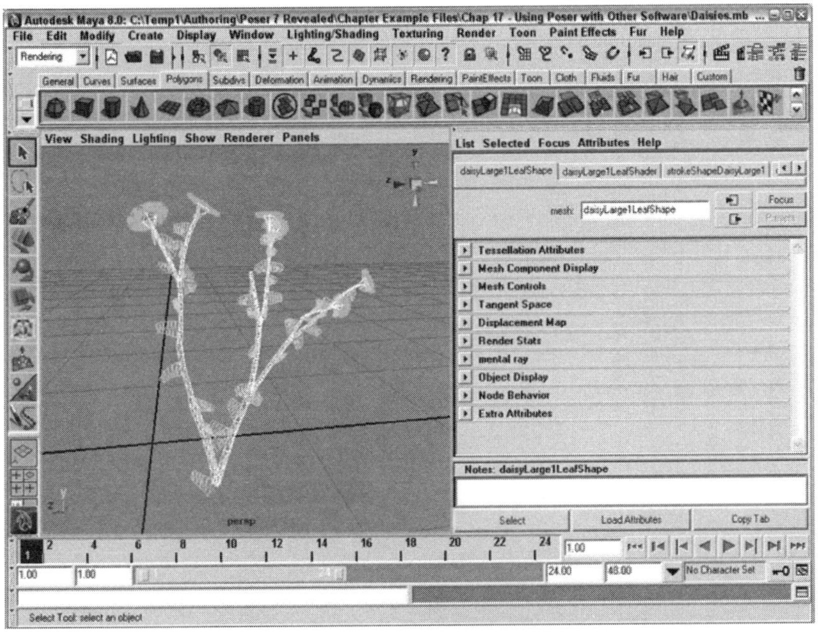

Import Maya Content into Poser

1. Start Maya and load a piece of content, such as a bunch of daisies, as shown in Figure 17-13.

2. Select the Window, Settings/Preferences, Plug-in Manager menu. In the Plug-in Manager, enable the Loaded option next to the objExport plug-in and click the Refresh button.

3. Select the File, Export All menu. Select a folder and name the file to be exported. Choose the OBJ export option from the File Type drop-down list and click the Export button.

4. Start Poser and select the File, Import, Wavefront OBJ menu. Select the Centered and Place on Floor option in the Import Options dialog box. Then locate and open the daisies file.

   The daisies are imported into Poser, as shown in Figure 17-14.

FIGURE 17-14

The daisies imported into Poser

RETOUCH IMAGES
IN PHOTOSHOP

What You'll Do

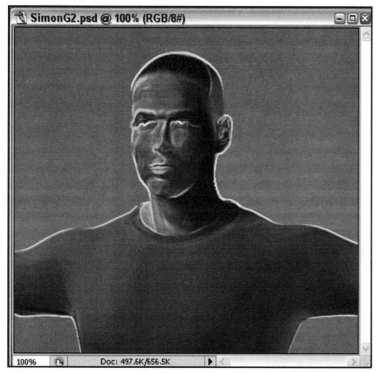

In this lesson, you learn how to export Poser images for retouching in Photoshop.

Although the final rendered images created in Poser are beautiful, there are times when you'll want to edit problems out of a rendered image rather than waiting another several hours for the image to re-render. Photoshop also includes several unique features that aren't easily created in Poser, such as Lens Flares.

Exporting Poser Images

Poser images can be exported in a couple of ways. From the Document Window, you can use the Export Image option in the pop-up menu to export the current image in the Document Window. This might be either the Preview panel or the Render panel, depending on which is selected.

You can also export images using the File, Export, Image menu. Both options allow the image to be exported using several different formats, including .PNG, .BMP, .TIF, .JPEG, .TGA, and .PSD. If you are opening the image file in Photoshop, the .PSD format is preferred. The .PSD format supports layers.

Removing Discontinuities

Although a rendered image typically won't have discontinuities, they may appear if a material texture isn't scaled correctly or perhaps if you forgot to turn off a light shadow that you didn't want. If you export the Preview panel, you might want to remove the ground plane lines.

Problem image areas can be easily removed in Photoshop using the various Clone and Healing brushes.

NOTE Even though the Photoshop (.PSD) format supports layers, when an image is exported using the .PSD format, the image is contained in a single background layer.

Patching Clothes

Another common problem that is often easier to fix in Photoshop than to correct and re-render is the problem that occurs when the skin pokes through cloth. Even though the Cloth Room does a great job draping cloth over a model, if the forces involved in the parameters are too extreme, the skin may be visible. Figure 17-15 shows a figure with this problem, even after using the Conform To command.

Clone and Healing brushes can quickly patch up this problem.

FIGURE 17-15
Skin poking through clothes

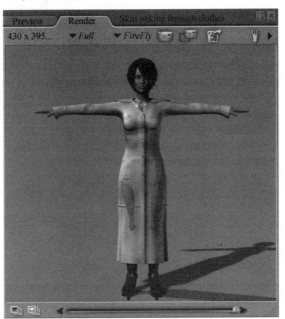

Adding Effects

Photoshop includes a number of effects that give the rendered image a new and interesting look that isn't possible by rendering. Figure 17-16 shows a rendered spaceship taken from Poser's Library that has been enhanced with a nice lens flare off its front canopy.

Photoshop's filters in particular can give the rendered image a painted look.

FIGURE 17-16
Added lens flare

1. Open the Skin poking through clothes.pz3 file using the File, Open menu.

2. Render the figure and use the File, Export, Image menu to export the image using the .PSD format.

3. Start Photoshop and open the exported image.

4. Zoom in on the problem area. Then select the Spot Healing brush and set the Diameter to around 8 pixels. Then lightly brush around the area where the skin is visible.

   The skin is hidden under the clothes, as shown in Figure 17-17. This process is much quicker than re-rendering the scene.

FIGURE 17-17
Skin through clothes fixed in Photoshop

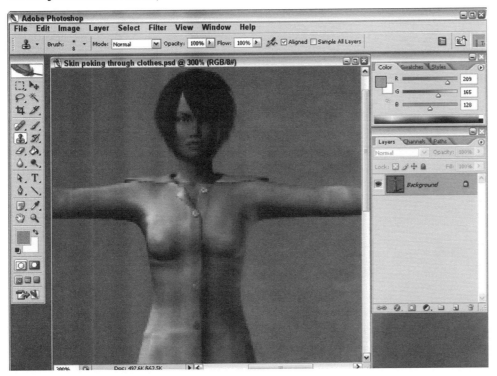

Use Photoshop to Add a Unique Look

1. Open Poser with the default figure visible.
2. Render the figure and use the File, Export, Image menu to export the image using the PSD format.
3. Start Photoshop and open the exported image.
4. Select the Filter, Brushed Strokes, Accented Edges menu to apply the filter to the rendered image.

   The filter gives the rendered image a unique look, as shown in Figure 17-18.

FIGURE 17-18

Photoshop filters give the rendered image a unique look

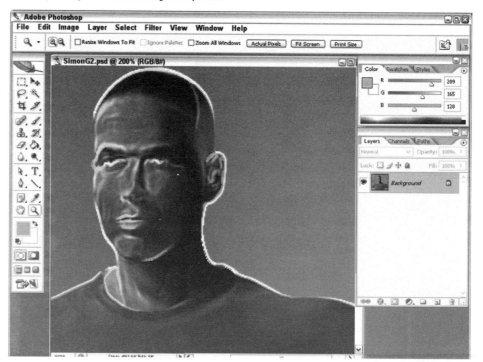

Chapter Summary

This chapter examined how Poser works with several other external packages, including several other e frontier products, 3D packages like 3ds Max and Maya, and image-editing packages such as Photoshop.

What You Have Learned

In this chapter, you

- Created custom clothes for Poser using Virtual Fashion.

- Loaded Poser figures into a Shade scene using the PoserFusion module.

- Loaded a Poser figure into Manga Studio.

- Exported a 3D object created in 3ds Max and Maya for importing into Poser.

- Exported rendered images for editing in Photoshop.

- Added special effects to a rendered image in Photoshop.

Key Terms from This Chapter

- **Virtual Fashion.** A software package that lets you create clothes in the same manner as clothes are made in real life.

- **Shade.** A 3D modeling and rendering application that works well with Poser using an integration module.

- **Manga Studio.** A software package used to create Manga comic pages.

- **3ds Max.** A popular 3D package.

- **Maya.** A popular 3D modeling package.

- **Photoshop.** A popular image-editing application.

chapter **18** **WRITING**
PYTHON SCRIPTS

1. Access pre-built scripts.

2. Edit Python scripts.

chapter 18 WRITING PYTHON SCRIPTS

Python is an interpreted, object-oriented scripting language that includes text commands for defining certain actions. **PoserPython** is an extension to the industry-standard Python scripting language that lets you extend and add new functionality to Poser.

You can write Poser scripts using any standard text editor, but the script commands must follow a specific syntax that the script interpreter can understand. You can learn this syntax using the Poser-Python Help files, which you can open using Help, PoserPython Help.

Poser scripts are executed using the Scripts menu. You can also run them using the File, Run Python Script menu command or by using the Python Scripts palette, which you open using the Window, Python Scripts menu command. You can open and run scripts that work with materials within the Wacros panel in the Shader Window.

Tools You'll Use

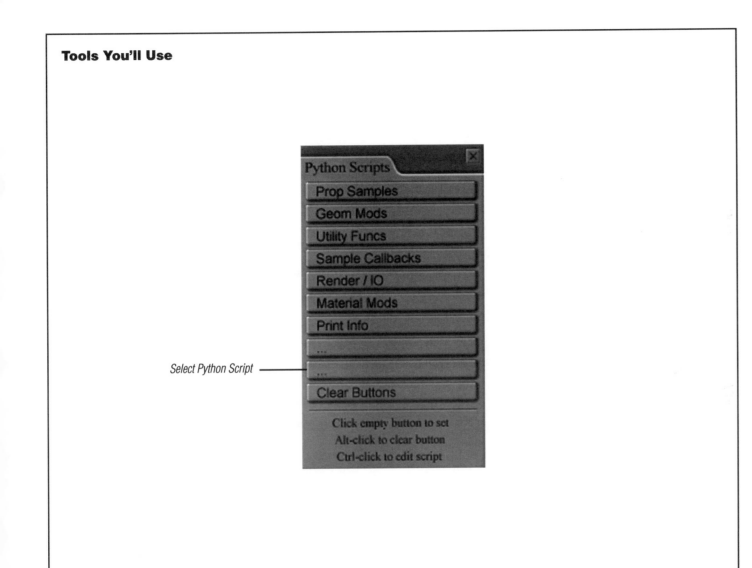

Select Python Script ——

ACCESS
PRE-BUILT SCRIPTS

What You'll Do

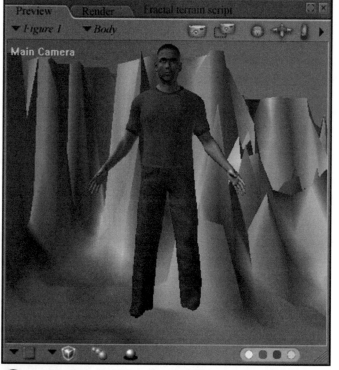

In this lesson, you learn how to access the various pre-built Python scripts.

You can execute PoserPython scripts within Poser in a couple of different ways. The easiest way to access existing Python scripts is with the Scripts menu. Another way is to use the File, Run Python Script menu command and another is with the Python Scripts palette.

NEW POSER 7 FEATURE
The Scripts menu is new to Poser 7.

Finding Default Python Scripts

Several default Python scripts are included with the default installation of Poser, and looking at these scripts is a good way to start to learn the Python syntax. To locate the default PoserPython scripts, look in the \Runtime\Python\poserScripts directory where Poser is installed. You can open and edit all Poser scripts that have the .PY file extension within a text editor.

Using the Scripts Menu

All Python scripts that are added to the PoserScripts/ScriptsMenu directory will automatically appear in the Scripts menu. If a folder exists within the PoserScripts/ScriptsMenu directory, the scripts contained in the folder will appear within a submenu in the Scripts menu.

> **NOTE** The PoserScripts directory also includes a wacros folder that holds all the Wacros scripts found in the Material Room's Shader window.

Using the Python Scripts Palette

You can also open the Python Scripts palette by selecting Window, Python Scripts. This palette, shown in Figure 18-1, includes several buttons. Each button can be attached to an external script. Clicking a script button executes the script, and clicking an empty button opens the Open dialog box where you can load a script for the button. Clicking a script button with the Alt/Option key pressed clears the selected button.

> **NOTE** Some of the buttons in the Python Scripts palette are simple scripts that open additional button sets.

Executing Scripts

Selecting File, Run Python Script makes an Open dialog box appear where you can select a script file to execute. This dialog box can open both Python source files with a .PY file extension and Python compiled files with the .PYC file extension.

Learning the Pre-Built Scripts

The available pre-built scripts are divided into several different categories. Some of these scripts will add simple props to the scene and others will give you access to utilities that can be helpful. The following sections list the available scripts and how they can be used.

FIGURE 18-1
Python Scripts palette

> **NOTE** Some scripts are only available in the Scripts menu and others are only available in the Scripts palette.

Learn the Prop Samples Scripts

Within the Prop Samples category are several scripts for creating props, including

- **Bucky Ball.** Adds a geometric Bucky Ball to the scene.
- **Tetra.** Adds a geometric tetrahedron to the scene.
- **Sinwaved Mesh.** Adds a sin wave mesh to the scene.
- **Fractal Terrain.** Adds a terrain plane to the scene.

Learn the Geom Mods Scripts

Within the Geom Mods category are several scripts for modifying the selected object, including

- **Randomize Figures.** Randomly repositions all the polygons that make up a figure to create an odd effect, shown in Figure 18-2.
- **Bulge Figures.** Causes the entire figure to be bulged along its normal vectors, resulting in a puffy figure, as shown in Figure 18-3.

- **Unimesh Demo.** Creates a prop from the current figure. The figure prop is a single mesh item without different body parts.

- **Copy Morph/Group data.** Creates a copy of the current morph target and/or group.

- **Check Paths of cr2/pz3.** Checks all the paths within the selected Poser file for missing files.

- **Randomize Morphs.** Creates a unique body style by randomizing all the available morph targets for the selected element.

- **Geometry Subdivide 2.** Increases the resolution of the selected element by subdividing all its polygons.

- **Random Expression.** Applies a random expression to the figure.

- **Shrink Figures.** The opposite of the Bulge Figure script. This script reduces the bulge of the muscles along the normal vectors.

Learn the Utility Functions Scripts

Within the Utility Functions category are several utility scripts for automatically changing settings, including

- **Drop Actor All Frames.** Drops the current actor to the ground in all frames. This is useful if you want to align the selected element to the ground for the entire animation.

- **Drop Fig All Frames.** Drops the entire figure to the ground in all frames. This is useful if you've animated a walk cycle that is above the ground plane.

- **Apply Gravity.** Enables gravity for the current selection to all simulations for all frames.

- **Copy Parameters.** Copies all keyframes from one parameter to another parameter.

- **Compress Files.** This utility lets you select a folder and automatically compress all the various Poser files found within the designated folder. You can also select to compress all .OBJ files that are found. Another option lets you delete the original files after they are compressed.

FIGURE 18-2
Randomized figure

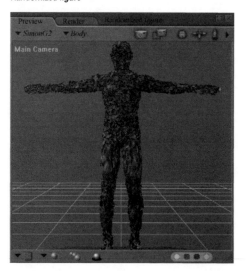

FIGURE 18-3
Bulged figure

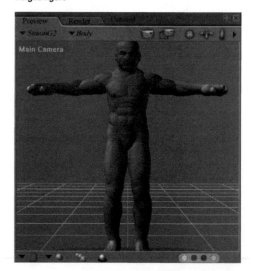

- **Uncompress Files.** This utility is the opposite of the Compress Files utility. It lets you select a folder to search for Poser files. All files that are found are uncompressed. You can also uncompress .OBJ files and delete the compressed file once it's uncompressed.

- **Delete All Lights.** Lets you quickly delete all the lights from the scene.

- **Collect Scene Inventory.** This utility lets you print a list of all the files currently opened in the scene, including scripts, texture maps, geometry files, morph target files, and backgrounds, as shown in Figure 18-4. This utility also includes an option to copy all these files to a specified folder. This is a great help if you need to collect all the files for a specific scene and you don't want to miss any texture files.

- **Convert to Universal Pose.** Poser 7 uses a Universal Pose format. This utility lets you select a folder, and all the poses within that folder will be converted to the new format. This lets you quickly update any older content.

- **Search and Replace Files.** This utility searches for problem files and replaces them with fixed files.

Learn the Sample Callbacks Scripts

Within the Sample Callbacks category are several scripts that return valuable information about the scene back to the debug window, including

- **Add Muscle Magnets.** Adds new magnet deformers to the left and right bicep muscles for the current figure.

- **Random Head Verts.** Randomizes all the vertices for the head polygons, creating a distorted localized mess.

FIGURE 18-4
Scene inventory list

- **Bend Arms by Frame.** Enables the Bend options for both arms in all frames.

- **World Space Print Vert.** Prints out the World-Space vertex coordinates for the selected element.

- **Print Event Callbacks.** Prints out all events that happen within the Poser interface.

- **Parameter Callback.** Prints all parameter changes that occur in the Poser interface.

Learn the Render Control Scripts

Within the Render Control category are several scripts that automate the exporting of certain file types and a valuable script for rendering individual passes, including

- **Mini-Me.** Creates a miniature version of the current figure by exporting the figure to the .OBJ format, and then importing it again using a different scale value, as shown in Figure 18-5.

- **Animated Trans.** This script lets you animate the transformations of the figure.

- **Export Flash.** This script searches a designated directory and converts all found Poser files to the Flash format automatically.

- **Export DXF.** This script exports the currently selected figure to the .DXF format, which can be done using the File, Export command. This script is provided as an example of an export script.

- **Calculate Depth of Field Focal Distance.** Prints the current focal distance value used for the depth of field effect where the camera is in focus.

- **Render Passes.** This script renders the current scene out into several passes, one for each light. You can also select to do a separate ambient lighting pass and a separate occlusion pass. These passes are saved into a designated directory where the light name is attached after the file name. These passes can then be used in a compositor to recreate and edit the lighting effects.

Learn the Material Mods Scripts

Within the Material Mods category are several scripts for creating props, including:

- **Set Materials.** The script sets the material inventory for the current scene.

- **Write Materials.** This script creates an inventory of all the materials used within a scene.

Learn the Print Info Scripts

Within the Print Info category are several scripts that output vital information to the debug window, including

- **Print Geometry Stats.** Prints the number of polygons and vertices included in each of the various body parts, as shown in Figure 18-6.

- **Scene Inventory.** Prints a quick list detailing the number of figures, body parts, props, lights, cameras, geometries, image maps, and bump maps.

- **List Files Used.** Prints all the files included in the current scene, including scripts, geometry, and texture files.

- **Figure Actor Info.** Prints a detailed list of the current selection, including its hierarchy, actor info, polygon and vertices totals, and all the polys and vertices for the remaining nonfigure actors in the

FIGURE 18-5
Miniature version of the figure

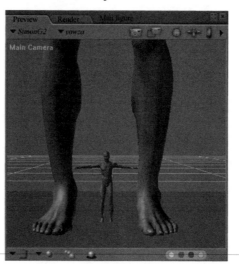

scene. It also includes the parameter values for each frame for the selected actor.

- **Check Figure Magnets.** Checks the integrity of all magnets within the current scene. Some content creators use complex manget rigs, and this script identifies any missing elements.

- **Print Figure WD Stats.** Prints the hip height and feet size for the current figure.

Some content creators use complex magnet rigs, and this script identifies any missing elements.

FIGURE 18-6
Geometry stats on each body part

printGeomStats		
Traps_lChest_DfmrZ	180 polys	162 verts
Traps_lCollar_DfmrB	9 polys	30 verts
Traps_lCollar_Dfmr	162 polys	336 verts
Traps_lCollar_DfmrZ	180 polys	162 verts
Glute_rButtock_Dfmr_Base	9 polys	30 verts
Glute_rButtock_Dfmr	162 polys	336 verts
Glute_rButtock_DfmrZ	180 polys	162 verts
Glute_rHip_DfmrB	9 polys	30 verts
Glute_rHip_Dfmr	162 polys	336 verts
Glute_rHip_DfmrZ	180 polys	162 verts
Glute_lHip_DfmrB	9 polys	30 verts
Glute_lHip_Dfmr	162 polys	336 verts
Glute_lHip_DfmrZ	180 polys	162 verts
Glute_lButtock_DfmrB	9 polys	30 verts
Glute_lButtock_Dfmr	162 polys	336 verts
Glute_lButtock_DfmrZ	180 polys	162 verts
Elbow_rForeArm_DfmrB	9 polys	30 verts
Elbow_rForeArm_Dfmr	162 polys	336 verts
Elbow_rForeArm_DfmrZ	180 polys	162 verts
Elbow_lForeArm_DfmrB	9 polys	30 verts
Elbow_lForeArm_Dfmr	162 polys	336 verts
Elbow_lForeArm_Dfmr_Zone	180 polys	162 verts
Pectoral_rCollar_DfmrB	9 polys	30 verts
Pectoral_rCollar_Dfmr	162 polys	336 verts
Pectoral_rCollar_DfmrZ	180 polys	162 verts
Pectoral_lCollar_DfmrB	9 polys	30 verts
Pectoral_lCollar_Dfmr	162 polys	336 verts
Pectoral_lCollar_DfmrZ	180 polys	162 verts

Run a Python Script

1. Open Poser with the default figure visible.
2. Choose File, Run Python Script.

   An Open dialog box appears.

3. Navigate to the \Runtime\Python\Poser-Scripts\CreateProps directory where Poser is installed.
4. Select the FractalTerrain.py file and click the Open button.

   A fractal terrain object is added to the scene, as shown in Figure 18-7.

5. Select File, Save As and save the file as **Fractal terrain script.pz3**.

Use the Python Scripts Palette

1. Open Poser with the default figure visible.
2. Choose Window, Python Scripts.

   The Python Scripts palette appears.

3. Click Print Info in the Python Scripts palette.

   A new set of buttons is loaded into the Python Scripts palette.

4. Click the Scene Inventory button.

   A dialog box opens that lists all the objects in the scene, as shown in Figure 18-8.

FIGURE 18-7
Fractal terrain script

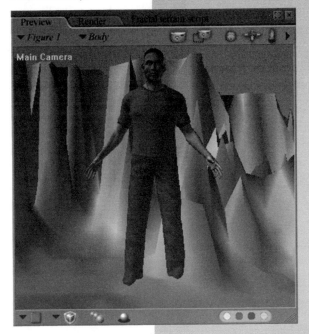

FIGURE 18-8
Bucky ball script

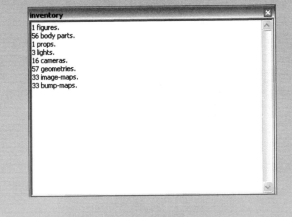

EDIT
PYTHON SCRIPTS

What You'll Do

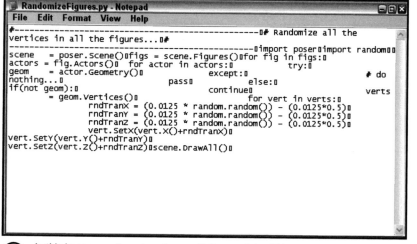

```
RandomizeFigures.py - Notepad
File  Edit  Format  View  Help
#----------------------------------------------------# Randomize all the
vertices in all the figures...#
----------------------------------------------import poserimport random
scene  = poser.Scene()figs = scene.Figures()for fig in figs:
actors = fig.Actors()  for actor in actors:          try:
geom   = actor.Geometry()             except:              # do
nothing...                     pass          else:
if(not geom):                   continue                verts
        = geom.Vertices()                   for vert in verts:
            rndTranX = (0.0125 * random.random()) - (0.0125*0.5)
            rndTranY = (0.0125 * random.random()) - (0.0125*0.5)
            rndTranZ = (0.0125 * random.random()) - (0.0125*0.5)
            vert.SetX(vert.X()+rndTranX)
vert.SetY(vert.Y()+rndTranY)
vert.SetZ(vert.Z()+rndTranZ)scene.DrawAll()
```

▶ *In this lesson, you learn how to open Python scripts within a text editor.*

You can open scripts available in the Python Scripts palette in the default text editor for editing by clicking the script button while holding the Ctrl/Command button down. Figure 18-9 shows the randomizeMorphs.py file opened within a text editor.

CAUTION Saving a script opened in a text editor from the Python Scripts palette will overwrite the existing script. If any changes are made to the script, save the file to a different file name, using File, Save As.

Editing Python Scripts

When a script is open within a text editor, you can change the function of the script by changing the commands, but it is important not to change the syntax of the script commands. When the script runs, it looks for specific commands and, if the syntax is misspelled or if the formatting is off, the script will throw an error.

You can often change the behavior of the script by simply changing the numeric values within the script.

Changing the Default Text Editor

When editing PoserPython scripts, the system's default text editor opens, but you can change the text editor that is used to edit PoserPython scripts using the Misc panel of the General Preferences dialog box, shown in Figure 18-10. You open the General Preferences dialog box by using Edit, General Preferences or by pressing Ctrl/Command+K. To change the Python Editor, click the Set Python Editor button and select the text editor you want to use.

Reinitializing Python

If you find that the Python engine is returning erroneous results, it could be that there is problem with how the data is being handled by the Poser interpreter. This can be easily corrected by simply resetting the Python engine using the File, Reinitialize Python menu.

FIGURE 18-9

Text editor

```
randomizeMorphs.py - Notepad
File  Edit  Format  View  Help
#------------------------------------------------------------
-
# This sample file will randomize all morph targets
# on the current actor
#------------------------------------------------------------
-
import random
import poser

scene = poser.Scene()

actor = scene.CurrentActor()

rememberFrame = scene.Frame()

for parm in actor.Parameters():
        if (parm.IsMorphTarget()):
                rndMagnitude = (0.75 * random.random()) - (0.75 *0.5)
                parm.SetValue(rndMagnitude)
actor.MarkGeomChanged()
scene.DrawAll()
```

FIGURE 18-10

Misc panel of the General Preferences dialog box

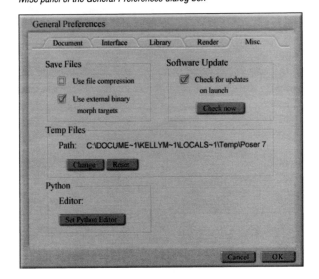

Open a Script for Editing

1. Open Poser with the default figure visible.
2. Choose Window, Python Scripts.

   The Python Scripts palette appears.
3. Click the Main button at the bottom of the palette, if necessary. Then, click the Geom Mods script in the Python Scripts palette.

   A new set of buttons is loaded into the Python Scripts palette.
4. Hold down the Ctrl/Command button and click the Randomize Figs button.

   The RandomizeFigures.py file is opened within the default text editor, as shown in Figure 18-11.

FIGURE 18-11

The RandomizeFigures.py script

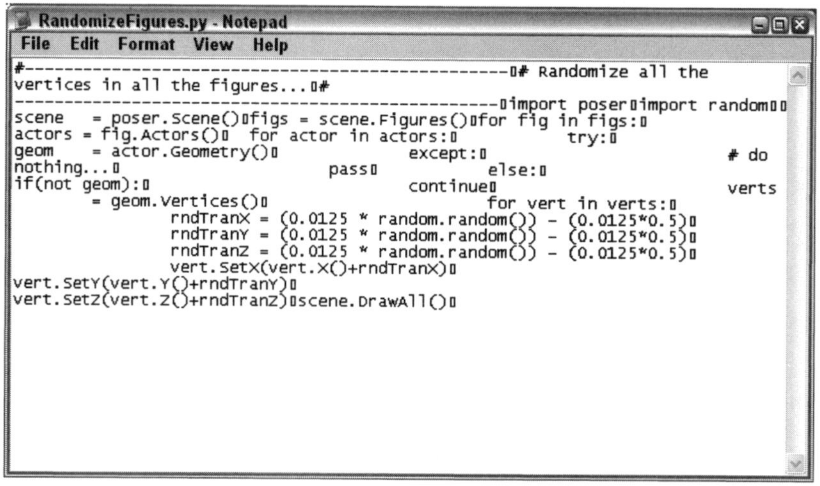
RandomizeFigures.py - Notepad
File Edit Format View Help
#--▯# Randomize all the
vertices in all the figures...▯#
--▯import poser▯import random▯▯
scene   = poser.Scene()▯figs = scene.Figures()▯for fig in figs:▯
actors = fig.Actors()▯ for actor in actors:▯   try:▯
geom   = actor.Geometry()▯   except:▯   # do
nothing...▯   pass▯   else:▯
if(not geom):▯   continue▯   verts
        = geom.Vertices()▯   for vert in verts:▯
                rndTranX = (0.0125 * random.random()) - (0.0125*0.5)▯
                rndTranY = (0.0125 * random.random()) - (0.0125*0.5)▯
                rndTranZ = (0.0125 * random.random()) - (0.0125*0.5)▯
                vert.SetX(vert.X()+rndTranX)▯
vert.SetY(vert.Y()+rndTranY)▯
vert.SetZ(vert.Z()+rndTranZ)▯scene.DrawAll()▯

CHAPTER REVIEW

Chapter Summary

This chapter introduced the interfaces used to load and execute PoserPython scripts, including the Scripts menu and the Scripts palette. It also introduces all the various scripts that ship with Poser. It also briefly showed how you can edit Python scripts using a text editor.

What You Have Learned

In this chapter, you

- Executed default scripts using the Python Scripts palette, the Scripts menu, and the File, Run Python Script menu command.

- Learned what the various default scripts do.

- Edited PoserPython scripts using the system's default text editor.

Key Terms from This Chapter

- Compiled file. A Python file that has been converted to a machine-savvy format that is no longer readable, but that executes quicker.

- PoserPython. An extension to the industry-standard Python scripting language that lets you extend and add new functionality to Poser.

- Python. An interpreted, object-oriented scripting language that includes text commands for defining certain actions.

- Python Scripts palette. An interface where you can load and execute Python scripts.

- Source file. An original text-based Python file that can be executed.

- Text editor. System software that is used to edit and save text files.

- Wacros. PoserPython scripts that deal specifically with materials.

appendix A NEW FEATURES
IN POSER 7

Poser has come a long way since its initial introduction and each version shows the software moving in totally new directions. At some point, you might begin to wonder if there will be any new features to add, but rest assured that the development team has great plans for the future as you take the time to understand and integrate the latest batch of new tools.

Major New Features

There are several new additions to Poser 7 that are classified as major improvements. These new features represent large shifts in how you will work with Poser and new tools that are worth exploring and mastering.

Multiple Undos

If you make a change and then another before you realize a mistake, you can now undo and redo most actions. The new multiple undo feature is a huge addition to Poser 7, and makes it possible to backtrack your work and take it in another direction. This feature is covered in Chapter 1, "Learning the Poser Interface."

Z-Buffer Selection List

If you are frustrated that in order to click and select a hidden body part, such as the middle finger, you need to rotate the camera, then you'll be happy to use the new Z-Buffer Selection list. If you click on an element in the Document Window, then all the elements that are under the cursor's position are listed, no matter if they are hidden behind another object in a menu that can be accessed by right-clicking. The menu lists all the parts under the current mouse cursor in order, from front to back. This feature is covered in Chapter 3, "Editing and Posing Figures."

Talk Designer

Poser 7's new Talk Designer lets you automate the process of facial animation and synching facial movements to a sound file. To make a figure speak, you simply need to load a sound file and a file that correlates to the morph targets for each of the sounds, and Poser does the rest automatically. It also includes the ability to control expressions, phonemes, eye blinks, and head movements. The Talk Designer is covered in detail in Chapter 15, "Lip Synching with Talk Designer."

Custom Morph Targets

The Morphing tool now includes a new Create panel that allows you to easily create custom morph targets using brushes. These brushes can push, pull, relax, and restore the object to its original shape. With several different brush styles, you can control the amount of falloff to work with, enabling you to paint subtle deformations or hard edges. You can also set the brush radius to work in broad areas or focus on tiny details. You can learn more about creating and working with morph targets in Chapter 14, "Morphing Figures and Using Deformers."

Animation Layers

Animation Layers let you work with non-linear animation by separating the animation sequences into different layers that can be recombined and mixed to create entirely new motions. Animation layers are covered along with the other animation features in Chapter 13, "Animating Figures and Scenes."

Improved FireFly Rendering

The FireFly rendering engine has been overhauled in Poser 7 and improved to work more efficiently with memory resources. With its new Tiled Texture Loading feature, textures are cached on the local hard drive. This frees up large amounts of memory that can be used to render images. The result is that the maximum rendering size that Poser 7 can handle is much larger. Texture filtering is now handled at the texture level instead of at the global level. FireFly is now multi-threaded, which enables it to render faster on multi-processor computers.

The improvements result in stability, better performance, and faster render speeds. You can learn about all these improvements in Chapter 16, "Rendering Scenes."

Ambient Occlusion

Although ambient occlusion isn't new to Poser 7, its implementation has been vastly improved, making it possible to render this effect in times that make it feasible. The new Irradiance Caching option lets you configure how much lighting detail is cached to improve render speeds. The new settings are covered in Chapter 7, "Adding Scene Lighting."

Shader Previews

Through the OpenGL display drivers, you can now see procedural material shaders rendered in the Document Window. This saves having to render a scene to check the texture. Preview textures can also be sized to high resolutions (up to 4096 by 4096 pixels) whether hardware shading is enabled or not. This new preview ability is covered in Chapter 8, "Creating and Applying Materials."

Content Collections

Content Collections are another panel added to the Library palette. This panel lets you create collections of content from a single source. These collections can also span multiple runtime libraries. Content Collections are covered in Chapter 2, "Using the Poser Library."

New Content

Just as with every recent Poser release, the Library palette comes pre-loaded with several tasty new selections of content, including two second generation (G2) figures—Simon and Sydney. Along with these new figures are entirely new sets of clothes, poses, expressions, etc. Much of the new content is displayed throughout the book, and the Library palette is covered in Chapter 2, "Using the Poser Library."

Minor New Features

In addition to the new major features are several improvements classified as minor. These won't change the way you work, but will leave you saying, "Aww, finally, they got it right." The list of minor features includes:

- **Intel Macintosh universal binary files.** Poser now runs natively on Intel Macintosh computers, which should speed up the program considerably for these systems.

- **HDRI file support.** Poser 7 includes support for High Dynamic Range (HDR) images. These are particularly important when used as image-based lighting (IBL) sources.

- **EXR file support.** Poser 7 can import images saved using the .EXR file format.

- **Quick Start guides.** The new Quick Start guides are lifesavers for beginners who want to learn the ins and outs of certain tasks in Poser 7. The available projects include Getting Started, Rendering Styles, Pose Figure, Add Props, and Lighting. Each provides a step-by-step set of instructions.

- **Scripts menu.** The new Scripts menu can be customized to include any

handy scripts you've downloaded or wrote yourself providing easy access.

- **Recent Files List.** Poser 7 keeps track of the last 10 files that you've opened and makes them available for selection in the Recent Files List.

- **Duplicate command.** The new Duplicate command creates a clone of the selected object automatically, without having to locate it in the Library. Even entire figures can be duplicated with a single command.

- **Universal Poses.** The new Universal Pose format lets you apply any biped figure's pose to another figure, regardless of the figure's skeleton and rigging. Existing poses are saved to the Library palette using this new format.

- **Dependent parameters.** Several parameters can be combined together into a single parameter that controls the figure's specific action.

- **Runtime Selection List.** The Library palette now includes pop-up lists that let you select a specific Runtime library without having to navigate up to the top of the current library.

POSER 7
KEYBOARD SHORTCUTS

If you can memorize even a partial set of these keyboard shortcuts, they will let you work much faster. They are worth the time to learn.

Menu Shortcuts

Command	Keyboard Shortcut
File, New	Ctrl/Command+N
File, Open	Ctrl/Command+O
File, Close	Ctrl/Command+W
File, Save	Ctrl/Command+S
File, Save As	Shift+Ctrl/Command+S
File, Print	Ctrl/Command+P
File, Quit	Ctrl/Command+Q
Edit, Undo	Ctrl/Command+Z
Edit, Redo	Shift+Ctrl/Command+Z
Edit, Cut	Ctrl/Command+X
Edit, Copy	Ctrl/Command+C
Edit, Paste	Ctrl/Command+V
Edit, Restore, Element	Ctrl/Command+E
Edit, Restore, Figure	Ctrl/Command+Shift+F
Edit, Restore, Lights	Ctrl/Command+Shift+L
Edit, Restore, Camera	Ctrl/Command+Shift+H
Edit, Restore, All	Ctrl/Command+A

Command	Keyboard Shortcut
Edit, Memorize, Element	Alt+Ctrl+E (Option+Command+E on the Mac)
Edit, Memorize, Figure	Alt+Ctrl+F (Option+Command+F on the Mac)
Edit, Memorize, Lights	Alt+Ctrl+L (Option+Command+L on the Mac)
Edit, Memorize, Camera	Alt+Ctrl+H (Option+Command+H on the Mac)
Edit, Memorize, All	Alt+Ctrl+A (Option+Command+A on the Mac)
Edit, General Preferences	Ctrl/Command+K
Figure, Drop to Floor	Ctrl/Command+D
Figure, Hide Figure	Ctrl/Command+H
Object, Properties	Ctrl/Command+I
Display, Camera View, Main Camera	Ctrl/Command+M
Display, Camera View, From Left	Ctrl/Command+;
Display, Camera View, From Right	Ctrl/Command+'
Display, Camera View, From Top	Ctrl/Command+T
Display, Camera View, From Front	Ctrl/Command+F
Display, Camera View, Face Camera	Ctrl/Command+=
Display, Camera View, Posing Camera	Ctrl/Command+,
Display, Camera View, Right Hand Camera	Ctrl/Command+[
Display, Camera View, Left Hand Camera	Ctrl/Command+]
Display, Camera View, Dolly Camera	Ctrl/Command+/
Display, Camera View, Main Camera	Ctrl/Command+M
Display, Camera View, Fly Around	Ctrl/Command+L
Display, Document Style, Silhouette	Ctrl/Command+1
Display, Document Style, Outline	Ctrl/Command+2
Display, Document Style, Wireframe	Ctrl/Command+3
Display, Document Style, Hidden Line	Ctrl/Command+4
Display, Document Style, Wireframe	Ctrl/Command+5
Display, Document Style, Flat Shaded	Ctrl/Command+6

(continued)

Command	Keyboard Shortcut
Display, Document Style, Cartoon with Lines	Ctrl/Command+7
Display, Document Style, Smooth Shaded	Ctrl/Command+8
Display, Document Style, Texture Shaded	Ctrl/Command+9
Display, Document Style, Silhouette	Alt+Ctrl+1 (Option+Command+1 on the Mac)
Display, Document Style, Outline	Alt+Ctrl+2 (Option+Command+2 on the Mac)
Display, Document Style, Wireframe	Alt+Ctrl+3 (Option+Command+3 on the Mac)
Display, Document Style, Hidden Line	Alt+Ctrl+4 (Option+Command+4 on the Mac)
Display, Document Style, Wireframe	Alt+Ctrl+5 (Option+Command+5 on the Mac)
Display, Document Style, Flat Shaded	Alt+Ctrl+6 (Option+Command+6 on the Mac)
Display, Document Style, Cartoon with Lines	Alt+Ctrl+7 (Option+Command+7 on the Mac)
Display, Document Style, Smooth Shaded	Alt+Ctrl+8 (Option+Command+8 on the Mac)
Display, Document Style, Texture Shaded	Alt+Ctrl+9 (Option+Command+9 on the Mac)
Display, Document Style, Silhouette	Shift+Ctrl/Command+1
Display, Document Style, Outline	Shift+Ctrl/Command+2
Display, Document Style, Wireframe	Shift+Ctrl/Command+3
Display, Document Style, Hidden Line	Shift+Ctrl/Command+4
Display, Document Style, Wireframe	Shift+Ctrl/Command+5
Display, Document Style, Flat Shaded	Shift+Ctrl/Command+6
Display, Document Style, Cartoon with Lines	Shift+Ctrl/Command+7
Display, Document Style, Smooth Shaded	Shift+Ctrl/Command+8
Display, Document Style, Texture Shaded	Shift+Ctrl/Command+9
Display, Depth Cue	Shift+Ctrl/Command+D
Display, Tracking, Bounding Boxes Only	Shift+Ctrl/Command+A
Display, Tracking, Fast Tracking	Shift+Ctrl/Command+X
Display, Tracking, Full Tracking	Shift+Ctrl/Command+C
Display, Show Background Picture	Ctrl/Command+B
Display, Guides, Ground Plane	Ctrl/Command+G
Display, Preview Drawing, OpenGL Hardware	Alt+Ctrl+O (Option+Command+O on the Mac)

(continued)

Command	Keyboard Shortcut
Display, Preview Drawing, SreeD Software	Alt+Ctrl+S (Option+Command+S on the Mac)
Render, Render	Ctrl/Command+R
Render, Area Render	Ctrl+Alt+N (Command+Option+N on the Mac)
Render, Antialias Document	Ctrl+Alt+R (Command+Option+R on the Mac)
Render, Render Settings	Ctrl/Command+Y
Render, Render Dimensions	Ctrl+Alt+D (Shift+Command+Y on the Mac)
Render, Materials	Ctrl/Command+U
Animation, Make Movie	Ctrl/Command+J
Window, Animation Palette	Shift+Ctrl/Command+V
Window, Graph	Shift+Ctrl/Command+G
Window, Libraries	Shift+Ctrl/Command+B
Window, Hierarchy Editor	Shift+Ctrl/Command+E
Window, Joint Editor	Shift+Ctrl/Command+J
Window, Walk Designer	Shift+Ctrl/Command+W
Window, Talk Designer	Shift+Ctrl/Command+K
Window, Python Scripts	Shift+Ctrl/Command+O
Window, Camera Controls	Shift+Ctrl/Command+R
Window, Preview Styles	Shift+Ctrl/Command+U
Window, Editing Tools	Shift+Ctrl/Command+T
Window, Light Controls	Shift+Ctrl/Command+I
Window, Memory Dots	Shift+Ctrl/Command+M
Window, Parameter Dials	Shift+Ctrl/Command+N
Window, Animation Controls	Shift+Ctrl/Command+P
Window, Show All Tools	Ctrl/Command+\
Window, Hide All Tools	Ctrl/Command+0
Window, Tool Titles	Ctrl/Command+-

Editing Tools Shortcuts

Tool	Keyboard Shortcut
Rotate	R
Twist	W
Translate/Pull	T
Translate In/Out	Z
Scale	S
Taper	P
Chain Break	L
Color	C

3ds Max. A popular 3D package.

3-point lighting. A basic lighting design that consists of a key, back, and fill light.

AIFF file. An audio format common on Macintosh computers.

Air damping. A cloth parameter value that defines how much the cloth group is affected by air currents, such as wind.

Ambient color. A global pervasive light color that is applied to the entire scene.

Ambient occlusion. An effect that diminishes ambient light from the scene, thus causing shadows to appear darker and providing more contrast for the rendered image.

Animation layer. An interface for dividing an animation sequence into several sections. Layers can be combined to create complex motions from simple isolated motions.

Animation set. A specific animation sequence that is named and saved to be reused on another figure.

Antialiasing. A process of smoothing rendered edges in order to remove any jagged edges.

Back light. A light positioned behind the scene to cast light on the edges of the scene objects.

Background image. An image that is set to appear behind the scene.

Base layer. The bottom-most layer that cannot be deleted or reduced in size.

Body part. The defined pieces that make up a figure.

Body part group. A set of polygons that shares the same name as the bone that is controlling it.

Bone. An invisible object that exists beneath the surface of the figure and defines how the attached body part moves as the bone is moved.

Bone Creation tool. A tool used to create and place new bones.

Bulge. The process of increasing a muscle's size as a joint's angle is decreased.

Bump map. A 2D bitmap image that adds a relief texture to the surface of an object, like an orange rind.

Camera Dots. An interface control used to remember and recall camera positions and properties.

Caricature. A silly drawing of a face that over-emphasizes a person's prominent features, such as a large nose, big ears, or a small mouth.

Chain Break tool. A tool used to prevent the movement of one object from moving a connected object from its current position.

Child. The following object in a hierarchy chain. Child objects can move independently of the parent object.

Choreographed group. A set of cloth vertices that can be animated as a group using keyframes.

Clipping plane. A plane positioned parallel to the camera that defines the border beyond which scene objects aren't visible.

Cloth density. A cloth parameter value that defines how heavy the cloth is per unit area.

Cloth Self-Friction. A cloth parameter value that defines how much friction the cloth has when rubbed against itself.

Cloth simulation. The process of calculating the position and motion of a cloth object as it is moved by forces and collides with various scene objects.

Clothify. The process of converting a prop object into a cloth object.

Clumpiness. The tendency of hair to clump together into groups.

Collision. An event that occurs when a vertex of a cloth object intersects with the polygon face of a scene object.

Compiled file. A Python file that has been converted to a machine-savvy format that is no longer readable, but that executes quicker.

Compressed file. The file that is reduced in size by compacting the data contained therein. Compressed files need to be uncompressed before they can be used. The decompression process happens automatically when Poser files are loaded.

Conforming clothes. Clothes or props that are designed to fit the given character exactly and to remain fitting as the figure's pose changes.

Conforming prop. An object that is deformed in order to fit the designated figure.

Constrained group. A cloth group of vertices that are constrained to not be moved by the dynamic simulation.

Content Collection. A group of content gathered together that can include content from several different categories.

Content Paradise. A Web site connected to Poser that lets users purchase and download custom content that can be used within Poser and other e frontier products.

Damping. The tendency of an object to resist bouncing after being set in motion. The opposite of springiness.

Deformer. An object used to deform the surface of body parts by moving vertices.

Depth cueing. An atmospheric effect that makes objects farther away in the scene appear hazier.

Depth of field. An optical effect that focuses the view at the focal point and gradually blurs all objects farther than the focal point.

Depth map shadows. Shadows that are calculated and the shadow information is saved in a depth map, resulting in shadows with blurred edges.

Diffuse color. The surface color emitted by an object.

Displacement map. A 2D bitmap image that controls the displacement of geometry objects.

Display ports. Additional sections of the Document Window that can display a different view of the scene.

Display styles. Render options for the Document Window.

Document Window. The main window interface where the posed figure is displayed.

Dolly. A camera motion that moves the view closer or farther from the scene.

Draping. The process of letting a cloth object fall to rest about a scene object.

Dynamic Friction. A cloth parameter value that is similar to Static Friction, except it defines the amount of force required to keep a moving object in motion.

Dynamics. The study of the motions of connected objects.

Editing Tools. A selection of tools used to manipulate and transform scene elements.

Element. Any scene object that can be selected, including body parts, props, cameras, and lights.

Ethnicity. The facial features that are inherent to a unique ethnic group, such as African-Americans, Europeans, and Asians.

Exporting. The process of saving Poser files to a format to be used by an external program.

Expression. When the face features are saved in a unique position to show different emotions.

Face shape. The underlying 3D geometry that the texture is mapped on in order to create the face.

Face texture map. An image that is wrapped about the head model to show details.

Figure. A character loaded into Poser that can be posed using the various interface controls.

Figure Circle control. A circle that surrounds the figure and enables the entire figure to be moved as one unit.

File format. The file type used to describe the contents of the file.

Fill light. A secondary light used to fill in the gaps of the scene.

FireFly render engine. The default rendering method for rendering images in Poser. This engine includes many advanced features, such as anti-aliasing, motion blur, and texture filtering.

Flash. A vector-based format commonly used to display images and movies on the Web.

Floating control. An interface object that isn't attached to the interface window and can be placed anywhere within the interface window.

Flyaround mode. A toggle mode that causes the camera to spin about the central axis of the current scene, animating its view from all angles.

Focal length. A camera property that changes the center focus point for the camera.

Fold Resistance. A cloth parameter value that defines how resistant the current cloth group is to folding.

Frame rate. The rate at which frames of an animation sequence are displayed. Higher frame rates result in smoother motion, but require more memory.

Friction. A force that resists the movement of one object over another.

F-stop. A camera setting that determines the size of the aperture and that affects the intensity of the blurring for a depth-of-field effect.

Genitalia. Male and female sex organs that can be visible or hidden.

Guide hairs. A sampling of hairs that show where the full set of hair will be located.

Hair density. The total number of hairs for a given hair group.

Hair growth group. A grouped selection of polygons that define where the hair is to be located.

Hair root. The end of the hair nearest the figure.

Hair Style tool. A tool that is used to style individual hairs or groups of selected hairs.

Hair tip. The end of the hair farthest away from the figure.

Hier file. Short for *hierarchy file*. An older file format based on hierarchical data used in Poser 3 to create figures.

Hierarchy. A linked chain of objects connected from parent to child.

High Dynamic Range (HDR) images. An image format that captures more detail about the lighting of the environment.

Highlight. The spot on an object where the light is reflected with the greatest intensity. Also known as a *specular* highlight.

IK chain. A set of hierarchically linked bones that are enabled using Inverse Kinematics, including root and goal objects.

Image-based lights (IBL). A light that illuminates the scene by deriving all light information from an image map.

Importing. The process of loading externally created files into Poser.

Inclusion and exclusion angles. Angles used to mark the polygons that are affected and unaffected by the joint's movement.

Infinite light. A light that simulates shining from an infinite distance so all light rays are parallel.

Interface. A set of controls used to interact with the software features.

Interpolation. A calculation process used to determine the intermediate position of objects between two keyframes.

Inverse Kinematics. A unique method of calculating the motion of linked objects that enables child objects to control the position and orientation of their parent object.

Irradiance Caching. The feature that caches lighting details into a buffer to decrease the render time for ambient occlusion scenes.

Joint. The base of a bone that marks the position between two bones where the body parts bend.

Joint Editor. A palette used to position and define the attributes of each bone and its relationship to the figure.

Key light. The main light in a scene used to cast shadows.

Keyboard shortcut. A key or set of keys that execute a command.

Keyframe. A defined state of an object at one point during an animation sequence that is used to interpolate motion.

Kinematics. The branch of physics that is used to calculate the movement of linked objects.

Kinkiness. The amount of curl in each hair.

Library. A collection of data that can be loaded into the scene.

Light probe. An environment image taken of a reflective sphere that holds lighting information about the entire environment.

Locked prop. A locked prop is one whose position and orientation is set and cannot be changed unless the object is unlocked.

Loop. A setting that causes an animation to play over and over.

Magnet. A deformer used to pull vertices away from an object.

Manga Studio. A software package used to create Manga comic pages.

Material group. A group of selected polygons that defines a region where similar materials are applied, such as a shirt or pants group.

Material node. A dialog box of material properties that can be connected to control another material value.

Maya. A popular 3D modeling package.

Morph target. A custom parameter that defines an object deformation that appears as a parameter in the Parameters palette.

Morphing tool. A tool used to sculpt the shape of a face.

Motion blur. A rendering option that blurs objects moving quickly in the scene.

Motion capture. A process of collecting motion data using a special sensor attached to real humans performing the action.

Normal. A nonrendered vector that extends from the center of each polygon face and is used to indicate the direction the polygon face is pointing.

Offset. The location of an imported prop as measured from the scene's origin point.

Opaque. The opposite of transparency. When objects cannot be seen through.

OpenGL. An option used to enable hardware acceleration for fast Document Window updates.

Origin. A point in the scene where the X, Y, and Z coordinate values are all 0.

Orphan polygons. Polygons that don't belong to a group.

Orthogonal camera. A camera that is positioned at the end of an axis and displays the scene as a 2D plane where all dimensions are accurate. Top, Bottom, Front, Back, Left, and Right are examples of orthogonal cameras.

Parent. The controlling object that a child object is attached to. When the parent moves, the child object moves with it.

PDF file. (Portable Document File) A document format created by Adobe used in Poser to view the Poser Reference Manual. PDF files require a Web browser or the Adobe Reader to read the files.

Perspective. An optical property that displays depth by having all object edges gradually converge to a point in the distance.

Phoneme. A set of common distinct sounds and the face motions required to create them. Phonemes in Poser include A, CH, E, F, TH, O, M, U, W, and L.

Photoshop. A popular image-editing application.

Pin tool. A tool used to prevent vertices from moving out of position.

Point light. A light that projects light rays in all directions equally.

Pose Dots. An interface control used to remember and recall a specific figure pose.

PoserPython. An extension of the industry-standard Python scripting language that lets you extend and add new functionality to Poser.

Posing camera. A camera that stays focused on the scene's selected figure.

Preferences. An interface for setting defaults and for configuring the interface.

Prop. Any external object added to the scene to enhance the final image. Props may include scenery, figure accessories, clothes, and hair.

Python. An interpreted, object-oriented scripting language that includes text commands for defining certain actions.

Python Scripts palette. An interface where you can load and execute Python scripts.

Quick start. An interface with step-by-step project guides for accomplishing specific tasks.

Ray-traced shadows. Shadows that are calculated using an accurate ray-tracing method that results in sharp edges.

Raytracing. A rendering method that calculates the scene by casting light rays into the scene and following these light rays as they bounce off objects. The results are accurately rendered shadows, reflections, and materials.

Render. The process of calculating the final look of all scene geometries, lights, materials, and textures into a final image.

Resampling. The process of reducing the total number of keys required to create a motion.

Retiming. The process of scaling animation keys so the relative spacing between adjacent keys remains constant.

Rig. The underlying bone skeleton used to control the position of the figure's body parts.

Rigging. The process of creating a bone skeleton and connecting it to the figure's model.

Rigid decorated group. A cloth group that is removed from the dynamic simulation and yet remains solid and is inflexible.

Room tabs. A set of tabs located at the top of the Poser interface that allows access to various feature interfaces.

Root node. The top-level material node.

Rotation. The process of spinning and reorienting an object within the scene.

Scaling. The process of changing the size of an object within the scene.

Sellion. That part of the nose that extends from its tip up between the eyes.

Shade. A 3D modeling and rendering application that works well with Poser using an integration module.

Shader Window. An interface found in the Material Room where new custom materials can be created.

Shadow camera. A camera that is positioned in the same location as a light.

Shadow map. A bitmap that includes all the computed shadows for the scene. Shadow maps can be reused to speed up rendering.

Shear Resistance. A cloth parameter value that defines how resistant the current cloth group is to shearing the surface against itself.

Side window handle. A simple control positioned on the side of the interface used to open another set of controls.

Simulation range. The number of frames that are included in the simulation marked by Start and End Frames.

Skeleton. A hierarchy of bones arranged to match the figure it controls.

Sketch Designer. An interface used to define brush strokes that are used to render a scene using the Sketch render engine.

Smart object. A piece of content that is parented to another object in the scene.

Smoothing group. A group of polygons smoothed between adjacent polygons without any hard edges.

Soft decorated group. A cloth group that is removed from the dynamic simulation and that can still flex and bend.

Source file. An original text-based Python file that can be executed.

Spotlight. A light that projects light within a cone of influence.

Springiness. The tendency of an object to bounce after being set in motion.

SreeD. An option used to enable software rendering that, although slower than the OpenGL option, produces high-quality previews.

Static Friction. A cloth parameter value that defines how much force is required to begin to move cloth over an object.

Stiffness. A property that makes hairs resist motion.

Stretch Damping. A cloth parameter value that defines how quickly the stretching of the cloth fades.

Stretch Resistance. A cloth parameter value that defines how resistant the current cloth group is to stretching.

Supplemental text. Text typed in to the Text Designer that matches the words in the sound file.

Symmetry. A property that occurs when one half of an object is identical to the opposite side.

Talk Designer. An interface used to automatically generate facial motions that are synched with a sound file.

Tapering. A scaling operation that changes the size of only one end of an object.

Temples. The portion of the face that lies between the ears and the eyes.

Text editor. System software that is used to edit and save text files.

Texture filtering. A process applied to 2D texture images to help avoid aliasing, moire patterns, and dropouts. It is also used to optimize performance when reading from a texture cache.

Texture map. An 2D image file that is wrapped about a surface.

Textured light. A light that projects a texture map onto the scene.

Thumbnail. A small image that displays the selected content.

Tool titles. The text that appears above each control set to help identify it.

Trackball. A ball-like control within the Camera Controls that rotates the scene.

Tracking mode. Modes that define the detail of the objects displayed in the Document Window.

Translation. The process of moving an object within the scene.

Transparency. A material property that defines how easy an object is to see through, like glass.

UI. User interface.

UI Dots. Interface controls used to remember and recall a specific interface configuration.

Undocked palette. A palette that is no longer constrained to the interface and that can float freely as a separate window.

Vanishing lines. Guide lines that lead from the edges of an object to the perspective converging point.

Virtual Fashion. A software package that lets you create clothes in the same manner as clothes are made in real life.

Viseme map. An XML-based file that defines the facial morph targets used to create the various phonemes.

Volume effect. An atmospheric effect that colors all scene objects with the designated color, much like fog.

Wacro. A custom PoserPython script used within the Shader Window to create new material types.

Walk cycle. A repeating set of frames that animate a figure walking.

WAV file. An audio format common on Windows computers.

Wave. A deformer used to deform surface vertices in a wave pattern.

Waveform. A visual display of a sound showing its volume per time.

Weld. An import option used to combine vertices with the same coordinates together.

Wind Force. A deformer used to add a wind force to the scene that is used by the hair and cloth simulations.

Z-Buffer. A portion of memory where the element's distance from the camera view is stored.

Zip archive. A compressed file format that reduces the size of files that need to be downloaded.

INDEX

INDEX

INDEX

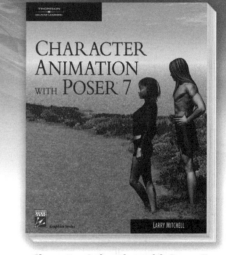